T0386776

JAN ULLRICH

Also by Daniel Friebe

MOUNTAIN HIGH: Europe's
50 Greatest Cycle Climbs

EDDY MERCKX: The Cannibal

MOUNTAIN HIGHER: Europe's Extreme,
Undiscovered and Unforgettable Cycle Climbs

DANIEL FRIEBE

JAN ULLRICH

THE BEST THERE NEVER WAS

MACMILLAN

First published 2022 by Macmillan
an imprint of Pan Macmillan
The Smithson, 6 Briset Street, London EC1M 5NR
EU representative: Macmillan Publishers Ireland Ltd, 1st Floor,
The Liffey Trust Centre, 117–126 Sheriff Street Upper,
Dublin 1, D01 YC43
Associated companies throughout the world
www.panmacmillan.com

ISBN 978-1-5098-0157-2 HB
ISBN 978-1-5098-4400-5 TPB

3 5 7 9 8 6 4

A CIP catalogue record for this book is available from the British Library.

Typeset by Jouve (UK), Milton Keynes
Printed and bound by CPI Group (UK) Ltd, Croydon, CR0 4YY

Visit **www.panmacmillan.com** to read more about all our books
and to buy them. You will also find features, author interviews and
news of any author events, and you can sign up for e-newsletters
so that you're always first to hear about our new releases.

Contents

CONTENTS

To Berlin.
May your arse remain in the garbage can,
and your head in the clouds.

JAN ULLRICH

Preface

The first thing I ever wrote about professional cycling was a sixth-form German project about Jan Ullrich. A few months earlier, I had sat gawping at a TV screen as, in the space of a quarter of an hour during the 1997 Tour de France's Pyrenean 'Queen Stage', Ullrich seemed to redraw the aesthetics and horizons of the sport. A sport that had known great dynasties before but never – as far as I knew or could even imagine – swivelled as professional cycling's destiny appeared to on that July afternoon. I was sixteen at the time – an age at which, as Julian Barnes wrote in his first novel *Metroland*, 'there were more meanings, more interpretations, a greater variety of available truths . . . Things contained more.' Among the other side effects of adolescence there is, indeed, an acute sensitization that embalms the images and ardours of that age in nostalgia later in life. Nonetheless, before commencing this book I already recalled, and now know for sure, that there were many others, and elders, upon whom Ullrich's performance in Andorra that day left the same imprint – the same thrill. With every strike of Ullrich's pedals came a thudding intuition that future and present tense had swapped places or bled together into one, indistinguishable, inconvertible truth: that from this day forth cycling would belong to Jan Ullrich of Team Telekom and Rostock.

To claim that the central or sole motivation for writing this biography was to understand only what went *wrong* would be reductive and also, from the outset, dismissive in the way that coverage of Ullrich has consistently been for the last fifteen years. It is hopefully not too big a spoiler to reveal that Jan Ullrich remains, per the annals and minus the caveats, Germany's greatest ever cyclist and also its only Tour de France winner. Moreover, there have been many meteors with similar, soaring trajectories and sharper descents – fellow phenoms who won cycling's great races at twenty-one and twenty-two and then faded into anonymity, whether overburdened by expectations or overtaken by their own hubris and, soon thereafter, their peers. Ullrich, by contrast, carried on winning and, if only at selected times every summer, achieving similar levels of excellence right up until his last dance in 2006. For a decade he also retained his status as a German national talisman. As such, as tempting at it has often proven to cast him as a flash-in-the-pan, a perennial groomsman, a misfit or a flop, bare statistics do not support that narrative. Neither can they explain a public affection that remained intact long after some of his most famous wins had been asterisked – a fondness that somehow emulsified the most contradictory ingredients; on one hand awe and the other a sympathy that eventually devolved into pity.

Over the course of his career, Ullrich's admirers were taken on a voyage between emotional extremities, in this sense becoming men and women after their hero's heart. The memoir he released in 2003 was called *Ganz oder Gar Nicht – All or Not At All* – and this was how he came to view or rationalize a life upon which everyone would at some point cast judgement. His close-season excesses became infamous, the subject of derision, and yet teammates marvelled at the sacrifices and exertions he annually undertook to correct his course. Every winter became its own cautionary tale, every springtime a new recovery memoir. As Ullrich's contemporary and fellow East German Jens Voigt once told the journalist Andreas Burkert, 'Characters like Ullrich fascinate people. They're right up in the heavens then they fall really, really deep, only to rise again. They go through life like normal people.'

In this book we will hear from others who extol Ullrich's 'everyman appeal', although one could easily make the opposite case – that it was his uncommonness that induced devotion among common men. Or, put another way, the feeling that, if Ullrich could only bring himself to do ordinary, mundane, everyman things – stay relatively fit in winter, control his appetite, handle his talent with care – he would one day reveal himself as the pedalling *übermensch*, superman, we glimpsed in 1997. He had demonstrated that potential once, and in subsequent years all who had witnessed it waited, enraptured, salivating at the prospect of a second look. As another contemporary, David Millar, put it to me, 'Jan was the ultimate missile that never got used. I think that's one of the things that makes his story so appealing: you had this guy who you felt could have nuked everyone and everything, but he ended up as almost this benign force. That almost makes him the perfect counterpoint to Armstrong.'

Ah, yes, Armstrong. He who shall not be mentioned. Not 'the disgraced Lance Armstrong' who occupies the public consciousness now, but rather the cyclist who was – without question and whatever we think about his redacted legacy – a force that steered, overshadowed and to a large extent defined Ullrich, at least in the public's eyes. 'Jan was my North Star,' Armstrong says – and the roles were also inverted. Some will bridle at the prominence afforded to Lance Armstrong's reminiscences on these pages – they want him forgotten, cancelled, deplatformed – but this book is no place to relitigate crimes acknowledged and punished years ago. Armstrong was the first interview I requested during the research process and, in style as much as substance, his retellings were also pitch-perfect reminders of the traits that made his generation-defining rivalry with Ullrich so compelling, in spite of a lopsided final scoreline. If Ullrich's story is of a would-be superman who lacked the Average Joe know-how to button on his cape, Armstrong stopped at nothing to escape and disguise his mortality – but ultimately could not hide his feet of clay.

There are those who contend it all ended in a moral, or immoral, stalemate – a resounding null and void, not just between Ullrich and Armstrong but between almost everyone who raced with and against them in the late nineties and early 2000s. The same people might even see poetic justice in the fact that some of the main material benefactors also ended up paying for an ethical bankruptcy. It is certainly sobering to reflect that, in the summer of 1999, the haut monde of international cycling indisputably consisted of five athletes – Frank Vandenbroucke, Marco Pantani, Lance Armstrong, Jan Ullrich and Mario Cipollini. A twenty-year check on that quintet today would make eye-wateringly grim reading, comprising as it does, respectively, two deaths by drug overdose; the most spectacular defrocking in the history of professional sport; Ullrich whose life had 'tipped from sporting into human tragedy', to borrow *Die Zeit*'s 2018 summation; and Cipollini who in 2022 was bracing himself for the third year of hearings in a case brought by his wife for assault and stalking charges, both of which he denies.

It is impossible to know how much and in what ways, subtle or otherwise, cycling brought chaos to these men's lives, having previously exalted and to a certain extent shaped them – as it does to everyone who falls under this sport's hypnotic spell. 'How do we know what is really happening in Jan's life, or anyone's? How can we judge them?' Bjarne Riis, Ullrich's old teammate, asked me. Riis is right. As another contemporary, Erwann Menthéour, lamented after seeing another scion of the same generation, Philippe Gaumont, follow his own drug- and dope-littered path to an early grave, 'These were guys riding 35,000 kilometres a year, people were in awe of them, and then all of a sudden they were treated like shits. And somewhere, even if they knew that they were only doing what everyone else did, those guys also had to look themselves in the mirror and feel shame, guilt, because that was what everyone was telling them that they should feel.'

Perhaps, then, we can favour compassion over condemnation, and humbly acknowledge that a biography is at best an artist's impression – while at the same time believing that it can satisfy a thirst for better, if not total understanding. In Ullrich's case, that craving is especially strong because of the affinities he inspired, but also because of the way his career ended and its largely unexplained, unseen postscript. Before that, there were already numerous barriers to knowing him better: physical, like the 1,400-kilometre electrified and barbed-wire fence behind which he grew up in the former East Germany; linguistic, in a sport long since colonized by French, Belgians, Dutch, Spanish and Italians, and which was becoming staunchly anglophone in the final years of his career; and cultural, in a professional world so paranoid and secretive, with its endemic 'omertà' or law of silence, that a childhood in the DDR may in some respects have served as the perfect preparation.

So there is a lot to discover. Ullrich committed his own memories to print in the aforementioned autobiography, *Ganz oder Gar Nicht*, in 2004 – though that truncated, carefully filtered, first-person perspective is but one piece in a complex puzzle. Ullrich didn't concern himself unduly with the legacies of the DDR, either in his own worldview or that of fellow Germans. He didn't explore the backgrounds, passions and opinions of his coaches and teammates. There were just a few bare lines pondering Armstrong's character, ending with the tart conclusion, 'I wouldn't like to be like him.' Doping was hardly mentioned. And, above all, he was writing before the thermonuclear blast in 2006 that liquidated what remained of his career, a large part of his identity and almost the entire sport in Germany, ahead of his related personal traumas in subsequent years. He was also writing a decade before Armstrong's own immolation, which torched and retrospectively rearranged the landscape of their generation even further.

A more complete analysis was therefore overdue. Throughout the process there were dozens who declined interviews or expressed their wish for the story – and Ullrich – to be left alone. In the main they were speaking out of kindness and concern for an old friend – but were also sometimes failing to acknowledge the widespread appetite for a non-judgemental re-evaluation. One chapter is entitled 'The Truth Will Set You Free' after a bible verse, a famous self-help bestseller and a pertinent engraving above the entrance of the University of Freiburg – but the maxim seemed not to have gained any traction among many of Ullrich's friends and former associates. Protective, suspicious and exasperated, they have come to believe that every pen is poisoned, every motive impure. They plead for Ullrich's honour to be restored but are too scared to argue his case lest they also incriminate themselves. As a result, a lot of what was always attractive about Ullrich – his warmth, his sense of humour, his generosity, his dazzling natural talent – has lost many of its most passionate and well-informed advocates. As the German journalist Michael Ostermann told me, 'When people actually meet him, they really love him, but part of the problem is that he doesn't speak and his friends won't speak either.'

Meaning that the catcalls have drowned out the hosannas, malicious tongues have outnumbered the voices of reason.

Fortunately there were still scores of character witnesses who have added layers, shades and new perspectives. Hopefully we are left with a portrait quite unlike the gaudy caricatures that are many fans' only keepsakes of Ullrich's decade in cycling's upper echelons.

A quarter of a century has passed since, to phrase it as the German media did at the time, a twenty-three-year-old, freckle-faced redhead created sporting history for his recently unified homeland – and a sixteen-year-old kid from a country with even less cycling heritage than Germany was among the millions watching, captivated. My innocence survived twelve months, until it was ripped away by the Festina doping scandal. Within three years I would begin a career in journalism that obliterated whatever romanticism was left, with its funereal procession of scandals over the next ten years culminating, yes, with He Who Has Already Been Mentioned.

I was not naive when I began working on this book, and there is certainly no excuse for being wide- or even misty-eyed today. Nevertheless, some of that 1997-vintage wonder is still alive in me, just as it is in others, and will probably never fade. After the Second World War, Germany committed to a long period of repentance and repair, but above all understanding, that they called *Vergangenheitsbewälti-gung*, literally 'coping with' or 'overcoming the past'. It took many forms, from war crimes trials to television documentaries and public monuments. But above all it was about learning. As an influential force behind the process, the judge Fritz Bauer, once said, 'Nothing belongs solely to the past, everything is contained within the present, and can still become the future.'[1]

The *Vergangenheitsbewältigung* of Jan Ullrich's life and times is a much less fraught and indeed comparatively trivial business, but there are some common themes. After two and a half decades, enough time has certainly now passed for more of the truth, and maybe even some reconciliation.

PART ONE

1

ARCALÍS

'It's Merckx!'

—*Raymond Poulidor*

On his third day as a professional cyclist, Jan Ullrich pedalled into Andorra and would have needed no explanation for why Louis Le Débonnaire had equated the encircling peaks and their canyons to the 'wild valleys of Hell' over a thousand years earlier. Ullrich saw a white line flow under his front wheel then took time to contemplate a result as bracing as the surrounding landscape. The winner of the third stage of the Setmana Catalana, or 'Catalan Week', Alex Zülle, had finished twenty-two minutes earlier. For the second time in two days, Ullrich could console himself only with having ridden in alongside the reigning Tour de France champion, Miguel Induráin. Otherwise, he admitted later, his first trip into the Principality and indeed his maiden voyage on the high seas of professional racing had been nothing less than 'depressing'.

Just over two years later, Jan Ullrich made his second journey into the Andorran mountains. This time things would go rather differently. Stage ten of the 1997 Tour de France, from Luchon to the Arcalís ski resort, was a monster at 242 kilometres. On the route were five Pyrenean passes, each glowing like hot coals in the July sunshine. Not that the heat was likely to faze Ullrich; the German press would later coin the term 'Ulle-Wetter' – 'Ullrich weather' – for those smouldering days when others wilted and he, the 'Sun King', as they also christened him, came alive.

As a child back in Rostock, he had not even been aware of the Tour de France's existence, much less watched it. For cyclists behind the Iron Curtain, a tour of the communist bloc, the Peace Race, represented the sport's pinnacle, its East German idols including Uwe Raab, Uwe Ampler or, long before them, Täve Schur. Ullrich had only caught his first, grainy glimpse of the Tour in July 1989, when he and a couple of other junior team members at Dynamo Berlin – the Stasi-affiliated multi-sports club they raced for – secretly adjusted the aerial on the tiny TV set in the common room of their dormitory block. They were lucky to witness arguably the most gripping Tour in the race's history, a seesawing three-week slugfest between the American Greg LeMond and Laurent Fignon of France.

Now, eight years on, he wasn't only riding cycling's most famous race but was widely fancied to win it. His repeated assertions that his teammate and the defending champion, Bjarne Riis, remained the Deutsche Telekom leader had been dismissed by the media as attempts to deflect pressure and curry favour with the Dane. On the morning of the first-day prologue in Rouen, *L'Équipe* had named Ullrich as its five-star favourite to take victory in Paris. He had, after all, finished runner-up to Riis the previous year. Pressure had also been building in the Deutsche Telekom camp over the first week and a half of racing; Ullrich's room-mate, Jens Heppner, had spoken for many of the Telekom riders when he told the twenty-three-year-old that he was stronger than Riis and should ride his own race on the road to Andorra. The team's directeurs sportifs, Walter Godefroot and Rudy Pevenage, had also tried to convince him, but Ullrich remained a reticent heir.

On the first four of those towering molochs – the passes of the Portet d'Aspet, the Port, the Envalira, and Ordino – he glanced continually over his shoulder or under an armpit to check Riis's position. Later, when two Festina riders, Richard Virenque and Laurent Dufaux, accelerated high up on the Ordino, Ullrich purred in their slipstream as he waited for Riis to arrive. A mere yeoman for much of his career, thirty-three-year-old Riis had astonished some sections of the cycling world with his domination of the 1996 Tour. In the last week of that race, though, he had started to flag as Ullrich became stronger. Heppner, for one, had been sure that Riis would never win another Tour after 1996.

Finally, with around ten kilometres to go, Riis drew alongside Ullrich.

Riis told him that if they wanted to win the Tour, they would have to attack.

Ullrich glanced across: 'What, you mean I should set the pace for you?'

Riis was going to have to spell it out. 'No,' he said, 'if you can, go for it.'

The East German – schooled to execute the orders of authority figures, weaned in an education system equating excellence with compliance – now hesitated. Or rather, he instinctively sought the blessing of a higher power – the Deutsche Telekom manager Walter Godefroot. On the pretext of needing a drink, he dropped back to his team car and leaned in to hear what Godefroot was barking out of the window.

'Give it a go! Try to attack!'

Moments later, he had swept past Riis and to the front of the sixteen-man group that was now sure to contest the stage win. Seeing the ten-kilometres-to-go banner, he rose out of the saddle and glided away from all but the Italian, Francesco Casagrande. He then paused again, as though assailed by second thoughts.

The doubts persisted until they reached El Serrat, a mountain hamlet of 180-odd inhabitants, one tiny chapel, three hotels, and two kinks in the road zigzagging towards Arcalís. On the first of those bends, the wide, graceful arc of Ullrich's pedal stroke betrayed no hint of aggression or even acceleration – but the group behind him shattered. Riis, Casagrande, then, finally, the last to submit to both gravity and Ullrich's diabolical rhythm, the Frenchman Richard Virenque.

Every professional sport lusts for heroes, and there is perhaps no more exhilarating moment than a performance heralding the arrival of a new virtuoso. Such events often come after a prelude – foretastes like Ullrich's a year earlier, the rumble of an era-defining talent as it stirs – or, much rarer, they arrive as sudden, blinding explosions. What they share is the ability to redraw a sport's landscape and its horizons within a matter of minutes, or even seconds. Just a few weeks earlier, in April 1997, Tiger Woods's twelve-shot victory in the US Masters had done just that, prompting *Sports Illustrated* to hail 'the week everything changed in golf'. Now, in Andorra, learned observers suggested Jan Ullrich was rescripting the future of another sport in an identical fashion.

Within a kilometre of his attack, Ullrich's advantage over Virenque had grown to a minute. Within three kilometres, it was heading towards two.

The rare spectacle of a twenty-three-year-old decimating his opposition on the first major climb of a Tour de France was accompanied by another uncommon occurrence further up the mountain. As Ullrich approached, a hundred or more journalists abandoned their laptops, tore mesmerized eyes from the TV monitors in the press room and hurried, en masse, across a car park and to the roadside barriers.

One of the reporters craning to see was Hartmut Scherzer. Scherzer had covered his first Tour two decades earlier, in 1977. He had written about and befriended Muhammed Ali, travelled to see him defeat Joe Frazier in the Thrilla in Manila, and two years later had the privilege of reporting on another historic occurrence on his first visit to the Tour: Scherzer's fellow Frankfurter, twenty-two-year-old Didi Thurau, taking the yellow jersey in the prologue and holding it for over two weeks, longer than any German before him.

But instinctively Scherzer knew this was different, not a cameo but a consecration. He watched Ullrich's silhouette appear from out of a tunnel, then glanced left and right at his colleagues, all beating their hands together like the fans. Only one spectator, standing, seemed completely impassive. The man was around Scherzer's age and his features – the plump, pursed lips, heavy brow and boot-shaped nose – would have been recognizable to anyone with even a loose grasp of Tour de France history in the 1960s and 1970s. Raymond Poulidor could not have known or imagined, that afternoon in Andorra, that Jan Ullrich would one day surpass the three second-place overall finishes in the Tour that had earned Poulidor an invidious nickname: 'The Eternal Runner-Up'.

When Ullrich had pounded past them and out of sight, and the journalists turned back towards the press centre, 'Poupou' was still propped against the barriers, processing what he had seen.

'C'est Merckx,' he said finally. 'C'est Merckx.'

Jan Ullrich was not yet Eddy Merckx, the winner of five Tours de France and the greatest male athlete ever to have climbed aboard a bicycle. He certainly had not done enough yet to justify Merckx's prediction before the Tour that he would be the 'rider of the century'. Nonetheless, for the heady quarter of an hour since his attack, no comparison had seemed too outlandish. How many Tours, based on what everyone was watching, would he end up winning? In the coming days, Bernard Hinault would tell the French press that Ullrich seemed predestined to join him, Merckx, Jacques Anquetil and Miguel Induráin as the only five-time winners – before probably going on to take a sixth or seventh. A few days later, Hinault had changed his mind; now he told *Der Spiegel* that Ullrich would be unbeatable for the next ten years.

Lance Armstrong, mid-recovery from testicular cancer, had visited the Tour that morning in Luchon. Armstrong caught a few minutes of the Arcalís stage on a TV monitor as he prepared to board a plane back to Texas. He disagreed with Hinault's prediction that Ullrich would beat all-comers for the next ten Tours. Armstrong thought Ullrich would 'destroy' them.

Another American, Greg LeMond, had climbed off his bike in 1994 and barely watched a Tour de France stage since. A three-time former champion, in retirement LeMond had grown increasingly disillusioned with what professional cycling had become, believing that the natural order had been completely disfigured, ruined, by that same venom that may also have curtailed his career: the banned but still undetectable hormone EPO being used by other riders.

LeMond, though, had heard about Ullrich. Curiosity now also drew him to a television screen to see for himself. In this instant, LeMond came to feel later, was everything that had enraptured him when he had seen the Tour for the first time, then when he had ridden it. There was everything that elevated cycling and the Tour out of the dimensions of mere sport.

In the last kilometre, even Ullrich began to suffer, but by then victory and its significance were secure. The sickly sweetheart of the French fans, Virenque, trailed home in second place, one minute and eight seconds adrift. To the reporters who thrust microphones towards him, Virenque said that the Pyrenean climbs suited Ullrich and that he may not be quite so strong in the Alps. A few moments later, he sat on the steps of his Festina team's camping car and buried his head in a towel, disgusted by what he'd seen.

While he didn't yet know it, Virenque would soon play a major role in turning Ullrich at Arcalís into a watershed for professional cycling. He had been the last to surrender on the mountain, but much more importantly, within a year he would help to change the lens through which the world watched the Tour forever as the central, pathetic figure of the Festina doping scandal. Ullrich's 500-watt rampage from El Serrat had been, physiologically speaking, the most prodigious effort the Tour had ever seen on a long climb (and still hasn't been surpassed in 2022), but it was also the last time that such a feat – the kind of which ninety-five years of Tour legend had been made – would be witnessed with undiluted awe. Hereafter – or, precisely, from the moment a Belgian customs officer opened the boot of Festina soigneur Willy Voet's Fiat Mare on the eve of the 1998 Tour – every dose of brilliance would come with an antidote of distrust.

For now, Riis confirmed his abdication by wrapping his arms around Ullrich and grinning for the cameras behind the podium. Ullrich was the strongest, he agreed. Ullrich could have dropped him the previous day at Loudenvielle, he also conceded. This was no lie: twenty-four hours earlier Ullrich had felt even better.

The 'New Giant' himself, as *L'Équipe* called him the next morning, could barely compute what had just happened. Lacking any linguistic common ground, the international media had already deduced from Ullrich's demeanour in and out of the saddle that they could safely paint from the usual palette of East German stereotypes: Ullrich was strong, silent, inscrutable. He now reinforced that image in his post-race press conference by showering them with clichés: he was 'delighted' that a 'dream had come true', but he was still taking 'one day at a time'. It was only 'half-time in the Tour'. There were still 'two time trials and the Alps to come'.

Back home, the reaction was also measured – for now. Ten days later, though, Germany would have its first Tour champion, cycling its new messiah, and Jan Ullrich – a twenty-three-year-old pure product of the East – the unlikely, unsolicited, unbearable role as a talisman for the unified Germany.

In 2009, an East Berliner named Mark Scheppert penned a collection of vignettes about children of the Deutsche Demokratische Republik and dedicated one chapter to what he called 'Generation Jan Ullrich'. Scheppert is almost exactly the same age as Ullrich. His father also worked for years as a cycling coach at the Dynamo Berlin club where Ullrich lived, studied and raced for three years before the end of the East.

Many of Scheppert's readers were people like him, offspring of the same 'Generation Jan Ullrich' – conflicted souls with a foot firmly in the before and after. Scheppert himself had seized every opportunity that freedom had offered after the Wall fell – travelling, partying and eventually dating a 'Wessi', a girl from the West. One morning in July 1997, Scheppert's sweetheart announced that she was taking him for a surprise weekend away. They boarded a train in Berlin's Hauptbahnhof and, several hours later, stepped into blinding Parisian sunlight. She had wanted a romantic weekend and that's what she would get – just not in the way that she expected. Choosing his moment carefully, Scheppert eventually broke the news that the Tour de France was finishing on the Champs-Élysées the very next day. More importantly, a cyclist whom his father had coached and Scheppert himself had once known was about to become the first ever German winner.

Scheppert tells me all of this on a wet September evening in a bar close to his home, and where he grew up, in Friedrichshain, East Berlin. All around us are the bearded hipsters and tattooed fashionistas who are modern Berlin's rank and file, and the land and times that gave birth to both Mark Scheppert and Jan Ullrich seem an awfully long way away.

Even today, that sun-kissed Parisian afternoon in July 1997 remains one of Scheppert's most vivid memories.

'One of the most powerful things I've ever experienced, for what it meant to us as East Germans. The Wall had fallen nearly ten years earlier, Germany was officially unified, but our identities were not. They were still fractured and fragmented in so many ways. People from the East held on to whatever they could – and one of their own succeeding on the world stage, like Ullrich was doing – brought a huge amount of inspiration, hope and, yes, nostalgia.

'Jan Ullrich gave the East a lot of pride, a lot of confidence,' he goes on. 'Franziska van Almsick, the swimmer, a few actors and actresses, one or two singers – they were all we had. When anyone from the East achieved anything, 17 million people celebrated the fact that they were one of us. They were proving that good things also happened in the East, that we weren't this embarrassing, good-for-nothing bastard child that the real Germany had been obliged to take into care. That we weren't just the Stasi. In 1997, Ullrich was still the kid from Rostock, and everyone in the East was proud of that. Even now, we cling to anything. For example, the footballer

Toni Kroos being the only Ossi [East German] to become world champion [in 2014]. The majority of the top sportsmen now were born in a unified Germany but for a very long time it was a big thing when someone from the East achieved something. For a lot of East Germans, Jan Ullrich was this figure of hope, someone who instilled a lot of self-confidence in us. No one from Germany had ever won the Tour de France before – but, more to the point, no one from the West had ever won it.'

2

ONE IN 17 MILLION

'He was obsessed, just frighteningly ambitious'

—*Peter Sager*

The greatest road cyclist that Germany has ever seen was a mistake, the result of a miscalculation not unlike the ones of which he would be accused in adulthood.

Or, rather, to put it more delicately and in terms Ullrich himself has employed, it was a 'happy accident' when his mother fell pregnant in the spring of 1973.[2] Marianne Ullrich (née Kaatz) had given birth to her first child, a baby boy named Stefan, a couple of years earlier. Both Stefan and Jan would grow up to somewhat resemble their father, Werner – Stefan with the same broad frame and brown hair, Jan inheriting his dad's downturned hazel eyes, while his finer, neatly pointed nose came from his mother. Werner had once also been a promising sportsman, cherry-picked by a forerunner of the ESA (*Einheitlichen Sichtungs und Auswahlsystem*) talent-identification programme that would one day reveal Stefan's aptitude for running, though not, as we'll discover, Jan's for cycling. Werner had chosen short-track speed-skating – or rather short-track speed-skating had been chosen for him. He won back-to-back junior East German championships in 1967 and 1968, and the following year was accepted into one of Berlin's residential sports clubs, the Berliner Turn-Sport-Club, or TSC. There he found the competition more intense and success harder to come by. He raced for the last time in February 1969 and soon thereafter returned to Rostock and a job in a cement works.

Marianne Kaatz had no notable sporting pedigree, though excelled in aspects of life that Werner, patently, would find beyond him in fatherhood and adulthood. Perhaps that partly explained the attraction – Werner felt that Marianne could somehow complete or correct him. Not that it was hard to succumb to her charm, as many guests did on a nightly basis in the village inn, the *Gasthof*, in Biestow, as she sped around the dining room distributing the local Rostocker Helles in giant glass tankards, plates of Mecklenburger rib roast and smiles. She was still a teenager when they met and, not long later, they were exchanging vows. Stefan was born soon afterwards. By this point Marianne already knew that she had married neither a model husband nor a model father. He drank – lots – and also occasionally turned violent. For men with such tendencies, army life can be a salvation, or a place for unpleasant traits to incubate. For his compulsory military service, Werner was stationed in Rostock – a blessing given that Marianne and the new-born Stefan were living with Marianne's parents in Biestow, just a few kilometres away. But even when he was on leave, Werner's visits to the cramped, two-bedroom, five-mark-a-month* cottage were unpredictable both in timing and for his mood. Marianne certainly hadn't banked on them adding to their 'family' when he suddenly reappeared in February 1973; but women in the DDR were advised to take a break from the contraceptive pill every two years and, well, the timing and destiny somehow conspired. Not quite nine months later, snow had come early to Germany's far north, and Jan Ullrich's arrival on the first Sunday of December also caught his parents somewhat by surprise. They would be rushed to hospital by Norbert Makowski, a neighbour, Marianne's parents Fritz and Ingeborg having taken the family car to the Christmas market in Rostock. A couple of hours later, at 7.15 p.m., Marianne Kaatz finally laid eyes on her second child – an eight-pound boy with a thick moquette of black hair. She would call him Jan.

The struggles of the ensuing years, Ullrich's 'difficult childhood', have become a tired and misleading trope even among German journalists, with popular generalizations about Rostock accounting for at least some of the inaccuracies. No one would dispute that there are richer, more elegant and less troubled German cities on both sides of

* East German marks.

the former divide. For many Germans, Rostock remains indissociable from one of the grimmest events in their post-reunification history – three days in August 1992 when a huge mob of neo-Nazis and other thugs laid siege to a dilapidated tower block housing hundreds of asylum seekers, pelting them, the building and the police with petrol bombs and stones. Even more shocking than the attack was that thousands of 'normal' Rostockers gathered to watch and in some cases applaud. An image of Rostock as the nation's cradle of right-wing extremism and thuggery solidified, and unfortunately is still periodically reinforced. One Saturday in October 2015, I am in town to seek out some of the key people and places in Jan Ullrich's early life story, while hundreds of others – only a few of them resembling a long-established, shaven-headed white supremacist identikit – are here for something else: the first major demonstration organized by the emerging right-wing Alternative für Deutschland (AfD) party against the German government's open migration policy. 'We are the people!' they shout – a suddenly fashionable bastardization of a famous motto from the 1989 Peaceful Revolution. 'Nazis raus!' a crowd of counter-protesters chorus back.

This depressing first impression notwithstanding, anyone who approaches Rostock for the first time expecting to find a grey, destitute Baltic Sea outpost of doom will be surprised. The city in fact has a proud maritime-mercantile past, its admission to the Hanseatic League in 1251 heralding an age of prosperity that lasted several centuries. It is also home to the oldest university in Northern Europe. As in bigger East German cities, most scars of extensive Allied bombardment during the Second World War are nowadays invisible to the untrained eye.

Even on a wet autumn morning, the lattice of pedestrianized streets that knits together the Stadtmitte offers a view of urban civility borrowed straight from a town planner's sketchbook – one of sterile yet orderly, understated prosperity. I drive out through the suburbs and see linden trees brushing the thatched roofs of cute bungalows or the windows of brightly painted mansions. In Lütten Klein, the vast phalanx of high-rises and concrete blocks that would become home for the Ullrichs in the mid-1980s, geraniums spill from balconies above cobbled streets lined with family saloons. If just over 12 per cent of Lütten Klein residents are currently unemployed, and the national average is half that, the district wears its problems under a brave disguise.

Appearances and reality were perhaps similarly at odds in the first years of Jan Ullrich's life. Or, rather, it seems that there were two distinct shades to Ullrich's world – the light personified and radiated by Marianne and her parents Fritz and Ingeborg, and the darkness cast by the shadow of Werner's worst side. Marianne had studied botany at a local college before Jan's arrival, and the young mother's days remained long and exhausting, beginning with a five a.m. alarm call, followed by a two-kilometre walk to Stefan's kindergarten, then lectures and tutorials and, finally, evening shifts at the *Gasthof* in Biestow. Monday to Friday. From January to December. Jan's arrival meant more sacrifices, not least because Werner remained a fitful presence, but Jan's later recollections were overwhelmingly happy ones – of nature walks and fishing trips with his granddad Fritz, of Ingeborg's baking, and how 'wonderful' it was to all be under one roof. As he said, 'Who, after all, doesn't like getting spoiled by their grandparents?'

They moved two or three kilometres south from Biestow when, having obtained her diploma, Marianne was taken on by the Papendorf agricultural cooperative, which also offered the family lodgings. Here, too, today, there is much that punctures the lie of Ullrich's joyless Eastern Bloc childhood. The village nestles to the south of Rostock, a tranquil isle amid lapping waves of green meadows. The drab, stereotypically East German apartment block where the Ullrichs lived is not hard to find; the three-storey breeze-block oblong is comfortably the ugliest building in the village, but only because the rest of Papendorf is so easy on the eye. Paint an Alpine peak on the skyline and we could be in Switzerland. Prime position in the village, on a hilltop directly above the Ullrichs' old apartment, is occupied by the house that Jan had built for his mother in 2003.

The home in which Jan Ullrich spent years five to thirteen was more modest, though amply suited to the lifestyle of a pre-teen and the older brother who combined the roles of partner in adventure and misadventure, idol and protector. Another sibling, Thomas, was born when Jan was four, Marianne and Werner's third child. From the window of their shared bedroom on the third floor, Jan and Stefan could look out over the communal garden and garages where they spent their happiest hours. A strip of gravel running parallel to the lawn was also where Jan rode a bicycle for the first time. He was five and a half – some fifteen years younger than the hallowed two-wheeler, a gearless kid's bike belonging to Stefan. Jan clung grimly to the handlebars while Werner gripped the back of the saddle and pushed his son forward. 'You're riding, you're riding!' Werner cried. Jan looked back, perhaps hoping to see the pride in his father's eyes . . . but instead crashed into a dustbin.

Ullrich noted later that it was one of his final experiences with his father – a sort of tragicomic metaphor, with a significant postscript.

Werner Ullrich stayed around just long enough, a few more months, to leave his son with another indelible souvenir – a scar just above the hairline, inflicted when Jan was six for some unspecified sleight or misdemeanour. In later years, the mark would still be visible when Jan cropped his hair short. Stefan had suffered worse and more frequent beatings, often when he was trying to protect Marianne. She would later explain to her sons that it had been 'a relief' when Werner finally agreed to move out of Papendorf, out of their life, and into a new house a few kilometres away. She told the journalist Andreas Burkert in 2003, 'We all suffered at his hands', without wishing to go into specifics. For a few months, Werner still sometimes came for the kids at weekends. The first Christmas, he left presents outside the front door. He was evidently given to selective acts of kindness or contrition. Like the time, just after Jan's fourth birthday, when he cross-country skied into Rostock on New Year's Eve and returned with an armful of fireworks for them to ring in 1978 in style. Soon, though, it had been so long since his last visit that Jan assumed they would never see him again – and was almost right.

Many years later, Jan Ullrich would say that he never missed having a father because he never truly felt as though he had one. He retained only a collection of hazy memories – and even they had to be suppressed or redacted. 'I wanted to have fond memories of my dad. Later I perhaps blocked out the fact that he drank too much, lost control – including of himself – and that he could be brutal with us as well as with our mother . . . I'm still amazed at how undramatic it seemed to me that our father had completely disappeared from our lives.'

Who knows, the heartache may have been greater had Werner's place not soon been taken by other men – part guardians, part role models.

Fritz, his granddad, was the first. Soon there would be another.

*

There is a little-known or acknowledged fact about Jan Ullrich and cycling that brings a sentimental smile to the face of his first ever coach, Peter Sager, even today.

'Had our paths not crossed,' Sager says, 'he would have been a runner. It was pure chance that he ended up being a cyclist.'

Such happenstance was not supposed to factor in the German Democratic Republic's grand sporting design. Sager still extols the merits of, almost pines for, the ESA talent-identification system that had been rolled out in 1973, the year of Ullrich's birth, and accelerated the DDR's land grab in international sporting competitions. West Germany had first recognized the DDR as an independent state in 1972, and that year's Olympics, in Munich no less, gave new impetus to the DDR's propagandist ambitions through sport. In Munich, competing for the first time under their own flag, they trounced and embarrassed the *Klassenfeind*, or 'class enemy', amassing sixty-six medals to West Germany's forty. The introduction the following year of the ESA was designed to widen the gulf, in parallel to an escalation in what became the world's most infamous state doping programme.

In September 1980, Jan Ullrich was one of nearly 300,000 East German six- and seven-year-olds walking through the gates of a primary school for the first time. At some point over the next year, most but not all of that number would be put through the first phase of ESA screening – height and weight measurements and coordination tests designed to root out candidates for success in gymnastics and swimming, the two Olympic sports in which teenagers regularly contended for medals.

Ullrich, the smallest in his class, had wriggled through a hole in that particular net. At some point in their third school year, most DDR children were submitted to the next phase of trials – a more rigorous battery of tests including a one-kilometre time trial on a closed road for which the qualifying time was two minutes. But in Ullrich's case, Peter Sager had got there first. Not thanks to some visionary protocol developed by DDR boffins but, as Sager tells me now, 'purely by fluke'.

'We had a winter cross-country running race coming up and, as a coach, you obviously have a certain amount of ambition and you want to win. But I had no one in the nine-year-olds' race, so I asked around, "Has anyone got a brother or a relative of some sort they could bring along?" Then Jan's older brother, Stefan, pipes up that he's got a brother. The race was on the Sunday in what we called the "new town" in Rostock. Jan was nine, had no training and won not only in his category but also the year above. It was a eureka moment for me. I told myself I had to coach this kid. Two or three weeks later, I'd got a bike ready for him and I took it to his house. "From today," I said, "you're a member of Dynamo Rostock West." That was the start of it all. From age nine to fifteen, I suppose he got the whole ABC of cycling from me.'

Sager is reminiscing in the front room of his house, a two-floor apartment reflecting the character of its humble, methodical owner on a quiet street a few blocks south of Rostock's town centre. Now in his seventies, he has the neighbourly air of a village carpenter or hardware-man, his round face bordered by two last strips of hair, his soft eyes the window into a kindly soul. His wife, Carola, brings us coffee and biscuits. For years, Jan Ullrich was one of the family here, often staying the night before races. To Carola and her husband, the received wisdom about Ullrich's 'difficult childhood' could sound like a personal affront. Carola maintains it is simply inaccurate. 'All of these stories about him growing up in poverty . . . it's nonsense. TV crews would come and film the worst parts of Rostock, then show Jan standing on the top step of the podium. They'd say, "Jan Ullrich went from this to this", as though it was some kind of rags to riches tale.'

Peter Sager's route into cycling had itself been a mazy journey made of chance encounters and blind turns. Born and raised in Wismar, a Rostock in miniature 50 kilometres west down the same Baltic Sea coastline towards Hamburg, Sager's first bike races were against the school bus taking his classmates to lessons in nearby Bobitz. He later trained as a shipbuilder before enrolling in the army. There he had to give up cycling due to heart problems but substituted it with judo, quickly becoming the champion of his battalion. As Sager says, though, 'the passion for cycling never went away'. He would eventually quit judo due to problems making his fighting weight, and attempt to rekindle his old love by buying a bike. He began coaching in Wismar, then moved to Rostock, where he joined the police. The motherlode of elite sport in the DDR, the Dynamo association existed under the aegis of the civilian police and the notorious Stasi, whose chief, Erich Mielke, was also Dynamo's president. In Rostock, having been urged to complete his formal training as a coach, Peter Sager would soon be one of the men responsible for finding and nurturing the young cyclists capable of graduating first to Dynamo's main star academy in Berlin – and later to glory for the DDR on the world stage.

Like his older brother Stefan, little Jan Ullrich could clearly run, but that was no guarantee of a glittering future on two wheels. Sager also didn't know at this point that he and Ullrich had something in common: aboard their bikes, Stefan and Jan had for months been racing their school bus to and from Grosse-Stove, just as Sager had between Bobitz and Wismar decades earlier.

'At the beginning, finding the talent is much more important than training it,' Sager notes now. 'As a coach I always tried to look for kids who had those fast-twitch muscle fibres, which you're born with or you're not. You can train endurance, but that speed is in the genes.' In 1986, Sager persuaded the city council to convert what was initially supposed to be a training facility for speed skaters on the west edge of Rostock into a 250-metre concrete bike track that would soon become the coach's lab, his factory, his canvas. 'Track work became the cornerstone of everything, and speed work in particular. It stands the slower kids in good stead and the ones with faster muscle fibres get even quicker.'

On 8 April 1984, under Sager's protective gaze, Jan Ullrich would take part in his first ever bicycle race. The venue was the Stephan-Jantzen-Ring in the Schmarl district of Rostock – a tarmac halo around a huge encampment of prefab concrete tower blocks that still stand today. The distance was 8.4 kilometres, or seven laps of the 'Ring'. The winner was Jan Ullrich.

Like other facets of the DDR sports system, how '*Nachwuchsportler*' or 'development athletes' were coached – and how much – has long been a source of fascination in the West. At age eleven, in his second season with Sager, Ullrich trained three times a week and raced at weekends, clocking up around 2,500 kilometres over the year. A favourite road ride took them south-west to Satow, over one of the few, unimposing hills in the region. The mileage increased considerably in Ullrich's third year with Sager and, by his final season at Dynamo Rostock, the near-daily road rides had lengthened from 30 to 70 kilometres and Ullrich's annual distance to well over 5,000 kilometres.

At the time, Dynamo Rostock West was one of around 1,500 designated training centres accommodating over 60,000 aspiring

DDR athletes across all sports, at the base layer of the DDR sporting pyramid. Ullrich's training group numbered twelve in the first year, eight in the second and four in the third and final year. After that, for Peter Sager to have fulfilled his mandate, at least one of his riders would have to qualify or, as the DDR functionaries termed it, be 'delegated' to Dynamo Berlin's residential *Kinder und Jugendsports-chule* (KJS), or academy. Sager insists that Dynamo's affiliation with the police and, by extension, the Stasi never posed any problems. 'I only ever had issues if I didn't get anybody delegated . . .'

With both Ullrich and a fellow scourge of Rostock junior races, André Korff, in Sager's class of 1984, he had no cause for concern. 'Jan was obsessed, frighteningly ambitious,' Sager says. He remembers pleading with Marianne to let Jan train when, once, as punishment for not doing his homework, she had barred him from riding his bike; Jan trampled up and down their linoleum kitchen floor in Stefan's running spikes in protest, compounding the original sin. 'He was a simple lad, who of course got up to mischief now and again,' Sager says. 'Sometimes you had to raise your voice. But when it came to cycling he never messed around. At school, yes – he might have skived off once or twice, not paid attention or tried to cheat in a test. That all comes with the territory. He wasn't a model pupil, wasn't especially sweet or kind. He messed around as much as any other kid. But that's also where you come into your own as a coach – keeping him on the straight and narrow.'

Sager says that Ullrich's competitive fire positively smouldered – whether he was riding a bike, kicking a football or doing press-ups in the gym. Initially around two thirds of his training was general athletic and gymnastic work – a cornerstone of the East German method but even more fundamental to Sager's curriculum, 'whether it was pull-ups, standing long jumps, jumping over obstacles or running through a metre of snow from the track to the New Town'. Sager had coached many kids who had graduated to Dynamo Berlin and gone on to compete nationally and internationally, but few had – as he puts it – 'been given so much by Mother Nature'.

The story sounds almost quaint, artless in Sager's anecdotal retelling, but of course the world would one day gasp in amazement and in some cases horror at what the eggheads of DDR sport had been hiding behind the Iron Curtain. There was a doping system of monstrous proportions, but also a breathtaking panoply of high-tech devices developed by the Research Institute for Physical Culture and Sport in Leipzig. They included the famous swimming flume invented in 1971 – a form of underwater treadmill for swimmers used by serial Olympic champions like Kornelia Ender and Barbara Krause. But the view lower down, among the grassroots of DDR sport, wasn't quite so impressive, particularly as the economy and with it an entire ideology creaked towards its eventual collapse in the mid-1980s. The Politburo's neglect of mass-participation sport had been a long-standing source of discontent stretching right back to the late 1950s, but increasingly every strata of DDR sport beneath the potentially medal-winning elite started to feel the squeeze. Peter Sager's office was located in an old coal cellar underneath Rostock's ice-hockey stadium, and in the adjoining room Sager had created the decidedly lo-fi 'sweatshop' where Ullrich, Korff and their Dynamo clubmates thrashed away on ergometers in winter. Sager had built the machines himself using dynamos rescued from a clapped-out old bus. Outside, on the track, while wrist-mounted heart-rate monitors were becoming all the rage, Sager simply placed his thumb on the inside of his rider's forearm, took a six-second pulse and multiplied by ten. By 1988, the DDR's sports ministry would be estimating that 30,000 racing bikes were needed to satisfy national demand, yet failing to ensure even a third of that rolled off production lines.

Of course, no one and nothing, not even a regime as determined to weaponize sporting success as the DDR, could buy the class Sager saw when Ullrich went to work in the saddle. 'It's just great when you see someone who looks at one with the bike like that,' Sager purrs. 'Some of them hang off the bike like a limp dishcloth. I also attached a lot of importance to aesthetics, which is basically the same as efficiency on the bike. I'd be following them in the car five days a week, just watching them from behind, barking instructions, or just adjustments, over a megaphone. If they start with bad habits when they're kids, you'll never get it out of them.'

By the end of 1986, Jan had turned thirteen and the Ullrichs had moved from Papendorf back to Rostock – into one of the 10,000 apartments that made up one of the DDR's largest high-rise housing developments, Lütten Klein. The views from their window were no longer of lush meadows rippling towards the North Sea but the dreary folds of a grey cityscape. There was at least more space in the flat for Jan and his younger brother Thomas, with Stefan now having been 'delegated' to Dynamo Berlin's athletics club. The Ullrichs were also climbing the social ladder, as much as that was possible under the DDR's conception of communism; Marianne's new job with the city council had brought her salary into line with the national average at the time – 1,100 marks a month.

Peace Race route maps ripped from *Junge Welt* and the *Neue Berliner Illustrierte* now hung on the wall in Jan's bedroom. Created in 1948 to help smooth relations between the Central European constituents of the Soviet Bloc, the two-week tour of Poland, Czechoslovakia and the DDR had become the biggest annual sporting event west of the Elbe – the communists' equivalent of the Tour de France, only with larger crowds and a keener sense of symbolism. Its stars – Uwe Raab, Uwe Ampler and the 1986 winner Olaf Ludwig – enjoyed God-like status in the DDR.

The first few months of 1987 would be vital for Ullrich's hopes of one day emulating those heroes. In the spring, he and André Korff were to face their judgement day – the trials to determine which young cyclists would be 'delegated' to a residential KJS, in their case, if selected, Dynamo Berlin. They had caused a sensation a few months earlier by leading Dynamo Rostock West to victory in the district championship four-man team time trial, then entering the under-17s event on a whim and finishing third. Peter Sager shows me a photograph of an even prouder moment from Ullrich's final months at Dynamo Rostock West; in it, we see three rows of young boys in identical cycling kit, interrupted only by a quartet in white jerseys adorned with the black, red and gold flag of East Germany and, printed on their chest, the year '1987'. Sager notes that Ullrich, Korff and their teammates Stefan Dassow and Jörg Papenfuß had just won the schoolboy 2,000-metre team pursuit national championship in Leipzig. Ullrich stands alongside the much taller Korff, looking distractedly to his left and towards Sager, whose smile in the picture resembles the one he wears now, the memory carrying him. 'National champions,' he says softly.

In order to secure their place in Berlin, Ullrich and Korff's by then enviable collection of trophies, medals, records and admirers would not suffice. 'Several factors came into play: first of all, sporting criteria; then medical; academic; and, back then, also political,' Sager explains. He recalls having to submit a report vouching for the thirteen-year-old Korff's ideological and political suitability, after family ties in the West had shown up in background checks. Dynamo officials would finally lower the red flag and allow Korff to take part in the trials, but, Sager concedes, 'That was not a very nice aspect of the whole thing, although we didn't fully realize it – it was just the way it was.'

The trials themselves consisted of a broad range of graded tests, many of them assessing general athletic and gymnastic, rather than cycling, performance. To help prepare his Dynamo Rostock West ensemble, in February Peter Sager had loaded his riders into his Barkas combi-van and headed to Wismar for a preparatory boot camp. Bike-riding was limited to track work or time on the rollers – and it was after one such session that Ullrich did something that will never feature in any almanac but has its own page in Peter Sager's personal anthology. 'They came off the rollers and I said, "Right, who can do a track stand?" Track stands are something every kid has to learn if he's going to race on the track, but most of them just topple over. So, if they could do it, I gave them a bar of chocolate. And that was that; I went off to cook their dinner, then, a while later, one of the kids suddenly bursts in: "Herr Sager, Jan's still standing . . ." It must have been half an hour. And he got a whole big box of chocolates for that. It was just that ability to handle the bike, which the examiners also looked at later in the KJS trials. And Jan hadn't trained it at all; it was pure talent.'

In his 2004 autobiography, it should be noted, Ullrich offered a different version of the same events: he claimed the track stand had lasted for one hour, thirteen minutes.

No one disputed that the kid was born to ride, although that genetic predisposition nearly turned into too much of a good thing later that same spring. In a medical check-up shortly before KJS selection weekend, a doctor in Rostock had noticed what he believed was an irregularity in Ullrich's heartbeat. Further tests were soon performed in Wismar by Gerd Dührkop, also doctor to then 400-metre world record holder Marita Koch. 'It could all have ended there,' says Sager. But Dührkop's conclusion was that Ullrich simply had an unusually large heart and slow pulse – also two indicia of his exceptional aerobic abilities.[3]

Just how remarkable those gifts were became evident at the KJS trials in Berlin. Much like a decathlon, these consisted of multiple events, each of which had been assigned their own performance-based points scale. Scores were also weighted for relative physical development, with thirteen-year-old Ullrich attributed a 'biological age' of just eleven. The most gruelling and in some ways most revealing discipline, the 3,000-metre run, was saved until last – and here Ullrich stunned everyone. 'The upper limit to score any points was thirteen minutes, thirty seconds,' Peter Sager explains. 'Well, I stood there with my clipboard and Jan was the only kid in the whole trials to run nine minutes something. You see that and it takes a while to process. He won the whole trial because of that run, was the best in the whole of East Germany. He didn't win it because of the cycling, but because of the 3,000 metres. The athletics coaches saw it and said to me, "Are you stupid? The kid has to be a runner, not a cyclist."'

Korff also made the cut, finishing third overall; Peter Sager's *Wunderkinder* were heading to Berlin – or rather would be back there, permanently, from the start of the school term the following September. Sadly for Ullrich, his older brother was heading in the opposite direction, out of Dynamo and back to Rostock – because the 'training conditions were better there', according to Jan. Over the next couple of years, Stefan would collect multiple DDR national junior titles in middle-distance events, only for knee injuries to drag him abruptly from the DDR medal factory's assembly line. Peter Sager believed cycling could have turned into a viable plan B, and was ready to make the older Ullrich his pet project in the autumn of 1989. 'He'd come to watch some track training sessions and had a few goes himself. He was also pretty handy. I'd got a bike ready for him . . . and then the Berlin Wall came down. He got on a bus, went off to somewhere in Spain, met a girl and that was it for his athletic career.'

Sager shrugs. Anyone like him, who has been training kids for nearly half a century, has seen many more stories of unfulfilled potential than fairy tales. This applies even to the Ullrich family. 'The youngest, Thomas, was the most talented of the lot. Crazy,' he says. 'But that's just how it goes. Thomas got injured . . . and it's in the head as well. As a coach you can have some influence, but ultimately it comes down to the athlete: "Do I take the right path or don't I?"'

Almost a decade to the day after Jan Ullrich's last races in the wine-red colours of Dynamo Rostock West, Peter Sager would watch him ride onto the Champs-Élysées in Paris wearing the *maillot jaune* of

Tour de France champion elect. At four the next morning, Ullrich was presenting Sager with the signed jersey that still hangs in Sager's porch and falling into his first coach's arms in a corridor of the Concorde-Lafayette hotel. 'Oh yes, that was emotional, but I must say that with André it was even more intense,' Sager says. André is André Greipel, the eleven-time Tour stage-winning sprinter who became Sager's next *alumnus excelsus*, after Ullrich, and with whom Sager maintains an even closer relationship. That day in 1997, Sager joked to the German television commentator Herbert Watterott that it was only down to him that Ullrich had become a cyclist and not a runner. Similarly, Sager once had to plead with Greipel not to ditch cycling in favour of football.

Asked to account for how, in an East German port city with an average annual temperature of 8 degrees Celsius and no prior tradition of producing leading cyclists, Sager alone has either discovered or weaned eight who went on to compete in the Tour de France, including Ullrich, he responds with typical self-effacement. 'As a coach, you can't work like someone sitting behind a desk or a work bench. That just doesn't fly . . . Some of what we did in the DDR was prescribed or dictated to us, and then we could put our own stamp on it. There was no better training programme than what we had in the DDR. I knew exactly how much speed work I needed to do, exactly how much endurance, how much I needed to do on skills and how much general athletics. The real art in the coaching was to get the message across. But as far as the programmes themselves went, there was nothing better. The training plans we followed are still being used in the UK, France, Italy and Australia.'

There is a recurring lament among former East German coaches, many of whom were 'exported' and enjoyed success all over the world after reunification. The DDR's sporting miracle, the paradox of a nation of 17 million that amassed 519 Olympic medals between 1968 and 1988 while West Germany's 60 million could muster only 253, is nowadays more often than not reduced to its bare chemical formulae, as though drugs were the system's only ammunition. This narrative ignores the extent to which that apparatus relied on massive funding, a talent-identification programme of unprecedented scale, political indoctrination, material incentives and, to a certain extent, fear of Stasi surveillance and reprisals. And also, in many cases, on scientific rigour, a canny eye and good coaching.

Peter Sager doesn't need reminding, in late 2015, that the many dimensions of the Jan Ullrich story have been conflated in exactly the same way. For detractors, Ullrich too is now synonymous with only one thing; they have neither the time nor inclination to parse causes and effects, heroes and villains, what Ullrich learned in the East and developed in the West. For some, Ullrich even became a locus of prejudice against the East in general, like drugs in DDR sport. As Mike Dennis and Jonathan Grix observe in *Sport Under Communism*: 'Post-unification condemnation of drug abuse as an intrinsic part of a dehumanizing and exploitative sports system, while not unjustified, is frequently turned into a stick with which to beat and demonize the DDR socio-political system as a whole.'[4]

The topic is an understandably bitter one for Peter Sager. How can it not be, when, as he says, 'the kids spent more time with me than they spent at home'? 'We were always away somewhere: five times a week then races at the weekend, when they also slept at my house or at one of my relatives' places.

'You can only really say with hindsight that things happened [in the DDR] that weren't exactly above board,' he goes on. 'Personally I didn't even know what doping was. In the junior categories there simply wasn't any of that. Or I knew nothing about it. I only read about it later – in books about Hamilton or Armstrong. Then suddenly the blindfold fell from my eyes. I just didn't think it was possible. Just crazy, what happened with Jan's generation . . .'

Sager's voice fades to a whisper, his gaze drifts to the middle of the room. He belongs to a generation of East Germans who have become accustomed to second-guessing memories they made in a land reduced to a caricature – a 'museum country' of quirky artefacts, brown furniture, bad weather and evil government. For the last three decades these once ordinary folk have been asked to rewrite or at least re-edit whole life stories, while knowing that no amount of conscious revisionism can alter certain realities – truths then and truths now.

For Peter Sager, one such keystone is that many years ago he 'discovered' a cyclist named Jan Ullrich.

Or, as he says now, 'The greatest I had – and there's no one else in the frame.'

3

DIPLOMATS IN TRACKSUITS

'Mr Gorbachev, open this gate! Mr Gorbachev, tear down this wall!'

—*Ronald Reagan*

The summer of 1987 was a memorable one for many among 'Generation Jan Ullrich', whether they lived on the East or West side of the Berlin Wall. In August, Ullrich's mum, Marianne, would drive him to the capital in her white Trabant, as excited as she was nervous about seeing her 'Jani' fly the family nest – and Ullrich landed in a city in a state of building ferment. A few weeks earlier, David Bowie had returned to West Berlin a decade after finding his creative oasis in the decrepit, still war-scarred doomscape ignored by empty suits in Bonn yet somehow fetishized by artists and musicians. A 'Disneyland for depressives', as the English record producer Mark Reeder calls it in the documentary, *B Movie: Lust & Sound in West Berlin*. A 'city with its arse in the garbage can', in the words of another famous and troubled Berlin émigré, Nick Cave.

The city had changed little since Bowie had moved out of his apartment in Schöneberg, but something was quietly stirring. That June, a three-day music festival celebrated Berlin's 750th birthday in the shadow of the Reichstag, naturally on the West side. But the 'death zone' bisecting the city was a more effective barrier to the venal ideas of capitalism than it was to sound – specifically, the message of hope and defiance that Bowie delivered with his rendition of 'Heroes'. He had recorded the song ten years earlier at a studio only a kilometre or two away, as an ode to a pair of separated lovers from the East and West.

The concert organizers boomed its chorus back over the Wall.

Before long, the hundreds of East Berliners who had gathered on their side of the Brandenburg Gate, many of them around Jan Ullrich's age, were crowing back: 'The Wall must go! The Wall must go!' As the DDR Volkspolizei stormed into the crowd with their truncheons, the chants continued – a sarcastic karaoke of the Soviet anthem, 'The Internationale', and noisy invocations of the reformist Soviet leader, Mikhail Gorbachev.

Six days later, US President Ronald Reagan stood in front of the Gate and addressed Gorbachev in a famous speech: 'Mr Gorbachev,' Reagan said, 'open this gate! Mr Gorbachev, tear down this wall!'

It would take two more years – and Jan Ullrich would spend them at the north-easternmost edge of a still very much divided city. His new home was a room on the seventh floor of a tower block not dissimilar from the one in which he had once lived in Rostock, among hundreds of others that had made a concrete honeycomb out of one half of the city skyline.

The dorm that Ullrich was to share with his old friend from Rostock and now fellow Dynamo Berlin undergraduate, André Korff, could best be described as spartan. Ullrich and Korff had called shotgun on the bunks, while a third room-mate, a fledgling track sprinter they knew as 'Schitti', would sleep on a single bed. They each had one shelf and a cupboard for clothes and other belongings. On the day of his arrival, Jan groaned with embarrassment when Marianne insisted on sticking around to help him unpack. He waited for her to leave before decorating the walls with posters: one of the 1987 Peace Race winner and Ullrich's future team manager, Olaf Ludwig, and another of an East Berlin-based athlete whom Ullrich and Korff admired for more than just her prowess in the long-jump pit – the future *Playboy* model Susen Tiedtke.

With his arrival at Dynamo Berlin, Ullrich had joined approximately 10,000 young East Germans on the middle rung of the DDR talent ladder – the twenty-five academies created to ensure a steady supply line of elite athletes to East Germany's sports clubs. Around 700 of the 3,500 sports club athletes would then typically meet the required standard to become a 'diplomat in a tracksuit' – the name informally given to the DDR team members called to embody and propagate the Marxist-Leninist ideology of the Socialist Unity Party of Germany (SED) by representing their homeland in competitions like the Olympic Games. Among these organizations, SV Dynamo was the behemoth, with both its own connected KJS, of which Ullrich was now an inductee, and, above that, the most successful of the DDR's twenty-five sports clubs. Had it competed at the 1972 Olympics in Munich as an independent nation, SV Dynamo would have finished ninth in the medal table. It was the pride of the East and certainly of Erich Mielke, its president, who from 1957 to the death of the DDR in 1989 served as the Minister for State Security, otherwise known as the secret police or the Stasi. The West German press dubbed Mielke the 'Master of Fear'.

Being 'delegated' to Dynamo did not necessarily align someone with the Stasi – but neither did it exempt them, in the final years of the DDR, from scrutiny by the estimated 3,000 informants (IMs) mandated solely to report back on matters relating to sport. Recent studies suggest that around one in sixteen of the 17 million people living in the DDR was a Stasi employee, an informant or someone who would willingly provide the Stasi with intelligence on a more casual basis. IMs were recruited among coaches, journalists, club officials and even athletes themselves. Any youngster at a training centre hoping to be delegated to a KJS would already have had to pass various kinds of background checks, including scrutiny of their family and even presumptions about their sexual orientation by IMs. One of the leading researchers into the DDR sport system, Giselher Spitzer, provides the example of eleven- and twelve-year-olds being required to maintain a detailed training log in which they would also have to write down their goals or sporting heroes. Any child who gave the name of a Westerner would have the page ripped out of the book and a note added to their file. All children in the system were referred to as a *Versuchsperson*: literally, a test subject.

On his first afternoon as a Dynamo Berlin undergrad, Jan Ullrich knew almost nothing of what awaited him – beyond the name of his new coach, Peter Becker. I nonetheless assume that Ullrich was less apprehensive than I am twenty-nine years later, on a balmy Tuesday night early in September, when Becker instructs me to report to his house on the outer edges of Prenzlauer Berg in north-east Berlin at six o'clock. The pre-agreed plan is for Becker to 'get to know' me, size up my intentions, then decide whether or not we will go ahead with a 'proper interview' the following day.

It doesn't sound altogether promising. The DDR sports system, its architects and enforcers, were as renowned for their secrecy as they were for their discipline. One epithet is almost ubiquitous in portrayals of Becker: he was, had always been, a *'harter Hund'* – literally a 'hard dog'. Meaning, I presume, that his bite will be as bad as his bark.

Twenty minutes after I have stepped apprehensively through his front gate and found him watering plants in the back garden that is his pride and joy, Becker has both hands locked firmly, painfully around my right forearm. He is also growling. It is less Chinese burn than Berliner vice.

'You see, a wolf gets you like this and rips your arm off,' Becker is telling me, gritting his teeth. 'People think the wolf is this cute, cuddly animal. "Save the Wolf!" *Pah!* The wolf is a fierce creature! Fierce! He looks as though he doesn't want to get too close, but he's watching. He's watching. Checking the colour of your clothes. Your scent. Deciding whether you'll make a good meal. A wolf needs three and a half kilos of meat a day . . .'

Becker releases his grip to raise an exclamatory finger.

'They're getting closer to Berlin every year. Every year. One of these days, you'll see . . .'

On that alarming note, Becker brings his arms to rest, folded, upon his chest, seemingly satisfied that he has made his point. He can now take off his overalls to reveal a faded black Team Telekom polo shirt that must be twenty years old. Becker himself has scarcely aged since we last saw him at races and in photographs a decade or so ago, invariably alongside Ullrich. His pelt is a snowier shade, but the hairline remains as luxuriant and the eyebrows just as bushy. Contrary to reputation, the old dog is also a warm, welcoming, avuncular host, albeit one who makes his point in a booming, sometimes unintelligibly pronounced Berlin accent, through a barrage of 'k's and 'j's. Any diffidence or hesitation on his part has nonetheless quickly disappeared, or is well concealed.

I have already learned, and will have it confirmed to me over the next four hours – then four more the following day – that Peter Becker loves to talk. The quite literally gripping tutorial on the migration habits of quadruped predators segues naturally from a question about Becker's plans for the following afternoon, and him announcing that he is off to hunt. He is a lifelong naturalist and graduate of forestry school, leading me to ponder but not ask how he reconciles his seemingly contradictory passions. Before we start talking – just *quatschen*, small talk, not a real interview yet, as he reminds me and himself – Becker insists on giving me a tour of his house. We go first to a living room that doubles as a taxidermy museum, its walls bedecked with stags' heads and wild boar snouts, its coffee tables patrolled by ornamental squirrels and ferrets. We then head downstairs, past more antlers, these ones rescued from the old DDR leader Erich Honecker's hunting lodge after reunification – another long story – and into a small office where Becker has filled several shelves with his cycling cups and trophies. Among them I spot a small glass disc mounted upon a piece of marble. The inscription underneath tells me this was Jan Ullrich's prize at Arcalís in 1997.

We go back upstairs, through to Becker's conservatory or 'winter garden', and onto the serious business – or, as he says, the small talk. A few hours later, the next morning, we are back in the same spot, and will be for the next several hours. Every once in a while Becker's wife will appear with refreshments – and they will be the only interruptions. It turns out that his arm didn't need much twisting. Once bitten, twice shy, both of mine remain hidden under the long sleeves of a thick sweater.

The story of how Peter Becker fell in love with cycling is, he tells me, a simple one to which nearly every child can relate. 'The flash of the spokes as they catch the sunlight. The gliding sensation. The speed. The tingle on your cheeks as skins breaks the air,' he coos. 'A kid is always fascinated by a bicycle . . .'

He saw his first one in 1949, at age eleven, in Bad Belzig, the town an hour west of Berlin where his family had sought refuge when the war broke out. Three years later, Becker and his classmates watched from the roadside as the Peace Race swooshed past their school, a shimmering blaze of metal, muscles and dreams. Soon, Becker was dismantling his stepfather's bike and attempting to rebuild it into an improvised racing machine like the Czech-made Favorit beauties he had seen propelling the members of a local club.

By this time, the East German road map to international sporting glory was beginning to take shape. In 1946, Erich Honecker, the future leader of the SED, had spoken of 'sport's power to put large sections of population under its spell'. Two years later, Honecker went further, or rather closer to an admission that athletics, football and other competitive physical endeavours would fulfil a key political role in the DDR, by stating that, 'Sport is not an end in itself, but a means to the end.' As the former gold medal-winning swimmer turned academic Andrew Strenk put it in the late 1970s, 'trade, commerce, diplomacy and negotiation were not available to the DDR for use in influencing the world beyond the borders of Eastern Europe [forcing them to] turn to sports as a medium of cultural diplomacy to obtain [their] foreign policy goals.'[5] In truth, it would eventually come to look less like diplomacy than cultural aggression, a kind of ideological as well as literal muscle-flexing designed to prove the transcendence of the 'socialist personality' and expose the evils of capitalism. Hitler had tried something similar with Nazism and the Berlin Olympics in 1936.

By 1968, SED memos would be equating elite athletes not to diplomats but to soldiers, their West Germany counterparts with the NATO guards at the border. But before that, one of the first, proud feathers in the cap of DDR sport had arrived via the 1955 edition of the Peace Race. Overnight, Täve Schur, its winner, became the DDR's first true sporting icon, and, Becker says, 'A Pied Piper for my generation – still today.' Schur was also a member of the SED and a parliamentarian who once declared that he owed everything he had achieved to his political party. Becker's own quest to emulate him on two wheels began in 1957, when he took part in his first race in the colours of Dynamo Potsdam. He would discover in time that he was a more effective teacher than practitioner, despite competing in races like the Little Peace Race for junior riders. Before calling time on his own racing career, Becker also had his first and he claims still solitary experience of 'doping' – a codeine-caffeine-ephedrine solution bought from a chemist and, at the time, commonly and legally used by cyclists. He insists it did nothing except leave him shivering in a ditch. And turn him into a lifelong opponent of chemical performance enhancement.

Becker's formal coaching career effectively began when he successfully applied to SV Dynamo in 1964, a year before a catalytic moment in East Germany's weaponization of elite sport: the pharmaceutical company, VEB Jenapharm, synthesizing Oral Turinabol, the testosterone-boosting anabolic steroid that later became the DDR coaches' *Wunderwaffe* – their wonder weapon. Becker was deployed two levels below the tip of the Dynamo performance pyramid, in the club's KJS. He went on to coach many of the young cyclists who brought Dynamo sixteen out of a possible seventeen DDR national titles in the school-age categories in 1968, before an argument with club officials resulted in his banishment to the boxing division until 1974.

By then, East German sportsmen and women were flourishing at world and Olympic level. Having had to compete in a joint, if not exactly 'unified' German team in every previous Olympics since the war, the DDR was recognized as an independent sporting nation for the first time at the 1968 Games in Mexico City – and shocked the world by finishing fifth in the medal table. Sweetest of all was the fact that West Germany languished three places further down the rankings. The 1972 Olympics would be even more important on account of where they would take place – Munich. The powerbrokers at SED headquarters feared that the noisy neighbours would use the opportunity to glorify or 'sportwash' their ignoble, fascistic instincts, and were determined to ruin the festivities. To that end, after some dabbling before 1968, primarily by athletes from Dynamo Berlin, in September 1970 the head of sports medicine for all of the DDR, Manfred Höppner, formerly gave his blessing to a plan of systematic and illegal doping. The result in Munich was the desired drubbing of the *Klassenfeind*, with the DDR claiming twenty golds to West Germany's thirteen. A valid detection method for anabolic steroids would arrive only four years later.

Peter Becker swears that his knowledge of Oral Turinabol went no further than 'hearsay'. Later, he tells me, well after Munich, experiments with this and other drugs on track cyclists were inconclusive or unsuccessful, which is a claim that many would dispute. 'They put us in the corner and they say [East German sport] was all just doping, but I always reject that,' Becker says. Instead, in the darkest age of DDR doping – the two decades up to reunification during which the DDR was never out of the top three in Olympic medals, summer or winter, but 10,000 athletes are thought to have been doped – Becker says that he was refining a method based on the most organic of philosophies: 'Nature gave us spring, summer, autumn and winter, and also day and night. We are living beings in an ecosystem and we have to abide by its laws.'

Meaning that, in the dorm rooms belonging to SV Dynamo, just as in the forests of north Brandenburg, only the strong would survive.

Becker's introductory monologue to Jan Ullrich and the other members of his Dynamo Berlin class of 1987 also contained a warning – though this one had nothing to do with drugs or indeed encroaching wolves: 'You no doubt think you're the biggest and best but now the serious stuff starts and second and third place don't mean anything any more. You're all starting from zero,' Becker told them.

Becker had encountered Ullrich for the first time a few months earlier, in November 1986, not on the road but in a cyclo-cross race in Potsdam, which Ullrich had won with ease. A month or so later, with Becker in attendance, Ullrich aced the KJS trials in Berlin that would determine the thirteen-year-old's sporting future. His results in many of the disciplines were remarkable, not least the sub-ten-minute 3,000-metre run which was the best in East Germany, but Peter Becker had paid equal attention to the football match as the athletics and even the cycling trials (a flying 200-metre, a two-kilometre time trial on the track and a ten-kilometre time trial on the road). 'I wanted to see the way a boy moved with and without the ball, his competitiveness, his work ethic and how much of a team player he was. In a match you can usually gauge someone's character.' In Ullrich's first few weeks at Dynamo Berlin, Becker was struck by some of the same attributes he had seen a few months earlier: 'His fighting spirit above all – as well as his ability to recover physically. But he was just desperate to make it, to become a really great rider.'

As already discussed, it was common practice in DDR sports schools to differentiate biological and chronological age, and Ullrich's arrival at Dynamo Berlin also coincided with a period of mounting concern about how much late-blooming talent was going to waste in the training centres, KJSs and sports clubs. Weighing barely 50 kilograms and under five feet tall, Ullrich was still awaiting his growth spurt – and Becker trained him and six others accordingly, with noticeably lighter workloads. As had been the case under Peter Sager in Rostock, cycling initially accounted for a relatively small proportion of the daily routine. Long hours were also spent on the basketball court, the football pitch, on gym mats and in the swimming pool.

Jan Schaffrath, who was trained and schooled at Dynamo's rival club, Turn-Sport-Club or TSC, and later became Ullrich's teammate at Telekom, says the most underrated facet of the DDR method was its variety. 'You can easily burn someone out if it's just cycling, cycling, cycling all year but we were doing all sorts, and I think that's maybe why a lot of the guys from the East ended up having very long careers – like Erik Zabel and Jens Voigt. Physically you also saw the legacy of it all later: [West German rider] Rolf Aldag used to say to me that he could tell who was East German and who was West German just by watching a sprint finish. The guys from the East had such incredible core strength from all the gym work they did that they barely moved on the bike.'

Peter Sager's belief that elegance and power on a bike were rarely if ever mutually exclusive had already shaped Ullrich's style. Now Becker only had to perfect it, as he explained in the book he wrote in 2004: 'Ulli* absolutely mastered that elegant way of riding, that aesthetic style I wanted. I always compare it with a musician. Only when he's truly grown up with the instrument, when it's really in him, can he then start to improvise with it. Ulli can do that. It's like he and the bike have been cast out of the same mould.'

The process of refinement was a time-consuming one. Ullrich would typically spend three to four hours on the bike every morning, then afternoons in the classroom at the Werner-Seelenbinder high school – or mornings behind a desk and afternoons in the gym or playing football. So it went, from Monday to Saturday (the DDR school week lasted six days). He would ride around 6,000 kilometres in his first year in Berlin, 9,000 in his second and 13,000 in his third. Training sessions were typically 60 to 80 kilometres long, most commonly into the thick forests or around the many lakes that dapple the east and north Brandenburg flatlands, then back to the big city. Sometimes Becker would take them to do intervals on the Großer Bunkerberg – an artificial hill built from Second World War rubble a

---

* Peter Becker was and still is apparently unique among Ullrich's friends and acquaintances in preferring the diminutive nickname 'Ulli' over the otherwise widely preferred 'Ulle'.

couple of kilometres from Dynamo's main campus in north-east Berlin.

Above all, Becker hopes that I have already grasped one thing – that he was never just some card-punching functionary mindlessly executing the dictates of the 'Party', the Dynamo leadership or the two government bodies which tussled for control of the sports schools – the Ministry for People's Education and the German Gymnastics and Sport Confederation of the DDR. Never was his training more effective, he says, than when its recipients were enjoying themselves. To that end, he made them box, ice-skate and play football in ankle-high snow. He took them cross-country skiing on the famous Kammloipe in the Ore mountain range bordering Czechoslovakia. They swam in lakes. And when they were forced inside, into the cavernous gym halls of the Hohenschönhausen campus, Becker would patrol up and down the line of stationary bikes, orchestrating a virtual road-race: 'Left turn, 200 metres downhill then sprint to get on the wheel!' All a far cry from the images of poker-faced cyborgs in gym vests used in Western documentaries to account for the East German sporting miracle.

'The way they'd give us training plans with targets and ratios was rubbish in many respects, but, among us coaches, we protected ourselves from that,' Becker explains. 'Back then, not everything was computer-processed, so we would write the figures down twice: one set of numbers for ourselves and one for the bosses. I carried on doing that right to the end. Simply gave them the training logs and figures that they wanted to see, while going on instinct and feel. If I'd always respected the plans, I would have had them out on the road in minus twelve degrees – but we had rotten clothing that was only made to be water repellent, not to keep them warm. That's where I put my foot down: I said, "Inside, warm shower, in the pool, then home and to bed." When I'd trained as a coach we'd always learned that health should be at the centre of everything. Later it looked as though it had become about performance at any price.'

Like with a lot of things in the DDR, Becker notes, noble ideas and desired effects had slowly drifted apart from real-world outcomes.

'We had this socialist system based on the idea that the national wealth was everyone's wealth, so no one could get rich at another person's expense. But there were these huge contradictions that were our brand of socialism's undoing. The whole notion of competition in society was bent out of shape. Just look at the food prices: a bread roll ended up costing the same in 1989 as it did in 1950 . . . I can't use the gross national product for things that are a big waste, like the military or the Stasi. That's where people started to be dissatisfied with the political system. They were promised wine and given water.'

The illusion of a socialist utopia had long since expired – but a hermetically sealed simulacrum did exist within the walls of clubs like Dynamo. Later, Ullrich's friends would notice the fondness with which he talked about the years he spent in East Berlin. 'I always had the impression that it was the best time of his life,' says Falk Nier, the tennis player who later became his manager. Others confirm that it went beyond the stereotypical *Ostalgie* – a romanticization of the pre-reunification years of which Easterners are often accused. Becker worked out quickly that Ullrich enjoyed and thrived within the framework of a rigid routine, just so long as he didn't have to create that structure himself.

'Of course they also got up to their mischief – like watching West German television, which was strictly forbidden,' Becker says. 'And there was other nonsense. Dares. Ride as fast they could towards a door and the one who braked last was the winner. Of course you're not supposed to know about these things but you start to play detective. "What have we got here then? Long black stripes in front of the door?" Skidmarks. Of course this was strictly forbidden. The door was glass, it would have shattered if they'd hit it – so no need to spell out how dangerous it could have been. Or when they were throwing water bombs out of the dorm window, and maybe the odd bottle. You try to educate them. Just imagine – you're a DDR champion and you go through a glass screen, cut your tendon and you can't ride a bike any more. Then they start to think about it a bit more . . .'

The topic of another kind of schooling – academic – and how much of it young East Germans received at the KJSs was a contentious one throughout the lifespan of the DDR. Officials had always maintained that the DDR's continued success on the international sporting stage hinged on their ability to not only prepare their athletes physically but also to bestow upon them the credos of the 'socialist personality'. This gave rise to a curriculum that eschewed French lessons in favour of Russian and prioritized *Staatsbürgerkunde* – long, prosaic lectures on the origins, political applications and inherent superiority of the Marxist-Leninist doctrine – as a bulwark against the evils of capitalist imperialism.

By his own admission 'really bad' in languages, Ullrich fared considerably better at maths and excelled in mechanics and lever equations according to his physics teacher. Not that his grades concerned him or any of his tutors unduly. As he said later, 'At the KJS, training was the focal point of everything, not schoolwork. If you got bad marks, it wasn't something to be proud of, but it wasn't a massive issue either. If you weren't performing in your sport, on the other hand, you'd be out of the door.'

On that score he had nothing to fear. At the end of his first year at Dynamo Berlin, he lined up in the B-Youth category in the DDR national road race championships. Ullrich was one of the smallest, slightest riders on the start line, but that was no disadvantage on a hilly course on the outskirts of Dresden. When André Korff crashed out early, Ullrich spied his opportunity, attacking on the final climb to take victory by over two minutes. His prize was a white jersey decorated with the black, red and gold bands of the national flag. He gave that to his grandfather, his most ardent and loyal supporter. He would also henceforth receive a monthly bursary of 100 marks given to all 'national level' athletes. Ullrich promptly informed his mum that he no longer needed the 30 marks pocket money she had previously sent to Berlin every few weeks.

One parental 'privilege' was still allowed – Marianne would still buy him ice cream when work brought her to Berlin and Jan would go to meet her in Alexanderplatz. He also still grudgingly acquiesced when, in the summer break after that first year at Dynamo Berlin, Marianne banned him from training on account of the heatwave on Germany's Baltic Sea coast and increasing concerns about the growing hole in the ozone layer. Becker was furious when Ullrich reported back to Berlin out of shape – and amazed when, in the first fitness tests of the new term, he was still among the best in the class. Ullrich admitted later that the experience set an unhelpful precedent; the title of his autobiography, *All or Not At All*, was also a neat summation of how, Ullrich believed, he could allow himself periods of almost complete inactivity if a short training binge undid the damage.

The highpoint of Ullrich's second year at Dynamo Berlin came in July 1989, when around 2,000 of the DDR's most talented junior athletes – of the nearly two million that had tried to qualify in local preliminary rounds – converged on Berlin for the event that exemplified the spirit, the reach and the goals of the DDR sport system as well as any other: the Spartakiade. First held in 1966, this miniature Olympics mimicked the pomp, media coverage and even the sheer scale of the actual games, with its packed 100,000-capacity venues and dazzling flag-waving ceremonies. The events were also designed to give future DDR Olympic hopefuls a taste of the patriotic honour and responsibilities for which they were ultimately being groomed. Hence, Ullrich's homework one day in the spring of 1989 was to write about his hopes for the Spartakiade, and he signed off with the vow to summon all of his 'discipline' and 'fighting spirit' to make Peter Becker and Dynamo proud. He finally took bronze in the four-man team time trial, but was outshone by his friend Korff, who won the road race. Throughout the week, Ullrich's thoughts had also been permeated with the technicoloured, intoxicating images of another sporting showcase, this one taking place on the other side of the Iron Curtain. The Tour de France was rip-roaring towards its most thrilling conclusion in decades, with one former winner, Laurent Fignon of France, leading another, the American Greg LeMond, by fifty seconds ahead of the final-day time trial. It was unthinkable that any DDR channel would broadcast or in most cases even so much as mention a race contested behind enemy lines. But, as Peter Becker says with a smile, 'They were sneaky – they were smart enough to play around with the aerial and pick up the Western channel, which wasn't blocked. They turned the volume down, had one of them guard the door . . .'

Ullrich later revealed the finer details of their counter-espionage, explaining how one of the posse would hide inside the cabinet on which the television was perched, ready to switch channels at a second's notice. Seconds were also what decided the Tour – eight of them being the difference when a devastated Fignon crossed the line, knowing that LeMond had overhauled him. Having supported LeMond throughout the Tour, Ullrich was euphoric, not to mention spellbound by the fleeting glimpse into another world that might as well have been another universe. As he put it: 'The rumours about the prize money, the garishness of the publicity caravan, the bright-coloured jerseys of the pro teams, the high-tech bikes – it all left an indelible mark on us while all seeming unimaginably far away.'

That summer was proving even more tumultuous than the one of Ullrich's arrival in Berlin two years earlier. In May, against the backdrop of Gorbachev's Glasnost (liberalization) and Perestroika (restructuring) in the Soviet Union and the worsening economic downturn in the DDR, Hungary began dismantling its border fence with Austria, creating the first puncture in the Soviet Bloc. Tens of thousands of East Germans seized their opportunity to either sneak into the West via this back door or seek asylum at the West German embassy in Budapest. Having already downgraded border crossings from 'crimes' to 'misdemeanours', in September the Hungarian government removed all formal opposition to DDR citizens exiting their land to enter Austria. Soon Czechoslovakia had followed suit and, with tension at home escalating, the SED leadership allowed fourteen trains crammed with DDR 'refugees' to travel through the East on their way from Prague to Bavaria and a new future on the 'other side'.

The scent of revolution was in the air, and it became ever more irresistible at a series of protests in the autumn, most notably in Leipzig and Berlin. With Ossis streaming out of the DDR and through the once ironclad Hungarian and Czech perimeters into Austria and West Germany, the SED began to implode. Erich Honecker, the party's leader since 1971, was ousted in mid-October, after which his successor, Egon Krenz, failed to dissuade the government's entire Cabinet from resigning on 7 November. The DDR had quite simply spiralled out of control.

Late in the afternoon of 9 November, in an otherwise routine press conference, an SED official made a muddled announcement about the DDR's intention to open its borders, and the lack of clarity over when exactly that would take effect led to huge crowds converging on the Berlin Wall. At 11.30 p.m., the first unobstructed crossings took place when, fearing a stampede and confused by the mixed messages of his superiors, a border guard at the checkpoint on Bornholmer Straße simply opened a gate and began letting people into the West. The Wall effectively 'fell' at that moment.

In November 2019, I am living in Berlin when the city and Germany celebrate the thirtieth anniversary of the moment when, as I keep reading in the papers, 'the fear switched sides'. This meant that a population living in the dark, sinister shadow of the Iron Curtain –

its paranoias and its repression – could finally emerge into the light, while many long-lost brothers and sisters suddenly required to welcome and reabsorb them gulped at the prospect. More simply put, when the DDR crumbled. The life-changing pivot that Germans, all Germans, whether 'Ossis' from the old East or 'Wessis' from the West, refer to simply as 'Die Wende' – the Turn, and which led in October 1990 to Germany's official reunification.

The subject is so ubiquitous in the conversations of most Germans over thirty that it scarcely seems to need a week of parties, exhibitions or public debates for remembrance. At the same time, I tell myself, never more than over these seven days is it apparent that what looks to outsiders like Germans' obsession with their own recent history, a form of collective PTSD, is truly a vain, never-ending attempt to *understand* the inexplicable and unconscionable. This process of introspection seems if anything to have become even more intense, more pressing and more confusing since the 2015 refugee crisis, when Chancellor Angela Merkel's open-door policy and particularly one three-word soundbite that has become a lightning rod – '*Wir schaffen das*' or 'we can do this' – exposed grave disunities in the way that Germans now view themselves, their past and their future, beyond and aside from the global rise of populism.

In Berlin, I see the struggles play out on a micro as well as a macro level: ordinary children of the East from 'ordinary' families who can't quite fathom how at the time life felt precisely that – ordinary – and who even today have to make an effort to correlate their memory with vulgar caricatures; friends' grandparents whose destinies were passed from the murderous hands of the Nazis into the grip of the Stasi; Berliners like the millennials and Gen Z-ers who surround me at a performance of East German punk music and poetry on the eve of the anniversary, in one of the key landmarks of the Berlin uprising, the Zionskirche in Mitte, and whose whimsical curiosity rather than a desire to relive and rejoice or grieve, it looks to me, is what has brought them here on a Friday night.

But I may also be wrong. A few days before the anniversary, the *Guardian* features a series of interviews with German writers. Maxim Leo, the former editor of the *Berliner Zeitung* and author of a famous memoir of family life in the East, says that the Germans aren't interested in figuring anything out at all: Westerners just want to know that they were on the right side of history and that Ossis are

a) exactly as the Wessis imagine and b) grateful. As a result, according to Leo, 'East Germans stopped explaining themselves ages ago. Sometimes they still point out hesitantly that it didn't rain all the time even in the DDR, that even under a dictatorship people were able to fall in love. That a genuinely normal life was possible even in a non-normal country. But then people in the West start wailing that the dictatorship is being played down, the DDR is being nostalgically transformed. So East Germans fall silent again, because what's the point?'

Or just maybe, as Dirk Michaelis, the lead singer of Karussell, whose 'Als ich fortging' became an anthem of the Wende, also says in the week of the anniversary, 'Describing how life in the DDR was is like trying explain the wind or a temperature.'

Jan Ullrich has never spoken at great length about what it all meant to him. Ullrich was a couple of months into his third year at Dynamo Berlin when, in a matter of days, tens of thousands of demonstrators in Leipzig turned to hundreds of thousands, and momentum behind what came to be known as the 'Peaceful Revolution' became overwhelming. His teacher in 'State Citizenship' lessons, Herr Beyer, was suddenly called to perform an almost impossible tightrope walk – still imparting the canons of a system whose collapse neared by the day and finally the hour. 'I would never have for a moment thought about joining the demonstrations,' Ullrich wrote in his autobiography in 2004. 'Why would I have? I wasn't interested in politics and was, probably without realizing it, simply pragmatic . . . Yes, I wanted to travel, but I wanted to fight for that freedom in sport not in a protest.'[6]

On the famous night itself, Ullrich and his classmates watched events unfold on a communal TV in their dorm in Hohenschönhausen, just as they had watched the 1989 Tour. The next day, Ullrich was due to return to Rostock for his monthly home visit but instead went to Friedrichstraße train station – previously a bolted door to the West that was now suddenly ajar. Every DDR citizen had the right to claim 100 deutsche marks to use in the West as 'greeting money', and Ullrich went to the first bank he saw to collect his. He then made a beeline for the closest department store and its sportswear aisle. In the DDR, there had been two brands of trainers – Germina or the marginally more exotic, Czech-made Botas. Now Ullrich reached for his first pair of Adidas, forgetting to look at the price – and was soon aghast to realize that he had spent his whole 100 deutsche marks.

Initially, bizarrely, not too much changed in the sports schools' day-to-day after November 1989, and certainly not before Germany's official reunification nearly a year later. In July 1990, Ullrich and Becker travelled to Middlesbrough in the United Kingdom for the world championships on both the road and track – and they fared better in the latter. Indeed, only a mistake by teammate Holger Schardt – leaving a gap on their inside as he prepared to lead Ullrich out – denied him a medal and possibly gold in the points race. 'Which,' Peter Becker says, 'may have been just as well, because he wasn't mature enough to deal with becoming a world champion.' Ullrich had also missed out on something else while in Middlesbrough: his high-school graduation ceremony.

He had at least enjoyed the honour of being one of the last athletes to represent East Germany in a world championship. After the first free DDR elections in March, the terms and timings of the final transition had been delineated – to be followed by a road map for dissolution of the much vaunted, soon-to-be controversial elite sports pyramid. Peter Becker was by now weighing an offer to become an estate agent against a proposal to carry on as before with Ullrich et al – and Becker took the latter option. The cyclists were allowed to remain in their boarding house in Hohenschönhausen and Becker even kept the Barkas van from which he loudly choreographed their training rides. As far as Ullrich was concerned, the main differences between DDR and united Germany were material – and welcome – ones. A bike shop in West Berlin had agreed to supply new, burgundy-coloured jerseys adorned with the SV Dynamo badge. Becker also secured the delivery of three sparkling new, Italian-made Bianchi bikes. They would be allocated to his three best prospects: André Korff, Michael Giebelmann and Jan Ullrich.

Ullrich's world was changing, expanding, just as, physically, he was undergoing his own transformation. Between his sixteenth and seventeenth birthdays, from December 1989 to December 1990, he grew twelve centimetres. 'I hadn't even heard of weight problems at this point,' he remarked later. In the second week of January 1991, he became the first former East German cyclist to win a medal in a 'unified' national competition when he took bronze in the German junior cyclo-cross championships – wearing Adidas trainers. A few weeks later he sported the colours of the united Germany for the first time in the cyclo-cross junior world championships in Gieten, finishing fifth.

Berlin, Germany and life in general were in a state of flux, but, interlaced with the bigger transitions of adolescence, the shifts possibly felt less profound to a young man still tethered to at least some vestiges of his former existence. Becker's hands-on training methods, for example, could apparently survive the implosion of the Eastern Bloc and the entire DDR sports system (including the much feted ESA talent-identification process) – and probably a nuclear war. 'When I'm training them, I'm there from the first minute – whether it's in the weights room, on the indoor trainer, the athletics track, if we're doing gymnastics or they're riding on the road,' Becker says. 'I'm hanging out of the window, telling them: "Small chainring, behind the car!"; or, 100 pedal revs per minute, at the heart rate I tell them. The only exception is when I do the first 50 kilometres with them out of Berlin, then turn around and tell them I'll see them back at base. Otherwise I'm with them from the first moment to the last.'

When Becker did loosen his grip, it often resulted in frustration. Like when Ullrich went to Tenerife for a national team training camp in the summer of 1991 and returned, according to Becker, 'sunburned and badly trained'. With Becker's hand firmly back on the tiller, Ullrich would win the 1991 Berlin district championships in cyclo-cross, on the track and team time trial. Having now officially left school, he and Korff also began apprenticeships at Niles machine tool factory in the north-east of Berlin. Mornings behind a workbench and afternoons on the bike added up to 'tiring and monotonous' days, Ullrich said later.

For many of Ullrich's contemporaries in the East, the door to adulthood had swung open at the same time as one leading to a land of new opportunity. Mark Scheppert's dad worked alongside Becker as a coach at Dynamo – indeed Becker had given Mark his first bike – and one day Scheppert would write a book, *Mauergewinner oder Ein Wessi des Ostens*, about the experiences of teenagers, like him and Ullrich, who he felt were the forgotten kids of the Peaceful Revolution. Scheppert's book is not a lament, more a reflection on the strange and in many respects exhilarating rope swing towards freedom that nonetheless left some 'Ossis' suspended between old and new, between their suddenly alienated parents and a false dreamland wire-fenced with suspicion and prejudice.

'In many ways, I don't feel different from kids who grew up in the West,' Scheppert says when we meet in 2015. 'On 4 November [1989] we were at the demonstration in Alexanderplatz, and it was touch and go, whether they would shoot or not. Dynamo was in a state of emergency. Maybe little Jan Ullrich didn't know it, lying in his boarding house, but my father and all of the other coaches at Dynamo were armed with revolvers. There were these Monday demonstrations, and the one in Leipzig, in particular, where it wasn't clear whether they were going to shoot or not . . . So it wasn't all just fireworks and celebrations. From October, November, December, everyone just remembers the pictures of people dancing on the Wall, but earlier it was very sketchy indeed. I had friends who were two years older and were in the NVA – the army – and they didn't even know that the Wall had fallen four weeks later. There was a complete news blackout. There was no information.

'But, yes, as far as what came next was concerned, it was the absolute best time for it to happen to my generation. I wasn't in the army yet, I was finishing school, no one was asking me to join the Stasi. We'd also not known any different as young kids: you went to the Baltic Sea on holiday and you didn't notice that you weren't in the USA. You didn't have the same toys as kids in the West but you had toys. Then the Wall fell and you could do everything. But then you also realized later that the Brandenburg Gate wasn't the door to paradise. I've lived in the "West" for long enough now to realize there were always backstabbers and corruption here too. The city and country were divided but really both sides had the same problems, humanity's problems. It was also really tough for my father's generation. He wasn't young, and from one day to the next in the March of 1990, he lost his job and had to go and find something else. He had a good reference, saying that he'd been a good coach at Dynamo, but he wasn't the man he'd been when he'd qualified. And in the West they thought everything coming from the East was just shit. They had to build a new life, whereas for my generation, Jan's generation, well, we thought life was just beginning.'

4

OVER THE RAINBOW

'I have a saying in my head: talents are often lazy'

—*Wolfgang Strohband*

From the moment Wolfgang Strohband opens the front door on a November morning in 2015, he personifies the *hanseatische Art* that journalists who dealt with him in Ullrich's peak years have told me to expect – an air of straight-backed, old-fashioned propriety for which businessmen of the Hanseatic cities of northern Germany – Hamburg, Lübeck and Bremen – have been well known and respected down the ages.

Everything in Strohband's home – from the parquet floor to the brass ornaments and photo frames on every surface – sparkles even in the gloom cast through the windows by the downpour outside. Strohband has suggested we talk at the small, square table in the centre of his dining room. In a few minutes, his slight, pleasantly fastidious wife, Inge, will arrive with coffee in the Strohbands' best china cups, and a plate of carefully arranged biscuits.

'I never understood why every journalist used to call me "the used car salesman". I was a BMW dealer, first and foremost. It used to drive my Inge crazy when she read that: "Ullrich's manager, the second-hand car dealer . . ."'

Wolfgang Strohband is smiling. He moves and speaks with a briskness and energy that bely his seventy-six years and does not seem like the kind to harbour grudges. Strohband also got used to being misunderstood and misrepresented, not to mention heavily criticized, in more than two decades of acting as Jan Ullrich's manager, financial advisor, friend and surrogate parent. Of all of the cod diagnoses of Ullrich's problems, maybe the most common was that he was 'badly advised'. Strohband has heard it so many times that nowadays the slur barely grazes his ego. 'They were good years. I also don't think I did too badly, setting Jan up for the future,' he surmises.

In many ways, the story of how Jan Ullrich came to Hamburg and to Strohband was a perfect post-Wende feel-good story – a tale of new opportunity, blessed happenstance and, yes, unification that until a few months earlier could not have come to pass. Strohband would be the latest in a curious lineage of paternal figures in the young Ullrich's life: after his grandfather, then Peter Sager and Peter Becker, another protective male influence to fill the void that Werner Ullrich had left. Strohband had been a member of the RG Hamburg cycling club since the mid-1950s, a once promising junior rider who eventually made his way in the world by selling four-wheeled vehicles rather than racing upon two. At the beginning of the 1990s, he had taken it upon himself to arrange a special present for the club's upcoming centenary: a team to compete in Germany's premier domestic competition, the Bundesliga. Strohband had also already found a prestigious sponsor in Panasonic, the Japanese electronics manufacturer which a few years earlier had whimsically begun making bikes because the son of the president dreamed of becoming a racing cyclist.

Strohband had money, a team name and identity, and just needed to source his riders and, perhaps even more important, someone to train and manage them. By this point, a few months on from reunification, coaches from the old DDR sports clubs had become one of the former East's few sought-after commodities, and Strohband coveted one for what he was planning in Hamburg. He made enquiries, was given some names, one of which was Peter Becker's. The pair then met in July 1991 at the German national 100-kilometre time trial championships in Forst, close to the Polish border, where Strohband gave Becker his pitch: he already had four riders in Hamburg and he wanted six more from what remained of Dynamo Berlin's juniors plus, if he was willing, Becker. Strohband would arrange a house on the outskirts of the city and apprenticeships similar to the ones his riders already had in Berlin. Becker only had to talk his wife into what turned out to be, in his words, four years of 'interrupted weekend romance'. He also had to persuade his riders and their families. Five eventually signed up for the adventure – Becker's son Erik, Michael Giebelmann, Ralf Grabsch, André Korff and Jan Ullrich. Early in January 1992, they travelled in a two-car convoy from Berlin towards a new home and future three hours away.

Only when they arrived in Hamburg did Wolfgang Strohband awkwardly reveal the first teething problem: the house, the team's future HQ, wasn't ready. Becker was unimpressed – and horrified when Strohband announced that, as a stopgap, they would be guests at a hotel belonging to one of Strohband's old cycling buddies . . . located on the Reeperbahn. Unquestionably Hamburg's most notorious street, probably Germany's and perhaps also Europe's, the Reeperbahn has long earned its nickname, *'die sündigste Meile'* – 'the most sinful mile' – with its unrelenting commitment to neon-lit debauchery, mainly in the form of brothels and sex shops. 'It was absolutely great for the boys, a bit embarrassing for me,' Strohband chuckles.

Peter Becker, meanwhile, was more concerned that the idyllic training roads that Strohband had raved about seemed as inaccessible as the choked carriageways in and out of Berlin. 'Getting through the city was an absolute catastrophe,' Becker tells me.

He was similarly appalled by the dining options. They included McDonald's – 'that papier-mâché food, my God' – and assorted other kebab houses and snack bars. Ullrich claimed in his autobiography years later that Becker introduced them to the local nightlife by organizing a visit to a strip bar. 'That story was totally invented,' Becker assures me. But he confirms that Ullrich did succumb to one vice – gambling. One day, while they waited for their takeaway pizzas at a regular haunt overlooking the Alster river, Ullrich fed a two-mark coin into one of the slot machines by the counter, and seconds later Becker heard a symphony of cascading coins. 'The lucky bugger – 465 deutsche marks, he won.' Ullrich gave Korff and Giebelmann 20 deutsche marks each while the rest was bundled into carrier bags and, sometime after that, into Ullrich's savings account.

Becker's boys were still officially homeless when, in mid-February, he drove them to the Costa Blanca for a training camp, having received assurances from Strohband that their new bolthole would be ready upon their return. It was – but only thanks to the round-the-clock efforts of the RG Hamburg members and their families. It was also taking Strohband longer than expected to organize the apprenticeships that were also part of his initial promise. Ullrich and Korff were shown around a BMW plant and offered positions there, only for the invitation to be withdrawn when Strohband and Peter Becker made it clear that their riders needed afternoons off to train. Finally, Strohband turned to another old cycling buddy and found them positions in a metalwork factory. Shifts started at seven in the morning and the work was not exactly varied. Ullrich described it later: 'Just filing, filing, filing, all day long. I would rather have ridden 500 kilometres.' What he called his 'final attempt to learn a proper trade' ended up lasting a few months, until the autumn of 1992. With their parents' blessing, Ullrich and Korff convinced Wolfgang Strohband that metallurgy's loss would be their team's gain, and the pair finally became full-time cyclists.

'I didn't even know which kids Peter Becker was bringing to Hamburg. Had no idea who Korff or Ullrich were. Becker told me that Ullrich was the best, but Korff had the most talent,' Strohband admits now. He, like others, was astonished by how quickly the Ossis settled into racing in their new environs. After a bruising debut in Hannover in March, ending with a furious pep talk from Peter Becker – 'The others are making fun of us!' – the victories soon began to multiply. On one weekend, Ullrich won a criterium near Hannover on the Friday, a race in the Harz mountains on the Saturday, then the Rund um den Kleinen Kiel on Sunday.

In general, in those first few months, Ullrich struck Strohband as a typical eighteen-year-old, as unremarkable off the bike as he was exceptional on it. 'He would come back from training and you'd find his kit lying on the floor as though it had just fallen off him, and it'd still be there hours later.' Ullrich occasionally wore an LA Kings baseball cap identical to the ones sported by the members of the controversial American hip-hop group N.W.A., but scarcely anything in his behaviour hinted at a rebellious streak, either explicit or suppressed. When not at the factory, or out on his bike, he would pass the time on Strohband's forecourt, 'just listening to the conversations I had with customers, how we sold the cars.'

What Strohband calls Ullrich's 'ambition with caveats' was channelled almost exclusively through the pedal stroke that, at the end of that first season, thanks to a pair of podium finishes on the qualifying weekend, helped earn the team promotion to the Bundesliga's first division.

'He was ambitious up to a point,' says Strohband. 'I have a saying in my head: talents are often lazy. They have the abilities but don't use them. For those kids everything was brand new. They were hungry for knowledge and were interested in everything. But Jan was someone who took the bike Giebelmann had prepared for him, sat on it, squeezed the brakes once and rode off. He didn't really bother about a lot of other things. He knew plenty about how to ride a bike, but to say that he was someone who had order and control in his life would have been inaccurate . . . Maybe it was a question of comfort. He came from the dorm in Berlin and you have to assume that he had some degree of independence. But he also must have been quite comfortable. He was very often very lucky with a lot of things in his life – you'd have to say that.'

Wolfgang Strohband had been so delighted with the émigrés' first season in the blue, yellow and red stripes of the Panasonic jerseys that he offered Ullrich, Korff and Grabsch interest-free credit on the purchase of three second-hand cars – in Ullrich's case a VW Golf. Ullrich celebrated his nineteenth birthday on 2 December by taking his new wheels all the way from Hamburg to his mum's house in Rostock. Shortly thereafter came the first driving misdemeanour in what would become quite a collection over the next twenty years – a speeding ticket that earned him a month-long ban.

Becker's brigade would prepare for the 1993 season as their coach's teams often had, on skis and snowshoes. From the pistes of the Austrian Alps they then headed to a training camp on the Costa Blanca. They would need to raise their game in the Bundesliga's top tier and did so emphatically. Ullrich scored podium finishes in races in Gütersloh and Dortmund, then tied up the Bundesliga overall individual title on a scorching summer weekend in Rheinland-Pfalz wine country, hammering to victory nearly three minutes ahead of the chasing peloton in Rhodt.

It was in the German national team jersey, though, that his performances in 1993 most caught the eye. In July, at the Bohemia Tour in the Czech Republic, he dazzled on every terrain, winning the decisive final-day time trial and the overall classification, the mountains prize and the honour of most aggressive rider. Such a virtuoso display would ordinarily have guaranteed a place in the German team for the 1993 amateur world championships in Oslo – had the national coach, Peter Weibel, not already ruled Ullrich out on the grounds that he was too young. It was not the first time that Weibel and Peter Becker had disagreed, and, finally, after heated negotiations, Weibel told Becker that Ullrich could attend a pre-worlds altitude training camp in Colorado – so long as he could get himself a ticket and be at the airport in Frankfurt for noon the following day. One call from Wolfgang Strohband to his travel agent and the next afternoon Ullrich was on the plane. Within days of arriving in Colorado, shoo-ins for the worlds team like Dirk Baldinger and Uwe Peschel could barely hold his wheel. 'If we're not careful, the little kid's gonna be world champion,' one of them said as a joke one day.

On their return to Germany, they all started the Regio-Tour, a week-long stage-race hopping back and forth across the Swiss and French borders. Ullrich's victory there banished whatever last doubts Weibel had about picking him for Norway – and yet within hours his selection was potentially placed in jeopardy by an event that Ullrich later described as the most upsetting of his young life. He had last seen his father flee at age seven and left home himself at thirteen, after which Jan had successfully anchored his identity to friends, teammates, a coach, two once-alien cities, Hamburg and Berlin, and above all to a sport which would soon become his job. But had anyone asked Jan Ullrich in 1993 to name his most powerful source of inspiration, the rock upon which he had built his sense of self, its past, present and future as a man and athlete, he would have had no hesitation in naming his maternal grandfather Fritz – who, he now learned, had suddenly passed away. Ullrich was shattered. At Weibel's urging, he immediately returned to Rostock, where he would attend a funeral for the first time. That Weibel had also sent him away with the news that he was selected for Oslo brought little solace. Not even when Marianne told him through tears how proud his grandfather would have been to watch him in Norway.

Ullrich would indeed feel over the next few days that his grand-dad was somehow observing, protecting him, bending fate in his favour. On the night before the race, Weibel confirmed which of the ten riders in the German squad would make up the six-man starting line-up for the amateur race* – and Ullrich's name was among them. Weibel also didn't believe in 'leaders'; Ullrich, like his teammates, would get his chance.

When it came to allocating room-mates in Norway, pairing Ullrich with Lutz Lehmann had been an obvious choice. Born in East Berlin in the early 1960s, Lehmann had been on a similar, DDR state-sponsored path to the one Ullrich would later tread before encountering a significant obstacle in the mid-1980s, when the Stasi discovered he had relatives in the West. Lehmann committed the mortal sin of requesting special permission for him and his then wife to join them. Not only was the application denied, Lehmann was thrown in jail in Berlin and could only 'buy' himself free a year later.

Nearly a decade on, he was the oldest member of the German team and therefore an ideal mentor to the pup of the litter. The pair had battled frequently and exchanged pleasantries in Bundesliga races, but in Colorado first, and then Norway, Lehmann had got to know a 'funny, laidback kid' who was also a 'force of nature' on the bike. Lehmann likes to tell the story of the Rund um Wiesbaden in March 1994, where he and Ullrich went wheel to wheel on the finishing straight but were both ultimately outsprinted by another rider, Jens Zemke. 'We were there waiting for the presentation, chatting, and I was saying to the other guys that I'd lacked a bit of freshness because I'd had a heavy training week and done 800 kilometres. Jan replies to this, dead serious, by saying that he wasn't on top of his game either because, well, he'd only ridden eighty kilometres. *Eighty.*'

Now, with the weather set fair, only on the last of ten laps of Oslo's southern suburbs did a natural selection occur. After a vain breakaway bid by the Belgian Axel Merckx, son of Eddy, a group of five finally, definitively pulled away on the final ascent of the Ekeberg climb, with Ullrich among them. The Italian team leader, Alessandro Bertolini, was also there, as were the Latvians, Kaspars Ozers and Arvis Piziks, and a Czech whom Ullrich had recognized even without glancing at the race numbers scrawled on a piece of tape on his handlebar stem – Lubor Tesař, whom Ullrich had narrowly beaten at the Bohemia Tour a few weeks before the worlds.

---

* The amateur men's race was an annual fixture at the UCI Road World Championships, usually held on the eve of the men's professional race, between 1921 and 1995. It was then replaced by an age-restricted 'Under-23' or 'Espoirs' race.

Peter Becker and Wolfgang Strohband had travelled to Norway with a few friends and cycling connections in their own improvised Jan Ullrich fan club. At the airport in Hamburg, Strohband responded to his wife's well wishes by joking that Ullrich winning was the last thing they needed, for 'then Jan would get really expensive' – Panasonic having not yet renewed their team sponsorship for the following year. Now, with the five escapees holding their lead, Strohband's prophecy was in danger of being realized.

The quintet sped into the final kilometre, out of reach of the chasing pack. Ullrich assumed that Tesař, who had competed in the previous year's Olympics on the track, would be the fastest finisher, and so stuck to his wheel. Which was where Ullrich stayed until, with 150 metres to go, Tesař surged and veered towards the barriers on the left side of the road, while Ullrich carried straight on into the open airspace. Seconds later he was raising his arms. Still three months shy of his twentieth birthday, he was the youngest world amateur champion since Eddy Merckx in 1964. Although riding for a unified Germany, Ullrich was also the sixth rider born and raised in the DDR to wear the rainbow jersey in the amateur category. The doyen of East German cycling, Täve Schur, had been the first in 1958.

Some of Ullrich's antecedents had faded or fizzled after world amateur titles, but esteemed observers believed that in Oslo they had witnessed the birth of a star. At home, comparisons were made with the last German to truly excel in the Tour de France, Didi Thurau. Peter Weibel, the German team coach, countered that Ullrich was a better climber than Thurau and that he might one day finish in the top ten of a three-week tour. Weibel died in 2019, which makes Lutz Lehmann reluctant to criticize; nonetheless, he says, it jarred to hear Weibel rhapsodize about a rider whom a few weeks earlier he had not wanted to select.

If anyone was sheepish when the German team celebrated that evening, it was Ullrich. The party would eventually spill out of the team hotel and into the streets of central Oslo, but it was only when they returned to their hotel in the early hours that Ullrich seemed to be really savouring his achievement, as he announced to Lehmann in their room that he would sleep in the rainbow jersey. The next day the whole team flew back to Frankfurt – except Ullrich, who was due in Hamburg for a TV interview. They all caught only glimpses of the men's professional road race ridden in desperate conditions, and won by a rider only two years Ullrich's senior: the American Lance Armstrong.

Wolfgang Strohband spent what remained of the weekend discussing Ullrich's future with, among others, the decorated former German rider, Rudi Altig, and Eddy Merckx. Altig was of the view that Ullrich should turn professional immediately. The manager of the Telekom team, Walter Godefroot, disagreed, telling Strohband that Ullrich should make the step up in 1995 . . . with Godefroot's Telekom team. This was also the timetable that Peter Becker had proposed, Becker believing that Ullrich would benefit from a season of racing with a target – in the form of those rainbow stripes – on his back and chest.

Strohband also now expected the Panasonic name to again adorn Ullrich's jersey in 1994. Upon his return to Germany, the electronics company appeared to reaffirm their commitment by inviting Strohband, Ullrich and Becker to a small celebration at the company offices. A twenty-minute highlight video of Ullrich's world-title winning ride was beamed by an overhead projector. 'When it ended, the head of advertising asked me what brand of bike Jan had ridden on. I couldn't catch my breath,' Strohband says. 'They had no idea their own company was even making bikes.'

On 31 August, Strohband travelled to Berlin for another meeting with Panasonic. That evening Ullrich was also in Berlin, taking part in the City Night exhibition race on the Kurfürstendamm, West Berlin's most iconic boulevard and a byword for revelry and excess since the 'Golden Twenties' of the Weimar Republic.

All Jan Ullrich intended to do on the Ku'damm on the last night of August 1993 was race his bike. But, as he rolled towards the start line, he heard a voice calling his name. He turned, and it took him a second or two to place facial features he had not seen for over ten years, which had changed but not beyond recognition: his father's. He rode over to the barrier and tentatively asked Werner Ullrich how he was, how he'd been. His dad didn't reply but Ullrich could see tears starting to well. 'Wow, Jan, it's nice to see you,' Werner said finally. The race was about to start, so Werner hurriedly scribbled his telephone number on a scrap of paper and handed it to his son. Ullrich shoved the note into his back pocket. 'Good luck!' his dad shouted as Ullrich rolled into the phalanx of riders waiting under the start banner.

Ullrich finally crossed the line a couple of hours later in third place. The heavens had opened and, by the end of its racing premiere, his rainbow jersey was drenched. The note in the back pocket was also reduced to soggy mush, the writing on it illegible. Ullrich had not given much thought to whether he would or would not call his dad. Now, anyway, the choice had been removed.

By his own later admission, Ullrich did not dwell unduly on the episode, and, over the ensuing days, weeks and months, the encounter seemed not to have affected or troubled him. Meanwhile, to Wolfgang Strohband's bafflement, Panasonic confirmed that they were withdrawing their backing (Müsing bikes would replace them) while other offers for a piece of Ullrich flooded in. One agent approached Strohband claiming that the Italian professional team, Polti, would pay a huge sum if Ullrich turned pro with them in 1994. 'The offer was so big that you thought you couldn't stand in his way,' Strohband says. In the end, though, he didn't even discuss the option with Ullrich, feeling, like Peter Becker, that he needed another year racing as an amateur. 'Jan riding abroad wouldn't have worked,' says Strohband now. 'He had to be developed slowly, not thrown into a pressure cooker.'

Whatever pitfalls, triumphs and adversities lay ahead for Jan Ullrich, he was not the only ambitious young sports nut making his way in Hamburg in 1994. That year, a journalism undergraduate from the city's university, Michael Ostermann, was doing a work placement with *Die Welt* newspaper when an editor asked for a volunteer to cover an event at which a local cycling team, RG Hamburg, was to present its new world champion. Ostermann duly went along, met Ullrich and filed the few lines that may or may not have made the paper the next day. Peter Becker was also in attendance and, Ostermann recalls, offered significantly better copy than the reticent main attraction. 'Becker couldn't have been more different from Ullrich,' Ostermann says. 'Peter was very outspoken and, well, let's say Jan was very happy to let others do his talking . . .'

This first impression was confirmed on the handful of other occasions Ostermann was sent on the same beat in 1994. He remembers one particular trip to the thatch-roofed, red-brick house near the airport where Ullrich and his teammates had been billeted for two years as particularly revealing, not because Ullrich was a loquacious interviewee. 'I can remember sitting there in the kitchen and really struggling to get him to talk,' Ostermann remembers. 'There was one question I asked him about a German amateur who had just crashed and been paralysed at the Baby Giro. He'd ended up in a wheelchair. This had happened right before the interview and Jan knew him from the national team. So I asked Jan how he felt about this and whether it would affect him in future. And the only thing Jan said was, "If you brake, you lose." I probed a little more, and eventually he explained that, if he thought about it, he wouldn't be able to race any more. But really he couldn't articulate it properly, so ended up using this cliché that all German cyclists use: *"Wer bremst, verliert."* It sounded insensitive but really it was typical of Jan when he's feeling insecure. He would just lapse into clichés.'

Ostermann would be writing about Ullrich for years thereafter – and recognizing the same traits he had noticed on those first meetings in Hamburg. Ullrich was invariably friendly, often endearingly down to earth, yet neither articulate nor confident enough to embroider interviews with rhetorical flourishes. Other riders would address journalists on first-name terms, even when they were only vaguely acquainted, while in the future Ullrich would see and speak to the same reporters dozens of times a year, every year, yet never step across that threshold of familiarity.

Peter Becker, a gifted or at least very willing communicator, came to feel with time that Ullrich's shyness was something that plagued him. It also baffled Becker, until one day Ullrich's mum told him a story. Once, when Jan was in kindergarten, she had given him the 20 marks they owed in fees to pass on to the teacher. 'Only instead of doing that, he hummed and hawed until the teacher looked his way, then he shoved the 20 marks into the snow and ran away . . . And exactly that – not making himself go towards other people – restricts him,' Becker says. 'But it also means that, with his pretty limited vocabulary, he doesn't come across well. Sometimes he has to put himself out there, though, and he feels awful doing it.'

In a country like Germany, and a city like Hamburg, there would be limited exposure for an amateur world champion cyclist, however eloquently he communicated. In one rare interview with a local paper, Ullrich even complained about a lack of recognition, that 'this city only seems interested in football, tennis and golf'. Nevertheless, in Ullrich, the town patently had an adoptive son well on his way to joining the global elite. In 1994, for the second season running, he would top the individual standings in the year-long cycling Bundesliga, underlining his credentials as the strongest under-23 rider in the land. He might also have successfully defended his amateur world road race title in Sicily had it not been for questionable decisions in the German team car. Two days later, he competed in the first ever world time trial championship – effectively as an amateur racing against professionals. Chris Boardman ran out winner, but Ullrich possibly caused an even bigger sensation than in Oslo by taking the bronze medal.

As the season drew to an end, so too did Ullrich's amateur career, and with it also his three years in Hamburg. He signed off in October with a final victory for Team Müsing in Frankfurt; within a few weeks he'd be heading down the Rhine Valley to a new home in the Black Forest. The pine-cloaked mountains surrounding Freiburg were laced with some of the best training roads in Germany and also blessed with the sunniest climate in the land, making the area a magnet for German pro riders and top amateurs. Ullrich had become a regular visitor thanks to his friendship with a local rider and his German national teammate, Dirk Baldinger, in whose home Ullrich would also spend his first few weeks in the south.

'Baldes' had beaten Ullrich to the German national amateur title in the summer of 1994 and, in November, a few weeks before Ullrich's move, was holding a party to celebrate. At one point in the evening, Ullrich saw his friend sitting at a table, surrounded by predominantly female old schoolmates, and decided to join them. A bumbled introduction – specifically something about 'all these pretty girls' – barely cracked let alone broke the ice, except with one of the women, a tall brunette who smiled and complimented Ullrich on a 'great first line'. She then invited him to take the seat next to her. Ullrich already knew that her name was Gaby and that she had gone to school with Baldinger. She told Jan that she'd seen him racing on TV, wearing a helmet that covered his hair. She was disappointed now to discover that the dark, flamboyant locks that she'd imagined were in real life rather shorter, less expansive and . . . a vivid shade of orange. Ullrich apologized. She said it didn't matter. She giggled.

When, later, they each described that first encounter to friends, both would say that they had simply 'clicked'. Ullrich was charmed by her peculiar south-western accent, with its flurries of 'sh' sounds and jovial, homely lilt. She seemed laidback, self-deprecating. Her parents owned a winery in nearby Merdingen, an idyllic cluster of half-timbered homes for 2,500 mostly lifelong inhabitants that in 1989 was voted Germany's prettiest village. From there it was also a short drive to the army barracks where she worked in the admin department. That was lucky, Ullrich had told her, because over the next few weeks he'd be doing his compulsory military service in the special athletes' division in nearby Todtnau. In no time they were agreeing to meet again, and, in fact, the very next afternoon Ullrich stood on the front step of the farmhouse where Gaby, her parents and grandparents lived, holding a bunch of flowers. They drove into the centre of Freiburg, drank hot chocolate, and talked for hours. That evening, when Ullrich dropped her off, they kissed under the stars and didn't want to let go. Before he went to bed, Ullrich would be on the phone, telling her how he was going to exaggerate the symptoms of a cold so he'd be signed off sick the next day and could see her again. Which is exactly what he did.

Years later, to *Bunte* magazine's probing about his taste in women, he replied that 'of course' Julia Roberts had a 'dream body' and Claudia Schiffer also 'isn't bad'. Gaby, though, would be his first true love. Hence, in December 1994, a mere month after their first meeting, he asked and then begged her to spend Christmas in Rostock with him and his mum. Finally, she agreed, and they set off on a nostalgia tour of the cities that had moulded him – Hamburg, Berlin and finally Rostock. For Christmas, Gaby gave him a silver earring which from that point on he never took from his left earlobe. The following March, they'd be moving into a thatched-roof cottage in the Burgunderweg, a few paces from the Gasthof Keller. The hub of village life, the inn was also run by a man who would soon set up Ullrich's first official fan club.

Wolfgang Strohband has barely, if ever, spoken to journalists since Jan Ullrich's retirement. He finally 'succumbed' to my request, enticed by the offer of reliving 'the Hamburg years' of what turned into a long partnership with Ullrich. 'The best years', Strohband still calls them, unfolding a warm, wistful smile.

There are many, in fact innumerable stories, some of which remained in the vault even when he and Ullrich were flying high.

Like the one about a good customer at Strohband's car dealership who happened to be a performer on the Reeperbahn, and who agreed to provide the 'entertainment' for an RG Hamburg end-of-year bash in return for Strohband dropping the price on her next BMW. The soirée ended up being one of the most memorable in the club's century or so of history, and definitely the only one featuring a striptease that, Strohband is at pains to stress, was 'all pretty tasteful'. Ullrich and the other boys from Berlin, certainly, 'thought it was absolutely great'.

Overall, in three years, Ullrich had doubtless grown up as both a man and athlete, although Strohband recognized vulnerabilities that would cause issues later on. He was a 'lovely, straightforward kid' who, even as a global superstar in his twenties and thirties, would visit the Strohbands at home and collapse into their sofa, like a student returning for the holidays.

'I had the feeling that his childhood hadn't been easy,' Strohband says. 'As a comparison: Jan and Korff are both from Rostock, were both discovered and developed as cyclists by Peter Sager, who was a really great coach . . . but their lives were quite different. Jan – problems with his dad, the mum who brought him up on her own, but then had to let him go. Whereas André had a really stable family life. It wasn't easy for Jan, with just his mum there, and his brother, but he came through it. Then went to Berlin and made his way . . .

'He just has the problem that he trusts people too easily. He's too gullible. He always thinks everything's just great – even today,' Strohband concludes.

Throughout the morning, rain has pummelled the window, bringing to mind a proverb about the city to which I had been introduced by a friend who grew up there: 'Nowhere does the grey sky shine more beautifully than in Hamburg.'

From what Wolfgang Strohband has told me, this city could teach Jan Ullrich nothing he didn't already know about a single-minded, perhaps self-destructive determination to see silver linings.

5

THE APPRENTICE

'As a bike rider you also have to be a pig,
and be a pig to other people as well'

—*Peter Becker*

Ask those who rode and worked for the Deutsche Telekom cycling team in the 1995 season to share their first impressions of Jan Ullrich, and a surprising number will speak of cleats, not physical feats.

That is, the cleats nailed to the bottom of Ullrich's cycling shoes.

The venue for Telekom's traditional pre-season training camp was the Hotel San Diego in El Arenal, Mallorca – the Balearic island so beloved of Germans that in 1993 parliament members and *Bild Zeitung* semi-seriously suggested that the government in Bonn simply buy it. The story gave rise to a moniker that survives to this day: the Seventeenth Bundesland. Regardless, settings might change, some of the faces too, but among the inalterable truths of these January get-togethers was the first-year pros' eagerness to impress.

In this season, Telekom were welcoming just one rookie: a red-headed, freckle-faced twenty-one-year-old from Rostock on the Baltic Sea, who also happened to be the amateur world champion in Oslo in 1993.

His second memorable feature – at least in the eyes of the more experienced teammates sizing him up in Mallorca – was an, ahem, relaxed attitude to equipment and particularly the shoe plates about which most pros are notoriously fastidious. Ullrich's were battered, misshapen, and obviously several months old. When one of them duly broke on a training session early in the camp, Ullrich completed the ride with one foot perfectly anchored, the other slipping and sliding as though balancing on a bar of soap.

One of the team's veteran riders, Udo Bölts, was aghast. Rolf Aldag would have been too, had he not already encountered Ullrich – and Ullrich's cleats – in the elevator of the German team hotel at those Oslo worlds two years earlier. 'Ach, maybe I should change these cleats,' Ullrich had ventured, surveying the plastic wreckage barely clinging to the bottom of his Adidas shoes. Forty-eight hours later, Ullrich returned to the German team hotel wearing the world champion's jersey and the same Adidas shoes, with the same death-trap cleats. 'They were a millimetre from being unusable,' Aldag remembers. 'Just imagine if they had gone in that sprint. It probably would have changed his whole career. And that's typical Jan: "*Ja*, if there's no one who will do it for me, I realize, but I don't really take it that seriously."'

Walter Godefroot had signed Ullrich on the strength of his cycling, not his bicycle or footwear maintenance, but Team Telekom's manager also knew that no amount of talent was a guarantee of success in the pro ranks. Godefroot had once been a prodigy himself, winning the Belgian national championship at age twenty-one. A serial 'victim' of Eddy Merckx, he nonetheless retired with a fine palmarès bejewelled by victories in the Tour of Flanders, Liège–Bastogne–Liège and Paris–Roubaix before becoming a directeur sportif. Late in 1991, finally, he was recruited by Deutsche Telekom to effectively take over the organization formerly known as Team Stuttgart.

Godefroot's hunched, dogged style had inspired Belgian journalists to christen him 'The Bulldog of Flanders' as a racer. In his second life as a team manager, his gentle, softly rounded features and oblong spectacles were a fatherly mask behind which lived a hard, working-class man in the best Flemish tradition. His parents, both factory workers, had struggled to stay above the poverty line after the war, instilling in their son the value of hard graft. When he was thirteen and bussed off to Switzerland on a trip organized and subsidized by the Catholic Church, his mum told him, 'This way you'll at least get to go that far once in your life. We never will.'

Cycling had finally taken Godefroot all over the globe, but his belief system hadn't wavered. The former Telekom rider Jörg Jaksche says riders who complained to Godefroot about illness could typic-ally expect a response like the one he once received: 'Ah, you're ill, Mr Jaksche? So you have cancer, because that's a real illness.' Rolf Aldag got similarly short shrift when he announced that he didn't want to ride the 1999 world championships, so angry was he at the International Cycling Union (UCI), the sport's governing body, over their organization of the previous year's event. 'So, Mr Aldag, you don't want to ride your bike any more? That can be arranged.' Need-less to say, Aldag soon reconsidered.

Another ex-Telekom rider, Brian Holm, remains deeply fond of Godefroot while admitting his man management wasn't to every-one's taste. 'Walter was a hard fuck. No small talk, but correct. Walter was the kind of guy who only called to fire you, not to ask how your kids were doing. I remember a Danish journalist asking Walter about sports psychologists. Walter looked over his glasses at him and said, "Psychologist? They can have one if they like . . . but they'd better also look for a new team. I don't need riders who need psychologists." Psychologists? Fuck off. That was Walter's attitude.'

Needless to say, then, Ullrich could expect Godefroot to be patient with him, but not to be mollycoddled. That had been clear when Godefroot learned that Ullrich would prepare for his first pro season with an altitude training camp in Mexico, and a curled bottom lip turned to a frown as he watched Ullrich struggle early in the year. As Rolf Aldag remembers in 2015, 'If he'd gone to Mexico and got com-pletely cooked, that was his fault and not theirs as far as the management was concerned.' Another Telekom rider, Jens Heppner, had also been with Ullrich in Mexico. 'And for quite a while Walter thought the whole altitude thing was bullshit,' Heppner recalls.

After illness in February, Ullrich finally made his racing debut at the Setmana Catalana in March 1995. He finished stage one way down the field but at least mildly amused and consoled by the fact that the four-time Tour de France champion, Miguel Induráin, had crossed the line next to him. The next four days were a bracing intro-duction to the world over which Induráin had reigned for the last half-decade. Ullrich finished the race in eightieth position overall, exhausted and chastised.

It was nothing new for a rookie, even one as gifted as Ullrich, to find the transition hard. Telekom was also no featherbed for a first-year pro, its results that season proving so lacklustre that the team's

very future seemed in danger. Walter Godefroot had grown increasingly restless throughout the spring, not least because the Société du
Tour de France appeared disinclined to even invite Telekom to the
1995 race. Godefroot's paymasters had already indicated that this
doomsday scenario would lead to them pulling their funding.

Ullrich's form was low on the list of Godefroot's most pressing
matters but a concern nonetheless. Late in the spring, Godefroot
decided to address it by dispatching one of his most reliable vassals,
Rolf Aldag, to the Black Forest to train with Ullrich and hopefully
impart some of his *savoir faire*. Another Telekom rider, Bert Dietz,
would join them.

Aldag checked into the small guest house that he often used as
a training base in the Schwarzwald, a few kilometres from chez Ullrich. At just gone nine the next day, Aldag's phone rang.

'*Ja*, it's Jan. It's raining here in Merdingen. What shall we do?'

Aldag peered out of his window. It was barely drizzling. Aldag
replied that they meet and ride as planned, to which Ullrich mumbled his consent.

They finally trained for four or five hours, with Aldag and Dietz
doing most of the pacemaking, and Ullrich all of the grumbling.

On the second morning, Aldag again laid out the itinerary – a
classic rodeo of old Black Forest favourites like the Notscherei, Feldberg and the Schauinsland. Ullrich rode slightly better and complained
a little less, though was still testing Aldag's patience. At nearly every
junction, Ullrich would turn to ask Aldag where they were heading
next, left or right. Finally, as the threesome swooped down towards
Freiburg, the distinctive terraced vineyards of the Kaiserstuhl mountain loomed on the skyline. 'Ah,' said Ullrich suddenly, 'there's the
Kaiserstuhl! And Merdingen. I know where we are now.'

Aldag glared back.

'I said to him, "What the hell are you doing? I mean, seriously?
How long have you been living here now? A year? And you didn't
have a clue where we were at any point today?" He said he'd basically been racing at weekends, thinking that he just needed to recover
at home. Then, when it got to Wednesday and Thursday and he felt
OK again, he'd be worried about tiring himself out for the following
weekend. So, really, he'd been in Merdingen that long and hardly
ever done any real training. This was the first time he'd done proper
riding on consecutive days.'

By the third day, the moans had suddenly stopped. On every climb, Dietz and Aldag were left gasping.

'And on the fourth morning, we had been due to meet on the valley road out of Merdingen, but Jan was coming from the opposite direction and he just rode straight past us. We had to call him back. He asked why we weren't going towards the climbs. I told him that it was a recovery day and that we were just going to do 100 kilometres through the Rhine Valley, then come home from the back side. He was kind of pissed off we weren't going into the hills. Anyway, that day Dietz and I were like Jan had been on the first day. We were just hanging on the whole time. That's when you realize what talent really looks like: it had taken him three days to build the form that we would in three weeks. There was just no way you could even compare to that.'

Jürgen Werner, another Telekom rider that season, says it was simple: 'Jan thrived on being surrounded by mates, camaraderie. He's a people person. He just didn't enjoy training on his own.' It was therefore logical that Ullrich had flourished in Berlin and Hamburg, living and training every day with club and teammates, but was finding the more self-sufficient lifestyle of the pro rider more difficult. Never before had he managed his own timetable, been his own taskmaster – and it showed. The extent to which he missed Peter Becker's gruffly reassuring presence became apparent when, after Aldag, Becker travelled to Merdingen for another bootcamp. After only a few sessions, with Becker barking instructions from his car, Ullrich was once again floating up the climbs.

Nonetheless, at the Classique des Alpes, a now defunct one-day race mimicking a Tour de France mountain stage, he trailed in eight minutes behind the leaders and made more of a mark with his gauche sense of humour than his cycling. His roommate, Brian Holm, remembers Ullrich being tickled by the name of the start town, Chambéry, and its phonetic similarity to a band, The Cranberries, who had recently topped the charts in Germany and struck many chords there with 'Zombie', a song about divisions in Ireland. 'And he sang that bloody song the whole time. In your heaaaad, in your heeeeeead . . . It was like a nightmare,' Holm recalls.

In the Tour of Switzerland two weeks later, Ullrich produced his best display to date in a Telekom jersey, finishing third on stage four to Wil. It could, would have been even better had he demonstrated a little more nous in the breakaway group that contested the stage win. 'He just wouldn't know any of the riders and he completely focused on the wrong rider,' Aldag remembers. 'I think he asked around who was the fastest and someone said Lombardi. But Jan wouldn't even know who that was. Even two years later he wouldn't have known most guys in the peloton or what their strengths were. He just didn't care.'

It was just as well that not every pro race was a test of tactical acumen. At the German time trial championship in Forst at the end of June, Ullrich simply pedalled harder and faster than any of his competitors – onto the top step of the podium and into the black-red-gold national champion's jersey. In his post-race interviews, he talked about the hard yards he had done to prepare on the climbs of the Black Forest and completely neglected to mention Peter Becker. Becker was so affronted that he decided, from now on, Ullrich could take care of his own training.

If that burst the champagne bubbles, a different party was pooped even more egregiously three days later. After a road race in which Telekom riders filled the first seven positions, with Udo Bölts the victor and Ullrich fourth, the company's CEO, Ron Sommer, interrupted the celebrations to warn Walter Godefroot that they would pull their sponsorship at the end of the year if the team didn't succeed at the Tour de France. Just days earlier, Godefroot had been informed that he would only be allowed to take two thirds of a team to the Tour, having been judged unworthy of a full invitation. The remaining three riders in a hybrid Italo-Germanic line-up would come from the ZG outfit managed by the moustachioed ringmaster, Gianni Savio.

First-year pros rarely ride the Tour, and Godefroot had never remotely considered selecting Ullrich. He stayed out of sight and out of mind while his teammates in France rode for Telekom's future and his. The pre-race ultimatum appeared to have the desired effect, as the sprinter Erik Zabel scored the first two stage wins of his Tour career. The Telekom execs were delighted – and promptly confirmed the team's survival into 1996.

Back in Merdingen, Ullrich watched the Tour on TV, fizzing with energy and impatience. 'So stupid – I was in the form of my life and had no way to show it,' he said later. He was back in action at the Vuelta a Burgos stage-race in early August, finishing an impressive twelfth overall. He rode even better to come second in the Tour du Limousin a week later. There, Brian Holm saw his callow Classique des Alpes roommate, the bad karaoke singer of two months earlier, leading some of the world's top riders a merry dance. 'I remember watching him one day there, just sitting on the brake hoods before the bunch sprint, so relaxed, on these tiny little roads, twisting left and right, and just thinking he looked born to ride a bike.'

Ullrich and Telekom hoped that he could build on that foundation in what was to be his first major tour, the Vuelta a España in September. The race began in Zaragoza – and immediately turned into a nightmare, as what had been a nagging toothache a few hours earlier turned into a flaming abscess by the end of the prologue time trial. Ullrich endured what he later described as 'torture' throughout the race's first week and never truly recovered, finally climbing off his bike in Andalusia on stage twelve.

And thus, midway through September, Jan Ullrich's first season as a professional cyclist drew to a premature and inglorious end.

Jan Ullrich had given few interviews in his first months on the job as a professional cyclist – but those which did make it into print, onto the airwaves or a screen contained subtle insights into his growing pains. He had started the year full of confidence, telling one journalist, Klaus Blume, that he aimed to ride the Tour de France in 1996 and intended to try and win it within four or five years. The extent to which spring and summer had brought a reality check, though, was obvious from what Ullrich was telling *Süddeutsche Zeitung* on the eve of the Vuelta, in an article discussing his early season 'depression'. 'I was really down, and I'd never been through that before,' Ullrich said. 'As an amateur I could win even when I wasn't fit. If you slack off for even just a week as a pro, you lose 50 per cent of your condition. As an amateur I was never that challenged.'

Godefroot had also been distinctly underwhelmed, despite boasting at the Tour that, in Erik Zabel and Ullrich, Telekom possessed two of the biggest talents in the cycling world. There were also no immediate signs that Ullrich was putting into practice what he had told the *Süddeutsche Zeitung* about taking greater care of his body in the future. In an autumn fitness test in Freiburg, his scores were worse than they had been at the same time the previous year.

Peter Becker's end-of-term report was damning: 'He hung like a bean.' Becker was also still seething about Ullrich's response to winning the national time trial championship in June, which had led to the breakdown of their relationship. 'I heard him talk about his training and say that he'd done it all by himself. I thought, OK, fine, have it your way. Then I went to him and told him, "Ulli, many congratulations. You did great. That's the last you'll see of me. All the best." At that point it was clear to me: the Ullrich chapter was over.'

It took Wolfgang Strohband's intervention for the bridge to be rebuilt – more precisely, at his manager's insistence, Ullrich travelling to Hamburg in the autumn and issuing Becker with a grovelling apology. Becker accepted and the two would resume their partnership ahead of the 1996 season. Years later, though, Becker would come to feel that Ullrich had learned and changed very little as a result of their fallout. His inability or refusal to shoulder certain responsibilities would continue to infuriate Becker – just as it sometimes had in Hamburg and Berlin. By way of an example, Becker tells me a story about a cracked handlebar stem that finally came apart at an under-23 race in Kiel in 1993 and landed Ullrich in hospital. Two of Ullrich's teammates had had the same issues with the same stems in the week or two before – but Ullrich assured Becker that he'd swapped his before the race. 'Ulli's away in a group, but then the two other kids in the break come through the finish line and Ulli's nowhere to be seen. Then, "Mr Becker, Ullrich has had a bad crash." The stem had just broken off. So off to the hospital I go. This is just before the Sachsen Rundfahrt, which is a key race before the worlds. I go in and the doctors tell me I have to be gentle with him, but Jan says he feels fine. I say, "Ulli, you're an idiot. I've left the others training on their own to come and see you. Because of your stupidity."'

Becker rocks back in his chair, shaking his head. It was simply maddening, he keeps telling me, to watch someone for whom he fulfilled an almost paternal role 'make their life twice as hard as it should be'.

'This way of overestimating himself that he has. This, "Ach no, it's OK, I can do it . . ."'

He sighs again.

'I mean, the kid has such a good heart. With animals, you should see him. I remember a dog at a training camp one year, how he lifted it up and stroked it. That's where you think that maybe he didn't get the love he needed from a father, say. His heart needed that. In

Hamburg, I was mum, dad and coach. There we talked about everything and I would also occasionally turn a blind eye if his room wasn't tidy. Of course not forgetting that as a bike rider you also have to be a pig, and be a pig to other people as well. But on the other hand, making things so hard for yourself, being so blind to certain things . . . that was totally unnecessary in my opinion.'

6

EUREKA!

'I'm sure Jan would have beaten Bjarne if he'd been allowed'

—*Jens Heppner*

'We never really talked that much. We didn't need to. That's the beauty of friendship. Of real teamwork, despite the fact there were seven years between us. That's what I like to remember.'

A quarter of a century has passed since Bjarne Riis first met Jan Ullrich – a timeframe long enough to define some people's lives and, in their cases, sufficient for multiple reinventions, both forced and voluntary, between retirements, marriages, divorces, fatherhood and public ignominies causing them to privately unravel.

Twenty-five long years from which, on a Friday afternoon in the spring of 2020, Bjarne Riis says that he would like to retain one thing: that he and Jan Ullrich could not have realized their dreams without each other.

In some ways, it is a pity that theirs was a bond based on actions more than words for, had they ever shared longer, deeper conversations, Riis and Ullrich might have realized they had a lot more in common than just being teammates at Telekom in the 1990s. Like Ullrich, Riis was also raised by only one of his parents and his grandparents. The Dane's mum and dad divorced when he was a year old, Riis staying with his father while mother and brother went to live in a commune, among other places. Years later, in his grandparents' home in Herning, Riis saw a photo of another little boy and was suddenly curious. 'That was your big brother Michael. He drowned,' the little Bjarne was told. There was no further explanation.

In his case, a fragmented childhood had forged a single-minded, taciturn personality at the antipodes of Ullrich's. 'I constantly developed myself and the things around me,' Riis says. 'That's still how I am today: I can't just let things be. I push people and I think that's a part of being professional. I know and see that not everyone's thinking like that but I don't care, because I believe in these things.'

The Ullrich that Riis slowly got to know after Riis signed for Telekom at the end of 1995 was 'ambitious, curious'. Later, says Riis, 'Jan changed.'

In their own ways, Riis and Ullrich would be the sensations of the 1996 cycling summer. They had made their first statements of intent the preceding winter, somewhat out of context – Jan Ullrich in a sauna, and Riis, Telekom's new big-money signing, a mock cowboy saloon at a theme park.

Telekom's veteran climber from the Pfalz region, Udo Bölts, had not known quite what to make of Ullrich in 1995. Bölts also cringed when he saw the clearly unwashed bike with which Ullrich had reported back for duty at a training camp in Fuerteventura ahead of what would be his second campaign in magenta and white. But Ullrich made a deeper impression on Bölts when they stepped into the sauna. Bölts stuck it out for barely twenty minutes; Ullrich lasted an hour, most of it spent with his eyes closed, a soupçon of a smile across his lips, on the hottest bench in the house.

It's possible, of course, that Ullrich was still chuckling to himself after a team gathering a couple of weeks earlier at the Elspe Festival amusement park in the hills of Sauerland, where Walter Godefroot had summoned the media to meet Riis, Telekom's new leader. A third-place finisher in the 1995 Tour, the thirty-one-year-old had played the solid yeoman for several seasons before morphing into a yellow jersey contender as he moved towards the twilight of his career. What had never changed was his intense, lugubrious disposition – more Nordic noir than Spaghetti Western, even now when Riis was throwing lassos and tossing horseshoes for a tacky photo op.

'We were in this sort of false saloon bar and we all got sent upstairs while the journalists got their time with Bjarne,' Rolf Aldag remembers. 'We were sitting up there, and for whatever reason you would hear what people said through the floorboards. At one point one of the journalists asked Bjarne what he thought about the Tour. "*Ja*, I think I can win it," he said. We all had to stop ourselves bursting out laughing, because we knew they could hear us downstairs. We were like, "Er, I'm not sure where you've been for the last five years, Bjarne, but Miguel Induráin is still riding. No one is ever going to beat him." The worst of it was that Bjarne kept saying it, all winter. We'd be like, "Yeah, congratulations, Bjarne. Good one." It became a running joke in the team. "Ah, you know Bjarne's going to win the Tour . . ." It was always guaranteed to get a laugh.'

If some at Telekom had doubts about Riis, he had also harboured a few about them upon joining the team from the Italian outfit Gewiss-Ballan. 'I said to him, "Bjarne, if you're good, the team will step up with you. There's Bölts, Heppner, Aldag, who are already competent riders, but if you're good they'll go to the next level,"' Walter Godefroot remembers. But Riis was initially aghast at some aspects of the reigning culture at Telekom. At one get-together that winter he had looked on in horror as a team dinner descended into a raucous, booze-fuelled food fight. The training was, as far as he was concerned, even worse. 'I'd do four or five hours but I did my homework – the efforts – whereas these guys were doing seven, eight hours, but it'd take them two more just to find any trace of a sprint or interval on their power files when they analysed them on the computer later. It was just hours, hours, hours with them,' Riis says now.

Ullrich's name hadn't featured in Walter Godefroot's sales pitch to his new leader, and indeed the Tour de France was not on Ullrich's race programme. Peter Becker's hope for the season was that Ullrich could continue his acclimatization to pro racing by targeting short stage-races – a waypoint to loftier goals in future years. Becker's Hamburg-based amateur team had now folded, meaning that his trips to Merdingen became more frequent. In the spring, Ullrich performed well at the Vuelta Valenciana, Criterium International and the Tour of the Basque Country. He would have done even better, Becker felt, had it not been for illness in March and February. The Telekom directeur sportif who had taken Ullrich under his wing at the Vuelta a España the previous autumn, a Belgian former rider named Rudy Pevenage, also believed he was starting to come of age.

Nothing in Riis's results, meanwhile, suggested that the teammates who had stifled their giggles in Sauerland would be proven wrong at the Tour. Only with hindsight does Rolf Aldag now look back on the GP Midi Libre in May as a pivotal moment not only in the Telekom's 1996 season, but also in the team's history.

And, by extension, as a turning point for Jan Ullrich.

'You only realized later how Bjarne was changing the culture of the team,' Aldag says. 'At the Midi Libre, we hated him so much. I think it took Udo Bölts a long time to forgive him.' Aldag goes on to paint a picture of Riis using his teammates like sled dogs, verbally whipping them into a seemingly gratuitous 90-kilometre pursuit on a stage in which a breakaway group had cut loose and Telekom had nothing to gain from hunting them down. 'I was almost crying on the bike,' Aldag says. 'We're all like, "What was that bonehead thinking? Why did he kill us?"'

Riis didn't go on to win the Midi Libre or even come close. But, says Aldag, 'that bonehead' had reminded his teammates that he was deadly serious about wanting to mix it with Induráin at the Tour.

'What you then realize is that it doesn't matter who's in the front – if you stay together and don't panic, you'll catch them. Your whole career you underperform because you never believe, then this guy comes along who's a strong believer – probably too much – and he changed the nature of the team. We were very defensive, quite pessimistic before that. But Bjarne had caused this shift that was definitely a big factor in what came next, also as far as Jan was concerned . . .'

Riis had experienced an epiphany of his own upon signing for Ariostea in 1992. Cycling was entering a new, scientific age, with Italian teams and, more specifically, their doctors its trailblazers. Upon moving from Ariostea to Gewiss in 1994, he had swapped one such *preparatore*, Luigi Cecchini, for another, Michele Ferrari, only to switch back to Cecchini after three months. Riis wrote in his auto-biography[7] that Cecchini played no part in his illegal drug use, whereas Ferrari would eventually receive two life-bans for doping-related offences, one from the Italian Olympic Committee in 2002 and one from the United States Anti-Doping Agency in 2012.[8] When he joined Telekom, Riis had been using EPO for over a year and brought with him an approach to not just training but also nutrition and what was euphemistically dubbed 'medical preparation' that Jens Heppner now describes, through a knowing smile, as 'very Italian'.

Whatever Heppner is or isn't implying, rumours about oscillations in Riis's blood values would one day earn him the nickname 'Mister Sixty Per Cent' – a reference to the alleged proportion of red cells in his blood at a time when the average 'natural' level was in the low forties, but illegal yet undetectable blood-booster EPO could push the number much higher. The more red cells a rider's blood contained, the more oxygen could be pumped to his muscles. Riis has always denied going to such extremes – despite finally, years later, conceding that EPO and various other forbidden potions, pills and ointments had indeed become part of his panoply.

At the Tour of Switzerland in June, his final stage-race before the Tour de France, Riis struggled through the first few days with a chest infection but didn't seem fazed. He announced to his teammates that he would test himself on the queen stage, the alpine blockbuster from Grindelwald to Frauenfeld. But that day he didn't even make it to the start-line. 'We only saw him again that night in the hotel,' Heppner recalls. 'He told us all goodbye and that he'd see us again at the Tour, which by the way he was going to win. We all just looked at each other in disbelief. But the whole year was like that. A bit . . . strange, shall we say.'

Meanwhile, relieved of his domestique duties by Riis's withdrawal, Ullrich finished second behind Udo Bölts in Frauenfeld, having sacrificed his chance of a breakthrough victory to man-mark . . . Lance Armstrong. Rudy Pevenage and the team doctor, Lothar Heinrich, had watched Ullrich pounding up the 10 per cent gradients of the Grosse Scheidegg, the climb that brushes past the Eiger's infamous north face, and gasped. 'It's like he's on a motorbike,' Pevenage said. Ullrich's performance was in fact so eye-catching that Pevenage called Walter Godefroot three times over the course of the afternoon. He thought they should take Ullrich to the Tour de France.

Godefroot had experienced a similar eureka moment with Ullrich a few weeks earlier, when the young German had done the job of three men as Telekom rode to set up Erik Zabel in a sprint stage at the Four Days of Dunkirk. This prompted Peter De Clercq of the Lotto team to drop back to the Telekom car and demand to know where Godefroot had found this 'monster'. Godefroot smiled. Now, though, he reminded Pevenage that Telekom's nine for the Tour had already been picked. The 'last' place was going to Riis's compatriot, Peter Meinert Nielsen.

It took one more week, and one more masterclass by Ullrich, to change Godefroot's mind. At the German national championships in the hills south of Stuttgart, Udo Bölts reckoned that Ullrich 'could have dropped everyone else in the race while picking his nose'. Instead, diplomatically, he let Christian Henn, his Telekom team-mate, escape to victory in the closing kilometres. But Ullrich's reward was a ticket to the Tour – specifically the one previously reserved for Meinert Nielsen.

There could be quibbles with Ullrich's lack of experience, but not with his talent or his form: in a fitness test at the University of Freiburg before leaving for the Tour, he scored a maximum aerobic power of 560 watts. It was the highest such value the Telekom doctors, Lothar Heinrich and Andreas Schmid, had ever seen.

The eighty-third Tour de France was to roll out of 's-Hertogenbosch in the Netherlands. For Telekom, the race began when Bjarne Riis put down his knife and fork and stood up midway through the team dinner on the eve of the race. Riis had finally found some form at the Danish national championships a week earlier, winning both the road race and the time trial, but Telekom also had a sprinter, Erik Zabel, whose two stage wins in 1995 had effectively secured their future. How the remainder of the team would share or divide roles was still moot – which was why Riis now decided to meet the issue head-on.

His compatriot, friend and domestique Brian Holm was listening. And, soon, wincing.

'He got up and basically said – again – that he could win the Tour,' Holm remembers. 'I knew Bjarne well, trained with him, and when I heard that I was thinking, *Oh, get fucked, Bjarne. Why the fuck have you said that?* My toes were curling. I hoped that he'd fall off and break his collarbone, because, to be honest, I thought we'd be wasting our time working for him. There were these two big groups in the team, one Erik's gang and one for Bjarne, and the two groups hardly talked to each other. It wasn't one big happy family. The only guy not in either group was Jan; they just told him to go as far as he could.'

Riis says now he 'wasn't really aware' of how little faith his team still had in him and wouldn't have cared even if he had. 'Because I believed in myself. Also, what was that going to change for me? Yeah, of course, in terms of them working for me, but it just meant I had to prove them wrong.'

Despite the misgivings, the Tour started well for Telekom, with Zabel sprinting to a stage win on day four. Riis's first major test would come four days later in the Alps, where most pundits had forecast two scenarios: one, the same script as the previous five Tours, all of which Miguel Induráin had won by asphyxiating or at least frustrating his rivals uphill and decimating them in time trials; or the much more remote possibility of the rider who had robbed Induráin of his world hour record at the end of 1994, Tony Rominger, now toppling the Spaniard in France.

What transpired was a stage peppered with dramas but transcended by one – Induráin cracking for the first time since his dominion at the Tour had been established in 1991. Rominger finished the stage in second and moved up to third on general classification, encircled by other pretenders to the seemingly now vacant throne. They included Bjarne Riis, who had been brilliantly assisted by the second youngest rider in the race, a twenty-two-year-old rookie named Jan Ullrich.

Two days later, again chauffeured by Ullrich, Riis staked his claim as Induráin's successor by winning at Sestriere and taking yellow. Ullrich himself climbed to fifth overall, just over a minute-and-a-half behind.

Slowly, Germans still revelling in the national football team's victory in Euro 96 a week earlier were beginning to take notice. Ullrich was also starting to enjoy himself. The German national coach, Peter Weibel, had given him an ultimatum – go to the Tour and he would be taking himself out of contention for the Olympic Games in Atlanta. Now, Ullrich was certain he had made the right decision. His choice had also proved financially astute, for on the first rest day, Wolfgang Strohband met Walter Godefroot to discuss a contract renewal that, when it was finally signed a few weeks later, would raise Ullrich's salary from 150,000 deutsche marks a year to over 600,000.

Jens Heppner remembers Ullrich signing the deal, but also that soliciting advice about bonus clauses and tax brackets was not exactly his room-mate's idea of pillow talk. 'His favourite topics of conversation were cars, women and cycling, although he didn't dwell too much on the racing itself. Unlike Bjarne, he wasn't spending his time going over power files or training logs on the computer. I used to try to get him to open a computer and go over some stuff but he was never interested; he wanted to be left in peace.' If Riis's milli-metric nit-picking over gear ratios and saddle height could drive his team mechanics to distraction, Ullrich typically issued one instruc-tion: 'I'll have the same as Bjarne.'

'At first he was quite curious, then I think he sort of learned, "Ach, Bjarne knows everything, Bjarne's thinking of everything, so I don't have to,"' Riis confirms. 'It was easy for him but also not the best thing because as a leader and as a young guy you need to learn what you want in your life. That's part of growing up as an athlete.'

Ullrich was briefly the *maillot jaune virtuel* when he slipped into a break on a tenth stage eventually won by Zabel. He then crashed after a tangle with a feed bag the following day, but survived that setback and the remaining stages in the Massif Central. On stage sixteen, Riis ordered him to set the pace on the lower slopes of the climb to Hautacam in the Pyrenees, and Ullrich, as usual, obliged. His pacesetting effected a first cull of the lead group while Riis moved up and down the line of his rivals, as though pondering the timing and style of their final execution. Moments later, with seven kilometres to go, he rose out of the saddle like Neptune from an unruly sea and obliterated them, going on to win by nearly a minute and to extend his lead on the overall standings to almost three. 'I think he wanted to crush us,' said the Festina rider Laurent Dufaux, one of those who had been, indeed, pulverized.

Ullrich excelled again the next day, the last in the Pyrenees. The stage had been designed as Induráin's apotheosis, arriving in the five-time winner's home city of Pamplona, but Ullrich helped turn it into a requiem, justifying what Induráin had said a few days earlier – Ullrich was a future champion. Ullrich now lay second overall, four minutes behind Riis heading into the 63-kilometre individual time trial from Bordeaux to Saint-Émilion on the penultimate day. Induráin had won all bar one of the Tour's long time trials since 1991 but, here, between row upon row of the world's most famous vineyards, Ullrich out-classed him. Perhaps even more galling than Ullrich's fifty-six-second margin of victory over the Spaniard was the nonchalance with which it had been achieved. For years, experts had swooned at the 'extra-terrestrial' bike and headgear with which Induráin seemed to enter a different orbit in time trials; here, to the aerodynamicists' horror, Ullrich had simply pulled on an old cotton racing cap and turned it backwards moments before rolling down the ramp.

So brilliant was Ullrich's performance that even Riis had appeared vulnerable – more ragged, more tired with every pedal stroke, while Ullrich seemed to be getting stronger. Riis finally conceded almost a minute in the last ten kilometres. This raised the question of how much more road Ullrich would have needed to overhaul the remaining one-minute, forty-one-second gap to the yellow jersey. Riis has always dismissed such conjecture, and Ullrich opined to Peter Becker after the Tour that Riis was simply stronger. But many in his team were confident then – and remain so now – that ten more kilometres might have been fatal. Walter Godefroot, for one, tells me, 'Jan could have won that Tour. He was stronger.' Udo Bölts has always concurred, as has Rolf Aldag, with some caveats. 'A few more days or a few more kilometres in the time trial, Jan would have won the Tour. I think Bjarne got it wrong mentally in that TT – he had such a big lead, so he started easy, like 48 kilometres an hour, then you start losing time, all of a sudden you're losing a lot, then you want to go faster but you can't any more, because even forty-eight hurts like hell after three weeks. Everything hurts double and, as strong as Bjarne is in his head, I think he really cracked. Even before that, at Hautacam when he was like, "Send it, Jan. Send it." . . . If Jan rides his own race there, he wins the Tour. At the same time, I think Bjarne really, really deserved to win because he took the lead and he put everything where it needed to be.'

Heppner, similarly, believes that, although Ullrich had the legs, the debate is complicated by ifs, buts and an epilogue that ultimately worked in Ullrich's favour.

'I'm sure Jan would have beaten him if he'd been allowed. I think everyone could see that. Jan was so good, but it probably also helped Jan not to win. Jan was very naive still. Bjarne was a role model and he listened to Bjarne. I think he learned a lot from him about rationing strength and energy over the three weeks. If it had been left to Jan, I think he would have just let rip at the bottom of the first mountain. You could see how economically he'd ridden from his performance in the Saint-Émilion TT. Initially we didn't know whether he'd ride one or two good mountain stages and then fall apart.'

At Telekom's victory party in Paris the next day, everyone was at least unanimous in acknowledging that they had been wrong to doubt their team leader. Erik Zabel, who had won two stages, stood up after dinner and apologized to Riis directly for not having believed in him. It was also true that for much of the season and the Tour a section of the Telekom team had not warmed to Riis. There was the day when, according to his masseur Jef D'Hont, he had found a banana in his feed bag and not the ham sandwich that he had requested, and flew into a rage on his return to the team hotel. Riis's diatribe had prompted D'Hont to retaliate by pushing Riis off his massage table. 'He was paranoid, chose the people he spoke to. He would hardly look in other people's direction. He considered himself a general,' D'Hont wrote years later in his memoir, *Memoires van een Wielerver-zorger*, which also contained many allegations of an altogether more serious nature – about Riis's doping – some of which Riis corroborated, others he has firmly rebutted.

Heppner also says that Riis cultivated an aloofness that occasionally tipped into arrogance. 'He pushed us and squeezed us every day, when he should have seen that he needed us and there were times when we should have been saving energy. But it was all the same to him. Jan was totally different.'

There were, it should be said, no complaints about Riis from Ullrich. Riis also thanked his understudy regularly, profusely, and still does today. 'Jan was super loyal to me, which is why I was also super loyal to him later,' Riis says. 'No one could get in between us and change that, although they tried. We never even had to discuss it – it just came naturally.'

After causing Riis a few nervous kilometres in Saint-Émilion, Ullrich looked and sounded almost embarrassed, telling the press he didn't want the yellow jersey, hadn't thought about it. Juxtaposed with Riis's imperious air, his modesty and naivety made him doubly charming. It was only seven years since East Berliners had taken pickaxes to the Wall while fifteen-year-old Ullrich slept in a dorm three kilometres away, and Walter Godefroot now told the media that Telekom's new prodigy had had to learn not only about professional cycling but the 'Western World'. When the media probed for finer details of Ullrich's backstory, Jan told them his mother still lived in Rostock and that he helped her out whenever and however he could. His dad had left them years ago. Where he was now, Ullrich had no idea.

Mum had been at the roadside – or at least somewhere close by, for the emotion at one point got too much – when Ullrich crossed the finish line on the Champs-Élysées. In the evening, she finally embraced her son in the lobby of the Concorde Lafayette, remarking that she had never seen him looking so thin – like 'skin and bone' as she put it. Peter Sager, who had travelled with her from Rostock, had to lend Ullrich his belt to stop his trousers falling down at the team's celebration dinner. Ullrich had never been so light since turning pro – 68 kilograms – and never would be again.

Peter Becker was also in the group of friends and family who had travelled from Rostock and Berlin. Becker noted with pride that Germany's two best overall results in the Tour had now been to a certain extent 'made in Berlin', Ullrich's second place equalling that of the Berliner Kurt Stöpel in 1932. As far as Becker was concerned, the two performances had also been achieved in the same spirit of noble toil – and Becker said as much to Telekom team doctor Lothar Heinrich when they met on the stairs of the Concorde Lafayette. 'You did really great work,' Becker told Heinrich, 'and I'm especially proud that it was all honest and clean.'

Becker says that, upon hearing this, the doctor 'stood up five centimetres taller'. Heinrich then snapped, 'Do you maybe think that I'd risk my medical licence?'

Becker was taken aback by his touchiness. He says he 'thought about that exchange a lot, later on.'

That Heinrich had detected a non-existent edge to Becker's compliment was a sign of the times. Just a few weeks after the 1996 Tour, Italian magistrates began investigating claims that, thanks to a tip-off, the teams participating in that year's Giro d'Italia in May had dodged a major, premeditated drugs bust on their return to Italy after the race start in Greece. Soon, following a trial at the Tour of Switzerland, the UCI was announcing that they intended to roll out a programme of blood tests and a 50 per cent haematocrit limit for the 1997 season – as a measure to protect riders' health, rather than detect doping. They called it the best, indeed maybe only available deterrent given that the doping substance du jour, EPO, couldn't be traced in urine tests. Others said it was a licence to dope, to saturate one's blood with oxygen-delivering red cells up to that 50 per cent threshold.

In Germany, these stories received little airplay. In the final week of the Tour, for the first time, reporters both on the ground and back in the newsrooms of Berlin, Munich, Hamburg and Cologne were busy asking whether Telekom's success and Ullrich's in particular might fuel a cycling 'boom' in Germany. Deemed unworthy of fielding a complete team in 1995, one year later Telekom had taken home five stages, the green and yellow jerseys and more prize money than any team in a single edition of the Tour's history. Cycling was Germany's second most popular participation sport, yet only twenty-fourth in terms of federation members. In Ullrich, there was now the hope they had found not only the country's first Tour winner in waiting but also someone who could convert a land of bike-racing agnostics into believers. As the journalist Guido Scholl would observe years later, Ullrich's kinfolk had 'instantly adopted him, for his appeal cut across class lines: there was as much about him to like for a manual labourer as there was for a university professor.'

His success in France had also led to the German national team selectors belatedly offering him a place at the Olympics. Ullrich declined and instead stayed at home to ride in and dominate the six-day Regio-Tour. Miguel Induráin had said during the Tour that Germany was effectively 'throwing away a medal' by not taking Ullrich to Atlanta; Induráin turned out to be the main beneficiary, winning gold in the time trial – the last major honour in a career that he officially ended the following winter.

It was also time for Ullrich to take a breather. By the time the 1997 Tour route was unveiled in late October, he was looking distinctly fuller of figure, though he reassured journalists that a little winter insulation was nothing new or alarming. 'It's just that in the past no one was interested,' he said, before adding that he had 'only' put on eight kilos. Team Telekom had also gained a different kind of 'weight', the company's sponsorship czar, Jürgen Kindervater, having confirmed that their budget in 1997 would climb from seven to ten million deutsche marks. The rise roughly equated with the 31 per cent the 1996 Tour had reportedly added to the company's brand recognition scores. 'Success has no price,' Kindervater declared – and Telekom fully intended to reign again in 1997. Riis would once more be their leader. Never mind that he had stood up at the team dinner in Paris and promised to one day repay Ullrich for his sacrifice.

That winter, Riis would have other concerns, bigger than and unrelated to Telekom's plans for the following summer. His marriage was about to fall apart and, moreover, a Danish television channel had repeated claims made two years earlier to *Der Spiegel* by the former Telekom rider Uwe Ampler, according to which Ampler had been unwittingly doped with EPO while at Telekom. It was an old story, though newly relevant, given that Telekom were also-rans in 1994 but had now become cycling's dominant power.

Riis's response was that he had heard of EPO but would never use it. 'He's an idiot and a liar,' said his compatriot Brian Holm – of Ampler, not Riis.

7

THE NEW GIANT

'In Andorra, the bell heralding the start of the Ullrich era rang. If he keeps his feet on the ground and chooses his entourage well, keeping the clowns and the weirdos away, he'll go very far'

—*Rudy Pevenage to* L'Équipe, *18 July 1997*

On a biting, electric-blue Saturday in January 2020, the Friedhof in Berlin's Heerstraße befits the name that Germans give to all of their burial grounds – literally a 'peace garden'. The low, dark marble grave of Germany's first ever Tour de France stage winner and the first German to wear the yellow jersey, Kurt Stöpel, barely tugs at the attention, but then here Stöpel is in illustrious company. The Nazis blocked a planned extension of the graveyard in the 1930s on account of the numerous Jews buried within the grounds and the fact that the cemetery would be visible from the nearby Olympic stadium. Today it is dotted with the remains of celebrated authors, painters and other luminaries such as Hermann Minkowski, Einstein's one-time teacher and among the most influential mathematicians of the nineteenth and twentieth centuries.

Kurt Stöpel took the yellow jersey on stage two of the 1932 Tour and went on to finish second overall, thereby planting a German flag near the top of the Tour's general classification for the first time. He later became an admired statesman of the international peloton, a rider so distinguished and erudite that the Tour director Henri Desgrange nicknamed him 'The Philosopher'. After the war, he authored a book about his experiences at the Tour, took a job at Berlin's French

Cultural Centre, then bought a taxi in which he chauffeured tourists around the sights of Berlin, giving history lessons in one of his five languages. His beloved wife died in 1995 and by all accounts it was a blow from which Kurt, by then in his late eighties, could not recover. On 11 June 1997, in the retirement home where he now seemed to be counting down his days, he reached for a bottle of cleaning fluid and took a swig. No one could say with certainty whether it was suicide, but his family did not rule it out.

At the time of his death, Stöpel's second place overall in 1932 remained the best ever finish by a German in a Tour de France. Jan Ullrich had matched it in 1996 and, twelve months later, cycling cognoscenti were tipping him to become, at twenty-three, Germany's first winner and the fourth youngest champion since the war. Eddy Merckx, winner of five Tours and 525 races in total in the 1960s and 1970s, had said in the build-up to the 1997 Tour that Ullrich could one day eclipse even his palmarès.

Peter Becker and the doctors at the University of Freiburg could vouch for Ullrich's perfect preparation. Twenty years later, as soon as the subject of the 1997 Tour is broached, Becker marches off in the direction of some private archive, leaving me alone with my cup of coffee on the porch overlooking his back garden in Berlin's Prenzlauer Berg. He returns a few minutes later clutching a graph that shows the results of Ullrich's final pre-Tour ergometer test. The date at the top of the sheet says 2 July 1997. 'As a coach, you dream about a graph like this,' Becker says, tracing the line with his finger.

In an interview the previous December, Becker had publicly accused Telekom of 'not moving with the times' and being 'methodically and medically stuck in the age of Father Jahn'. Jahn's doctrines were designed to train a generation of Germans to repel a Napoleonic invasion at the start of the nineteenth century. The inference – or accusation – was clear: Ullrich had finally succeeded in 1996, and would in 1997, only because Becker was again at his side.

More important, Becker also acknowledged, was that in the six months before the Tour Ullrich had lost just five days of riding to illness, banking 23,800 kilometres since the previous December, including 10,600 in races. Heading into his last stage-race tune-up, the Tour of Switzerland in June, Ullrich had not yet won in 1997 but his results were following another one of those satisfyingly smooth, rising arcs. In Switzerland, that first victory also arrived, on stage three to Kandersteg. It would be followed ten days later by an even more ominous display: in the German national championship road race in the eastern suburbs of Bonn, Telekom riders filled six of the top seven positions, but Ullrich was in a class of his own, powering away from stablemates Rolf Aldag, Erik Zabel and Christian Henn on the final ascent of the decisive, cobbled climb to win by nearly a minute.

The new Kaiser looked unstoppable – and yet he also remained shackled both to the edicts of his team and to his own subservient instincts. Walter Godefroot had set out early in the year and kept repeating that the defending champion, Bjarne Riis, would again be the team's leader at the Tour, and Ullrich his deputy. Riis echoed him, although the Dane also betrayed some anxiety at his pre-race press conference in Rouen, admitting he didn't know how Ullrich felt 'deep down' about the established order in the team.

Publicly and privately, Ullrich continued to profess his loyalty, much to some teammates' bemusement. After Ullrich's second place in the prologue time trial behind Chris Boardman, Jens Heppner whispered to Udo Bölts that Riis would have no chance if Ullrich was ever set free.

An incident late on stage one to Forges-les-Eaux brought the question into even sharper focus. Riis was caught behind a pile-up in the closing kilometres and found himself momentarily isolated. Some teammates were aware of the crash but also saw Riis getting up, apparently untroubled, while others rode on, oblivious. A few minutes later, when Riis had still not reappeared in the bunch, Udo Bölts radioed the team car to ask for instructions, but Walter Godefroot was busy helping to untangle Riis. The only person left in the Telekom 'cockpit' was their VIP guest for the day, the politician Rudolf Scharping. Scharping considered himself a cycling aficionado, and that year was also penning daily Tour columns for *Bild Zeitung* – but Bölts could not sensibly defer to a middle-aged man whose idea of a bike-ride was 15 kilometres to the nearest *Kaffeehaus*. So he, Heppner and Georg Totschnig all focused on protecting Jan Ullrich.

'Riis was furious,' Walter Godefroot remembers. 'That night, I told Rudy we needed to have a meeting. The riders were having their massages but I said, "No, right now, meeting." I asked Heppner why he hadn't waited, asked all of them, while knowing the answer: they have more faith in Jan and they like Jan more. Riders will always do more for a guy they like. After fifteen minutes everyone suddenly falls silent and it's the end of the meeting. Then they all leave, I turn to Rudy and I say that was it for Bjarne: I knew he wouldn't win a second Tour. His time was up.'

Under cross-examination by his team boss, Jens Heppner had kept his true feelings to himself. Now, he says, 'It was obvious after Forges-les-Eaux that Bjarne couldn't win. And Jan couldn't have been more relaxed. There was only one guy on the team who could win the Tour.'

Unbeknownst to even most of his teammates, Riis had been in turmoil even before the incident, indeed before the Tour had started in Rouen. After winning the Tour the previous summer he had gone to the Olympics in Atlanta, where he had met and would soon fall in love with one of the Danish handball team's star players, Anne Dorthe Tanderup. Riis was still married to another woman, but it was in Tanderup that he would confide in his long, daily phone calls from France, as his dream of a second Tour victory faded. He also suspected Rudy Pevenage of leading a whispering campaign to get Ullrich sworn in as Telekom's leader. Riis and his friend Brian Holm had taken to calling Pevenage the 'Cookie Monster' when they discovered that he had been checking riders' rooms for biscuits and other 'unauthorized' snacks at training camps. Holm had warned Riis that the 'Cookie Monster' would one day betray him. And Holm had been right, Riis now believed.

In the first Pyrenean stage to Loudenvielle, Riis couldn't live with the pace set by the Festina team and their leader Richard Virenque on the ascent of the Col de Val Louron-Azet – and Ullrich promptly fastened himself to Virenque's rear wheel, in the hope that Riis could recover. But he couldn't and didn't, finally conceding forty more seconds to the Virenque and Ullrich group and slumping to fourth place on general classification. That night, Walter Godefroot assured the press the Telekom hierarchy and strategy hadn't changed: Riis remained the number one.

In a team meeting, Godefroot told his riders something else: Ullrich would no longer have to sacrifice himself for Riis.

*

At Gasthof Keller in Merdingen, the corks flew a full quarter of an hour before Ullrich crossed the line in Arcalís – when he rode under the five-kilometre banner in glorious, imperious, seemingly generation-defining solitude. Erich, the owner, had first met Ullrich in 1991, on one of the youngster's first trips to train in the Black Forest. Now in his forties, Keller sat in the front row of the cinema he had created for the Tour in the main bar, in his Telekom racing jersey, leading a chorus of 'Jan Ullrich, you're the champ!'

Whenever Jan was home in Merdingen, Erich would jump aboard a scooter and off they would both ride, into the hills above Merdingen, with Ullrich's front wheel and Erich's back one millimetres apart. Freiburg's 1,800 annual hours of sun and selection box of climbs made it a popular destination for leading German riders, and Keller had watched, driven or ridden with many of them on the same roads. But none could punish, purge and transform themselves like Ullrich in the run-up to a three-week race. A few days before setting off for the 1997 Tour, he and Gaby had dropped in on Keller to celebrate Ullrich's German national title with a glass of red wine. After two sips, Ullrich had shaken his head, smiled at Keller and admitted that he was already half-cut.

Over the next few days of the Tour, the local elixir, a fizzy red called Merdinger Bühl, would continue to flow, and the afternoon crowd in Keller's bar to swell as Ullrich's position began to look impregnable. L'Équipe called him 'The New Giant' on the morning after Arcalís. One by one, newspapers from across the globe now offered their own superlatives. Writing in La Repubblica, Gianni Mura argued that, contrary to popular opinion, the outcome of the 1997 Tour was still laden with suspense. Yes, said Mura, one doubt persisted: 'Will Ullrich just win the Tour or absolutely destroy the opposition?'

By the end of the stage twelve time trial around Saint-Étienne most were leaning towards the latter. Walter Godefroot had been joking when he told Ullrich to pass Richard Virenque, who had set off three minutes before him, on the Frenchman's left-hand side, to spook him. Ullrich hadn't understood the joke and also didn't much care for mind games; overtake Virenque Ullrich did – but on his right. It took the time trial of Virenque's life to finish second. That was also now his position on general classification, nearly six minutes down on Ullrich. Only five riders had completed the Saint-Étienne course within four minutes of Ullrich's time. Not since Miguel Induráin's towering ride in Luxembourg five years earlier had a Tour time trial seen such domination.

Unintentionally, Ullrich had done some of his best work in those interviews and team briefings early in the race, Rolf Aldag believes now. When others tried to exalt him, Ullrich had deflected compliments, praised rivals and teammates, abdicated all personal ambition. 'That was the smartest thing he could have done,' says Aldag. 'Internally, we knew he was going to be the man, but he kept the pressure off by saying that Bjarne was the defending champion, and also not forcing anything or asking for anything special from us as teammates.'

With the Alps looming, Ullrich finally had no choice but to embrace the responsibilities of both race and team leader – and, unbeknownst to almost everyone outside the Telekom bubble, it quickly became a rocky ride. He added to his lead in the first alpine stage to Alpe d'Huez, finishing second behind Marco Pantani and extending his advantage over Virenque to more than six minutes. But, on their way off the mountain in the Telekom team car that evening, Walter Godefroot sneaked a glance at Ullrich in the passenger seat as fans started to press against the bumper and the windows, straining to glimpse the new Messiah. Godefroot thought Ullrich looked terrified.

Jens Heppner and Hagen Boßdorf could both also sense Ullrich's relief when, every night, he finally retreated to the sanctuary of the team hotel, after the press conferences and the dope tests, the autographs and the photos. Boßdorf, a reporter for German TV network ARD, was acting as ghostwriter for a Tour diary that would later be published in Ullrich's name. Sometimes it was eleven at night before they sat down for a few minutes to jot down Ullrich's thoughts and observations from the day. Boßdorf could see fatigue starting to grip him. To this were added the fears which Ullrich could hide from world on the other side of the camera lenses and crash barriers, but not his roommate Heppner. 'He was getting more and more stressed. He was terrified of crashing, above all. The talk in the media about him winning for the next ten years was also unsettling him. He knew that he couldn't justify that as long as he hadn't won even one Tour. That terrorized him, as did the attacks, which we and he had to respond to, as the race leader. He became scared of crashing, of getting ill . . . it was extreme.'

To German journalists, Ullrich's anxiousness looked more like endearing giddiness, a naiveté that seemed to say more about his age than it did about any inherent vulnerability. Meanwhile, without a lingua franca or any real familiarity with his origin story, the foreign press had decided that here came another unflappable, monosyllabic tyrant in the same mould as Induráin, or the embodiment of a one-dimensional East German stereotype. Ullrich himself could offer precious little insight into either his personal history or how the hysteria was affecting him, apart from repeating that everything – the crowds, the attention, the accolades – was *Wahnsinn*, pure madness. At a media day at his home in Merdingen before the Tour, asked why he hadn't wanted to attend the previous year's German sports personality of the year awards, he had replied, 'I simply don't have the time to be a star.'

Now he didn't have any say in the matter.

Virenque tried to test him on the last two alpine stages, winning at Courchevel, but crossing the line with Ullrich in his shadow. Riis was enduring a miserable Tour but had made good on his promise to repay the favours of the previous year, saving Ullrich on the Col de la Madeleine. The next day the *maillot jaune* looked more assured on the road to Morzine, never leaving Virenque's back wheel on the steepest mountain pass of the Tour and the last climb in the Alps, the Col de Joux Plane.

With a cushion of nearly seven minutes, he looked home and dry – and not only because, from Morzine, the Tour was heading over the German border to Freiburg. But one of Ullrich's fears had turned into a self-fulfilling prophesy: he was starting to fall ill. His mother and Peter Sager had both come from Rostock to see him after stage seventeen, starting in Freiburg and finishing in Colmar, and Gaby was also waiting at the finish line. But that evening Ullrich was in a hurry to get back to the team hotel to speak with Rudy Pevenage. He had been struggling to breathe on what had been a relatively straightforward day only skirting the Vosges mountains. He feared he could implode on the much harder next stage. Festina had surely noticed and were no doubt preparing to take one last, wild swing at Telekom, with Riis also complaining of stomach problems. Pevenage agreed that it was time to call in some favours.

Ullrich's travails the following day – and the way Udo Bölts rescued him – have become a famous chapter in German cycling folklore. In particular, the message Bölts growled on the Col du Hundsruck when Ullrich pleaded with him to slow down – '*Quäl dich, du sau!*', literally 'Suffer, you pig!' – turned into a national sporting aphorism, not to mention the title of Bölts's autobiography. Festina had set about breaking Ullrich, and with 90 kilometres and the ascent of the Ballon to come, Virenque held a half-minute lead over the yellow jersey. The Frenchman was joined by two teammates and an assortment of the best riders in the race, while Ullrich had lost all of his Telekom domestiques except Bölts. A coup was taking shape until, one by one, Virenque's breakaway companions declined to help him. Finally, after several kilometres of futile remonstrations, Virenque ordered his teammates Didier Rous and Pascal Hervé to ride away to the stage victory while the group's momentum dissolved and Ullrich caught Virenque.

Still frothing, Virenque refused to answer Italian reporters' questions at the finish line because 'their riders' were 'wheel-suckers'. By which he meant Marco Pantani, who hadn't helped him – and even, the Festina team manager revealed later, declined a sizeable cash offer to do so, not for tactical reasons but because he found Virenque insufferable. Moreover, one of Rudy Pevenage's 'courtesy calls' the previous night had been to Fausto Pinarello, Telekom's bike sponsor and also that of the Spanish Banesto team. Their riders had also been conspicuous by their unwillingness to help Virenque.

From Banesto's point of view it would also turn into a worthwhile quid pro quo: the following day, according to Pevenage's account years later, Ullrich 'let' the Banesto (and Pinarello) rider Abraham Olano win the final time trial.

Earlier in the Tour, during one of their nightly phone calls, Gaby had asked Ullrich if he had any idea what euphoria he was whipping up in Germany. He didn't – and there was nothing Gaby could say to accurately convey, as she put it, 'how crazy people are going'. The last time Ullrich had watched the Tour on TV, in 1995, the total race and its related broadcasts had accounted for just 131 hours of airtime on domestic networks in Germany. In 1997, that figure had risen to 530 hours. Having estimated in 1996 that their screen time equated to 23 million marks in advertising spend, in 1997 Telekom would calculate it was worth nearly four times that.

Until only a few months earlier, as Rolf Aldag puts it, Telekom had been 'just a company you called up when you got overcharged on your phone bill', a faceless utility provider that even the then CEO Ron Sommer admits was widely 'hated' by its customers and mocked on satirical TV shows. Now, suddenly, T-shirts, key rings and baseball caps emblazoned with the company logo were selling out in the ten T-Punkt shops Telekom had opened in major German cities. When Sommer was asked whether Telekom would renew and increase its commitment, he replied that they would be 'stupid' not to.

'It was total euphoria,' says Jürgen Kindervater, Telekom's then Head of Communications. Where once Telekom's association with a team of also-rans had been questioned even in the company's boardroom, now Kindervater was suddenly being hailed as a genius. 'Just imagine,' he says, 'the state broadcaster, ARD, moved its whole schedule around to accommodate a special fifteen-minute bulletin from the Tour that went out every night after the main evening news. That'd be absolutely inconceivable now.'

It also beggared belief that a twenty-three-year-old was about to win the Tour by the widest margin since Laurent Fignon in 1984 – nearly ten minutes. Virenque said that Ullrich's wobble in the Vosges had convinced him the tables could be turned the following year, but prevailing wisdom suggested otherwise. It had, after all, been one of the more mountainous Tours of the past decade, with its time trial in the Massif Central and two stages in the Vosges in addition to the usual slog through the Pyrenees and Alps. An older, more mature Ullrich on a more orthodox route, with two flat time trials, would surely wreak even more destruction, à la Induráin in the first half of the nineties. Indeed, opponents, pundits and fans spent much of the last week debating not whether Ullrich would win this Tour but over how many editions he could layer an inevitable dynasty. For every Bernard Hinault predicting seven victories, there was an Eddy Merckx who had talked about ten even before the race left Rouen. Never since the first of 'The Cannibal's' five Tour wins in 1969 had cycling and the Tour seemed so clearly to stand on the brink of redefinition at the hands, or legs, of one rider.

The final procession to Paris offered further evidence of one transformation that was already complete – Telekom's. Walter Gode-froot's men in magenta had won the team classification, and Erik Zabel's second place in the bunch gallop up the Champs-Élysées also

brought him his second consecutive green jersey. With these accolades, four stage wins in total and Ullrich's yellow jersey, they had
amassed over 700,000 deutsche marks in prize money – another
record.

'All I've done is ride a bike for three weeks,' Ullrich shrugged as
the plaudits rained down. Messages from Chancellor Helmut Kohl
and Germany's 'other' head of state, its footballing Kaiser, Franz
Beckenbauer; gushing homages from Michael Schumacher and Katarina Witt. The prestige of the admirers confirmed Ullrich's entry to
the high society of German sport. Yet it was also the stoic nature of
his endeavour, his modesty in interviews, the perceived quaintness
of his sport, at least in the eyes of the uninitiated audience east
of the Rhine, that had made such an impact. There were immediate
comparisons with Boris Becker's first Wimbledon victory and the
'tennis fever' it had created.

Germany's newest darling resembled that early version of Becker
in more than just hair colour, before the money and the models that
eventually led one of Becker's rivals, Ivan Lendl, to brand him 'the
limousine radical'. 'He has suddenly woken interest in a competition
that occasionally turns into a test of the soul, among a population
whose 63 million bicycles are mainly used for Sunday leisure jaunts
or trips to the bakery,' wrote Michael Reinsch in the *Frankfurter
Allgemeine Zeitung*, describing a sudden awakening almost identical
in nature to the one the United Kingdom would experience with
Bradley Wiggins's Tour victory in 2012. 'Ullrich's suffering and his
exploits and those of his rivals have restored some perspective to
sport showbusiness. Other athletes don't work for seven hours a day
at the outer edge of their capacities, exhausted and faced with the
constant risk of crashes and illness. And despite this, seven-figure
salaries are as rare in cycling as they are routine in football, tennis,
Formula 1 and boxing.'

Ullrich had begun the summer of 1997 virtually unknown to the
wider German public and was to end it as the greatest sportsman they
had ever seen. Those same Germans, or at least those who partici-
pated in a *Der Spiegel* survey in September, would say so. Recency
bias no doubt played its part, and 1997 had been a controversial and
in the end unsuccessful vintage for Schumacher and a disastrous one
for the ageing Becker. Steffi Graf had not won a single Grand Slam
tournament for the first season in a decade. Nonetheless, the German

people spoke resoundingly: the *Radmessias*, the 'cycling messiah' from Rostock, claimed 16 per cent of the vote to Schumacher's thirteen, Becker's ten, Graf's nine. Of the twenty-four most famous active German sports personalities, Ullrich was also credited with by far the highest 'likability rating'. The piece quoted esteemed sociologists, including one who suggested that athletes, far more than writers, musicians and artists, 'showcased the values of ancient humanity'. It scarcely mattered, said *Der Spiegel* tartly, if 'personality-wise, they're a zero out of ten, which seems to be the case with Ullrich.'

Riis had been Denmark's first Tour winner a year earlier, and the scenes that followed served as an appetizer for what now awaited Ullrich in Germany. 'I felt like the fucking president,' says Brian Holm of the frenzy that he experienced at Riis's side a year earlier. 'It was far too early for Jan to win the Tour, if you ask me,' Riis acquiesces now. 'He wasn't mature enough. He had no idea what was coming.'

Riis had been one of the first to embrace Ullrich when he crossed the finish line in Paris and, Ullrich said, fear melted into relief. '*Unglaublich* – unbelievable,' Ullrich had gasped. 'Unbelievable,' Riis had replied.

The next day, a crowd of 30,000 people packed into the Marktplatz in Bonn and watched the 1996 Tour champion present his successor with the yellow jersey on the steps of the old town hall. Ullrich then boarded a private jet and flew to London for the presentation of a special edition Tag Heuer watch commemorating his victory. Two days later, he began a run of seventeen criterium or city-circuit races that sent him hightailing all around Europe, commanding five-figure appearance fees for each outing. One day in August, Jens Heppner hosted an autograph-signing session for Ullrich in the cheese shop Heppner owned with his wife in a usually tranquil village close to the Belgian border. Heppner told the local police to expect around 150 people, and they duly dispatched three officers to help out with marshalling and 'crowd control'. The final attendance was nearly 5,000. Ullrich would end up having to take cover behind the Blauschimmel bries and the Camemberts as fans grabbed, pawed and prodded, shrieking with excitement. 'It was total madness,' Heppner remembers.

A few days later, he witnessed a similar scene at a criterium in Heerlen, Holland. That day he told journalist Klaus Blume he feared 'that Jan will simply pack everything away and go home with Gaby'.

Ullrich's manager, Wolfgang Strohband, says his own mobile telephone bill for July 1997 served as an accurate Richter scale for the
commotion back in Germany. '3,000 deutsche marks . . . until Telekom sorted me out.' A year earlier he had waited for offers to pour
in after the Tour but few arrived, whereas now Strohband was
engulfed by a 'tsunami', as he puts it. He discussed how best to surf
it with friends, like the manager of the Hamburg-based Ukrainian
boxers, the Klitschko brothers, and with football agents. 'But I'd have
to explain to them that cyclists would sometimes be training eight
hours a day. They didn't have time for autograph signings every day.'
Finally, Strohband settled on a limited cadre of top-tier sponsors,
each of which would be graced with fifteen hours of Ullrich's time
per year. Deals were soon being struck with Adidas for apparel, Tag
Heuer for watches, Schwartau for cereal bars, Nestlé for mineral
water, Audi for cars and, most controversially when it was first
reported years later, state broadcaster ARD, who would henceforth
receive preferential access to the new national treasure. Adidas were
believed to be shelling out half a million deutsche marks a year,
whereas ARD had signed on for around 200,000. The combined
value of the contracts would see Ullrich's annual earnings soar into
the millions. His 600,000-deutsche-mark deal with Telekom had one
season left to run, but in December Telekom announced that it had
been replaced with a four-year extension which was the longest and
reportedly most lucrative arrangement in the professional peloton.

When we meet at his home in Hamburg in 2015, Strohband
baulks at the suggestion that it all may have been too much for
Ullrich – not the money, clearly, but what came with it. 'I can't
believe that he was overwhelmed. The endorsement contracts
included clauses about first-class travel and timetables to be
respected, all so that Jan only had to concentrate on riding his bike.'

In the immediate wake of the Tour, with 'Ullrich fever' at its
acme, there was also no noticeable downturn in his performances.
On the contrary, in his first official race after the Tour, the Luk-Cup
in Bühl, he attacked from an eight-man group on the final climb and
triumphed alone. Then, at the championship of Zürich a week later,
he did his best to manage expectations by reminding journalists that
he had been 'up to his ears since the Tour' – and yet still finished
second on maybe the hardest single-day race route in cycling. A
week later, half a million people came primarily to see Ullrich at the

HEW Cyclassics one-day race in his former adoptive home city, Hamburg. On terrain seemingly ill-suited to his abilities, Ullrich still outclassed and rode away from his opposition.

Soon Ullrich's teammate, Erik Zabel, would be opining that Ullrich was doing cycling in Germany no favours, meaning that his popularity was overshadowing everything and everyone else. Some smelled jealousy in those comments, others genuine concern – and, regardless, it was worth considering whether Ullrich wasn't inflicting a counterintuitive form of self-harm. For while doubts persisted over the breadth, sustainability and exact nature of whatever boom or mania Ullrich had unleashed, he had already lured new fans into a fundamental misapprehension: based on what they had seen in July and August, Ullrich had turned recent converts onto a sport in which the strongest, most talented, most feted rider would also generally be the man crossing the line first, usually having scattered his rivals across mountainsides and valleys. Would the neophytes remain captivated by, or even tolerate, those more humdrum but inevitable periods when his toil went unrewarded?

Later, Ullrich would indeed learn that every pedestal comes with a precipice – and even now there were occasional glimpses over the cliff edge. His post-Tour lap of honour and his season ended at the GP Breitling, a time trial in Karlsruhe ridden in pairs. When he and his partner Rolf Aldag finished third, Ullrich was booed. 'They expect me to win every race,' he lamented. He hoped that the fans would 'develop their knowledge a little bit in future'.

They would indeed deepen their understanding over subsequent years, but, buttressed by partisan bias, their expectations for Ullrich were and would remain dauntingly high. Which wasn't altogether surprising, says Giovanni Lombardi, one of his teammates at the 1997 Tour. 'Sure, people said he was going to break this record and that record, win this many Tours, but that was only a reflection of what he'd done in the Tour, especially in Andorra. He'd made a fool of everyone in the mountains and again in the time trials. You also looked at the riders he'd beaten, and by how much: Virenque, what, nine minutes down, the rest nowhere . . . It was really hard to see how or why he wasn't going to be kicking everyone's head in for the next ten years.'

Initially, Ullrich's Telekom teammates received many of the perks and few of the pressures associated with 'Ulle-mania', at least compared to him. The financial future of their team was suddenly assured, and recognition of their efforts didn't end with the numbers on their payslips. 'It was really crazy after that Tour,' says Rolf Aldag. 'We all went to Bonn, and you have the mayor, and we're like rock stars. You need an Audi? You get an Audi. Free, of course. I think I do actually understand what it's like for footballers because it did grow to that level for us. You know, going out to restaurants and not even needing your wallet because you know it's on the house. You were just so respected. We have this prize on German television, the Bambi award, which is the biggest prize you can win – and they gave it to us for the best afternoon's entertainment, so completely unrelated to cycling. I was sitting there with Harrison Ford and people like this . . . I think it was really, really over the top and it wasn't normal. It was also against our nature because there's no real culture for German cycling. We had Didi Thurau and Gregor Braun, Rudi Altig and Rolf Gölz, but we didn't have races with a long history or tradition, where people would come just because it was cycling.'

For journeymen domestiques whose careers had until then been parables of service and abnegation, everything that glittered could be considered gold. Aldag believes that, conversely, it was all much harder for Ullrich partly because of the intensity of the spotlight and for reasons linked to his personality. It hadn't previously mattered when, out of absentmindedness, he forgot to bring money with him on training rides, and Aldag or someone else had to shout him a drink when he insisted they stop at a cafe. Or that he didn't know or really care how much air the mechanics put in his tyres. Now, though, the same endearing insouciance wouldn't fly; he had to take responsibility and did so, says Aldag, in a way that sometimes proved counterproductive. 'That whole thing of being a celebrity turned against him and made his life so much more difficult. He wasn't a leader in general but once in a while he made very strong statements. "This is how we want to do it . . ." Not in 1996, but from 1997 he had a pretty clear opinion on things and you couldn't change his mind. But the question is, how do you develop your opinion? I think later on that was the tricky part again, with the people around him. I'm not so sure that his own opinion always developed out of his own thoughts, but rather than from other people who talked him into something.'

*

Whatever challenges lay ahead, Jan Ullrich had known one thing when he climbed off his bike at the GP Breitling in September, thus ending his season: he was tired and needed a holiday. To which sun-kissed destination he and Gaby were to escape, Ullrich declined to reveal. He hoped reporters would understand that he had shared enough of his life and thoughts over the previous few weeks.

Unfortunately, the media did finally catch up with him, though not in the way that Ullrich had anticipated. He and Gaby were on their way to the airport, making their secret getaway to Turkey, when his phone rang and Wolfgang Strohband's name flashed onto the display. There was bad news, Strohband its bearer: the French newspaper, *L'Équipe*, had published a story alleging that two major players in the 1996 Tour had also failed out-of-competition drug tests carried out by national testing agencies shortly before that race, and that the UCI had neglected to name or sanction either athlete. The claim seemed fanciful, vague . . . until the 1996 Olympic road race champion, Pascal Richard, said in an interview with the Swiss tabloid *Blick* that the mystery dopers were Bjarne Riis and Jan Ullrich.

Lacking any robust evidence, Richard's accusation was relatively easy to discredit – and discredited Richard was by the UCI. 'Pascal Richard is a stupid cyclist. Every year some idiot comes out of the woodwork,' bristled the UCI president Hein Verbruggen. Soon Richard would also be writing Ullrich a letter of apology, explaining that he had been misquoted.

Ullrich didn't look at a single German newspaper or indeed watch the news while he was in Turkey, and the storm had passed by the time he came home. Nonetheless, it had been a reminder that with his new status would come a new level of scrutiny. Which, some would have argued, was long overdue. It turned out that Ullrich could not have tested positive in the spring of 1996 because the national anti-doping body hadn't been able to locate or test him until 11 August of that year. The agency's former chairman told the *Frankfurter Allgemeine Zeitung* that Ullrich hadn't exactly refused a test, since that would have resulted in a ban. But 'the way it all happened wasn't exactly all above board.'[9]

Another rumour was also swirling, albeit only in the echo chamber of the pro peloton: the night before his victory in Bühl in August 1997, there had been another vain attempt to trace Ullrich for a dope test at the hotel where Telekom were staying. Officially, the testers

were told that he had been waylaid at a fan event hundreds of kilometres away; in reality, Ullrich had been hurriedly booked into
accommodation a few kilometres from his team's appointed billet.[10]

These were worrying developments – or could have been for
German fans paying close attention. For it was still uncertain at this
point whether fears aired after the Tour by Wolfgang Strohband and
Erik Zabel, among others, would be realized – namely that, as Strohband said, 'It's a Jan Ullrich boom rather than a cycling boom.'
Throughout the months of July and August, Strohband had closely
monitored membership numbers at his club, RG Hamburg. Fifteen new applications hardly suggested Bayern Munich would be
quaking.

Some potential new supporters may already have been put off by
what they had read in *Der Spiegel* two weeks before the Tour. A
recently retired or, to be more accurate, banned journeyman pro
named Jörg Paffrath had opened up to the magazine about what he
said was the sordid reality of a jobbing cyclist, and certainly of his life
before a positive test in 1996. Scarcely anyone, Paffrath said, could
'ride the Tour de France on water and pasta'. Most, in his experience,
were also fuelled by EPO, growth hormone and steroids.

Via their press department, Telekom had dismissed Paffrath's
claims as the bitter testimony of a second-rate dropout. A fortnight
or so later, while Jan Ullrich was dominating the Tour, the head of
sports medicine at the University of Freiburg and the overseer of
Telekom's medical programme, Joseph Keul, further reassured the
German public: yes, EPO was used by cyclists, but the potential gains
were minimal.

And, Keul said, there was certainly, certainly no one at Telekom
taking the drug.

8

HUNGER GAMES

'Basically you gain weight in the winter if you eat too much.
It's not rocket science'

—*Brian Holm*

Rudy Pevenage knew they had a problem when he looked inside the fridge. One Jan Ullrich Tour de France victory was behind them and the next was surely a year away, but what Pevenage had seen over the previous few hours gave him pause. Ullrich had come to Pevenage's house for a meal but after his second helping, then his third, it had begun to feel more like a looting. As Pevenage said later, 'It's scary, the way he eats . . . After a big lunch, he carried on eating all afternoon until he'd cleaned out my fridge. It was a few days after the Tour and I let it go because he was thin enough to haunt houses. But I realized then that his appetite is stronger than he is. Jan loves food as much as cycling.'

Ullrich's mother, Marianne Kaatz, half blamed herself. Jan was five days old when she stood by and watched his older brother, Stefan, shove a chocolate snowman into his tiny mouth. Jan later joked his sweet tooth probably grew its first roots then and there. Later, when Jan was a teenager, Peter Sager had motivated his young charges with an incentive scheme he called 'Chocolate for victories'. And, as the best in the class, Ullrich filled his chops.

Regardless of how and where the 'problem' had originated, in Jan Ullrich's first months as a reigning Tour champion, it remained largely unacknowledged until deep into the winter. His holiday to

Turkey in October had mainly been an opportunity to 'laze around' in the sun. On his return, he looked decidedly cherubic visiting a cycling club in Löhne in late October and at the Bambi gala in Cologne later that evening. But at the Bambi event, Ullrich was also, for the first time in weeks and months, far from the most famous face in the room. Neither the Spice Girls nor Harrison Ford stopped to say hello – and they certainly didn't tell him he had put on weight.

A training camp in Lanzarote followed and there Ullrich had no qualms about removing his shirt to reveal the soft contours of a fading six-pack during a game of beach volleyball. The contrast between his skeletal July iteration and present silhouette was again noticeable when a montage of his best moments from the Tour played on the big screen at the ARD German sports personality of the year awards in Ludwigsberg at the beginning of December – and the *Süddeutsche Zeitung* referred to his 'little pot belly' in a report the next day. The key number of that night was not the ten kilos Ullrich said he would lose in time for the Tour but his 3,225-point margin over the second-placed athlete in the poll of 1,313 German sports journalists. Clearly Wolfgang Strohband had been right a few weeks earlier when he had told the press that only Boris Becker's first Wimbledon victory had resonated anything like as loudly among German sporting milestones – never mind that it bore all the hallmarks of a fickle infatuation.

To anyone squinting disapprovingly at his waistline over the next few weeks, Ullrich replied matter-of-factly that it was always the same at this time of year. In the winter preceding his first pro season he had 'absolutely stuffed his face', according to Peter Becker. To correct the mistake, it had taken a special intervention from Becker – '150-kilometre rides through the Black Forest with Peter on only water, no bread, that nearly finished him,' as Wolfgang Strohband tells me.

The next two years had been better, but then Ullrich had been allowed to quietly hibernate at home. Now, he trundled from one prize ceremony to the next, grazing on canapés and red wine. 'He likes food, we all know that,' says Rolf Aldag, 'but he also just likes to sit with people – not necessarily be on stage in front of people, in the spotlight, but he likes to be honoured for what he's done. Then what do you do if you have seven invitations for seven nights in a week to go for dinner? Do you go and have a salad, say, "That fillet steak's nice but I'm not going to eat it"? Somehow he became a celebrity, every-one wanted a piece of him, and everyone gave him something. Of course, if you like a bottle of good red wine and people send you three bottles a week – "Here's a good bottle to say congratulations for the Tour. You can drink it in front of the open fire . . ." – you're going to open it. Plus he was living on a vineyard . . .

'So, knowing him,' Aldag continues, 'would he go grocery shop-ping, or take the trouble to go to a vineyard? No, it wasn't important enough for him. But if he had it at home, he would drink it. As opposed to when he was living in Hamburg and no one was going shopping for him. Then he was super lean. He probably just came back from training rides and had a bowl of muesli.'

Another Telekom rider, Jens Heppner, had gone with Ullrich on a skiing trip to Austria before Christmas. This was also where Hepp-ner realized that Ullrich's were not just the usual end-of-season indulgences. 'He ate to excess, drank to excess, hardly slept and we stayed too long: ten days, when four would have been enough,' Heppner remembers. 'Then we went straight from there to a team meeting which lasted four days and where, again, there was no train-ing and we ate and drank a lot.'

After meetings in the autumn and certainly by the time they reconvened for their annual training camp in Mallorca in January, Ullrich's weight was the talk of the team. Now Brian Holm under-stood what Ullrich had meant when he had confided in the Dane a few months earlier. 'I could remember him talking to me about his weight, saying he'd go on a diet for three days, then he'd be sitting there watching television and suddenly not be able to resist any more. He'd take his car – an Opel Calibra, I think – and just drive to the petrol station to load up on junk food. He said he'd eat and eat and eat, then feel guilty afterwards – which of course I'd done as well a few times.'

In Mallorca, there was no more hiding. The German media had descended, and Ullrich and Telekom were faced with a choice of whether to respond with white lies, excuses or humour. Ullrich's claim that the surplus amounted to no more than five kilos belonged in the first category, his blaming two bouts of illness before Christmas arguably in the second. As for jokes, even Erik Zabel tried to lighten the mood by quipping to the assembled reporters that, once upon a time, the Telekom directeurs sportifs would have removed Ullrich's suitcase from his room and told him to come back when he looked like a bike rider.

Brian Holm can well imagine Walter Godefroot's reaction at the time being even blunter. 'Walter wouldn't even try to control Jan's eating. He was like, "You either listen or fuck off."'

In truth, Godefroot was mainly irked at having been kept in the dark. He knew that Ullrich had overindulged and perhaps undertrained, but not to the tune of nearly 20 kilos – more than three times what would be deemed a normal post-season slide. That is indeed the scarcely believable figure that Peter Becker remembers – correcting me when I suggest that, having finished the 1997 Tour weighing 68 or 69 kilos, Ullrich had ballooned to 85 by early 1998. 'More than 85!' Becker bellows. 'More like 90!'

The tipping point came, says Godefroot, with a belated call from the Telekom doctors in Freiburg.

'Ultimately he's a bit bone idle,' Godefroot says. 'He's not bad when he only has to do his job and there are no distractions, but everyone always says yes to Jan. Either no one tells me or they tell me after everyone else. So, anyway, when he'd put on 20 kilos, then I finally get the message: Walter, you have to speak to Jan. He had an appointment in Freiburg to do a test. He says he can come at nine o' clock the next day. But he doesn't come. When I find out, I say to Lothar or Schmid [Lothar Heinrich and Andreas Schmid, Telekom's doctors], "This isn't possible. Are you just fans?" When I've got an appointment in hospital, I'm fifteen minutes early so the doctor doesn't have to wait for me. But no one says anything. Becker, who usually had a big mouth, just turns away and says nothing. So Jan does whatever he wants.'

That 'whatever' would soon spawn countless more or less apocryphal tales. The most legendary (though also widely corroborated) went that Ullrich loved nothing more than to snack on Nutella – that is, not spread it on toast, but put a whole jar in the microwave and drink the resulting DIY 'hot chocolate' through a straw.

He started his 1998 season as planned at the Challenge Mallorca in early February, but results and performances over the weeks that followed were disastrous. His best finish in five Spanish stage-races before the end of April was seventy-eighth. He abandoned Tirreno–Adriatico in the first hour of the first stage, having arrived in Italy with a chest infection. But it was Ullrich's waist that L'Équipe said was 'as hotly discussed as Naomi Campbell's'. An article in the same paper also suggested that Ullrich's condition was unworthy of a Tour winner, to which Ullrich retorted tartly that they had used a picture that was several weeks old, which was also hardly worthy of a newspaper of *L'Équipe*'s prestige.

Regardless, the team leader's illnesses, withdrawals and race programme rejigs soon became a source of frustration to more than just Telekom's management. Giovanni Lombardi spent whole days of the Vuelta a Aragon by Ullrich's side, way off the back of the peloton, but says 'it was impossible to get angry with him because, as a guy, he was pure gold.' Others sometimes felt differently. 'It was frustrating at times,' says Rolf Aldag, 'because he'd be getting dropped on the first climb of those races – Basque Country, Valencia – and we'd have to stay with him, going a lot slower than we wanted. Instead of building our form we were being brought down to his level. Walter would be sending me to stay and train with Jan and I'd know that wasn't what I particularly needed. On the other hand, I said to myself that tenth place in the Tour would earn me 2,000 euros, or maybe 5,000 euros, so almost nothing, and for that I'd have to spit blood for three weeks. Jan was the only rider we had who was capable of winning the Tour or even of finishing second or third, and so it made total sense.'

Even so, Aldag concedes, in early 1998 in particular Ullrich tested the patience of even his most devoted teammates. 'You're like, "Get your shit together, Jan." Or, to the management, "Look, you know he's not going to be ready, so stop entering these races or force him to be ready. But don't dump this shit on us."'

In Mallorca in January, Peter Becker had watched in dismay as Ullrich shovelled helping after helping onto his plate at the hotel buffet. Aldag also remembers Ullrich's prodigious breakfasts becoming as much of a feature of Telekom's Mallorca camps as hill repeats in the Tramuntana mountains. 'He would eat so much muesli that you thought he had to throw up. There's no way that stays inside him. If we go riding, in an hour and a half . . . no one can handle that. You wouldn't be able to breathe. It was that sticky muesli that you soak for a whole day and you can build a house with it. You really wouldn't want to be in the toilet after him.'

But if Ullrich's appetite could leave mouths agape then so, in spring, could his ability to suppress or override it. Aldag recalls training camps when his evening meals would consist of a few leaves of lettuce. 'He'd do his six hours of riding, then have his salad. And the next day muesli again. Doing that, with that workload, you'd just die. You'd never have any energy . . . but Jan just got better and better. Which was proof that, whatever he did, he was just so talented. You couldn't compare him to anyone.'

Finally, at a certain point in the spring, Ullrich did begin to turn the oil tanker around – as he began to shed some of his cargo. His Tour victory the previous summer had spurred Telekom to set up a development squad in Ullrich's name, with Peter Becker as its coach. The project was partly viewed by Walter Godefroot as a way to stop Becker meddling in the affairs of the main team, but, with Ullrich's Tour defence just weeks away, Becker was dispatched to the Black Forest to attempt to salvage the seemingly unsalvageable. Over three weeks in May, Ullrich wowed his old coach with feats of endurance that were in many ways far more impressive than anything he had done the previous July. Whether the approach was healthy or sensible was another matter. 'Imagine having to lose 15 or 20 kilos between the start of the spring classics and the Tour,' Becker says. 'How can you hope to do that? You've got to fit in sessions behind the car, time in the mountains, interval training . . .'

Becker shakes his head, half in awe, half in exasperation.

'He got away with it but it could have gone very wrong. With his joints, for example, given how heavy he was. But somehow the kid found a way.'

Respectable displays in the Vuelta a Castilla y Leon, Classique des Alpes, Tour of Switzerland, Route du Sud and, finally, his traditional pre-Tour fitness test in Freiburg confirmed that Ullrich was ready for the Tour – or at least within five kilos of his 1997 weight, and nearly as powerful. The football World Cup in France had further helped him by pushing the Grand Départ back by a week, almost to the middle of July. In fact, the race wouldn't arrive on French soil until the third stage, for the Grand Départ was to set out from Dublin, Ireland. At Telekom's pre-race press conference, Ullrich lied that he had never been worried about his condition. He supposed ten riders could potentially win the Tour, one of whom was his teammate Bjarne Riis. The bookmakers, meanwhile, had Ullrich as their overwhelming, even-odds favourite. Richard Virenque was his scarcely credible closest challenger, out at 8–1.

Scarcely credible was certainly right about Virenque. The big news on the eve of the race came not from Telekom or even Ireland but a customs posting on the Franco–Belgian border. There, a masseur working for Virenque's Festina team, Wily Voet, had been arrested following a search of the Fiat he was driving to the start of the Tour. The vehicle contained over 400 doses of banned drugs, including 235 vials of EPO. For years, experts had speculated about – and in some cases produced solid evidence for – a hidden but encroaching plague in professional cycling: EPO's magical, blood-oxygenating properties could supposedly turn sprinters into climbers, donkeys into racehorses, team doctors into sorcerers. The hormone was also undetectable in routine urine tests, meaning it was impossible to gauge just how many riders were using it. Now, Festina and Virenque would be allowed to start the Tour while Voet languished in jail, but their protests of innocence – particularly the claim that the drugs were for someone else – sounded like a lie with short legs. They also raised a disturbing question: if the dimensions of Voet's stash suggested that all or at least most of the Festina riders were his patients-cum-pin cushions, what did that imply about the other riders in the field?

While doubts about the veracity of what fans and journalists would be watching took their time to solidify, most could at least agree that a successful Ullrich title defence appeared the most likely outcome for the 1998 Tour. With Voet deciding to tell the truth after three days in police custody, Virenque and his Festina teammate and fellow podium aspirant Alex Zülle started the race in Dublin but were surely unlikely to finish it. Meanwhile, the Italian climber Marco Pantani doddered around the prologue time trial course to last place. Pantani had won the Giro d'Italia in June and spent the next fortnight eating pizza and hitting the discos near his home on Italy's Adriatic coast. He manifested no real intention of riding the Tour – until one day when he was training with the veteran domestique Roberto Conti in the hills overlooking Rimini, they stopped at a water fountain, and Conti turned to his mate and suggested they 'go to France to beat Ullrich'. Pantani hesitated for a moment then finally said yes to the going to France part. As for beating Ullrich, well, they would have to see.

Ullrich's sixth place in the prologue, five seconds behind winner Chris Boardman, said little either way about his form. A dreary procession of flat stages taking the peloton south through Ireland and down the north-west corner of France offered similarly little insight – and produced no significant time-gaps between the main contenders. Nevertheless, Ullrich's prospects looked good after his crushing display in the time trial to Gare de Corrèze on stage seven to reclaim the yellow jersey he had last worn in Paris the previous year. He led the general classification by over a minute, a position that the Tour organizers had strengthened further by finally expelling Festina, their team manager having at last admitted the drugs in Willy Voet's car were destined for his riders. Ullrich's path to victory looked unencumbered, despite the as yet unacknowledged danger lurking, or languishing, in forty-third place, over five minutes down – Marco Pantani. The sylph-like Italian duly skipped away on the first day in the Pyrenees to gain half a minute, then seized on an Ullrich puncture to win the following afternoon at Plateau de Beille and claw back nearly two minutes more. He now trailed Ullrich by only three minutes with the Alps looming.

As *Libération*'s correspondent wrote later, stage fifteen of the 1998 Tour had truly begun in the middle of the night before, when darkness fell upon the mighty alpine summits encircling Grenoble and wind and rain had lashed the windows in the hotels where the riders were trying to sleep. The forecast had made grim reading, but nothing like what greeted Jan Ullrich when he woke. The most daunting climb on the day's *parcours* was also the highest of the Tour, the 2,645-metre Col du Galibier. The Galibier is to the French Alps what the Tourmalet is to the Pyrenees – the grandest, most venerable climb in the range and one of the Tour's topographical crown jewels. The former's infamy was cemented on the race's maiden ascent in 1910, when Octave Lapize snarled at the race organizers Henri Desgrange and Alphonse Steines that they were 'murderers'. A year later, for the human rights abuse that was the Galibier's Tour premiere, riders called Desgrange and Steines 'bandits'.

Pantani knew before they even started rolling where he would strike. The Galibier's north–south traverse gains height slowly, stealthily, emerging from Valloire and into a vast groove in which the village nestles, as though hiding under the turned-up collar of a giant, rocky overcoat. The road steepens as it begins to corkscrew at Plan Lachat, and it was here that Pantani had decided to make his move – into a fog of icy rain so dense that within seconds he had vanished. The summit was still five and a half kilometres away, Les Deux Alpes and the finish-line nearly fifty. Telekom had talked that morning about staying patient, and about the wretched conditions calling for even cooler heads. When Pantani surged, Ullrich's legs told him to go while his head said to stay – and so he didn't move. Soon, while the Italian skittered up the last hairpins before the pass and the air turned thinner, Ullrich was panting. By the time the dim outline of his yellow jersey appeared through the murk at the summit, two minutes forty seconds had passed since the shivering fans had seen Pantani.

By this point, Walter Godefroot in the first team car and Rudy Pevenage in the second were fretting. Two weeks earlier, the race hadn't yet left Ireland and Pantani could have been cut adrift, guillotined out of the general classification, when he was dropped in crosswinds on stage three to Cork. Only the then yellow jersey Chris Boardman's crash and the ensuing ceasefire a few minutes later had saved him. There would be various other occasions over the next few days when Pantani could be seen barely holding on. As Pevenage says ruefully, 'We should have got rid of Pantani in that first week. He'd lost a minute in the prologue, which to us was a sign that he wouldn't be a factor. Then in the first week, he was getting dropped on the flat and we just didn't twist the knife.'

The implications of that mistake now began to reveal themselves – and were compounded by another error. 'Bjarne had said in the morning that the Galibier was too far from the finish, so we shouldn't try to cover any attacks there: he or Udo Bölts would do it if necessary,' Pevenage explains. 'So we get halfway up the Galibier, Pantani attacks, and Jan doesn't follow. Why? Because Bjarne said in the morning he shouldn't panic. Jan's told me many times since then that he could easily have followed.'

Bölts and Riis had in fact already been dropped before Pantani launched himself. Soon they were reunited with Ullrich, only because, almost at the exact moment when Pantani's lead on the road surpassed his deficit on the general classification, making him the *maillot jaune virtuel*, Ullrich punctured. As he had done after flatting at the foot of the Plateau de Beille climb in the Pyrenees a few days earlier, Ullrich got back on his bike and immediately began thrashing at the pedals, draining his lungs of oxygen. Meanwhile, Pantani had caught and passed the remnants of earlier breakaways and crossed the line alone, his arms outstretched, his expression

almost mournful – like a religious figurine tackily rushed out to commemorate the atrocity that he had just inflicted. Back down the
mountain Ullrich was flanked by Bölts and Riis, advancing at a funereal pace. The cheekbones that had resurfaced sometime in June lay
suddenly buried beneath two thick folds of skin, each of them plotting deep, diminishing curves that finished close to Ullrich's ears.

The stopwatch when he crossed the line said that he had lost
eight minutes, fifty-seven seconds to Pantani. On the general classification, the Italian was now nearly six minutes ahead of Ullrich, who
had also been overtaken by Bobby Julich and Fernando Escartín.

How could anyone explain such a collapse? How could Ullrich?
One or two old scribes had looked quizzically up from their laptops
when, in his press conference the previous afternoon, Ullrich had
insisted on thanking his teammates 'whether I win the Tour or not'.
That had sounded oddly pessimistic at the time. Now he allowed his
soigneur to swaddle him in towels and blankets, sought shelter in his
team's camping car and left others to speculate. Meanwhile, Udo
Bölts thought back to the morning, when he had watched Ullrich cut
the sleeves off the yellow rain cape supplied by the race organizers.
On the Galibier later, Bölts also noticed that Ullrich had run out of
the maltodextrin drink that would ordinarily be his last source of fuel
on a stage like this. Bölts asked whether he needed anything and
Ullrich said no; he had been doing longer rides, with less sustenance,
for weeks in the run-up to the Tour.

Hagen Boßdorf had returned to the Tour as one of a nearly fifty-
strong delegation from German national channels ARD and ZDF –
and the anchor of ARD's nightly fifteen-minute dispatch from France.
As the ghostwriter of Ullrich's tour diary the previous year, Boßdorf
had generally found the job of teasing out Ullrich's most pertinent
musings rewarding but tough going. Now, Telekom's press officer
instructed Boßdorf – quite firmly – that of course Jan would not be
available for an interview from the team hotel that night. Whereupon Boßdorf called Ullrich directly – and, to Boßdorf's pleasant
surprise, Ullrich obliged.

'It was the best interview he ever gave,' Boßdorf says. 'He was so
honest about everything that had gone wrong, everything that he'd
done wrong – and that's what people loved about him at that time.
For once his guard was completely down.'

In the *Süddeutsche Zeitung* the next day, the journalist Peter

Burghardt pointed out that Ullrich's debacle had occurred on 27 July, the one-year anniversary of his enthronement on the Champs-Élysées. Burghardt also wondered whether losing the Tour and some of the aura he'd carried for the last twelve months hadn't also brought some kind of relief for Ullrich. 'Recently he's seemed edgy, anxious, annoyed. As though hunted,' Burghardt wrote. 'The 27th of July must have liberated him somehow. It looked as though he'd lost not only a yellow shirt in Haute Savoie but the lead vest he'd been wearing.'

If Ullrich's reaction had indeed endeared him to the German public, it also impressed his teammates. Over dinner, he apologized to them for failing to capitalize on their hard work. Bölts wrote in his autobiography that, on that evening, Ullrich 'moved up three levels in my estimation'.[11]

Ullrich could pinpoint some of his mistakes immediately. Others revealed themselves later, and were almost too numerous to list when he came to write another book with Boßdorf a few years later: the short-lived, panicked pursuit of Michael Boogerd and Christophe Rinero three kilometres before Pantani's attack, which had unhinged Riis and Bölts; how unusually hungry he had been early in the stage – a sure warning that his reserves were depleted; not asking for a rain jacket until halfway down the Galibier, unlike Pantani who had stopped at the top of the climb to pull his on; concentrating so hard on the descent that he forgot to eat and suffered the dreaded *fringale* or 'hunger knock' – a particularly undigestible irony given what had happened in the winter and spring. On which note, yes, Ullrich did also admit, his extreme efforts to lose weight both before and during the Tour had played their part.

It was doubly frustrating for Walter Godefroot and Rudy Pevenage that, within a couple of hours of hobbling into the team hotel, he looked reinvigorated. It had taken a hot bath, three bowls of muesli, six bananas and a call to his mother to say, literally, 'I'm alive'. 'He had recovered completely,' Pevenage says. 'If the weather had been "normal" that day, there's no doubt he would have won the Tour.' The next day, Ullrich rubber-stamped that hypothesis with a mighty attack on the Col de la Madeleine, which only Pantani was able to follow. The pair would sprint for the stage win in Albertville, with Ullrich taking his second bouquet of the Tour.

Four days later, on the penultimate stage, Pantani faced the

hardly daunting task of defending that six-minute advantage in a
55-kilometre time trial. He cruised home while Ullrich took his third
stage win of the race – one more than he had managed a year
earlier.

Despite Ullrich's second place, Telekom would still welcome him and
the rest of 'Germany's team' home with a party at the company headquarters in Bonn the day after the Tour. They would also take out
full-page advertisements in all of the main German broadsheets to
congratulate their riders on something perhaps even more important
than any stage win or other accolade. 'Well done, clean performance,
boys!' – said the missive, firmly planting Telekom's magenta flag on
the Tour's moral high ground, its ethical Galibier. Pantani had ended
the Tour not only as the race winner but in the improbable role of
its 'saviour', to use the exact terminology employed by race director
Jean-Marie Leblanc. Alas, nine months later Pantani would fail a
blood test on the penultimate day of the 1999 Giro d'Italia, indicating that he had used EPO. This would prompt Ullrich to tell the
journalist Andreas Burkert that he felt 'almost like the true champion
of the 1998 Tour'.

How might his future have panned out had he actually won for
a second time, if his Les Deux Alpes nightmare could have been ex-
punged or re-edited? That question was and remains much more
difficult to answer than the business of identifying where and how,
in the summer of 1998, Jan Ullrich's career path had pivoted irrevocably. Jens Heppner says now that of course, in truth, the shift
began around the time when Ullrich was eating Rudy Pevenage out
of house and home in the late summer of 1997. During this period –
a victory lap lasting several weeks and alternating lucrative exhibition races, the more serious ones on Ullrich's regular race programme,
autograph signings and TV appearances – Heppner was frequently
at Ullrich's side and witnessed his young teammate's struggle to ride,
rather than be engulfed by, a tidal wave of newfound popularity and
scrutiny. And even earlier than that, in the last week of the 1997
Tour, Heppner had got a sense of Ullrich's likely coping capacities. 'I
think that probably said a lot about how he was going to deal with
the stress of it all,' Heppner agrees. 'He was under pressure there
and, suddenly, he couldn't free his head and he got nervous.

'After the 1997 Tour we did a dozen or so criterium races in

Holland and Jan stayed at mine,' Heppner goes on. 'We organized the fan event at my cheese shop in Aachen and it was pandemonium. I thought they were going to start smashing the windows . . . And that all bothered Jan. He didn't feel free any more. It was a massive change for him. You'd be with him in a cafe, he'd have cake in his mouth and people would be coming up to the table, asking for autographs. I'd have to tell them to at least let him finish eating. And that caused him an enormous amount of stress. He needed his peace and quiet. For three weeks straight his face had been front and centre on people's TVs. We tried to shield him as much as possible but there was only so much you could do. At the criteriums he'd always be tucked in behind me when we walked and rode around, but you couldn't hide him completely. Then we'd be at my house in the forest, upstairs, we'd look out the window and see journalists waiting there. I'd have to tell them to go away. He liked his own space, being alone – and yet he couldn't deal with the whole commotion on his own either. Everything was done for him – whether it was cooking or washing. He was like a kid.'

All of which begs the question of whether the pressure may have become even more intense, and Ullrich's difficulties even more acute, if Les Deux Alpes hadn't happened and he had chalked up Tour win two in 1998. Heppner says not and that, instead, Ullrich's faltering build-up to the 1998 Tour set in motion a vicious cycle of mistrust, worry and rebellion that soon became a toxic spiral. 'He liked eating, really liked eating, sweet things and everything else, but he didn't have the same issues with weight before he turned pro. Back then he just used to eat when he was hungry, but a normal amount. Then he came to Telekom and suddenly Godefroot and the doctors or masseurs were watching and on his back, saying he shouldn't be eating cake and this and that. Whenever he wasn't allowed to do something, it became a problem. I think when he was on his own he just kept eating out of a kind of anxiety about what he wouldn't be allowed to do at races or training camps. All the damage was done at home: he ate a lot and trained a little. To compound that, he's someone who naturally puts on weight quickly when he's not doing much. He could put on six or seven kilos in the blink of an eye. But I think the biggest problem was people trying to "ban" him from eating the stuff he liked. He couldn't cope with that. It was the same with stress: whenever he was told that he had to do something, he got agitated and nothing worked any more.'

It was a sign of unenlightened times that Ullrich's weight would become the subject of widespread mirth, cruel taunts and, for Ullrich, greater anguish than his mockers imagined. Equally, while he was perhaps the most prominent rider to grapple with the same issue, he was certainly not the first in a sport where body image was rarely broached but where the arbitration between power and weight could sentence a career. It did precisely that to Dario Pieri, a Paris–Roubaix and Tour of Flanders runner-up who ultimately retired early in 2006, at age thirty, after years of struggling to stay lean. 'A bike rider doesn't smoke, doesn't drink, so what's left as an outlet?' Pieri asks. 'You're also used to eating lots every day, because you're burning so many calories. All it takes is for you to eat a bit more and train a bit less and it gets out of control. The stress of doing it every year also just builds and builds. You get to the point where the will to make those sacrifices just dissolves.'

Brian Holm broadly, bluntly agrees: 'I think [Jan's] problem was his appetite. That simple. You really need to be disciplined . . . and, yeah, well, Jan was a hungry boy.'

Whether Ullrich's was 'comfort' or 'emotional' eating – the 'pressure valve' that another teammate, Giovanni Lombardi, describes – there was no denying that the 1998 Tour had been a stressful one for him and indeed for professional cycling. A Grande Boucle which started with Willy Voet's arrest had degenerated into a 'Tour de Farce' or 'Race of Disgrace', as the journalists had dubbed it by the end.

Jean-Marie Leblanc, the race director, was just relieved that they had made it to Paris – although in his mind it had resembled a journey to a different city: 'The Tour was our road to Damascus,' Leblanc said. Meaning that over the previous three weeks cycling had finally steered itself out of iniquity, into a new age of enlightenment and towards redemption.

9

THE TRUTH WILL SET YOU FREE

'Our riders can't have been using EPO'

—*Professor Joseph Keul to Jürgen Kindervater*

Twenty-two years after one of its strangest days, the Tour de France takes me back to one of its unlikeliest cult locations at the midway point of one of its most curious editions.

Gare de Corrèze is a train station with no obvious reason to exist, lost in 'La France Profonde', encircled by oak woods and cattle farms, its catchment area a smattering of gabled houses with large gardens. There is no nearby church or central square, no pulse of village life – just a road leading to a busy roundabout that serves as the nucleus of whatever community exists here.

Who knows why, in 1998, the Société du Tour de France decided to locate the finish line of a time trial in this no man's land two hours east of Bordeaux? And who would have predicted what would have occurred in a dime-a-dozen cafe overlooking that same roundabout?

In July 1998, the Festina scandal was said to have laid bare cycling's long-festering doping plague. In 2020, it is a real pandemic threatening humanity, not only cycling, and reducing the sport's biggest celebration event to a zombified September cortège through populations fearing for their lives.

Dominique Espinasse, the owner of Le Domino, would not usually need to consult a calendar to know it was Tour time. Usually, he can tell it's July by the steady stream of journalists or Lycra-clad 'dark tourists' – cycling fans who want to know, want to see where one of

the bleakest chapters in the sport's recent history played out. Whenever they arrive, Espinasse laboriously explains – as he does to me
now from behind the perspex shield over his bar – that the cafe didn't
belong to him then, that he bought it a few years later from Gilberte
'Guillou' Boulegue, from whom it took its name at the time, 'Chez
Guillou'. If they ask, which they always do, he'll point to what used to
be a small back room where Jean-Marie Leblanc confirmed to Richard
Virenque that he and his Festina teammates were no longer welcome
at the 1998 Tour. Espinasse will then notice their disappointment when
all they see now is a pizza oven. He'll smile apologetically and confirm that there are no photos on the wall because Madame Boulegue
took them when she left – even the ones of Virenque when he returned
a few months later for an aperitif that probably felt like an exorcism.

No one talks about who pulled on the yellow jersey later that
same afternoon. And Espinasse wouldn't be able to tell you that it
was Jan Ullrich.

Telekom's Head of Communications, Jürgen Kindervater, spent
that second weekend of the 1998 Tour vacillating between triumphalism and concern. Triumphalism because Ullrich's path to a
second consecutive victory now looked gloriously unobstructed. After
the last of the Pyrenean stages, Kindervater asked the whole Telekom
team to sign the plaster cast wrapped around the left hand he had
injured before travelling to France. It would make a great a souvenir
if, as most expected, Ullrich held on for a second consecutive Tour win.

But for that to happen the Tour needed to make it to Paris, which
was no foregone conclusion. Behind them, Festina had left a mael-
strom of recrimination and suspicion. On the day of Ullrich's TT win,
newspapers and TV networks from all over the world published
quotes from Gérald Gremion, the former doctor of a Swiss professional team, who had said in an interview that 99 per cent of riders
were doping. Within days, that claim appeared to have been further
corroborated by a raid on the Dutch TVM team and the seizure of
104 ampoules of EPO.

Publicly, Kindervater was dismissive – telling the *Süddeutsche Zeitung*, 'Now all of the rats are coming out of their holes' – but he was
rattled enough to pick up the phone and call a doctor whose opinion
he did respect, Joseph Keul. The director of the sports medicine department at the University of Freiburg, Keul was also nominally Telekom's
head doctor, though much less hands-on than Lothar Heinrich and

Andreas Schmid. In their conversations, Keul confirmed what Kindervater already thought: Gremion was well wide of the mark. As Keul had told *Der Spiegel* when they published the similarly sweeping allegations about drug use in the peloton by the former pro Jörg Paffrath in 1997, EPO was neither dangerous nor particularly useful.

Later, in an email, Keul also explained to Kindervater how he knew that no one at Telekom was taking EPO. 'Our data on Telekom riders show haematocrit scores of 45%–50%,' the professor wrote. 'These are the same numbers we saw in blood tests between 1980 and 1990, when no EPO was available.'

Nevertheless, on the weekend of Festina's expulsion, Keul and Kindervater began working on a plan. Despite various attempts, numerous pilots and research projects, the world of sport had thus far failed to produce a valid method of EPO detection – and so Keul and Kindervater would do it themselves, or at least try to contribute. Keul came up with a list of suggestions about this and other ways to combat doping and put them in a two-page letter to Kindervater, dated 29 July, three days before the end of the Tour. Professor Keul had a further 'happy announcement' for Kindervater, he wrote: 'Since the last time we spoke I've given five TV and nine radio interviews in which I was able to make clear that our Telekom team is under our control and doesn't take doping products – and that it would be impossible under the terms of their Telekom contract.'

It was assurances like this by men like Keul that emboldened Kindervater and his colleagues to take out their 'Well done, clean performance, boys!' advert in the German papers the day after the Tour reached Paris. Kindervater liked one of Keul's proposals in particular – that Telekom create and lead a group of team sponsors in research that would finally result in an EPO test being approved. Keul suggested calling it *Dopingfreier Sport* – 'Doping-free Sport'. Kindervater was so enamoured with the idea that, even with no other teams or sponsors signed up, he was soon agreeing to commit 450,000 deutsche marks a year for three years. The money would be spent, at Keul's discretion, on research grants, extra testing for the Telekom riders and twice-yearly conferences for doctors, coaches and even journalists.

Most in the media saw *Dopingfreier Sport* as a noble endeavour. Or, if they didn't, wouldn't let on. Kindervater was, after all, a powerful man – according to the 2003 book *Die Stille Macht, Lobbyismus in Deutschland*, 'one of the most powerful in Germany', given that

Telekom's marketing budget was the biggest in the land. His list of achievements was extensive, with the team's success over the previous three year's typifying his Midas touch. It had been a band of underperforming minnows when Kindervater and Telekom decided to invest, in 1991. Six years later Ullrich's Tour victory had put the corporate logo on German TV screens for a total of sixty-seven hours in a single month.

That branding – the capital T and its magenta colour – was Kindervater's crowning glory and is still, a quarter of a century on, among the most recognizable visual identities in the corporate world. Its mastermind had barely even seen a bike race on TV before 1991, though became a distant – he says 'dispassionate' – observer of the team's fortunes, or more often misfortunes, in their first few seasons. 'I'd go to the team presentation but Jan Ullrich was just another name. Bölts, Kummer, Ullrich . . . I knew they were great athletes but that was it.'

Since 1996, however, Kindervater had been a regular visitor to the Tour – a discreet, calming presence behind his thin-framed oval glasses and under his neat thatch of fine white hair. As he tells me now, 'the cycling team had changed the image of the company', so it was also natural that Kindervater had cosied up. As he did, nothing had shaken the faith that he had placed in Professor Keul and the Uniklinik in Freiburg back when the team was launched. 'In the Uniklinik Freiburg we had a medical institution which, as far as we were concerned, was second to none in Germany. With Professor Keul, the Uniklinik had treated the Davis Cup team, the German Olympic team, the German cross-country skiing team . . . We had total confidence because there was nothing better as far as we knew. For me, the Uniklinik was like the Bundesgericht – above everything.'

Keul and the Uniklinik could certainly boast a distinguished pedigree, not that it was entirely untainted. It also would not have taken a cynic to point out that Germany had often been in the vanguard of drug development and experimentation, in sport and beyond, with noble and ignoble outcomes. A chemist from Ludwigsburg, Felix Hoffman, was after all credited with synthesizing both aspirin and heroin within the space of a fortnight shortly before the turn of the twentieth century. Drug consumption had then exploded in the aftermath of the First World War, partly due to tariffs imposed on imported 'remedies' like coffee, vanilla and pepper by the Treaty of Versailles. By the 1920s, Germany was producing more morphine than any other country on earth, 80 per cent of its cocaine and 98 per cent of its heroin – which Bayer marketed as a wonder-tonic for children and an effective treatment for over forty conditions, including insanity and nymphomania.

At one point in the Second World War, Wehrmacht generals believed – and wrote in internal memos, according to Norman Ohler's *Blitzed* – that a drug and not a missile or the Luftwaffe would ultimately defeat the Allies and facilitate their 'Final Solution'. Their little miracle was a pill called Pervitin, a form of methamphetamine. German soldiers knew it as *Panzerschokolade* or 'Tank chocolate'. It had fuelled the invasion of Poland and felt like a cure for tiredness.

Experiments to see whether Pervitin had the same effect on athletes took place in 1954 . . . at the Uniklinik in Freiburg. The trials suggested *Panzerschokolade* could indeed improve performances by 23 per cent. It would allegedly propel the West German football team to victory in that year's World Cup, according to a study by researchers at Berlin's Humboldt University in 2013.

In 1954, Joseph Keul was a promising 1,500-metre runner and medicine undergraduate whose success in the sporting arena would eventually come as a doctor, not an athlete. He began working for the German Olympic team in 1960 and became its head doctor twenty years later. Athletes loved him, critics rounded on him – even well before Telekom took the decision to entrust their cycling team's medical care to Keul and Freiburg in 1991.

Over several months between 1976 and 1977 in particular, his was a familiar face in West German newspapers and on television, as questions about the growing influence of drugs on elite sport were suddenly brought into focus by the Montreal Olympics. Keul's public stance was clear . . . yet somehow still ambivalent: anabolic steroids like the ones thought to have played at least a role in East German athletes' success in Canada should not be recommended, not least because they were banned. Equally, Keul could not say in good conscience that they were 'dangerous'. He also argued in a radio debate in October 1976 that there was a difference between performance enhancement with steroids and 'performance stabilization' – for example, 'restoring' testosterone levels depleted by training. In 1977, Keul would argue that blood transfusions could not be considered doping, either – not because they were not yet banned, but because they had no effect on athletes' performances.

Times would change, science evolve . . . but some of Keul's claims as well as his ethics remained confusing. At the 1988 Winter Olympics in Calgary, 'Erythropoietin' was an obscure-sounding, unspellable hormone still several years from notoriety. But there was already something familiar about the way in which the professor dismissed the drug's looming threat. 'It's not dangerous if used correctly,' he told the German news agency DPA.

Three years later, Team Telekom saw the light of day within months of a book by the former discus thrower Brigitte Berendonk accusing Keul of not only doping athletes with steroids but also lying about their dangerous side effects. In a meeting, the vice president of the German Sports Federation (DSB), Manfred von Richthofen, told the head of the German Olympic Committee that Keul must be fired – 'and was more or less politely shown the door myself,' Von Richthofen later reported.

Thus, Joseph Keul retained his status as the éminence grise of sports medicine in Germany. He was also the chief guarantor of Telekom riders' health and, more than ever thanks to *Dopingfreier Sport* after the 1998 Tour, their sporting credibility.

'We just wanted to be as active as possible in fighting doping,' Jürgen Kindervater assures me. 'We knew Dr Keul's story and we also got him to explain. When the DDR was dominating international sport, the West German Home Office started to look at how it could compete. From there they started looking at which substances could be used that weren't on the banned list. That's what Keul always told us. And we were assured that forbidden substances had never been used . . . I can't believe that Keul wanted to deceive us.'

What no one disputed at the end of the 1998 Tour de France was that professional cycling needed a new moral compass. New weapons in the war on drugs. A new spirit of fair play, transparency and honesty.

In short, it needed the essence of the motto carved in large gold letters above the University of Freiburg's red-brick collegiate building, the same words that Jesus had addressed to the Jews in a verse of the New Testament: 'DIE WAHRHEIT WIRD EUCH FREI MACHEN' – 'The truth will set you free.'

PART TWO

10

LANCE

'Okay, game on. No prisoners. Everybody's going down'

—*Lance Armstrong*

Lance Armstrong's silhouette appears suddenly, urgently in the hall-way, underneath the enormous map of Texas by contemporary artist Tom Sachs that greets every visitor to his Austin home.

He has instructed me over email to get here at just gone eleven on this early spring day in 2015. His partner of eight years, a blonde-haired biology graduate from Colorado named Anna Hansen, has answered the door. She has warmly ushered me in and promised that Lance won't be long. In the meantime, she asks, do I know Mark Higgins, Lance's long-time manager, who has also just appeared over her shoulder? I doubt Higgins will remember me from back in the day, so I shake his hand and leave it at that. The three of us then exchange pleasantries – about when I got to the US, my Airbnb on the other side of town, the run Anna's about to do – until the approaching jangle of golf clubs announces Armstrong's arrival.

We have never properly met, unless one counts the uncivilized ping-pong of barked questions and answers in finish-line scrums and press conferences. Despite this, Armstrong doesn't appear particu-larly wary. On the contrary.

'Man, look at you! Hey, look at this guy, Anna! Look at the Eng-lishman! Short sleeves? Dude, have you seen the weather? You're going to be cold. Sure you don't want a jacket? You got your clubs? Shoes? You got balls?'

'Yeah,' Anna interjects, 'because he's only got one ball.'

Armstrong has heard this one before, many times before, but still the laughter comes. 'She's good, huh? Real good.'

He grabs a waterproof jacket and golf shoes. Adidas, not Nike. Swooshes have been banned – literally covered up or thrown out of his garage – ever since the day in 2012 when, beginning with the Oregon-based sportswear giant, one by one eight of Armstrong's eleven personal sponsors announced that they were ditching him over doping allegations. Conservative estimates put the future earnings Armstrong lost in the space of twenty-four hours at about $35 million. 'That was a pretty bad day,' Armstrong conceded to Oprah Winfrey a few months later. His baseball cap today bears the name not of a sports apparel company but an Aspen eatery, Cache Cache. The restaurant was another waypoint on Armstrong's *Via Crucis* – the scene of a supposedly chance altercation with former teammate Tyler Hamilton in May 2011, a few days after Hamilton had blown a bit more of Armstrong's cover on the *60 Minutes* TV show. That night, Armstrong's alleged threat that he would 'destroy' Hamilton on the witness stand and was going to make his life 'a living hell' represented a final act of defiance, a last stand at the Alamo. And here too Texas would lose out in the end.

Armstrong drives us to the course in his black SUV. The questions, his not mine, begin almost before we leave the driveway: So why a book on Jan? Who have you spoken to? Did he go through some of the same shit? You think he's doing OK?

Over email, Armstrong has already made his fondness for Ullrich clear. A book on Jan? Cool. Wanna come and see me? You bet. Golf? Bring your A-game. Then, after the rat-a-tat-tat of two- and three-word replies, a significantly longer missive, and the warning: 'And just for the record, not sure what your angle is with regards to Jan, but I wanna make it clear that I love Jan Ullrich. I respected him as a rival and cherished our time on the road together. I will not utter one negative word about him. So if you're writing a hatchet piece (which I don't think you are) then don't bother flying to Texas.'

After around twenty minutes, we pull into the parking lot of the Barton Creek resort. Back when Armstrong was a teenager in Plano, Texas, there were two country clubs in town – one, kind of scruffy, on the east side of Highway 75, and another, a glistening, manicured playground for rich Republicans, on the west. An old pal, Scott Eder, told the French magazine *Pédale* in 2013 that the highway symbolized Plano's class divide. 'Even if he wasn't thinking about conquering the world, he wanted the same clothes as the kids on the west. He wanted to live on the other side of the highway.'

Recent troubles notwithstanding, Armstrong has made it across the breach – but still appears to revel in the role of punkish arriviste. He is more at home talking smack with the teenage valet than etiquette with the on-course stewards. As we warm up on the range, he answers a call on his mobile in a familiar, spiky tone: 'Don't bore us, get to the chorus. I'm about to tee off . . .' He then pulls out a wireless speaker, jams it into the cup holder in our golf cart and lets Springsteen serenade us to the first tee.

Despite his protestations to the contrary, Armstrong is a decent, well-coached golfer. His teacher, Chuck Cook, has played swing guru to major champions including Tom Kite, Keegan Bradley and the late Payne Stewart. Armstrong crams in over 200 rounds a year, usually for much more money than the fifty bucks being staked today. His backswing is fast, mechanical and tight, not unlike his old pedalling style. On and around the greens, he epitomizes that old maxim – that, in golf, you drive for show and putt for dough.

He says that golf provides both focus and escapism. Not that he ever can or seems to want to switch off. He is larger than life and relentlessly engaging company. On every tee, the wait for the three-ball in front gives him a few minutes to spin his wheels: on the meeting with his nemesis, US Anti-Doping Agency (USADA) chief Travis Tygart, that is secretly scheduled for the day after our game; on his kids; on being sick of Austin, 'because everyone here's got a Lance Armstrong story'; on Tyler Hamilton and how 'he was always the one pushing it, wanting to do crazy shit'; on the 'arrogance and stupidity' of his comeback – 'the stupidest thing I've ever done'; on how Michele Ferrari, Armstrong's most vilified aide, was 'the fucking man' when it came to training; on how he's got another story for me in a minute – 'Just wait until I hit this shot.'

Then, as his ball is still bounding across the turf 230 or 240 yards away – 'I don't hit it long, I'm always playing defence' – he's straight back into the flow, or rather back at the hideaway in Hawaii that he's recently had to sell to cover legal fees. 'What were we saying? Oh, my house in Hawaii? Yeah, Floyd took that.'

Indeed, the topic to which he returns most often and is clearly causing him considerable anguish is the 'whistle-blower' lawsuit brought by former teammate Floyd Landis. Armstrong hopes and believes it will finally end in 'about a year, give or take', with victory, if you can call it that.[*] 'It's all just bullshit,' Armstrong says as we wait on one hole, kicking dirt off his spikes. 'I've paid enough now. I mean, come on. Now it's just . . . bullshit.'

'Bullshit' is also what he thinks of the way the media is still portraying him, in March 2015, two years on from USADA. 'You know the one I hate? "The disgraced Lance Armstrong". Disgraced? Disgraced?? *Really?* Ask Hinault. Ask Merckx. Ask anyone I raced with who won those Tours. Come up with something else . . .'

What would he suggest?

'I don't know,' he says. 'How about, "The Controversial Lance Armstrong"? Just not "disgraced". I mean, come on . . .'

At moments like these, Armstrong sounds wounded, diminished in his once ironclad vainglory. But that is because this war is old and maybe now unwinnable. Going forward, it'll be a question of picking his battles.

On one hole, a course steward admonishes us for driving our buggy off the cart path. Armstrong nods in acknowledgement, then turns away, muttering, 'It was those women in front who snitched on us. Did you see that? Unbelievable.'

A minute later, he is still indignant. 'Those tittle-tattlers. No one likes a snitch . . .'

Sometimes, I suspect, he gets a kick out of playing the part.

It doesn't take Lance Armstrong's goading about the long carry over a lake to Barton Creek's Par 5 18th – 'Go for it, dude! Don't poop your pants . . .' – for me to know that this is a man who believes in the value of taking risks.

In the late summer of 1996, three years after becoming the third youngest professional world road race champion of all time in Oslo, Lance Armstrong remained one of the hottest properties in the sport of professional cycling, despite his clear limitations in the long-form, mountain-laden three-week tours. That year's Tour de France had been particularly disappointing for Armstrong, as he climbed off his

---

[*]   The case would not, in fact, end for another three years, with an April 2018 settlement that saw Landis paid $5 million.

bike, feeling wasted, after only a week of racing. Three months later, on 8 October, Armstrong ended his season in a conference room in Austin, telling the world through sobs that he had been diagnosed with testicular cancer. He had undergone his first chemo session just hours before addressing the media.

Oncologists at MD Anderson hospital in Houston gave him less than a 50 per cent chance of survival. The ensuing treatment was punishing. At one point, his haematocrit dropped to 25 per cent. Only a prescribed course of EPO, the banned elixir of his earlier and later athletic life, stopped him from dying.

By January 1997, Armstrong had completed a twelve-week course of chemo and, remarkably, was already pedalling. The question of whether he was still a bike *racer* awaited an answer. In the summer of 1996, Armstrong had agreed a two-year, $1.25 million-a-season contract with the French team, Cofidis, but a return to competition would still represent another almighty roll of the dice; an insurance policy with Lloyds of London stipulated that he could earn $1.5 million over the next five years, tax-free, as long as he didn't race again. True to form and character, Armstrong gambled.

Cofidis, for their part, informed Armstrong that their contractual obligations in 1997 and 1998 were now contingent upon him passing a full medical exam. He – a man who had once declined an invitation to meet the king of Norway because his mother wasn't on the ticket – told them to get fucked. As he would put it to *Playboy* in 2005: 'Through my illness I learned rejection. I was written off. That was the moment I thought, *Okay, game on. No prisoners. Everybody's going down.*'

Finally, the US Postal team bit on his agent's pitch – a soul-stirring albeit niche comeback story that casual sports fans didn't need a degree in modern languages or PhD in bicycle mechanics to understand. By December, Armstrong was going to Spain to see his old doctor, Michele Ferrari, having his blood drawn (haematocrit 41 per cent) and mapping out a strategy for 1998. Hell, he only needed to race once, maybe a couple of times, then quit and the world would gasp – which is what he nearly did after abandoning Paris–Nice in March. For a few weeks thereafter, he played golf and guzzled Tex-Mex until an epiphany of sorts on a training ride in Carolina's Blue Ridge Mountains a few weeks later. As he would soon be writing in his autobiography: 'As I rode upward, I reflected on my life, back to all points, my childhood, my early races, my illness, and how it changed me. Maybe it was the primitive act of climbing that made me confront the issues I'd been evading for weeks. It was time to quit stalling, I realized.'[12]

A couple of months later he was finishing fourth in the Vuelta a España – by far his best result to date in a three-week tour. One day in Spain, the recently retired Belgian rider Johan Bruyneel, who was working as a TV pundit, commended Armstrong on his ride. Armstrong returned the compliment by suggesting to the US Postal management that Bruyneel would be an ideal candidate for the position of directeur sportif.

Bruyneel accepted the offer. Soon he was sending Armstrong an email that he signed off with the tantalizing line: 'You will look great on the podium of the Tour de France next year.'

We're now back in Armstrong's SUV, picking our way through the school-run traffic, on our way to his mansion on the west side of downtown Austin. He won our golf game on the seventeenth, holing a clutch putt for birdie. He says he intends to brag about the victory on Twitter. When I request that he doesn't, he seems hurt. 'What, you don't want to be associated with me?'

Thankfully, finally, we're soon back to discussing the real reason for my visit to Texas.

'When I got that mail from Johan, I thought, *Hmm, kinda cool. I've never thought about that necessarily.* The thing was, I had no idea how I was going to measure up against Jan in 1999. The only thing I could use to get a sense of what that level was like was talking to Kevin Livingston. He had climbed well in that '98 Tour and trained with me every day in 1999. We'd go out on training rides that winter and then next spring and I'd tell Kevin, "I've really gotta work on my descending, because I'm going to be getting dropped on the climbs. I'll have to catch up on the downhills . . ." But of course he'd done all the climbs with those guys in '98, and he'd look at me, like, "Dude, you're not getting dropped on the climbs."

'As for Ferrari, he would never . . . Ferrari was always very guarded on his predictions. You'd have an amazing test, an amazing lead-up to the Tour, and he'd look at you with a straight face and go, "You'll be close." He would never say, "You're going to kill them. You're going to win by X amount." He was always very humble about it. And this would drive me crazy sometimes. I'd be like, "What? Did you not see the test I just did?" But that wasn't his style. That's also what makes him what he is.'

In the spring of 2015, I also meet Johan Bruyneel in London, where he lived for several years with his Spanish wife and young family. He tells me that he too had felt Ullrich would dominate the Tour after 1997, but that view had changed by early 1999, when he was ready to unleash Armstrong.

'There was nothing to back up what we were thinking in the spring of 1999 except that fourth place in the Tour of Spain . . . but you don't necessarily need to have been racing against these guys. I can remember a reconnaissance ride we did in the Pyrenees in the April of 1999. I had just retired, so I could easily compare what I could do with what I saw from Lance, and I remember thinking, *This guy's gonna win the Tour. Doesn't matter what the other guys do. This guy's got it.* Or if it wasn't Lance, I thought the guy who beat him was going to win the Tour.

'Of course, Ullrich was always a fear,' Bruyneel goes on. 'He was the only guy we were scared of. You knew that physically he was super powerful and that, if he got everything right, he was going to win. But he never got everything right. I can remember the Tour of the Basque Country, the same April, in 1999, thinking it was just unbelievable, how out of shape he was. He was the last guy in front of the broom wagon. He was just huge. After that I thought we had less to worry about.'

As soon as we're in the door, Armstrong beckons me through the hall and invites me to take a seat at his kitchen table. Asks whether I'd like a beer. I hesitate but the fridge door is already half open. He grabs two bottles of Shiner Bock, the beer with which he'd always celebrate his return home after a stint of racing in Europe. He sits down and slides one of the bottles across the tabletop. Asks where were we, in the car.

Ah, yeah, Ullrich – we were finally talking about Jan.

'So yeah,' Armstrong picks up. 'I could see the media was exasperated. Like, "When's he going to get his shit together?" But it endeared him to the fans – I mean, versus this robotic American.'

Armstrong takes a swig. Stretches his right arm towards me and places his hand palm-down on the marble.

'I mean, they could say what they wanted about Jan . . . but he was the North Star. There's your quote. And it's true. He was the standard. He was the bar. Basso, wonderful guy. Klöden, Beloki . . . sure. But Jan? Jan gets me up early. Jan stops me having a beer. OK, there were years when he didn't come through, but he was what I used to set my standards by. Nobody else.

'I'll tell you my favourite Jan story. Do you know about the 2005 victory party? This is my favourite story. This is Jan Ullrich. And this is why I love him. So we do the 2005 Tour, and I catch him in the prologue, which is just surreal, man. I go off the ramp, I nearly fucking unclip and fall off the front of the bike, I clip back in, then it's just that straight shot out to Fuck-Knows-Where . . .'

'Noirmoutier.'

'Right, Noir-whatever. Anyway, Johan can see what's happening. I hear him on the radio like, "You're catching him." Which I don't really believe. But I keep going, and I'm getting closer and closer, until finally I can see him. And part of me was, like, I can't go by this guy, I'm going to beat him over the next three weeks, but I can't go by him here. But I did. So anyways, we do the Tour – which was meaningless for me, because I'd broken the record, there were no bonuses. I was just doing one more Tour so the team would get two more years of Discovery Channel sponsoring us. Then we get to Paris and we have our big party in the Crillon or Musée d'Orsay or Ritz – I can't even remember where the fuck it was. Anyway, like an hour before this starts, our press guy, Jogi Müller, calls me and says he just got a call from Jan's press guy and, you're not going to believe this, but Jan wants to come and speak tonight. I said, "What, at our party?" He said yeah. And you know Jan's English was not that good. But I say, "Allllriiight then . . ."'

Another swig. Bottle down. He's jumped ahead, way ahead in the timeline, we're now in 2005, at the end not the beginning, but I don't interrupt.

'. . . So this motherfucker rolls up, into a crowd of 600 rabid Americans. And this guy, in his bad English – you could have heard a pin drop. He takes the mic, talks to me, makes a toast to me, talks to the crowd, because I was retiring, that was it for me, and he just sends me out. I mean, dude . . .'

Armstrong is shaking his head.

'Dude . . . it was one of the nicest things anybody's ever done for me.'

Armstrong has stopped shaking his head. Now he is pinching the peak of his Cache Cache baseball cap to cover his eyes, though it can't conceal the trickle of saltwater down his cheeks.

Armstrong is crying.

Lance Armstrong is in his kitchen, sobbing, because Jan Ullrich's few words of mangled English ten years ago were among the nicest things anyone's ever done for him, in his forty-four years of being Lance Armstrong.

For exactly twenty-four seconds, no one speaks.

'Yeah,' he says finally. 'Kinda funny, ain't it?'

11

PROMISES

'Doping, in my opinion, is when someone gets caught'

—*Jan Ullrich*

In the first months of 1999, Lance Armstrong did not figure among Jan Ullrich's main preoccupations, for all that the American's performances at the Vuelta the previous autumn had placed him among his likely antagonists for the Tour.

It was the previous year's races and their aftermath that were mainly worrying Telekom and Ullrich, as the aftershocks of the Festina scandal continued to rattle the cycling world. Telekom's palpable smugness at having ducked the most serious scrutiny, those 'Well done, clean performance, boys!' adverts in the German press, had not won them many friends. The Swiss rider Rolf Järmann summed up the mood in the peloton thus: 'At the moment, everyone's hoping that Telekom doesn't win the Tour. No one's demanding some sort of confession, but they shouldn't be making out they're the big, clean, paragons of virtue.'

If statements like this suggested cycling's old law of silence had fractured, the deference, some would say complicity, of a media totally reliant on access also showed some cracks. German coverage of the scandal continued to be particularly strident. When, in December 1998, Richard Virenque was confronted with laboratory proof that he had in fact been doping just like his Festina teammates, Germany's most stiff-lipped daily newspaper, the *Frankfurter Allgemeine*

Zeitung, greeted the news with the headline: 'The liar Richard Virenque retires'.

As Telekom gathered for their annual post-Christmas training camp in Mallorca in January, bad news struck closer to home. A Danish TV documentary had laid out compelling reasons to believe that the Telekom team member who the previous July had acted as an unofficial riders' spokesman, Bjarne Riis, was himself an inveterate user of doping substances. One of the programme-makers, Niels Christian Jung, had worked as a soigneur at the 1995 Tour of Denmark and collected used syringes left in the hotel rooms of several teams, including Riis's – Gewiss-Ballan. Jung kept the needles and sent them off for analysis after the 1998 Tour. Some contained traces of EPO. There was nothing to indicate that Riis had been among the recipients of the drugs, but Jung's colleague, Olav Saning, a Danish journalist of the year, had also gained access to Riis's medical data from the 1995 Tour. His haematocrit on the rest-day had been 56.3 – a figure that could only be indicative either of EPO use or serious illness, Denmark's leading EPO expert told the programme.

Long-serving Telekom riders like Erik Zabel remembered years when there would be exactly one picture taken at their annual Mallorca training camp: the team photo snapped by a member of staff. The media presence had naturally swelled since Riis's Tour win in 1996 and Ullrich's in 1997, but now, partly as a result of the revelations from Denmark, the team hotel in Palma was besieged. In a press conference, Riis said that he was 'sick of being a toy for the media to play with' and batted away their calls for him to publish his blood values. Meanwhile, Ullrich moaned that he was fed up of being stopped by reporters on his way out of the team dining room, of being asked whether he had time for 'one question, just one question', that was invariably about doping. Ullrich told one journalist he could understand why Riis wouldn't want to release his blood values: his rivals might discover his 'secrets', ingenuous hacks like the one Ullrich now revealed – that he put on extra kilos over the winter to make his training harder. Ullrich also offered that the Festina riders may have been unwittingly doped. The 235 ampoules of EPO, 120 amphetamine capsules, 60 doses of testosterone and 82 vials of human growth hormone found in their soigneur Willy Voet's car might have been meant for someone else, perhaps bodybuilders, he suggested. Never mind that Voet had been driving to the Tour de

France. Or that Ullrich had spelled out a troubling credo in another interview with the *Frankfurter Allgemeine* two years earlier: 'Doping, in my opinion, is when someone gets caught.'

The relative serenity of previous years' camps had been replaced by an all-encompassing paranoia. Questioned about his race programme, Ullrich said that he probably wouldn't race in France before the Tour in case an aspirin got him arrested and put in jail. If he felt unduly scrutinized, it wasn't helped by the fact that, having scrupulously watched his weight at training camps in Lanzarote in November and California in December, he had lapsed into familiar patterns after Christmas. In Mallorca, it was hard to tell where his cheeks ended and the double-chin spilling over his jersey collar began. The annual battle with the bulge suffered a further setback when he spent two days at the camp in bed recovering from a cold. This would be followed by more illness at the start of February, plus a wisdom tooth extraction.

Rudy Pevenage said later that the tone for a wretched start to the year had been set in Mallorca when, on the traditional walk with visiting wives and girlfriends, Jan's partner, Gaby, stumbled and broke her foot.

For one rider in the Balearics, a troubling sense of déjà vu was hard to reconcile with the fact he had officially been with Telekom for only a couple of weeks.

The team had signed Jörg Jaksche for 300,000 deutsche marks a year on the back of the sinewy twenty-two-year-old Bavarian's impressive debut at the Tour de France in 1998. Many observers had raised eyebrows two years earlier when Jaksche, one of Germany's top young talents, turned professional in a team from Italy sponsored by the electrical goods manufacturer Polti. But it was, in at least one respect, an inspired choice: while other teams at the 1998 Tour de France scrambled to dispense with their drugs, Jaksche and his teammates found that the drum of a Polti vacuum cleaner used to clean their team vehicles was the perfect hiding place for vials of EPO.

Clean and naive when he arrived at Polti, Jaksche was quickly introduced to the grubby realities of cycling at the top level in the late nineties. When he rode well at Paris–Nice in the spring of his first season, Jaksche says his Italian team manager asked him what drugs he was taking. When he responded with a blank look, the boss gleefully announced that he was going to tear up Jaksche's two-year contract and offer him one for five instead. Soon, Jaksche was 'losing his virginity' with a first dose of EPO before the 1997 Tour of Switzerland. An introduction to human growth hormone and testosterone followed soon thereafter. In fleeting moments of anxiety, Jaksche found comfort in the knowledge that bodybuilders took doses of growth hormone twenty times bigger. It was also about speculating to accumulate: at Polti the 'bonus' for a top-twenty finish was not having to pick up the tab for one's own medicine.

Polti's erstwhile manager, Gianluigi Stanga, has called the allegation that he in any way encouraged, oversaw or abetted Jaksche's doping 'absurd'. Nonetheless, at his first training camp for Polti, Jaksche says he had been taken aside to discuss legal vitamin injections, a gateway that he says ultimately led to him taking banned substances. Now, in Mallorca, Walter Godefroot summoned his class of 1999 to a conference room in the team hotel and appeared to Jaksche to do a similar dance around a subject that they all knew was unavoidable. Godefroot's official line was that, after what had happened at the previous year's Tour, no banned drugs would be taken, transported or tolerated. The message seemed clear – and yet Jaksche detected an underlying ambiguity exacerbated by its delivery. 'Walter spoke in his hilarious Flemish-German hybrid. We'd end up turning to Rudy Pevenage and being like, "Rudy, can you please tell us what the fuck he's trying to say?" Then Rudy, who spoke a few languages, would translate.'

Godefroot's German, it should be noted, can't be faulted in 2015 when, reacting to Jaksche's recollection of events, he sniffs that Jaksche 'was known in the team as *"Der Mülleimer* – the Garbage Can". Why? He took everything.'

Regardless, Jaksche says, the months immediately following the Festina scandal had demonstrated that the prevailing lingua franca of professional cycling was one which rarely married actions with words. 'In the 1998 Vuelta I heard that absolutely nothing had changed. In Spain, you could line up ten syringes on your windscreen and the Guardia Civil wouldn't stop you. There was one well-known Spanish rider whose private courier for his drugs was one of the police motorbike escorts for the race.'

Jaksche meets me in April 2015 in a crowded, Italian-themed bar nestled just behind Munich's town hall. Now thirty-six, retired and still single, he lives over the border in Austria and is a habitué of the Bavarian capital, though not particularly at home among the mink coat and Boss slacks brigade reputed to reign here. 'You meet a girl here and the first thing she wants to know is what car you drive. And if it isn't a Mercedes or a Porsche . . .' he'll muse later.

Jaksche didn't immediately feel comfortable at Telekom in 1999 either. The educated son of well-to-do doctors, he suspected that he was simply too school for cool – or at least too different from the other riders. 'When I came onto the team, from the first training camp the older guys mocked me because I was a potential threat for a place in the Tour team, but also sometimes because I came from a richer family. Some of the guys were stopping school at fourteen or fifteen and then just thinking about becoming a pro. It was a macho environment. There were times when you would be rooming with someone and he would just fart next to you, or burp next to you. For them it was totally normal.'

It was curious, though, how the usually boorish could become models of discretion regarding one topic in particular. After the warnings from Godefroot – which Jaksche had decided not to take at face value – he says that one day in Mallorca Pevenage quietly asked him what 'other things' besides training they had done at Polti. When Jaksche replied that he had taken EPO and human growth hormone, he says Pevenage casually instructed him to 'talk to the team doctors'. This at least is Jaksche's version of a conversation that Pevenage says never took place. Also according to Jaksche, the team doctor, Lothar Heinrich, later informed him that he could supply Jaksche with 'EPO' or 'E', as they referred to it. Over the next two years, on multiple occasions, Heinrich would use a post or courier service to send doping products from Freiburg to the train station in Ansbach in Bavaria, close to Jaksche's home. Jaksche simply had to supply a code to collect his package.

Jaksche remembers two main sources of teeth-gnashing among the Telekom management at that Mallorca camp – one, the allegations against Riis and, two, Ullrich's weight. The team had recruited a nutritionist for the 1999 season, nominally to help the whole team but with the primary brief of keeping Ullrich in check. But Jaksche says that the arrangement shed more light on the Telekom leader's personality than it did centimetres from his waistline. 'This lady came and gave everyone a set of scales and you had to weigh every meal and write down what it was before you ate. We were supposed to do this for seven days because she wanted to observe our habits. Well, on the first day Jan was very precise: he weighed and wrote everything down. Then on the second day he didn't write anything. We asked why. "Ah, because every day I'll eat the same thing," he said. And that was Jan. That explains a lot.

'Lance was always looking for the right people to have around him,' Jaksche continues. 'He wanted to have people around him who, in certain things, were much better informed than him. Jan just didn't want any stress. He always wanted a Walter Godefroot or a Rudy Pevenage, because Rudy was like a father, whereas Lance didn't care about that. He wanted the investment banker, the best doctor. He was always hungry for information. Jan was also curious . . . about ice cream. Red wine and ice cream. I saw him eating two litres of ice cream in under an hour at that training camp in Mallorca.'

It was therefore no surprise that the pattern of the previous spring repeated itself when Ullrich started racing. He grovelled through two stages of the Challenge Mallorca and three out of four at the GP Telecom de Portugal before pulling out of the Vuelta Valenciana, the Vuelta a Murcia and Milan–Sanremo. He then abandoned the Setmana Catalana after four days while lying second-to-last on general classification, fifty-seven minutes behind the race leader.

Publicly, Ullrich sounded sanguine about his second consecutive winter of discontent. He told Hartmut Scherzer of the *Frankfurter Allgemeine Zeitung* that 'no one cares if I am fifteenth or one hundredth in the Vuelta a Aragon in April.' To believe, though, that these were the debonair musings of a man at peace with himself and his craft would have been naive. In March, Telekom were rocked again when an Italian judge summoned Riis to explain some of the evidence presented on Danish TV two months earlier. Meanwhile, a French former rider and doper turned whistle-blowing author, Erwann Menthéour, accused Ullrich of having diluted his blood to pass a UCI health check on the morning of the stage to Les Deux Alpes that had cost him the 1998 Tour. This, Menthéour told a major French newspaper, would explain why Ullrich's face had looked so unnaturally swollen – and maybe why he'd performed so poorly.

Who knows which of these factors, if any, pushed Jan Ullrich beyond some kind of coping threshold. Rudy Pevenage thinks that he was at home in Geraardsbergen in Belgium watching a cyclo-cross race on TV when Ullrich called him with an announcement. That would place it before the end of February. In Ullrich's own autobiography he refers to a 'Sunday in April'.

What Pevenage does remember for sure is what Ullrich said.

'Rudy, it's Jan. I'm giving up. Retiring.'

If the question of how to coax the best out of Jan Ullrich had challenged and sometimes befuddled the Telekom bosses since he turned professional in 1995, now came the most critical test of their asset management to date. Ullrich would finally soon change his mind and carry on racing – but the wobble revealed much about the insecurities that would continue to dog him. It could also be argued that Ullrich would never have reached this existential impasse had his minders protected and learned how to nurture him sooner – and better.

Ullrich certainly knew by now that pity parties were not Walter Godefroot's style. When I ask Godefroot about Ullrich's crisis of motivation in 1999, his response is wholly, witheringly in character. 'Jan wanted to stop several times. I just said, OK, if he doesn't want to do it any more, don't do it. I wasn't going to earn any less money. Maybe Telekom would have pulled out. That's possible. But I didn't owe my livelihood to Jan. I owed it to the success of the team, to everyone's work, the whole structure. I always say – it sounds extreme – but the masseurs and mechanics are more important than the rider. When someone offers a rider 1,000 euros more, off he goes, whereas I'd been working with some of the other staff for twenty, twenty-five years.'

Unlike him, Godefroot tells me, Pevenage, Becker and even Telekom Head of Communications Jürgen Kindervater were 'Jan Ullrich fans'. Brian Holm goes even further: 'Ullrich was also Pevenage's son. I think Rudy fell in love with him a bit.'

But Pevenage's devotion didn't necessarily make him any more qualified or able to lift Ullrich either. Away from races, he would often call Ullrich's number and the phone would ring out. Pevenage sometimes noticed how Ullrich's moods seemed to mirror the weather and wondered whether he didn't suffer from seasonal affective disorder, SAD, or clinical depression. It was also hard to know whether the eating and sometimes drinking were symptoms or causes of the same malaise. With so many diverging opinions about what was needed, set against Ullrich's insistence that he knew best, a crossfire of confusion was frequently the result.

After the previous season's debacle, it was perhaps also understandable that Godefroot et al initially defaulted to a disciplinarian, controlling approach. Within days of his phone call to Pevenage, Ullrich sat in an emergency meeting with Godefroot, Pevenage and Wolfgang Strohband agreeing that, yes, he would carry on riding – and that he would stick to a more rigid regimen than in previous years. Ullrich outlined the strategy in his 2004 autobiography: 'We came up with the idea of the "babysitter system", a round-the-clock system of care, control and motivation, involving my directeurs sportifs, doctors, manager, PR men and soigneurs. It was all absolutely perfect . . . but its success or failure would depend entirely on me.'[13]

The featherbedding may have offended Godefroot's hard-nosed instincts, but he recognized that it was Telekom's best shot at saving Ullrich. Freedom, he had decided, posed a bigger problem than discipline to someone who had grown up behind the Berlin Wall. As he tells me, 'Ullrich had learned in the DDR that the boss was the boss, that an order was an order.'

As far as Godefroot and many others were concerned, one man, Peter Becker, embodied what Ullrich had brought with him from the East – everything that he had learned, the dogmas that had encoded themselves into his DNA and all that was hopelessly, risibly outdated behind Germany's great divide. In a nation where four fifths of children were in all-day nurseries and being weaned on the precepts of the 'socialist personality' by their first birthday, it was true to say that pedagogy carried enormous influence – but a cliché to assume that every teacher or coach blindly, unthinkingly preached an identical doctrine. As detailed in Chapter 3, throughout his career Becker had struggled to reconcile the directives handed down by his superiors, steeped in their one-size-fits-all ideology, with what he observed in the gym and the velodrome. At SV Dynamo he had developed a habit of writing down two sets of figures in his training logs – one real that he kept to himself and one doctored to hit the targets and quotas ordained by his Sektionleitung. As also alluded to earlier, he was even banished to SV Dynamo's boxing division for four years in the early 1970s after offering uninvited, unappreciated criticism of club officials in an appraisal. Becker maintains that, by and large, he based his method on 'feel'. 'It was all so dogmatic,' he says. 'And these buzz-words they always used – "Socialistic", "The Collective", "Knowledge Sharing". There were so many contradictions in it all. Why did they have to make their and our lives so difficult?'

He was not, then, the Lenin-worshipping stooge that Godefroot and others perhaps imagined – and he also knew Ullrich the athlete better than anyone. Nonetheless, even he had been oblivious to some of the forces dragging Ullrich down.

'I was down in Merdingen with him one day and he told me he had something to tell me. So he tells me he's quitting, ending his career. He tells me he has so many problems, so many issues. I say, OK, we'll do the 180 kilometres we planned for today, otherwise we'll be behind our schedule. Then, I say, you can have a shower, come and find me in my hotel and we'll talk it all out, get to the bottom of exactly what it is that's bothering you. We pulled his bike out, went training as normal and talked everything through in the afternoon. And there he told me a few things that really shocked me. I couldn't quite believe what I was hearing. He told me none of it could leave the room. He ultimately took my advice and carried on racing. But who's to say that these issues didn't also prevent him from putting in the work he needed to put in on a more regular basis?

'It had nothing to do with the team,' Becker stresses. 'These were private problems. It also had nothing to do with his girlfriend. But they were real, deep problems, and what he told me brought tears of rage to my eyes. Unbelievable. That was an example where I say that the lad had a personality that just wasn't fully mature yet, that couldn't stand back from a situation, take decisions, lead himself in the right direction.'

In a six-hour interview over two days at his house in Berlin, Becker will frequently criticize Ullrich and lament a partial break-down in their relationship. Regrets and even recriminations still gnaw at him – though not at his loyalty.

'I won't say what the problems were,' he says again, finally. 'It was a promise that I'll take to my grave.'

Whatever precisely was troubling Jan Ullrich in those early months of 1999, Peter Becker also knew that there were broader issues that possibly went ignored or were misunderstood. Common preconceptions about how life had been for East German's pre-reunification were accompanied, ten years after its demolition, by similar platitudes about how Ossis now felt and what they needed to thrive in the West. But as the author Mark Scheppert, who meditated on the limbo of 'Generation Jan Ullrich', wrote, those born in the late 1960s and 1970s were in truth as different from their parents as their parents had been from their contemporaries in the East. 'We were neither East nor West, meat nor fish,' Scheppert says.

Ullrich's fellow Ossi and roommate at Telekom, Jens Heppner, had wrestled with the same contradictions in a nowhere zone between different generations, beyond a new line bifurcating old fantasies about a promised land and a bracing reality. Scheppert's assertion that 'The Brandenburg Gate wasn't a door to paradise' rang equally true for Heppner. Having retired in 2002, East Germany's last ever road race champion once owned two cheese shops in Aachen, but nowadays runs an altitude fitness centre in the basement of his house in Kelmis, on the other side of the German–Belgian border. On a wet morning late in 2015, we sit in his dining room overlooking the dank fields of eastern Wallonia, contemplating the fundamental misconceptions that had given birth to the 'babysitter system' and, equally, before that, to Wessis' ideas about their estranged cousins on the other side of the river Elbe.

'When Jan called Rudy and told him he wanted to give up, I can remember that at that point he was really heavy and he had no more motivation, partly because of the pressure he was being put under, I think,' Heppner says. 'Walter wanted me to go and stay at his house, but I couldn't watch him twenty-four hours a day. It got so bad that the soigneurs started sneaking into our room to check whether he had cakes or gummy bears in his suitcase. He didn't take that well at all. He railed against it, said he was a free man, that he should be left alone, left to live his life. Maybe there were some echoes of the DDR as well – he felt like he was back there, where everything was a duty and an obligation. I also had that at first, after the Wende. In the East everything you did seemed like an obligation, then the Wende came and a directeur sportif was still coming and telling you to do certain things. That was hard for us to get our heads around. We'd been sold this idea of a free society. You still knew that you were responsible for your own future, that if you didn't work you would lose your job, but that idea of obligation still jarred. I know that Jan hadn't spent as long in the system as me, but that legacy and that mentality shift also played its part with him, I think.'

Some of Ullrich's lack of discipline and self-leadership, Heppner nevertheless concedes, may have had more to do with nature than nurture.

'Whenever he wasn't allowed to do something, it became a problem,' Heppner says. 'Any obligation – be it to train, to win, to lose weight. He'd go home, shut himself away and everyone could go whistle. He wanted to be left alone. I always used to say he needed a longer leash – that you couldn't be prescriptive with him. Or he needed to be talked into things in a different way. Ideally, Jan would have been able to communicate to Walter what worked best for him, but Walter was also a businessman and he was under pressure from Telekom, who had paid a lot of money and wanted bang for their buck. Also, from Walter's point of view, if a guy says that he's spending his days eating chocolate but he'll stop as long as you don't nag him, how do you take that leap of faith?'

If Walter Godefroot, Rudy Pevenage et al believed that one meeting of several minds was all it had taken to give Jan Ullrich's career a hard reset in April 1999, early signs of an upturn in his performances were hard to discern.

The Amstel Gold Race, the Rund um den Henninger Turm and the Rund um Köln all came and went without great encouragement. At the Bayern Rundfahrt in May, Ullrich did rather better, finishing fourteenth on the final general classification and playing a key role in teammate Rolf Aldag's overall victory. The Deutschland Tour was to set out from Berlin the following week. Ullrich declared that his goal was at least one stage win.

His race ended up lasting two and a half days. At the Berlin team presentation, Telekom's riders had walked on stage to the theme music of the hit German detective series *Der Kommissar, The Police Inspector* – but 30 kilometres from the end of stage three in Bielefeld, Ullrich sat on the tarmac, bloodied and dazed, looking like a victim of grievous bodily harm. A touch of wheels with another Telekom rider, Udo Bölts, had sent him sprawling, head first and without a helmet to protect him. Lothar Heinrich, the Telekom doctor, said that he had been fortunate to escape with just some cuts and mild discomfort in his right knee.

Ullrich returned to the Black Forest hopeful that this latest set-back was a minor one. Meanwhile, a reminder of the long, still haunting shadow cast by the previous summer's Festina scandal arrived from Italy in the first week of June, as Marco Pantani was sensationally kicked out of the Giro d'Italia thirty-six hours before what looked like a certain victory. Pantani had failed a blood test, strongly indicating that his feats in the Alps and Dolomites had been fuelled by EPO. In Italy, where Pantani's Giro–Tour double in 1998 had turned an already popular cyclist into a national icon, the news caused a seismic shock.

The same weekend, three investigative journalists working for Germany's leading news magazine, *Der Spiegel*, were doing final checks and tweaking the last proofs of a story that had been in the works since the Festina scandal the previous summer. It would finally go to press on 14 June, the eve of the Tour of Switzerland. *'Die Werte Spielen Verrückt'* – 'The Values Are Playing Tricks' – was the title. The text, spread over several pages, was devastating for Telekom and Ullrich.

Drawing on information from multiple sources and 'team insiders', the authors laid out persuasive evidence for a systematic doping programme at Telekom. A shuddering first line set the tone: 'In the doping-plagued world sport of professional cycling, Team Deutsche Telekom presents itself as an oasis of clean sport, but now the facade is crumbling.' There followed details of a doping programme on a par with Festina's, described to *Der Spiegel* by 'former team members': injections of EPO, or 'Vitamin E' as it was internally known, that had begun in 1994 and since become *de rigueur*; copious use of human growth hormone, or 'Vitamin G'; a cocktail of other drugs – nineteen in total – administered according to a monthly timetable reproduced in the article; a system designed and funded by the team management but executed by the soigneurs with nicknames like 'Dr Schiwago' and decades-long experience as syringe-wielding factotums; well-practised protocols for disposing of used needles and diluting riders' blood to avoid the fate just suffered by Pantani.

Far from being spared the guilt by association, Ullrich was the target of specific allegations. In August 1997, *Der Spiegel* claimed, Ullrich's unusually high haematocrit on the day before the Luk–Bühl Cup one-day race in southern Germany had sent Walter Godefroot into a panic. 'Jan's values are going crazy,' were supposedly

Godefroot's exact words, giving *Der Spiegel* their headline. Ullrich was immediately booked into a hotel away from the rest of the Telekom team, just in case the UCI testers or 'vampires' came calling. Telekom's official excuse, if required, would be that Ullrich had been delayed by an autograph-signing session after a criterium race in Aachen. Thus they could forego the emergency measures that Ullrich and other riders had used in the past, which included lying with ones feet in the air, against a wall, for fifteen minutes. On more than one occasion, Ullrich had allegedly dropped off to sleep while performing the manoeuvre, forcing his roommate to duck as he keeled over.

Jaksche says that Walter Godefroot now broke one of his golden rules: he directly addressed the issue of doping with his riders. Specifically, according to Jaksche, Godefroot told him to stop whatever he was doing, whatever he was using, and that they couldn't take any risks whatsoever at the Tour de France starting in just a few weeks. Jaksche maintains that he obeyed the command – but that others at Telekom did not.

The journalists behind the scoop were enduring a few sleepless nights of their own – and not only because Ullrich's manager, Wolfgang Strohband, had vowed to sue *Der Spiegel*. One of two main sources for the story, Dieter Quarz, had worked for five years in Cologne's world-famous anti-doping laboratory while at the same time coaching and dispensing his knowledge of drugs and testing to under-23 racers, effectively a gamekeeper moonlighting as poacher. When one of his clients, Dirk Müller, scored a contract with Telekom for the 1998 season, Quarz was allowed to attend the team's preseason training camp in Mallorca – and it was there that he had garnered much of the information that had now appeared in *Der Spiegel*. Not only was Quarz not exactly the 'team insider' described in the magazine, he had also purportedly asked for several changes to the story's first draft – and *Der Spiegel* had not made them. Even worse, the day after the story's publication, Quarz heard a knock at the front door and found police with search warrants waiting outside. The original matchmaker between Quarz and *Der Spiegel*, and a man who over the next few years would become Telekom's nemesis, the microbiologist Werner Franke, had tipped off Düsseldorf's public prosecution service about Quarz's links to doping.

The credibility of *Der Spiegel*'s exposé was in jeopardy, and Quarz soon completely distanced himself from the allegations. Meanwhile,

Ullrich had retained a libel lawyer who had fought and won cases for, among others, Claudia Schiffer and Princess Caroline of Monaco. There could only be one outcome, one winner of the case finally filed in September. *Der Spiegel* would finally have to print a long apology and a statement under oath from Ullrich that he had never taken banned substances and 'particularly not EPO'. They also undertook not to accuse Jan Ullrich or Telekom for the next fourteen years. This despite the fact that, independently of the legal case, the authors of '*Die Werte Spielen Verrückt*' had travelled to Belgium in September 1999 and met with the former Telekom masseur Jef D'Hont, who gave them even more damning material than had appeared in the first article. D'Hont, though, would finally go cold on *Der Spiegel*'s offer of a book deal, coincidentally – or not – around the time Telekom took on his son as a soigneur.

The Telekom team itself had also filed a lawsuit against *Der Spiegel*. This led to the magazine's publisher finally settling out of court. Perhaps even more damagingly, three years after inviting a group of *Der Spiegel* journalists on an all-expenses-paid trip to Paris to see Ullrich win the 1997 Tour, Telekom cut 1.3 million euros from their expenditure on advertising in *Der Spiegel* and sister publications for the year 2000, although claimed this had nothing to do with editorial direction.

Going forward, rather than incentivizing other media outlets to look more closely at Telekom, the whole saga did the opposite. Meanwhile, Telekom could continue a charm offensive that had begun in 1998 after the Festina scandal. In January, one of the team's best friends in the highest of places, the German defence minister Rudolf Scharping, had been a guest at the team's training camp in Mallorca at exactly the time when Danish television was accusing Bjarne Riis. Scharping told the press at the time that Telekom was the victim of some form of media vendetta. Within hours, the head of Telekom's medical team, Joseph Keul, was emailing Scharping to invite him for a guided tour and full suite of health checks at the Freiburg University Clinic.

Three days after *Der Spiegel* had tried to take an axe to the team's reputation, Jan Ullrich pulled to the side of the road and climbed off his bike close to the Areuse Gorge, a majestic canyon criss-crossed by ancient stone bridges near Neuchâtel. Stage two of the Tour of

Switzerland was just 70 kilometres old and they had been painful ones for Ullrich. The right knee that he had bumped in his crash in the Deutschland Tour still throbbed; the bigger the gear he tried to push, the worse his discomfort. 'If it doesn't go away in the next few days and I can't train then we'll have to see about the Tour de France,' he told journalists.

By the weekend, after scans, he and Telekom had their answer – Ullrich had damaged the meniscus in his right knee. Riding the Tour was out of the question. As it was for Bjarne Riis. The Dane had crashed on the ride to a stage start in Switzerland, prolonging Telekom's wretched run.

As much as he sounded beleaguered, privately, Ullrich may have felt a lapping wave of relief. The *Der Spiegel* article had awoken old fears and, above all, the same compulsion to escape that had taken hold during the spring. He intimated to Gaby that perhaps his enforced lay-off should melt into an early retirement. She listened sympathetically – but also asked how else he intended to spend the rest of his life. This, Ullrich couldn't answer.

The next morning, regional German newspapers covered the Ullrich story alongside a half-page advertisement taken out by Telekom, crowing 'WE STAND BY OUR TEAM!' Referring to 'an article in a magazine that tried to connect our team to doping', the missive went on to request that members of the German public 'do not jump to conclusions about a single rider or the team'.

As they tried to control the narrative off the road, on it, the team's Tour was saved by the Italian climber Giuseppe Guerini's stage win at Alpe d'Huez and Erik Zabel's fourth consecutive green jersey. In the race for yellow, in Ullrich and Pantani's absence, and with the race organizers heralding a 'Tour of Renewal' after the bloodbath of the previous year, Lance Armstrong obliged with what he called a 'miracle' and others hailed as the greatest sports story ever told – but was to some minds, already, a shameless exercise in science fiction, a grim fairy tale.

Ullrich observed Armstrong's 'comeback of the century' from afar – and with a certain emotional distance. He enjoyed holidays in Austria with Tobias Steinhauser, a journeyman pro from Bavaria, then stayed for a few days with Bjarne Riis in Tuscany. Riis said he was crazy to be considering retirement. Ullrich had also inched towards that conclusion and finally informed Walter Godefroot that he intended to ride on at a meeting in Brussels in August. Having hesitated at first, he responded favourably to Godefroot's offer to ride the Vuelta a España. It would help, they both agreed, to lay the groundwork for a fruitful 2000 season.

The Vuelta rolled out of Murcia in the south-east corner of Spain on 4 September, and a callow Telekom line-up reflected the team and Ullrich's limited ambitions. He remained out of sight, out of mind for the first few stages, until the peloton began climbing into the sierras that are western Spain's last lines of natural fortification before the land ripples into Portugal. Ullrich scaled the first two bona fide mountain passes of the Vuelta among the leaders and then stunned everyone by leading home a twenty-three-man group in Ciudad Rodrigo to take stage five. It was his first victory of any description since the 1998 Tour, the first in a bunch sprint since his amateur days. His insistence that he was treating the Vuelta as an extended training camp suddenly rang hollow, all the more so after his second place behind Abraham Olano in the long time trial to Salamanca the following day took Ullrich to second on the overall standings, a minute behind Olano.

Ullrich slipped back slightly on stage eight, the premiere of a climb whose obnoxious steepness brought it overnight, worldwide notoriety – the Alto de l'Angliru. But the next big test came on an ascent that had elevated Ullrich to global superstardom – the mountain road to the Arcalís ski resort in Andorra where, in the 1997 Tour de France, Ullrich had announced himself as cycling's next dominant figure. Now the recital was less emphatic and the plaudits more measured, but in one respect history had repeated itself: Olano capitulated, and Ullrich took over the race leader's jersey.

Years later, in his autobiography, Ullrich wrote about the 1999 Vuelta in terms that suggested his passion for professional cycling had been reignited in Spain. He felt unburdened, liberated of the stresses of the previous few months. Meanwhile, to the Spanish journalists covering the race, Ullrich looked, on the contrary, joyless and poker-faced. The *ABC* newspaper's correspondent, José Carlos Carabias, interviewed him in Murcia on the eve of Vuelta and wrote of an 'odyssey . . . a kind of persecution' which, between the wait and delaying tactics of his entourage, had 'lasted four hours – all for fourteen questions'. Carabias found Ullrich to be 'passionless, shy, a touch melancholic . . . like a frightened mouse.'

Ullrich's countryman, the sprinter Marcel Wüst, had won four stages and led the race for two days in the first week – and yet would soon be reminded that, as he says, 'in Germany, cycling was three things – Jan Ullrich, the Tour de France and Telekom'. 'I do all that in the first week and nobody gives a fuck. There are two German journalists at the Vuelta. Then Jan takes the jersey and suddenly there are twenty. I was like, "Hey, guys, thanks for showing up last week and writing three lines about me in your paper." I was grown up enough by then to make it sound funny, but I also sort of meant it.'

Even Wüst had to concede, though, that a glimpse of Ullrich in full flight was worth anyone's airfare. A rider whose career straddled the dynasties of Jacques Anquetil and Eddy Merckx, the Italian Vittorio Adorni, once said that the key difference between those two riders lay in how they affected the senses rather than the course of the sport's history; Adorni was in equal measure haunted and mesmerized by Anquetil's stealth, the way he could silently cut through a peloton like a dagger through human flesh; Merckx, meanwhile, came and went with a commotion, a turbulence which years later moved another Italian contemporary, Giancarlo Ferretti, to recall the angry rustle of a 'one-man forest fire'.

Ullrich possessed neither Anquetil's finesse nor Merckx's ballast, but a hybrid not dissimilar to his most recent predecessor on the cathedra of the major tours, Miguel Induráin. What most impressed about Ullrich, the Italian journalist Gianni Mura had written during the 1997 Tour, was the 'power and effortlessness' of his pedal stroke. 'He looked like a postman . . . a motorized postman,' Mura observed. Reminiscent, Mura thought, of Merckx during his first Tour win in 1969. Certainly 'more than just a rider on his bike'.

At the 1999 Vuelta, for the first time since that scramble for new superlatives in July 1997, Ullrich was purring on the roads. 'He had that smoothness back. Just so super relaxed and super determined, like the result was never in doubt,' says Marcel Wüst. Three mountain stages remained – and in none of them would he appear unduly flustered. Telekom's porous, teetering flotilla could offer little resistance against the Spanish armadas of Banesto, Kelme and Vitalicio Seguros, and yet its captain, Ullrich, emerged from every battle windswept, weary but defiantly afloat. After the final mountaintop finish of the race to the Alto de Abantos, Ullrich's closest challenger, the Spaniard Igor González de Galdeano, had narrowed his deficit to

The block of flats in Papendorf where Ullrich lived between the ages of five and thirteen, and (*above*) the communal garden where he learned to ride a bike.

Ullrich and his teammates, André Korff, Stefan Dassow and Jörg Papenfuß, line up with their Dynamo Rostock West clubmates after their 2,000-metre team pursuit schoolboy national championship victory in 1987. Ullrich stands in the centre, looking to his left, while Peter Sager is at the end of the same row.

Ullrich, aged seventeen, on his way to fifth place in the 1991 cyclo-cross junior world championships in Gieten, the Netherlands.

Two years later, Ullrich took gold and the rainbow jersey in the 1993 amateur world championship road race in Oslo.

Peter Sager, Ullrich's first ever cycling coach, at home in Rostock.

Peter Becker, Ullrich's coach from 1987 until 2002, signs a copy of his autobiography at his home in Berlin in September 2015.

Jan and Gaby Weis, his first long-term partner, pose in front of the town hall in Merdingen in 1997.

Ullrich (*left*) and Lance Armstrong in the 1996 Tour de France, weeks before Armstrong's diagnosis with testicular cancer.

Posing with Bjarne Riis (*centre*) and Erik Zabel (*left*) during a rest day that year.

Telekom directeur sportif Walter Godefroot (*left*)
and the company's CEO Ron Sommer in 1997.

Jan (*in second place*) shadowing Richard Virenque on the first stage in the
Pyrenees at the 1997 Tour de France, the day before he took the yellow jersey.

Above: Racing in yellow, with Bjarne Riis behind him, on stage fourteen of the 1997 Tour to Courchevel.

Right: A rare moment of respite on the same stage.

(*From left*) Jens Heppner, Peter Becker, Jan Ullrich and Walter Godefroot are given a heroes' reception in a packed Marktplatz in Bonn in 1997.

Ullrich with his mother after stage seventeen of the 1997 Tour to Colmar.

Already looking decidedly fuller-figured, alongside directeur sportif Rudy Pevenage (*centre*) and Erik Zabel (*left*) at the presentation of the 1998 Tour de France, just three months after his 1997 triumph.

under a minute. But Galdeano's last remaining 'chance' came in the penultimate-day time trial in Ávila – and, there, Ullrich dominated. His margin of victory on the stage ran to nearly three minutes, his cushion over Galdeano in the general classification as the race rolled into Madrid stood at over four.

Thus Jan Ullrich became the third German to triumph in the Vuelta a España, after Rudi Altig and Rolf Wolfshohl, the 1962 and 1965 champions. To Ullrich's teammates in Spain, the three weeks had served as a dazzling reminder of his crystalline talent. The hours spent carrying water bottles, counselling and sheltering Ullrich from the wind had given Rolf Aldag the time and further cause to ponder how much of Ullrich's brilliance was inborn and how much had been moulded, refined, polished. 'It was the combination of power and style that was so impressive,' Aldag says. 'Never out of the saddle, just killing people with his rhythm. Obviously the time trial skills were just really impressive. You could have chased him with a whole team and not really caught him. And looking so stylish. It's maybe a little bit the legacy of the athletic training they did in the DDR. You could hang Jens Heppner on a tree and he would do fifty pull-ups, whereas in the West we only knew how to ride our bikes. We could barely even hang from the tree.

'That was also what you saw on the bike. If you saw Jens Heppner, or Olaf Ludwig, or Uwe Ampler or Jan, the way they sat on the bike, they were like robots. They looked identical at 20 kph, 30 kph or 60 kph. That's really impressive, and I think that was the real benefit of what they did at school. Whereas, in the West, I left school at fifteen, went to the factory at sixteen, was going to work at six a.m. then back at three p.m. What do you do then? Core stability or ride your bike? You ride your bike and do nothing else. The trade-off is that your body can only do this one thing, while they had their first athletic lesson before they went to school for three hours, then had a break, went riding for four hours, then went for another two hours to school. So Jan was just a really good overall athlete, otherwise he couldn't have been able to look that good on the bike.'

Ullrich's physical gifts had of course never been in question. It was how he used them that occasionally vexed less gifted colleagues like Aldag.

'It was always really funny, how he defended himself and how he argued once in a while. He would say, "You know, I really don't understand you guys. I see it like this: it's like a glass of water that's full in the winter, really full. You guys are tipping a little bit, a little bit, then when you get to the Tour it's already half empty. What I do is keep it completely full until the Tour, then empty it all at once. I'm not better than you are. I'm just smarter." And he was really convinced that was the truth, to defend his laziness in the winter. If you're not talented and you hear Jan say this, you actually get quite angry. "You really think that you have the same talent as us and are just more dedicated to the Tour de France? OK, Jan. Thank you very much . . . but what I think is your motor is just four times bigger than ours." But, he'd be sitting there, really convinced his theory was the truth.'

Jörg Jaksche had often been the last of Ullrich's lieutenants to buckle in one of the most mountainous Vueltas for years. All these years later, Jaksche's affection for Ullrich is tempered with the frustration that often came with serving him as a teammate.

'Jan was a very nice guy, very humble,' Jaksche says. 'The only negative thing I could say about him is that he sometimes didn't stand up and take a position. That was often missing with Jan – just standing up and showing personality. This was also the reason, I think, why the team wasn't super successful, because Jan couldn't give the team direction and momentum.'

Jaksche recounts one episode from the Vuelta to underline his point.

'There was one summit finish where Olano got dropped. I was having a good day, so ten kilometres before the last climb I asked Jan whether he also felt good. He nodded, so I say, "Why don't I go as fast as I can to the bottom of the last climb, and you just hold on?" Because I could see that Olano was struggling slightly. Jan hears this, thinks about it for a second, then says, "Yeah, but why?" I'm like, "Er, so you can drop Olano?" "Ah, OK," he replies. It was like his mind was somewhere else.

'You really had to spell it out to him. It was sometimes funny but sometimes you were also thinking, *Come on, man*. At the same time, what Jan could do with his body was just phenomenal.'

That would again be evident two weeks after the Vuelta, at the world championships in north-east Italy, where the time trial was to be Ullrich's main objective. A gently undulating 50.8-kilometre route into the Prosecco vineyards to the north of Treviso, then back towards the city, suited him perfectly. As widely predicted, he proved too strong for the competition – although a journeyman Swede, Michael Andersson, caused a shock by finishing second, just fourteen seconds behind Ullrich's time. Telekom's bike sponsor, Pinarello, is based just a few kilometres outside Treviso's city walls, and they honoured Ullrich's victory by inviting him to a celebration dinner with other illustrious former Pinarello 'ambassadors'. One of them, Miguel Induráin, said that Ullrich's recent results proved that he had turned a corner: he was 'no longer just strong in the legs, but also in the head as well'.

Rudy Pevenage also spoke of a transformation, a sudden jolt forward into adulthood. Ullrich had apparently learned an important lesson – in future, he needed to do more racing and less training to stay in shape. To one reporter enquiring about how these changes would affect how he approached the coming winter, Ullrich responded with a laugh and the vow that 'Fat Jan', as he called himself, wouldn't be making a reappearance this year or indeed ever again.

The new, purportedly unrecognizable Ullrich more or less single-handedly dragged the road race peloton up the last ascent of the Torricelle hill three days later, only for a rank outsider, the twenty-three-year-old Oscar Freire, to pull off an unfathomable heist as the front group of eleven swept into the last 600 metres. Freire had missed even more of the season than Ullrich due to his own knee problems. Many of the commentators who broke the news of his victory from the television gantry overlooking the finish line had never even heard of him. 'I had no idea who he was,' Ullrich also conceded after finishing eighth.

Overall, Ullrich's late summer and autumn had exceeded expectations, and the recurring, overriding theme of his interviews in Italy had been the rekindling of his love for cycling. In the same articles, it was frequently pointed out that Ullrich was still a couple of months short of his twenty-fifth birthday; while the talk of a ten-year reign after the 1997 Tour had proven premature, he was still a young man in cycling terms, still primed, with his new mindset, to shape an époque in professional cycling.

Equally, the previous three months had been a mixed blessing. Ullrich would admit the following spring that he had rediscovered his best form so quickly over the summer that it had reinforced bad habits – most notably the conviction that he could ride himself into form in a matter of weeks.

In other words, Peter Becker's this time, the giddy glory of his Vuelta success and TT gold in Italy had exacerbated what Becker calls Ullrich's 'certain self-overestimation'. 'You get kids who climb trees without having a clue how to do it, yet they somehow succeed. And that puts them in danger. They develop this conviction: I can do this. But really, actually, they haven't mastered it. That's how it works with Ulli.'

To use Becker's metaphor, never was Ullrich at greater risk than when gaily swinging from the highest branches, as at the end of the 1999 season, the torments of the spring long forgotten.

Other worries were also fading from memory. Telekom's main accusers, *Der Spiegel*, had been gagged and other naysayers deterred. A positive test for one of Ullrich's Telekom teammates, Christian Henn, at the Bayern Rundfahrt was dismissed as the folly of a lone wolf.* Even the microbiologist Werner Franke, who had helped *Der Spiegel* with their investigation in June and made it his mission to expose Telekom, was now publicly avowing his trust in the team's Freiburg medical staff.

So would end a season that had seen a series of near epiphanies turn into missed opportunities: for Jan Ullrich, who had extracted the wrong lessons from a disastrous winter and spring; for the Telekom bigwigs in Bonn who, rather than take *Der Spiegel*'s allegations seriously, opened fire on the messengers. And for cycling at large, which rather than believing in myths like the 'Tour of Renewal', ought to have realized the daunting proportions of the plague uncovered the previous year.

Back in the present day, flanked on all sides by denizens of Munich's cocktail-sipping *Schickeria* – the name given here to the city's fashionistas and scenesters since the late 1970s – Jörg Jaksche and I are reliving cycling's age of drugs and decadence.

Andreas Burkert, a long-serving journalist for *Süddeutsche Zeitung*, has joined us. To anyone familiar with Burkert's work and with Jaksche's career path, this may seem incongruous. Burkert was for many years the German media's most dogged and prolific reporter

---

* Christian Henn admitted using EPO to *Süddeutsche Zeitung*, 26 May 2007.

on doping in cycling, and Jaksche would one day wind up among his 'victims'. As they've explained to me, though, hunter and hunted finally discovered they had much in common – most notably their interest in how cycling had sucked in, chewed up and spat out a generation of promising young athletes. Yesterday, Andreas attended Jaksche's graduation from finance school. They are a little like big and little brother – Burkert a decade or so older, a few inches taller, one or two wider, and bald. Andreas chides Jörg over his love life; Jörg pokes fun at Andreas for going 'over to the dark side', to a job as communications chief for Bayern Munich's basketball team.

They'll riff off each other seamlessly, fascinatingly, for as long as the bar is still serving negronis – but the conversation keeps coming back to the same subjects. Jan Ullrich, doping and the Germans.

'I think the difference, Jörg, is that in France or Belgium they've had scandals too in the past but they're cycling countries . . .'

'They're also mainly Catholic. And if you're a Catholic you can go to church and say these are my sins, and they forgive you.'

'Jörg's right, but partly because of what happened with the Nazis, there's always this desperation to pick away at why things happened here, to find who was guilty. Which can also be a very good thing . . .'

'Ja, and if you put up a German flag in your garden, up until a few years ago, everyone would call you a Nazi, or at least a nationalist . . .'

'The turning point was the World Cup in 2006. Then suddenly you were allowed to be proud of being German.'

They both fall silent for a second. In few places is nationhood as frequently or intensely debated as in Germany, and yet connecting certain dots, or threads in this narrative, still gives Andreas and Jörg pause.

'The Germans want to have that image of [being] technologically advanced, hard-working, clean, transparent,' Jörg picks up. 'We want people to think a German car is advanced because of German engineering, hard work, no cheating – not like a Ferrari that will fall apart after 100,000 kilometres or whatever. This is the German way. Hey, Andreas?'

'Ja, Germans are very moral . . .'

'. . . and this is because of the war.'

'For sure.'

12

REALITY CHECK

'That's great. We got the cancer guy to win
the Tour, but now the real guys are back'

—*Lance Armstrong*

'Jan, can you not just lay off the chocolate a bit?'

These words, delivered by Jens Heppner to his friend and team-mate Jan Ullrich one day in the spring of 2000, sounded less like Heppner's usual brotherly counsel and more like an admonishment. All of the promises of the 1999 autumn, Ullrich's vow that 'Fat Jan' would never return, the good intentions and New Year's resolutions, had petered out into a much more familiar loop of illness, infections, antibiotics and lethargy. Once again, the first four months of the year had come and gone with Ullrich's withdrawals and enforced schedule changes having outnumbered his days of competition. He had 'successfully' completed one race, the Tour of Murcia (in ninety-third position overall). For the first time, Ullrich was training with an SRM power meter – but as ever it was gravity and oxygen, not watts through the pedals, that were his undoing. One day at the January Mallorca camp, Udo Bölts had walked in on Ullrich thrashing away on an indoor trainer, noticed the overhang of his belly, seen the sweat rolling down his brow and over the edge of his chin – and thought what he could see was a hopelessly unfit teammate straining to hit respectable numbers. Bölts then sneaked a glance at Ullrich's power meter. The display read 450 watts.

No, power was definitely not Jan's problem.

The SRM device hadn't been Ullrich's only change for the new millennium. Mario Kummer, a teammate in Ullrich's debut Tour in 1996, had been a member of Telekom's coaching staff since the end of his racing career in 1998. Now, Kummer was to be Ullrich's chief minder for the 2000 season, or to use a term that Telekom had employed the previous season, his 'babysitter'. Kummer recalls the weeks spent in Merdingen, where Ullrich and Gaby had moved into their new 'dream home' the preceding winter, with fond nostalgia. Not that Ullrich didn't also occasionally test his patience.

'We'd agree a time of nine o'clock to go training, and I'd be there at nine on the dot, on his front step, just hoping he'd open the door. He always did, but he'd be in his pyjamas, and then, as casual as you like, he'd say, "Kummi, let's just have a coffee first." Finally we'd get out the door and go training at ten thirty, eleven . . .

'I'd known him in 1996 and 1997 and he was a different person [in 2000],' Kummer continues. 'It was harder to motivate him. I know that the team tried everything. But motivation has to come from within.'

The fresh memory of Ullrich's rip-roaring end to 1999 – and of how expediently it had been achieved – brought him at least a limited period of grace. Walter Godefroot was also happily distracted by Telekom's best start to a season for years. Central to it were the rider some pundits had hurried to anoint as the new Ullrich, Andreas Klöden, and Telekom's other star and in many ways its anti-Ullrich, Erik Zabel. While Klöden won both Paris–Nice and the Tour of the Basque Country, Zabel rattled off a succession of minor victories and two major ones, in Milan–Sanremo and the Amstel Gold Race. As ever with Zabel, it was minimum fuss, maximum grunt – the diametric opposite of what Godefroot was used to seeing from Ullrich. 'Walter was a huge fan of Zabel. That was his son. Zabel was everything Ullrich wasn't,' Brian Holm observes.

Another long-time teammate of both riders at Telekom, Giovanni Lombardi, says that if Godefroot or anyone else could have 'screwed Erik's head onto Jan's body, they would have had Eddy Merckx'.

Merckx himself was one of the pundits who now weighed in on Ullrich's perennial early season struggles. The most decorated rider of all time reckoned Ullrich had 'a mental weakness' that was perhaps the result of 'being under pressure to perform too early when he was growing up in East Germany'. Ullrich dismissed such beermat psychoanalysis, but a further inquest followed his return to competition in late May at the Midi Libre. There, wearing the rainbow skinsuit of world champion, he was caught by his 'minute man' in a 26-kilometre time trial on the fourth day. On the fifth, he finished in the last group on the road, thirty minutes off the pace. On day six, he crossed the finish line in a Telekom team car.

At the start of the Deutschland Tour the following week, Godefroot seemed finally to be losing his rag. Whether Ullrich would ever become a model pro, Godefroot said gloomily while tapping the side of his head, would depend only on his 'grey matter'.

Ullrich himself told the press he had no more than three or four kilos to lose in the five weeks before the Tour. The Vuelta in 1999 had proved how quickly he could get into form. Besides, what did they want? 'For me to be a sportsman who only thinks about his job for 365 days a year and eats strictly fat-free foods?' The very notion seemed far-fetched. After all, he said, 'It doesn't matter how you achieve the success.'

The rider who most thought would be his biggest rival come the Tour would have agreed with that sentiment, and certainly exemplified it. Lance Armstrong had suffered his own setbacks in the spring of 2000, crashing on a training ride in the Pyrenees in May. But by comparison with Ullrich's, the first half of Armstrong's season had still been ominously smooth. Their paths were due to cross for the first and last time in their respective Tour build-ups on the first Saturday of June at the Classique des Alpes – a now defunct one-day race mimicking a Tour de France mountain stage. They duly took their place on the start line in Aix-les-Bains and rolled through the neutralized zone only for Ullrich to climb off his bike before he even reached the start line proper. The back spasms that had begun at the Deutschland Tour had made a sudden reappearance, making it impossible for him to even do up the Velcro straps on his shoes.

With still no direct confrontation in a meaningful setting, it was hard to know how Armstrong and Ullrich would measure up even if the latter could shape up in time for the Tour. The aesthetic contrast between their two styles certainly offered few clues. In his second autobiography, *Every Second Counts*, Armstrong himself described Ullrich as a 'big, pantherish rider, while I looked, someone said, like a cat climbing a tree'.[14] In May, Armstrong's coach, or at least the man he presented as such, Chris Carmichael, also reached for a zoological metaphor as he described how he had reinvented Armstrong post-cancer to *Outside* magazine. 'Lance is a small rider, compared with Miguel Induráin. Induráin has larger muscle mass, meaning he can use bigger gears. Lance needed to break this work into smaller segments. It's like lifting 300 pounds. If you're a gorilla, you can lift it all at once, but if you're a little guy, you'd be better off lifting 100 pounds three times. In Lance's case, it meant he had to pedal faster.'

It sounded simple, perhaps simply ingenious, but there was another story, an alternative and untold version of this already dubious narrative. On a Tuesday in June, while Ullrich was competing in – and helping Telekom to win – a team time trial at the Tour of Switzerland, Armstrong, his US Postal directeur sportif Johan Bruyneel and teammates Kevin Livingston and Tyler Hamilton were boarding a private plane in Nice and flying across the Mediterranean to Valencia. Near there, Hamilton reported later, Armstrong's real guru – not Carmichael but the Italian sports doctor Michele Ferrari – was waiting for the travelling party in a large, conference centre-style hotel overlooking the beach of Les Gavines. The US Postal team doctor, Luis del Moral – or '*El Gato Negro*', 'the black cat', as he was only semi-affectionately known by his patients – and the team's coach, José 'Pepe' Martí, were also in attendance. According to Hamilton, between them, Martí, Ferrari and Del Moral proceeded to draw blood from the three riders with the intention of re-infusing it at the Tour de France in a just a couple of weeks' time.[15] In the USADA reasoned decision that twelve years later summarized the evidence leading to Armstrong's conviction as a drugs cheat, the account of this episode is pithily footnoted with a quote from Bruyneel's autobiography: 'The Tour has always brought out the best and the worst in humankind.'[16]

The 'worst' in this case was a doping technique that most assumed to be obsolete. It is widely documented that the practice of transfusing blood to boost the supply of oxygen to muscles was adopted, if not pioneered, by Finnish distance runners in the 1970s. A secret weapon at first, the method quickly gained traction and had become relatively common by the 1984 Olympics in Los Angeles, where the US track cycling team were among its users. In 1986, finally, belatedly, the International Olympic Committee banned blood transfusions despite not being able to detect them. But their best deterrent was neither the testing nor the Olympic ideal; rather, it was the difficulty, the danger and the sheer grisliness of the process, which involved either cold-storing one's own blood and then injecting it or, even more chillingly, 'filling up' with someone else's. The first reports outing the American track cyclists in LA had spoken of 'vampirism'.

Luckily for the cheats and unluckily for their sports, there would soon be a much better and less gory alternative. In 1983, an American pharmaceutical company, Amgen, cloned the gene for human erythropoietin – a hormone secreted by the kidneys to stimulate the production of those precious oxygen-carrying, performance-enhancing red blood cells. Five years later, in 1988, a synthetic or recombinant form of erythropoietin was approved in Europe for the treatment of anaemia. In June 1989, Amgen launched its EPO drug in the USA. The IOC added EPO to its banned list the following year. The UCI followed suit in 1991.

The question of when, precisely, EPO was first given to athletes has fascinated sports historians for decades. A flurry of deaths among Belgian and Dutch cyclists beginning in December 1987 and stretching to 1993 has been commonly described as the ugly tidemark of the drug's first wave, but evidence remains patchy. The same could be said about rumours centring on the 1988 Calgary Winter Olympics and Francesco Conconi, the University of Ferrara professor and mentor to Michele Ferrari. The Italian anti-doping expert who first exposed Conconi's use of EPO to dope cyclists, Alessandro Donati, tells me he thinks Conconi started to give athletes EPO 'at some point in 1988, between the late spring and the summer, largely abandoning blood transfusions'.[17]

Certainly, athletes were a lot quicker to embrace EPO than sports lawmakers to combat it – and this was partly due to Conconi. For years in the early 1990s, including while serving as the president of the UCI's medical commission, the professor told the International Olympic Committee he was developing a method to detect the drug when, in fact, he was using it for a different kind of experiment – doping some of the world's top cyclists and, bizarrely, himself.[18] This was judge Franca Oliva's conclusion at the end of a trial that finished in 2003 with Conconi's acquittal because the statute of limitations had lapsed '[although] the crime took place'. Other, genuine attempts to come up with a test either made painfully slow progress or failed, and by the mid-1990s endurance sports were in the grip of an EPO pandemic. The danger to an athlete's health could be managed, the risk of getting caught was zero. Years later, Lance Armstrong put it in a nutshell: 'We had a drug that was totally undetectable, unbelievably beneficial, and most would say, if monitored by a doctor, totally safe. What were we all gonna do? Trust me. We're all in.'

Armstrong had regularly used EPO, among other substances, even before his diagnosis with testicular cancer in 1996. When he returned to racing in 1998, his body had changed shape but his morals and illegal medical regimen remained much the same. Jörg Jaksche says Telekom stopped bringing EPO to races in 1999 – and US Postal had been sufficiently perturbed by the previous year's Festina scandal to do the same. But while Rudy Pevenage makes the dubious claim that Telekom riders gave up the drug altogether, no one would try to argue today that, in July 1999, EPO was not part of Armstrong and US Postal's chemical arsenal during their first Tour win.

The following spring, the cycling world was abuzz with anticipation of Armstrong and Ullrich's first mano a mano at the Tour – and about a development that could have more far-reaching consequences: finally, a French research team had reportedly cracked the EPO code, come up with a way to find its fingerprint in urine. Their paper was published in the journal *Nature* on 8 June 2000. Coincidentally, Armstrong lost his leader's jersey on Mont Ventoux in the Dauphiné Libéré that afternoon.

A few days later, Armstrong and his two most vaunted teammates were flying to Valencia to get their blood banked. Ultimately, the UCI would decide at the last minute not to give the new EPO test its world premiere at the Tour, but Armstrong and Dr Ferrari had not wanted to take the risk. They would go old-school, medieval – back to the guts and gore of doping's Middle Ages.

'Frankenstein-ish', as Tyler Hamilton described it.

Miraculously, not only did Jan Ullrich make it to the start of the Tour, but he fairly swaggered into France at the end of June. In the Tour of Switzerland he had worn the leader's jersey for three days and eventually finished fifth. A few days later, he starred in a Telekom procession at the German National Road Race championship, giving teammate Rolf Aldag a limousine ride to the title. He suddenly looked lean, motivated and capable of challenging Armstrong.

According to the Telekom doctor, Lothar Heinrich, Ullrich's fitness test at the University of Freiburg on the Tuesday before the Tour yielded his best results since 1997. Ullrich had also reached his target weight. But what exactly was that? In pre-race interviews, Heinrich and Ullrich put the magic number at 74 kilograms – and journalists nodded. Never mind that Ullrich had told some of the same writers just a few weeks earlier that his Tour weight was between 70 and 73 kilograms. Or that, according to Peter Becker, by the end of the 1996 and 1997 races, he had been a skeletal 68 kilograms.

Rolf Aldag was left scratching his head. 'His "perfect" Tour weight changed by about five kilos over time,' Aldag says. 'I know that he weighed around 69 kilos at the end of the Tour when he won it. He was super lean. And he'd started that Tour at seventy-one. So that was his perfect weight. But the next year, suddenly, they were saying seventy-three was a really good weight for Jan. They even put that out publicly. I always wondered why no one ever looked this up. It went to seventy-four, then eventually seventy-five and seventy-six, and he was "good". You're like, *Hang on, he's five kilos heavier than when he won the Tour.* OK, he could gain some muscle, but he has to get oxygen to it, so how can that ever be good?'

The venue for the traditional pre-race team presentation and for the stage one time trial the following day was the Futuroscope theme park just outside Poitiers. Ullrich walked onto a stage overlooked by a 3D cinema and 45-metre space needle – and, in the process, gave Lance Armstrong a heartening glimpse into the futures of the two respective riders.

'In 2000 I was the defending champion, but it also had this stigma that Ullrich wasn't there and Pantani wasn't there,' Armstrong says. 'People said '99 was an easy Tour, or that I would have been third if they'd raced. So the impression among the fans, in the press room probably, and also in the peloton was, "That's great. We got the cancer guy to win the Tour, but now the real guys are back." There were two big stories: not just Jan but also Pantani. And Jan was not fit. He was looking pretty bad. I knew that I would have to take time out of him early because he'd come in – and he'd do this often, like in the Vuelta – and by the end he'd be skinny. But I could just look at him and see he wasn't fit. For sure. Just his face, then at the team presentation, absolutely . . .'

The possibility that Ullrich and Telekom had found a different way of dealing with the looming threat of an EPO test didn't faze Armstrong then and doesn't seem to strike him as particularly relevant now. 'We also knew what was going on with Jan because Jörg Jaksche always told everybody . . .' he says dismissively, half in jest.

'Anyway, whatever,' Armstrong picks up brusquely, 'I knew I had to strike early while Jan was still trying to lose a few kilos.'

Not much could be gleaned from the 16-kilometre first-day time trial and Armstrong's second place behind the British debutant, David Millar, twelve seconds ahead of Ullrich. Even a 70-kilometre team time trial to Saint Nazaire three days later was far from conclusive, as US Postal's 'blue train' gained forty seconds over Ullrich and Telekom. Meanwhile, Pantani leaked over five minutes on general classification over the first seven days but would still be declared 'the winner of the first week' by Walter Godefroot. The Italian had overhauled a bigger deficit in the Pyrenees and Alps in 1998.

The first mountain stage of this Tour took the peloton to Hautacam, a dark, brooding moloch of a Pyrenean climb overlooking Lourdes. A dense mist had enveloped the lower slopes, and through it, Armstrong responded to an attack from Pantani by dancing into the Italian's slipstream and away from Ullrich in a phosphorescent blur of flesh and metal. So long revered for his twinkle-toed pedalling style, Pantani seemed stuck to the mountainside as Armstrong shimmied clear alone. Behind them both, Ullrich lumbered. The stylistic gulf translated into a numerical abyss by the end of the day, with Armstrong suddenly over four minutes ahead of Ullrich and the Tour – pundits agreed – as good as over after ten stages.

Trying hard to keep his euphoria in check, Armstrong half lied that a bad day could result in losses of fifteen minutes or more on Mont Ventoux, where he and Ullrich would have their rematch in three days. He then found a quiet moment to call the individual whose opinion he valued most: his doctor, Michele Ferrari.

Expecting confetti, what he got was a cold shower.

'People talked a lot about me always making a big statement in the first mountain stage of the Tour . . . but it just ended up working out that way,' Armstrong says. 'It wasn't like it was a team mandate or plan. I guess those opportunities just presented themselves in Sestriere in 1999 and Hautacam in 2000, because of weather. I was always better in the colder weather. I ran hot, so on a scorching day it was always hard for me to do an effort. Also, just to set the tone for the race, get a cushion . . . you know, those efforts are impressive to watch on TV, and they get people talking, but they're really not that smart – and this is where we get to Ferrari. I get onto our little camper after the stage, I call Ferrari and I'm thinking this guy's gonna be like, "That was amazing! Way to go, Lance!" But I ask him what he thinks and he replies in this low voice, "You made a big mistake."

'I say to him, "What are you talking about? I won by fucking four minutes." But he just went on, "Big mistake. That was too good. Guys are going to be on you now." He had to balance the tactics and the politics in the peloton, but also what the authorities probably thought. He just thought that was a mistake, to come out with such an obvious show of strength. Also, forget the politics and all of that, he also always had the view – because I did it every year, and he'd tell me every time – that you paid for those efforts. He'd straight up say it to your face: "You will pay for that effort. Don't think you won't because you will. This is a three-week race and this is the first day in the mountains . . ." Sure enough, I did later.'

Ferrari was right on at least one score. The previous year, Armstrong's performance in the first mountain stage to Sestriere had inspired innuendo-laden headlines like *L'Équipe*'s 'On Another Planet'. It had also given impetus to sleuthing journalists who, just a few days later, would uncover his use of a banned corticosteroid. Officially, he had emerged victorious and unsullied from the 1999 Tour, but, now, twelve months later, he had put a large down payment on a second win after just one mountain stage and had rivals comparing him to a jumbo jet. In a few days, a pair of French journalists would be following their intuition and, from a safe distance, an unmarked car driven by US Postal staff members. They tailed the vehicle to a lay-by in the Alps and filmed its occupants dumping rubbish bags. Among the trash were syringe wrappers, 160 of them, plus packaging for a substance with a strange name, Actovegin, and even stranger derivation – the blood of foetal cows. The discovery would eventually lead to a French government investigation that lasted over a year. US Postal were finally cleared because the product wasn't banned. But the scent of suspicion around Armstrong had become a little more pungent.

Ferrari had seen it coming. Not that it altered US Postal's plans for the rest of the 2000 Tour. Their rest day was partly spent injecting the blood removed a month earlier in Valencia. Replenished and refreshed, Armstrong took a further half-minute out of Ullrich the following afternoon on Mont Ventoux. So much for him losing a quarter of an hour.

Perversely, though, Ullrich's sole moment of glory in the 2000 Tour was also to come partly as a result of what had occurred on the 'Giant of Provence'. Armstrong had said previously of the Ventoux: 'It doesn't like me and I don't like it.' Now, having coasted in half a wheel behind Pantani, gifting the Italian the stage win, Armstrong made a new enemy; instead of thanking the American, Pantani claimed that he had simply been the stronger man. And this sent Armstrong into a rage.

First, he mocked Pantani's big ears by calling him 'Elefantino' and comparing him unfavourably to 'the gentleman' Ullrich. He then downgraded the Italian to 'a little shit-starter' after Pantani's second stage win at Courchevel. Finally, two days later, on the final mountain stage of the Tour at Morzine, Pantani launched not just an attack on the first of five passes on the route but something he hoped could turn into a revolution – setting out to overturn his nine-minute deficit on general classification and overthrow Armstrong.

One of Armstrong's then teammates, Frankie Andreu, will never forget Armstrong's reaction.

'I'd never seen Lance so excited, so riled up. We were chasing like crazy, right on our limit, but Lance was like, "Let him go, let him go! Fuck, yes. We're gonna kill him! This is fucking *great*!" He figured Pantani was going to be away all day, then blow up, just explode, and we were going to blow by and kill him. I can remember going up to him, and Kevin Livingston going up to him, telling him he had to remember to eat but it was like he didn't want to hear us. Total tunnel vision. "Man, this is gonna be great. It's gonna be great! We're gonna kill him!" Just so . . . gung-ho. Eventually, of course, we did catch him – but we'd ridden ourselves into the ground. Then we get to the final climb, the Joux Plane, and look what came next . . .'

It became a footnote, an inconsequential tangent in the story of the 2000 Tour, but in the career of Jan Ullrich the moment was significant: four kilometres from the summit of the Col de Joux Plane, as the gradient stiffened, Armstrong's legs seemed to lock and Jan Ullrich pulled away. A minute or two later, a couple of hairpins higher, the gap was yawning and Armstrong floundering, in the grip of the dreaded hunger knock. It was a crisis like this that he had meant when he had talked about 'maybe losing fifteen minutes' after Hautacam. It was also this, as well as prying eyes, that Ferrari had feared.

Years later, it would emerge that Ferrari, whose partnership with Armstrong was still not public knowledge in 2000, had counselled Johan Bruyneel, Armstrong and US Postal on how to respond to Pantani's attack via a phone call to Bruyneel's team car.

Armstrong finally lost over a minute and a half to Ullrich – and ended the day apologizing to his teammates for his own act of self-sabotage. 'He barely finished the stage . . .' says Andreu. 'He said he knew he could have lost the Tour.' The rest of us were like, 'No shit!'

'I definitely got wrapped in the Pantani thing that day,' Armstrong confirms. 'I was distracted, paying attention to Pantani and not eating. And the whole thing just totally backfired. Not only that, but we got to the bottom of the Joux Plane and I told Kevin Livingston just to blow it apart. I remember that I was alone then all of a sudden Jan comes back and I'm like, *Huh. That's strange. That's not supposed to happen.* Then I'm on Jan's wheel and I'm thinking, *Man, this don't feel so good.* Then you're dropped. Oh, it was terrible. Then the next minute you're in full-on crisis mode. Then it's cut to Johan seeing it on the TV in the car, and he says, "Lance, you have a seven-minute lead. You do not need to panic." But of course, you're thinking, *Fucking seven minutes is going to be gone like that.*'

Salvation came from an unlikely source – an old friend and teammate of Pantani, Roberto Conti, who handed Armstrong two energy gels as they crested the Joux Plane together.

'He gave me them for free! For free!' Armstrong splutters. 'I'm not saying you'd usually have to pay him, but, you know, I mean the guy's just saved your Tour . . .'

It would have been even better for Ullrich had he not lost precious seconds and his chance of a stage win due to his brake pads wearing out and forcing him into a bike change as he began the descent into Morzine. He had, though, restored some pride and some credibility, even in his own mind, to the trope of Ullrich versus Armstrong as the rivalry of a generation. He could one day beat Armstrong, he was sure, given that he was finishing second having drawn on 'only 80 per cent' of his potential, as he told the press. 'My weight problems in winter really have to stop now,' he added – a rare public self-reproach. But Walter Godefroot had heard it all before, and made his feelings known on the rest day in Provence: contrary to what the 1999 Vuelta had led them to believe, ten weeks of sacrifice every season was not enough, not even for Ullrich.

His third second place in four appearances at the Tour was therefore filed away as semi-failure. The collective memory of Arcalís in 1997 remained powerfully intact, like the reductive, prejudicial myth of a profligate whizz-kid who was more gifted than Armstrong. 'Purely body-wise, he was the biggest talent,' says Rolf Aldag, 'but then we come into this complete opposite thing with Lance. I think that's what made it so interesting: people really believe, rightly or wrongly, that Jan was the biggest physical talent and Lance was by far the biggest mental talent. In Germany it turned out to be a little unfair. It was all "He's lazy, he doesn't do this or that . . ." But if you really break it down, it's like, can you really blame him for that? We all have certain talents and we all have certain weaknesses. Definitely that was one of his weaknesses: he definitely wasn't as uncompromising as Lance. But what if he just can't be like that? It's against his nature. His genes. What if Lance and Jan had equal talents, just different ones?'

Despite the many warnings and Godefroot's insistence that things had to change, the late summer and autumn of 2000 would send the same mixed messages as the previous year's Vuelta, in much the same way: reinforcing the notion that Ullrich was the best cyclist on the planet – but also a lazy one. Before the Olympic Games in Sydney, Ullrich went to the Vuelta as the defending champion but with his focus very much on topping-up his post-Tour fitness in time for Australia. He completed eleven stages in Spain, his most important result being the one displayed on his bathroom scales; according to Peter Becker, Ullrich was leaving the Vuelta 'underweight'.

For Becker, Ullrich and anyone else who had grown up in the East, the Olympics were more than just a joyous quadrennial congress of sport and cultures. Ever since the advent of the DDR, sport had been used as a delivery drug for the 'socialist personality' that the regime sought to instil in its people – and as a megaphone to broadcast its message. The role of the DDR's 'diplomats in tracksuits' in international competition was less about cultivating relationships beyond the Iron Curtain than proving the inherent superiority of the socialist corpus and animus.

It was clearly another world and another Germany after reunification, but to Ossis the Olympics retained a different cachet and bestirred sharper patriotic emotions than those experienced by Wessis or their opponents on the track, pitch or in the pool. Ullrich would admit it years later: 'For us who grew up in the East, the Games are extra special.'

Walter Godefroot went with Ullrich to Sydney and noticed something he found curious: Ullrich seemed different, more relaxed than in his usual environment at Telekom. Godefroot would finally put it down as an unconscious craving for Ullrich's former, simpler existence in a breeze-block dormitory in Berlin's Sportforum. 'I can remember standing with him at the Olympics in Sydney, and him pointing to the Olympic Village. "That's real sport," he said. I'll never forget that. It reminded him of the DDR. Jan's a super athlete but everything that comes with that is too much for him. He needed to be shut away like that.'

Peter Becker had reconnoitred the Sydney route a year earlier and returned to Germany with vital insight, notably into the importance of the wind direction on the only significant climb on the road race circuit. The German team was to consist of four Telekom riders – Ullrich, Klöden, Rolf Aldag and Erik Zabel – plus the larger-than-life Berliner, Jens Voigt. On the eve of the race, Zabel and Ullrich sat down to discuss how to distribute roles and resources, given that both were potential winners. They finally, amicably, decided that until the last lap of the 17-kilometre circuit Ullrich would have a licence to attack but that he would lead out Zabel should his attempts fail. Riders who had seen Ullrich in the Olympic Village remarked on his gauntness, which was accentuated by an aggressively short hairstyle. 'My English isn't that great, and I just kept saying "shorter, shorter!" Then the guy took the whole lot off,' Ullrich said of his visit to a local hairdresser.

He was grinning again when, on the day of the 240-kilometre road race, as they made their way to the start, rain hammered against the windows of the German team's minibus – and he joked with Andreas Klöden that they might as well head straight for the airport. Fortunately, Lothar Heinrich, the Telekom and German team doctor, was soon calling to say the sun had just come out over the race route – and wind was also whistling down the climb in Centennial Park. Just as Peter Becker had predicted.

Two laps from the end none of the favourites – not Armstrong, not Ullrich, not Zabel nor one of the fancied classics specialists – had yet made their move. With his freedom ticket about to expire, Ullrich finally bolted out of the peloton and onto the Centennial Park climb, as per Becker's advice. Halfway up the hill, Ullrich turned to see Klöden and the Kazakh, Alexander Vinokourov, pursuing him, and more daylight between them and the field. A Telekom employee and teammate for the rest of the year, Vinokourov had trained with the German team at their holding camp in Brisbane – and had given the frequency of the Kazakh team's intercom radio to Rudy Pevenage. Hence, Pevenage, a Belgian, was standing in a gazebo close to the finish line directing both Germany and Kazakhstan's Olympic cyclists over his walkie-talkie. Meanwhile, Lance Armstrong was, for once, oddly out of the loop. He hadn't seen Ullrich's attack and was livid when he found out.

At the front of the race, Ullrich, Klöden and Vinokourov turned the remaining lap into a Telekom team time trial. Soon, their advantage was unassailable and they were discussing who would take which medal, finally deciding Ullrich would get the gold, Vinokourov silver and Klöden bronze. Not everyone appreciated the cosy German–Kazakh alliance. 'If Hitler and Stalin had co-operated in the same way, there would have been no Eastern Front,' sniffed the *Sydney Morning Herald*.

Peter Becker had undoubtedly been one of the architects not only of Ullrich's success but also Germany's, having spent a key week with Klöden and Ullrich in Merdingen after their withdrawals from the Vuelta. Becker hadn't made it to Australia but watched on TV and, initially, rejoiced. A decade and a half later in his home in Berlin, though, at the mere mention of Sydney, Becker's brow creases.

'There, for the first time in my career as a coach, I shed tears. But not tears of joy. No, tears because he gave an interview and there wasn't a mention, not a word of thanks to his coach in Germany. Just "I, I, I . . ."'

A similar fallout after the German time trial championship in 1995 had apparently neither changed Ullrich nor lowered Becker's expectations. When Becker and I meet in late 2015, they are years into another impasse in their relationship. It pains Becker to criticize, he says, but he also wants to press home the point that, when people said Ullrich was 'badly advised', they didn't understand that Ullrich's worst advisor has often been himself.

'At the end of the day, given all that he's experienced and the way he is, he's not a bad person. I don't want people to take that message. But the mistakes that he makes, this immaturity of his, the way he mishandles situations, all that damaged him so much and cost him and his career so dearly.'

Jan Ullrich might have gone home from Australia with two gold medals, but the wind that had been key to his success in the road race conspired against him three days later in the time trial. As the TT world champion and in-form rider, Ullrich seemed destined to avenge Armstrong's Tour de France win on the 46-kilometre course – and yet, to everyone's surprise, it was neither of the demiurges who finally prevailed. Armstrong's US Postal teammate, Viatcheslav Ekimov, had taken advantage of an early start time and gentler breeze to relegate Ullrich to the silver medal and Armstrong to the bronze.

Germany ended the Sydney Games behind only the USA, Russia, China and the host nation in the medal table, but overall it had been a strange and sobering year for German sport. In January, twenty-one months after beginning in Berlin, the trials of the doctors, coaches and officials who had masterminded the East German state doping system produced one of its most shocking moments when the lawyer, Michael Lerner, told Lothar Kipke that he was 'the Joseph Mengele of the DDR doping system'. The comparison with a Nazi doctor nicknamed 'The Angel of Death', the perpetrator of unspeakable crimes at Auschwitz, seemed questionable in its taste and proportion, and Lerner later regretted it. Nonetheless, the twelve former athletes whom he represented, and whose children bore the legacy of Kipke's treatments in their assorted disabilities, appreciated the power of his emotion.

Earlier in the hearings, it had been the turn of former SV Dynamo Berlin swimming coach Rolf Gläser. At the 1976 Olympics in Montreal, Gläser infamously responded to a question about his female swimmers' unusually deep voices with the quip: 'They came to swim, not sing.' Twenty-odd years later, from the witness box in an oak-panelled courtroom in Berlin, one of his former lab animals,

Christiane Knacke-Sommer, pulled out the bronze medal that she had won at the 1980 Moscow Games and slung it to the floor. The echo was as chilling as the words Knacke-Sommer said next: 'They destroyed my body and my mind. They even poisoned my medal . . . It is worthless and a terrible embarrassment to all Germans.'

On the afternoon of 18 July 2000, Jan Ullrich was dropping Lance Armstrong on the Col de Joux Plane when judge Dirk Dickhaus handed the two main brains behind 'State Planning Theme 14.25', Manfred Höppner and Manfred Ewald, eighteen- and twenty-two-month suspended jail terms. 'I have nothing to add. I stand by what I did and I am grateful,' mumbled Ewald when the judge asked him for a closing remark.

The final months of the trials had been charged with a harrying urgency owing to the fact that the statute of limitations on crimes committed in the former DDR was to run out in October. In total, seventeen coaches or doctors ended up receiving suspended jail sentences. Thirty were made to pay financial penalties. In all, it seemed a meagre tariff for a system estimated to have dispensed two million doses of anabolic steroids a year and to have employed 600 doctors and technicians solely to coordinate State Planning Theme 14.25. They had reportedly doped around 10,000 athletes without their knowledge over two and a half decades.

Jan Ullrich has always maintained that he was one of the lucky ones, that he escaped the DDR's moral and pharmaceutical depravities. Peter Becker, likewise, forcefully tells me that he kept his charges well away from 'diesen Dreck' – 'this muck'.

Shortly after visiting and spending almost two days with Becker, I continue my journey into the historical hinterland – and now disbanded Vaterland – that gave birth to Jan Ullrich via a tiny upstairs office in an apartment building in Berlin's Prenzlauer Berg. Here, encircled by floor-to-ceiling shelves stuffed with the paper files that tell an alternative version of East Germany's sporting miracle, Katrin Kanitz is explaining to me how she became a part of the medal factory's human toll. Once, before the Wall fell, Kanitz was among East Germany's and indeed the world's leading figure skaters – a statuesque, brown-haired Katarina Witt-doppelgänger with similar pedigree. Lately she's been spending her days in this room working for the Doping Opfer Hilfe – the organization set up in 1999 to morally and financially support the victims of State Planning Theme 14.25.

Kanitz retired at age eighteen after missing out on the 1988 Calgary Winter Olympics with a knee injury likely to have been precipitated by her unwitting use of the steroid Turinabol. She tells me she was 'dropped like a hot potato' by her coach and shunned by her parents. She suddenly had the feeling of being catapulted into adulthood before tasting adolescence, this while Germany was undergoing its own seismic, developmental shift. Years later, in 1997, Kanitz was studying, reinventing herself, just about muddling through when a letter from the police bureau in Thüringen dropped through her letterbox. One line in the text would change her life forever. 'They said they'd found a disk and on it I was recorded as having received Turinabol.'

Kanitz doesn't know to what extent this bombshell was to blame, whether it was the drugs themselves, or how much was to do with her parents, her private life or the process of *Sozialisation* – socialization – in the East. She can only say that, in 2001, she began suffering psychotic episodes and still needs anti-psychotic medicine 'to live a normal life' today. Professor Werner Franke, the archduke of anti-doping in Germany, is among those who believe that anabolic steroids could trigger conditions like Kanitz's years later. Kanitz would rather not speculate, but sees and hears on a daily basis from others like her just how deleterious the drug's effects could be. 'Damage to the heart, liver, kidney, pancreas. Busted joints. A hundred per cent of the people affected have knee, shoulder and back issues. I don't know the percentage, but a very large number of the women have breast cancer, which is scientifically proven to be a side effect of Turinabol . . .' she explains.

Kanitz and I speak for over an hour, about her story, about the shame that stops others like her coming forward, and about how a symbolic, belated but still heartfelt recognition of their suffering often means more to victims than financial compensation. At best, they can expect to receive 10,500 euros from the German state and roughly the same amount from Jenapharm, the company which created Oral Turinabol and is still in business today. For some, the cash barely covers a few months of prescriptions.

Cycling has been curiously neglected in the process of piecing together exactly which DDR sorcerers gave which drugs to which athletes. Nevertheless, like all Ossis, Katrin Kanitz knows Jan Ullrich and what he represents. She has also, she says, learned that there are universal truths which apply to everyone who grew up in the East, in a society both built on and torn apart by secrecy.

'When you tell your own story, you also learn about other people. That's also why I'm open about my own journey. I can understand that he, for example, might not want to open up in the same way. But that's really not smart. It's a chance to grow. That's my experience. You don't have to explain everything but if you start being open, talking about your feelings and how certain decisions were taken – you start to grow through that.'

13

UNTOUCHABLE

'Pressure was always the problem with Jan, even when no
one was putting him under any'

—*Walter Godefroot*

Rudy Pevenage, Jan Ullrich's long-time directeur sportif and friend, agrees to speak to me because Johan Bruyneel, Lance Armstrong's long-time directeur sportif and friend, has asked him on my behalf. At the time, it will be the first interview that Pevenage has given for years. It is also years since he has been seen at a bike race.

In the first years of the twenty-first century the Tour de France was essentially a duopoly presided over by Pevenage and Bruyneel, who also happened to live in the same village. As Lance Armstrong will put it to me: 'I mean, the whole incestuousness of it. Rudy, Johan, all the soigneurs and mechanics, all living within a kilometre or two of each other. That's like saying, I mean, for many of those Tours, the whole power structure in cycling was concentrated in this one fucking neighbourhood in Belgium. It's just weird.'

It is also a coincidence that the aforementioned neighbourhood was world famous among cycling fans for reasons that had little to do with Bruyneel or Pevenage. In 1950, for the first time, the organizers of the Tour of Flanders sent their race through and out of the town of Geraardsbergen via a cobbled track so severely inclined that locals referred to it not as a street but a wall, or 'muur'. Before long it had become so notorious that further appellation was unnecessary. It was just – and remains today – *the* Muur.

Pevenage was born in Geraardsbergen and never really left. After years of lucrative success as Telekom and Ullrich's directeur sportif, he established his fief on a leafy residential street five minutes' walk from the top of the Muur, in a mock-Tuscan villa with swimming pool in the back garden and giant terracotta urns on the front step. Bruyneel grew up in the far west of Flanders in Izegem, a few kilometres from the French border and another of cycling's *lieux sacrés*, the velodrome in which the annual Paris–Roubaix classic race finishes its journey. In the early 2000s, he masterminded the US Postal team and the Lance Armstrong empire from a key point on the route of another classic; if Pevenage could open his front door in Geraardsbergen and stroll to the brow of the Tour of Flanders' second-to-last climb, the Muur, Bruyneel's home looked out over the last hill of the Flanders route, the Bosberg.

Many of the fans, the amateur pilgrims on wheels, who come to the Muur pause beside the Chapel of Our Lady of the Oudenberg at the top or stumble into Hemelrijk restaurant across the road. And it is here that Rudy Pevenage instructs me to meet him at noon on the eve of the 2015 Tour of Flanders.

The first thing one notices about Pevenage these days is that he has lost weight since the era when he would typically be seen in a white Deutsche Telekom polo shirt, with an arm around Ullrich's shoulder. Following his retirement as a racer in the late 1980s, Pevenage's meagre, visible concessions to middle-age had been the slow fade of his surviving wreath of fine blonde hair to a white moquette, and his heavily freckled cheeks and midriff curving gently outwards. Today, though, he suddenly looks a frail sixty-one-year-old. In the spring of 2014, he'll tell me, he was battling with throat cancer – and losing. Twelve months on, his voice is still halting and hoarse. The old glint has left his eyes and his walk and gestures seem slow and deliberate. At least, happily, the tumour has gone and his health, he says, is improving.

We take our place in a quiet corner of the restaurant, away from the clatter of cutlery and cyclists' cleats. After a few minutes of niceties and Pevenage establishing some ground rules, a waiter arrives to take our order. Pevenage asks for a steak tartare listed on the menu as 'The American'.

How apt.

Fifteen years ago, Jan Ullrich's double 'victory' over Lance

Armstrong in the Sydney Olympics had renewed his faith and that of his entourage, including Pevenage. As Pevenage saw it, only two things stood in Ullrich's path to world domination: Ullrich himself and . . . the American.

'I tried everything to get Jan to beat Armstrong,' Pevenage sighs. 'I'd be talking to him in winter like Micky to Rocky Balboa. But Jan would just say, "I'm Jan Ullrich and that's it." He had a problem in his head when he saw Armstrong spin his legs, that's for sure. I did too. Because I knew Armstrong before his illness. He was a classics rider. He was the kind of guy who would win a medium mountain stage after a big mountain stage. Then he got ill, came back and it was a different Armstrong. I didn't really understand . . . I still say that if you'd put Jan and Lance in quarantine for a month before a Tour de France, it's Jan who'll win the Tour.'

Pevenage wasn't the only one at Telekom who wished that Ullrich was a little bit more like his arch-rival. Walter Godefroot had tried in vain to tease out Ullrich's killer instinct only to finally decide he was wasting his time. 'I remember Jan saying to Rudy after Pantani had beaten him in the 1998 Tour and he'd lost all those minutes in the cold, "Ach, well, Marco's had a lot of bad luck in his life." He said this in the team meeting. I couldn't believe it. It was almost as though he was happy to have that pressure off him. He wasn't a warrior. He wasn't a Hinault, a Merckx. Jan was everyone's friend.'

Bobby Julich – a preppy, bespectacled American whom Armstrong privately dismissed as a 'choad' – was, besides Pantani, Ullrich's toughest opponent in that 1998 Tour.* Julich and Ullrich barely knew each other, but, over the course of the three weeks, Julich would be struck by Ullrich's friendliness whenever they found themselves side-by-side in the peloton. During one stage, Julich complimented Ullrich on his Tag Heuer watch, to which Ullrich replied that he had a spare one that Julich could have.

The gift never materialized, but when they reached Paris, Ullrich lay second and Julich third – for the American an astonishing and life-changing result. There was, though, one more surprise, as Julich told Richard Moore in an interview for the book *Étape*. 'I was in the hotel that everyone goes to in Paris, the Concorde Lafayette, all dressed up. I was with my mom and dad and my dad is, like, "Oh my god, there's

---

* Nowadays Julich and Armstrong are friends.

Jan Ullrich." And there was Ullrich with his girlfriend, Gaby, and a million people around him [. . .] He spots me, races up and says, "Wait right there." He races through the people, all trying to get a piece of him, and back up to his room. In a few minutes he's back with this beautiful Tag Heuer watch. I still have it to this day.'

Another former rider, Jan Schaffrath, also volunteers a story about a watch as an Ullrich character reference. In 1997, Schaffrath was a bashful *stagiaire*, a mere triallist for the final weeks of Telekom's season, when one day he got the call to make up the numbers on the set of the telecommunications giant's latest TV commercial. The stars of the show were Jan Ullrich, Udo Bölts and Jens Heppner, the creative brief a goofy set-piece whereby the quartet would ride side-by-side and pass a ringing mobile phone down the line to Ullrich. It would be hours before they nailed a take, as Schaffrath could tell by glancing over at the hands on Ullrich's wristwatch, a special edition Adidas had made to commemorate his Tour win. 'It wasn't the fanciest or most expensive watch in the world,' Schaffrath says, 'but my eyes must have been as big as plates, because Jan saw me and said, "You like this watch? You can have it." He took it off and gave it to me on the spot. I went home that night proud as punch.'

By most accounts, Armstrong could also be generous with teammates – but rivals were a different matter. If Ullrich was 'the bar, the standard, what I had to beat', it stood to reason that he would also become an obsession. Tyler Hamilton describes in his autobiography how Armstrong would trawl the internet or mine his contacts for information, any information, about his opponents – especially Ullrich. 'For a while Lance had so much information I thought he had someone working for him – I pictured a young intern in a cubicle somewhere, compiling reports. But after a while I realized it was all Lance. He needed to gather the information so he could turn it into motivational fuel.'[19]

Hamilton's seemingly apocryphal line about Armstrong employing 'spies' in fact carries more than a grain of truth. As Armstrong tells me in Austin: 'I mostly did the Dauphiné and Jan did Switzerland . . . so Ferrari would drive to Switzerland and wear a little disguise. I don't know what kind of disguise exactly, but he'd stand on the side of the road, just on top of a climb, and watch Jan go past. He could look at Ullrich, just see his face and know exactly where Jan was. Then he'd give me the report.'

Johan Bruyneel laughs at the image of the world's most mytholo-
gized, vilified sports doctor peering over the brow of a Swiss
mountain pass – and over a pair of thick-rimmed fake glasses – as
Jan Ullrich obliviously turtled past. Bruyneel and I meet in a wine
bar in London's Sloane Square in March 2015, a few days before my
appointment with Pevenage. At the time of our conversation, Bruyneel has been living between London and Madrid for several years,
having left Belgium and Geraardsbergen. Soon, in addition to the
legal issues arising from USADA's reasoned decision, he'll be dealing
with a painful divorce and separation from his children. He looks
weary, but comes alive at the mention of a Cold War whose competing nerve centres were not Washington and Moscow but two
inconspicuous houses 'a few hundred metres apart' in a town in east
Flanders.

'Rudy and I were colleagues, but more rivals than colleagues,' he
says. 'There was just a cordial communication when we saw each
other, but you had to measure your words very carefully. We would
never have shared anything.'

Everything that Bruyneel was able to glean – at races, training
camps, or from behind the net curtain at home – he fed straight back
to Armstrong. Extra gasoline on his already smouldering fire of curiosity, ambition and fuck you.

'I remember Ferrari going to spy on Ullrich,' Bruyneel says. 'That
did happen. It became just such a habit between Lance and I to get
information about him. Just anything. I knew a lot of guys in Belgium who were connected to Telekom . . . The German press, lots of
people who talk.'

I say that Armstrong has also mentioned other riders. Jaksche,
for example.

'Yes! He wasn't at Telekom long but guys who have been on the
team keep connections . . . Anyway, knowing Lance, he needed a
certain bad vibe between him and somebody else, to outperform
them. He took every little thing to create that bad situation. And I
would do that too. I didn't exactly invent things, but I knew how he
worked, how his system worked, so wherever I was, I would try to
exaggerate it a little bit. If Ullrich said something in the press, I
would exaggerate it.'

*

Jan Ullrich had at least left one scuff mark on Armstrong's suit of armour ahead of the 2001 racing season. Having asked Bruyneel and US Postal for a pay rise and been dissatisfied with their offer, Armstrong's long-serving domestique and one of his closest friends, Kevin Livingston, had quit the team. Livingston wanted more cash and more freedom, and decided he would get both at the British Linda McCartney team. That logic proved to be sounder than the Linda McCartney team's foundations: by late January, the team was broke and broken, forcing its contracted riders to find employment elsewhere. Livingston got snapped up by Telekom.

Armstrong was, to say the least, unimpressed. It was, he said in the press, akin to the Gulf War general Norman Schwarzkopf defecting to Communist China.

I ask Rudy Pevenage whether one motivation for signing Livingston was to plunder intelligence on Armstrong and Postal. Pevenage shakes his head and says that, in fact, Livingston – a quiet, private character – never volunteered any. When I later put the same question to Walter Godefroot, he smiles and offers a more layered response: 'We don't only sign him so that he can tell us what's going on in Armstrong's team . . . but he's also useful in that regard.'

Armstrong now concedes that he dealt with the split rashly. Years earlier, the Missourian had moved to Austin to be close to Armstrong, but in the months before he left Postal, Livingston said at the time they had 'grown apart'. Armstrong disputes this, telling me that it was only towards the end of 2000, when Livingston demanded more money than Postal were willing to pay, that their friendship fractured. It was also a sense of betrayal, the feeling that his old pal had 'flicked' him, rather than any anxiety about what Livingston might reveal, that enraged Armstrong. 'I was pissed with Kevin for a while. It wasn't about him sharing secrets. I mean, *secrets*? There were no secrets. You mean medical secrets? Telekom knew everything anyway. That wasn't my concern. It was just, we had been very close friends. He'd been on Motorola [Armstrong's team from 1992–96], been like a big brother, and it felt just like a slap in the face to have him leave. But looking back, I could have dealt with it better. Looking back, I did that with a lot of relationships – kind of cut it all off. Anyway, he was better on the road for me in 1999 and 2000 than he was in 2001.'

It would be interesting to hear Livingston's own thoughts, but he doesn't respond to my emails requesting an interview. Over the years and particularly after his shock early retirement from racing in 2002, he and Armstrong patched things up to the extent that, when I visit Texas in spring 2015, Livingston is offering a bike-fitting service out of the basement of Armstrong's Austin shop, Mellow Johnny's. I go there unannounced in the hope that Livingston will at least hear me out. I spot a shop clerk, tell him why I'm here, to which the colleague responds that he'll go and fetch Kevin. A minute or two later, the same gentleman returns to uneasily tell me that, no luck, it turns out Kevin's not around.

When I relate all of this to Armstrong the next day, he shakes his head. 'I don't get it,' he mutters. His efforts to solicit Livingston on my behalf come to nothing.

At the time, Livingston's defection was perceived as the latest sign that maybe Ullrich and Telekom were finally getting serious. After three catastrophic winters, it was decided that, in 2001, Ullrich would finally commit to the credo prescribed by Walter Godefroot at the Tour the previous summer: total professionalism in all four seasons, and not only a few weeks in June, July and August. It would all start with a training camp in South Africa before Christmas, followed by another in Mallorca in the New Year, then a second trip to the Cape. Between the beginning of December and the second week of January, Ullrich racked up 3,000 kilometres. In Mallorca, he sounded determined, feisty. 'Lance Armstrong doesn't know anything about how I train,' he sniffed in one interview, apparently piqued by Armstrong's comments the previous summer.

The volume of Ullrich's training had been the subject of scrutiny for several years, but now attention also turned to the methodology. In particular, Armstrong's high-cadence blitzkrieg at Hautacam in the 2000 Tour had prompted some to question whether Ullrich wasn't stuck in the dark ages, old dogmas that he had presumably learned in the East. Armstrong appeared to personify a new way – twenty-first century high-tech, the spirit of Silicon Valley that both infused and partially funded the US Postal team, given that it was where the team's main backer, Thom Weisel, had made his fortune.

Ullrich, meanwhile, embodied the antediluvian methods of a political and sporting system so backward-looking that it had fallen into ruin and scorn. The pedal strokes of the two riders were the animated mirror images not only of their respective approaches but the worlds from which they came: Armstrong fast, efficient, ruthless; Ullrich slow, ponderous, intransigent.

Ullrich's coach, Peter Becker, rolls his eyes at what he still sees as reductionism bordering on xenophobia. Rudy Pevenage has told me that Ullrich's low cadence 'was Peter Becker's way, the East German way'. Pevenage also claims 'everyone wanted Jan to change, except Becker'. But Becker says this is nonsense, and that he even encouraged Ullrich to mimic Armstrong – but was repeatedly ignored. In his 2004 autobiography, Ullrich himself writes about whole training sessions on his favourite Black Forest roads dedicated to learning 'spin' like Armstrong.[20] On some of them he even had his nemesis's old sidekick, Livingston, giving him tips. He also talks about Becker wanting him to alternate between climbing in and out of the saddle, to vary the muscle groups he was using and lessen fatigue. It was Ullrich who had quickly decided that neither technique was for him – the 90 rpm cadence because 'it made my heart rate shoot up and I was exhausted far too quickly', and the short bursts *en danseuse*, out of the saddle, because he thought that he could more easily maintain a steady, fast tempo sitting down. Ullrich believed he could kill Armstrong with consistent power. 'I didn't even want to attempt a compromise,' he wrote. 'A tennis player wouldn't switch from right- to left-handed midway through Wimbledon,' he said on another occasion.

Peter Becker's features crumple painfully at the mere mention of a subject that, to his mind, became a dog whistle used to turn critics against him. He points out that in 1996 and 1997 commentators had drooled over Ullrich's graceful, fluid pedalling motion – and they were the seasons at Telekom when Becker and Ullrich had collaborated most closely. Becker was an easy East German to stereotype – a sometimes gruff, steel-haired Berliner. But he was also his own man, not some brainwashed Socialist Party functionary. This is what Becker wants me to grasp.

There is something else Becker says we shouldn't overlook: that Ullrich rode the way he did partly not only out of stubbornness but also ego and sheer machismo. In his memoir of the years he spent coaching Tiger Woods, *The Big Miss*, Hank Haney argues compellingly that Woods's obsession with distance off the tee – another supposed badge of masculinity to go with the golfer's sudden fixation with retraining as a Navy SEAL – both hampered his game and caused the multiple injuries that have derailed his bid to surpass Jack Nicklaus's record of eighteen major championships.

Peter Becker tells me that similarly vain and virile impulses were driving and hampering Ullrich.

'I spoke with Ulli about the issue of his gears and his cadence. He simply wanted – this is what I firmly believe – to prove to himself and to others what gears he was capable of pushing. That was what motivated it, deep down. But, yes, he's got unbelievable power. He'd always been able to turn a gear over, but he didn't always do that before. Normally it's absolute poison for a rider. Then there was the issue of the delays in his preparation, and the fact that in the early season he would suddenly find himself riding with guys doing 100 or 110 revs per minute. There, you soon notice that it's a lot easier to stick with the group at 80 revs per minute. Sooner or later, though, a moment comes when you have to spin your legs, only you haven't trained that, so you go to an even bigger gear. That's one cause. The other is that stubbornness. One year I was with him at the Luk Cup in Bühl in southern Germany. It was all captured on camera: you see me turn around and walk away in disgust. I couldn't believe what I was seeing. How the hell can you go uphill in a gear like that? Not even a beginner does that. You can't ride a bike like that. But by that point he'd long since stopped listening to me.'

Upon hearing this, others would argue that turning inwards had simply become Ullrich's default martial art when he felt bombarded with often conflicting opinions. For the 2001 season, Godefroot, Pevenage, Ullrich's manager Wolfgang Strohband and the Telekom doctors at the University of Freiburg had doubled down on the 'baby-sitter system', which they had now even publicly given that name. A resolution was made: Ullrich must never be left to his own devices – or vices. By the time he competed for the first time in 2001 at the Vuelta a Murcia, he had clocked up 15,000 kilometres since his first training camp of the winter in December. He even looked relatively svelte, his trips to South Africa around Christmas having kept him at a safe distance from seasonal creature comforts like Gaby's mum's cakes and sausage soup.

Poor results in a fitness test at the University of Freiburg in March indicated, though, that appearances were deceiving. In interviews, he lapsed back into familiar old excuses and blandishments, exemplified by what he told journalist Hartmut Scherzer in April: 'I can lose five or six kilos in the blink of an eye. It's just like firing up an engine.' Meanwhile, Armstrong was trying to persuade the same reporters that he didn't have the opposite problem – that he hadn't found form too early, having roared into the spring with a second place at the Amstel Gold Race.

By the summer, Armstrong's agent would be bragging to *Texas Monthly* that his client could now charge double Bill Clinton's fee for keynote speeches – a further revenue stream to go with the $5 million a year Armstrong was now pocketing from endorsements and a 'basic' wage from US Postal creeping towards eight figures. Here, too, Ullrich was struggling to keep pace, for all that, at a press conference on 1 May in Frankfurt, he and Telekom announced that he would wear their colours at least until the end of 2003. His salary would also rise to around two million euros, placing him behind only Armstrong in cycling's league table of top earners. Earlier the same day, 1.5 million German fans had lined the route of the Rund Um den Henninger Turm, most of them to see Ullrich. In Ullrich's eyes, his 1997 Tour may have created unfair expectations, but business in German cycling was booming. The new president of the German Cycling Federation (BDR), Sylvia Schenk, said upon her election that a process had 'begun with Jan Ullrich . . . and [Germany] can now proudly call itself a cycling nation.' There was evidence of that wherever one looked: at the national tour, which had died in the mid-1980s amid court battles over who would pay for traffic policing, but was now bringing around seven million Germans to the roadside after its rebirth in 1999; the fact that Germany would suddenly have three elite professional teams in 2002, with Team Coast and Team Gerolsteiner both upscaling budget and ambitions; or at how the hours annually dedicated to bike racing by German television had spiked from 535 in 1994 to 1,060 in 1997 – and remained on the same high plateau.

The Pied Piper was Ullrich, yet he seemed barely able to look after himself, let alone the future of his sport in a country which had never allowed sporadic flirtations to mature into an enduring affinity for pro cycling. He had committed his future to Telekom while at the same time acknowledging that the 'babysitter system' had become suffocating – and counterproductive. 'There was always a doctor being sent to weigh me, or a training partner to check up on me,' he said later. As had already been the case in 1999, he felt both over-scrutinized and affronted by how little Telekom appeared to trust him. Walter Godefroot remembers, 'I used to go to the soigneurs' room and one of them, Dieter Ruthenberg, "Eule" as we called him, would be there massaging Jan. I'd have something to say to Jan but, when I spoke, he'd just turn to face the other way on the massage table and not say a word. Eule would whisper to me that I should just leave him in peace. Pressure was always the problem with Jan, even when no one was putting him under any.'

Fumbling for their annual quick fix, Ullrich and Telekom decided for the first time in his career that he should race in the Giro d'Italia in May. He would have no designs on overall victory. Instead, he would treat the three weeks as an extended training camp.

Things went serenely enough before the race paused for its one and only rest day in the Ligurian port of Sanremo. A few days earlier, the Italian drugs squad, the NAS, had already visited a number of hotel rooms just vacated by Giro riders in Montevarchi, finding numerous empty syringes and blister packs. Now they descended upon Sanremo to conduct a raid of extraordinary scale and shock value at the Hotel des Anglais, where Ullrich and Telekom were among the guests. Marco Pantani's Mercatone Uno team were in the same hotel – and soon agents would be foraging in the bushes and flowerbeds outside for a bag allegedly hidden there by Pantani's personal soigneur.

One member of the NAS didn't even need to look for evidence – a syringe hit him as it flew out of a bedroom window. A rider on the Tacconi Sport team, Giuseppe Di Grande, allegedly decided the safest way to dispose of incriminating material was not to throw the drugs into the garden but himself; Di Grande was intercepted just as he was getting airborne.

In 2004, Ullrich recalled what *La Gazzetta dello Sport* the next day described as 'The Giro's Darkest Night': 'Two officers began searching my room. In one cardboard box they made a discovery that clearly made quite an impression on them: an inhaler, a huge syringe and a yellow liquid. They immediately called two of their colleagues into the room to proudly show them what they'd found. Rudy Pevenage, who speaks Italian, explained to them that it was apparatus and medication for completely harmless inhalations that I needed every night because I was ill . . . The whole room was ransacked. Every bit of medication they found was noted down and confiscated. That included vitamin pills, antibiotics and two doses of cortisone. I wanted to tell them that I had a bad cold and needed these medicines but they weren't interested. I wanted to show them the certificate I've had since 1996, which allows me to take cortisone to treat symptoms of exercise-induced asthma. But they didn't want to see anything.'

In an interview a few days before the raid, Ullrich had advocated life bans for convicted dopers. Now, reports in Italian newspapers claimed that the NAS had needed four pages to itemize what they had found in his room, including salbutamol, theophylline, corticoids and various other drops, pills and pomades.

All told, the NAS had seized medicines from eighty-one riders and numerous team doctors, including Telekom's Lothar Heinrich. In Heinrich's room they found Pulmicort, a corticosteroid authorized with a medical certificate. There were also high-dose caffeine pills that Heinrich said had helped keep him awake on a flight to Europe from Florida.

Stage eighteen would finally be cancelled amid threats by the peloton that they would stop racing altogether. The following day, when the Giro did resume, the rider lying second on general classification, Dario Frigo, was sent home and fired by his team for attempting to dope with what he believed was synthetic haemoglobin but turned out to be distilled water.

Frigo's ejection infuriated Ullrich, he told *Der Spiegel*. He was also incensed that the NAS had confiscated the cortisone he was allowed to use to treat his asthma, per a therapeutic use exemption approved by the UCI.

The *Der Spiegel* interview was followed by another one, on television, with Germany's most popular sports programme, *Sportschau*. Hartmut Scherzer, a journalist who had covered cycling for German newspapers and agencies since the 1970s, watched it and cringed.

'Jan sort of corresponded to the Rostock stereotype,' Scherzer says. 'He didn't talk much, and he was insecure. He hated press conferences. Hated interviews. Anyway, there, Frigo was suspended and on the Saturday night, *Sportschau* had a live link-up to the hotel where Ullrich was and they interviewed him from Mainz. What did he think about Frigo, and the police, etcetera? I can remember his exact words: "All of those black sheep like Frigo should be suspended for life." I was in the hotel, sitting with Rudy Pevenage, and when Rudy heard this he put his head in his hands. Unfortunately, Jan doesn't think about what he's doing or saying. That's always been his problem. Plus, besides Rudy, no one was really looking after him.'

Ultimately, when in August the investigating magistrate in Florence opened proceedings against fifty-two individuals, Ullrich was not among them. Questions remained, like the legitimacy of Telekom spokesman Olaf Ludwig's claim Ullrich suffered from a pine-pollen allergy that had been well documented for years. Or who was right – the former Festina soigneur Willy Voet, who ridiculed the pollen-allergy alibi in an interview on German national TV, or Ullrich, who claimed that he was going to sue Voet. And, finally, why Heinrich had mentioned Kevin Livingston's asthma in interviews but not Ullrich's.

Months later, Ullrich's file would be reopened and passed to the German National Cycling Federation, who finally decided that neither he nor Heinrich had any case to answer. The UCI's medical commission agreed, thus officially quashing the idea that Ullrich had been using cortisone not to treat asthma but enhance his performance – and specifically to trim fat, which is among the drug's side effects. Anyway, as Telekom's Head of Communications, Jürgen Kindervater, had said after Sanremo, 'organized doping would be impossible at Telekom.'

Ullrich finished the Giro in a lowly fifty-second place but at least confident that the race had put him firmly on the right track for the Tour. He hoped now that 'The Tour passes off without doping' – something that, given what had occurred in Sanremo, seemed improbable. The start of the 2001 season had seen the long-awaited introduction of a test for EPO – and it had taken just four months to claim its first victim, the Dane Bo Hamburger. There would surely have been more, but the shadowy gurus who for years had been leveraging cycling's moral bankruptcy already had their clients well briefed.

Lance Armstrong, of course, knew the whole playbook. He spoke openly to teammates about the intricacies of the test and how to avoid getting caught. To that end, he had concocted a bulletproof plan of micro-dosing, time at altitude to boost the body's natural EPO production and muddle the test, and intravenous injections

with a small detection window. Or so Armstrong believed. Tyler
Hamilton first made the claim that Armstrong tested positive for EPO
in the 2001 Tour of Switzerland in his book, *The Secret Race*, then
repeated it to the United States Anti-Doping Agency years later.
According to Hamilton, Armstrong matter-of-factly informed him of
his positive test on the morning of the final stage in Switzerland.
Hamilton also claims Armstrong told him there would be no repercussions because his 'people had been in touch with the UCI'.
Another of Armstrong's US Postal teammates at the time, Floyd
Landis, has also alleged Armstrong spoke to him about 'paying off'
the UCI to cover up the positive test. The UCI strongly denied this,
although USADA did conclude, based on several sources, that Armstrong had indeed given a sample in Switzerland which, if not
sanctionable, was certainly suspicious. And he was definitely doping.

Armstrong doesn't disagree with that bottom line, though he
does tell me in 2015 that some reporting of the episode has left him
confused. 'I don't remember the Tour of Switzerland thing as it's
been described. It was the first year they were supposedly using this
test, and you had guys going, "Are they? Are they not? I don't think
they are . . ." And basically carrying on. Meanwhile, the UCI was
looking at the samples, going, "Oh fuck . . ." If you see a test result
there's a band going through the middle, like a music graph, and it's
where you put the band among the dots. They were still trying to
figure out where that band should go; I think they knew where they
thought it should go, but if they put it there, they have like fifty posi-
tives on their hands. So they're going, "Fuck, what are we going to
do?" So they're either adjusting the band or they're calling these guys
and telling them, "Hey, you've got to be careful." That call never
came to me, though. It might have gone to Johan . . .

'In any case,' he says finally, 'it didn't affect what we did.'

The final standings after ten stages in Switzerland said that Armstrong had stayed ahead of his competition and also the law. Or
above it. He looked in ominous form going into the Tour de France
but so, for once, did Ullrich. At the German national championships
in Bad Dürrheim, he powered away from Erik Zabel in the final two
kilometres to ensure that he would ride the Tour with the black, red
and gold colours of the German national flag across his chest, as he
had in 1997. After collecting his jersey on the podium, Ullrich had

jumped on his bike and ridden home to Merdingen – a 75-kilometre encore . . . after a 210-kilometre race.

At the Tour's team presentation in Dunkirk a few days later, his *sveltesse* didn't pass unnoticed. One of Armstrong's US Postal imperial guard, Christian Vande Velde, gulped. 'It was my first Tour, and I just was standing there, looking at his body, his legs, and I turned to George Hincapie and said, "Holy fuck, we're in trouble." I mean, his veins were like garden hoses. I said to George, "That guy is a fucking mutant. He's going to fucking kill us." I was speechless. And he was wearing leg warmers. You could see these veins through his leg warmers.'

Premiered in the 1952 edition, the first Tour to enjoy daily TV coverage, Alpe d'Huez is nowadays referred to as cycling's 'Hollywood' climb – and Ullrich and Armstrong were to star in the first blockbuster of the 2001 race on stage ten. Both men found themselves in unfamiliar positions, over thirteen minutes down on surprise *maillot jaune* François Simon. Two days earlier, in torrential rain and polar temperatures, Telekom and US Postal had engaged in a blinking contest on the road through the Jura mountains to Pontarlier, allowing a fourteen-man group including Simon to gain thirty-five minutes.

What occurred next has become a fabled chapter in the Tour's mythology. The widely accepted, oft-corroborated version goes that, after feigning weakness for much of the stage, Armstrong tore off his pain mask and committed an act of rare savagery on the lower slopes of Alpe d'Huez to win the stage and bury Ullrich. Worse, he looked over his shoulder and into Ullrich's eyes as he launched the attack. As though wanting a visual keepsake of the distress being inflicted – a souvenir of Ullrich's humiliation, a polaroid to allegorize their 'rivalry', a painting that would hang in his mental gallery like his own private, sanguinary Caravaggio.

'The Look', the image, the moment, was instantly christened.

Back in the smaller of the Hemelrijk restaurant's two dining rooms in Geraardsbergen, Rudy Pevenage is chewing on the first mouthfuls of his 'Américain' when I broach 2001 and Alpe d'Huez. The topic itself causes Pevenage a curious kind of indigestion, for to the ignominy of defeat, on this occasion, was added the embarrassment of being fooled – or at least of Armstrong having given that impression.

For this act of deception, Armstrong and US Postal didn't use drugs or blood – only the airwaves. Intercom radios. These devices had quickly become popular in professional cycling since their introduction by the team for which Armstrong rode in the early and mid-1990s, Motorola. Via matchbox-sized receivers tucked into jersey pockets and connected to two-way mics, riders and their directeurs sportifs could relay real-time information back and forth between the peloton and team cars, which were also equipped with TV monitors. Purists complained they had changed cycling for the worse, breeding a generation of 'radio-controlled' riders who showed no initiative. Less well known or hotly debated by the general public was the fact that some directeurs had become adept at 'hacking' the frequencies of rival teams' radios and eavesdropping on their tactics. As they were in most things, Bruyneel, Armstrong and US Postal had been in the vanguard of this form of espionage.

Telekom, a team sponsored by a telecommunications company with 50 billion euros turnover a year and with two stars, Erik Zabel and Jan Ullrich, raised under a regime that used to allocate $1 billion a year to spying on its own citizens, had been comparatively slow to cotton on.

Pevenage assures me that by 2001 and certainly at Alpe d'Huez, he was doing to Bruyneel, his nosy Geraardsbergen neighbour, what Bruyneel was doing to him. It had, though, taken the input of another wily operator, Vicente Belda of the Kelme team, to bring him up to speed.

'Maybe we were a bit naive,' he concedes. 'I found out what was happening at the 2000 Vuelta. Oscar Sevilla was one of the Kelme leaders, and I used to be quite friendly with Vicente Belda, their directeur sportif. In the stage to Albacete, there was a lot of wind, and Sevilla was competing for the overall. Belda was scared that the wind was going to split the race, so he came and asked whether we could help Sevilla. He said that, in return, he'd tell me a secret that I'd be able to use the following year at the Tour . . . So, at the start of the Tour in 2001, Belda gave me US Postal's frequency. I had no idea before that. But it worked, because after that I could hear Bruyneel.'

The satisfaction was short-lived, for Pevenage had sensed for a while that Bruyneel was onto Pevenage being onto him. Just as Telekom had recruited their man from behind enemy lines in Kevin

Livingston, US Postal had also mined the Telekom brain trust by signing up Ullrich's former mechanic, Jean-Marc Vandenberghe. Vandenberghe had kept a lot of his old contacts at Telekom, and Pevenage suspected news travelled quickly down that particular grapevine. Not that Bruyneel would have been surprised. 'You know that everyone's listening to everybody, and there's just no way around that,' he says. Which Armstrong echoes: 'Pevenage was listening, but we were listening to him. Every day. Every year . . . I assumed everyone was listening to everyone.'

In Bruyneel's pre-race briefing in Aix-les-Bains that morning, he at least hinted that it may be a good day to lay a trap that he and Armstrong had been plotting for some time. Armstrong would puff and pant, fake a 'pain face', Telekom would see and start making the pace – thus sparing US Postal some spade work. Then, Armstrong would strike.

'That day, there was one big climb, Madeleine, then another one, Glandon, and then Alpe d'Huez,' Armstrong remembers. 'So we get to the Madeleine – and this is me just being typical me, an egomaniac, because I'd won two Tours and I was feeling good – we get there, and I'm like, *If anyone's going to set the tempo on the climbs, it's us.* But we hit that climb and they go to the front . . .'

Armstrong frowns and cocks his head to one side, mimicking his reaction at the time.

'I'm like, *What? This is our Tour. Look at these motherfuckers. What are they thinking? This is my road. I say who sets the tempo . . .* And it was Kevin. Kevin, Klöden, just driving it for Telekom. So I'm thinking, *OK, what am I going to do? I've got an idea: I'm just going to fool them.* So I just stayed by the TV motorbike. I never stayed at the back; usually I'd be right on the front, right on the wheel. But this time I stayed at the back and, when I heard the motos coming, I'd give a little more of a grimace. And I knew they were listening, so I got on the radio and said, "Johan, something's wrong. I don't feel good. We've got two more climbs and I'm suffering." At this point, Johan doesn't know yet that I've gone with the bluff. Next thing, Johan hears Rudy on the radio. "Lance told Johan he's suffering. Give it more gas!"'

Here, Bruyneel's recollection of events and Armstrong's diverge. Bruyneel downplays the influence of whatever messages were being relayed on the radio waves, believing instead that Pevenage was fooled by Armstrong's repertoire of gulps, of grimaces on his dash-board TV screen. Regardless, it seemed to be working – as US Postal's Spanish climber, José Luis 'Chechu' Rubiera, confirmed to Bruyneel.

'Chechu was coming back a few times for bottles, and he was winking at me and telling me that Lance was super. Rudy didn't know. He thought Lance was bad. Otherwise why would Telekom have kept on riding?'

In his kitchen in Texas, Armstrong is fully re-immersing himself in the moment.

'So, yeah, then Johan comes on again, like, "What's happening?? Are you OK??!" I tell him I'm definitely not, that something's not right, so Rudy will hear. But then I drifted back and called the car, and [team owner Tom] Weisel was in there. He comes up and I wink at them. They're like, "What?" And I wink again. Then they knew that I was just fucking with them. Then it continued on the next climb. We had good guys – Rubiera, [Roberto] Heras – but those Spanish dudes didn't really speak much English, and my Spanish isn't great, but I made up this thing: "*Esperamos, miramos, decidimos, atacamos.*" – "We wait, we look, we decide and then we attack." I told them that and they loved that shit. Chechu was like, "What's this guy talking about?" And Heras just spoke no English. But they loved that shit.'

As Armstrong's bravado was reaching its zenith, so the perception of Ullrich and Telekom as his half-witted whipping boys was about to receive further corroboration. For what it is worth, Pevenage is still adamant that they didn't get fooled, telling me he was immediately suspicious of Armstrong's huffing and puffing, contrary to what some of his Telekom riders were telling him. 'We should have attacked before the Alpe,' he says. 'We knew that Lance was always going to be stronger than Jan on the Alpe. I knew that he was bluff-ing. What could we have done anyway? We rode to toughen up the race . . . Armstrong was just stronger. It's not true to say that we fell into his trap.'

Ullrich later also claimed the idea they'd been tricked was 'non-sense', while conceding that Livingston and Klöden had got carried away. At one point, another Telekom rider, Alexander Vinokourov, had gone back to the team car to get drinks and been forced into a breathless chase to deliver them, so hard were his teammates riding on the front. Vinokourov had hurled one of the bottles against a rock face in a fit of rage.

Then, within moments of Livingston leading the peloton onto the first ramps of the Alpe, it was time for the big reveal. Rubiera surged to the front and unleashed Armstrong from out of his slipstream, like a magician swishing back his silk. It was in this instant, before his murderous flourish, that Armstrong gave Ullrich 'The Look'.

His margin of victory was staggering – one minute and fifty-nine seconds over Ullrich, the result of having set the fifth fastest time ever for the 13.8-kilometre ascent of the Alpe. Ullrich was one of those who had gone quicker – by twenty-three seconds in 1997. But that was then, when Ullrich was two or three kilograms lighter and Armstrong was still recovering from cancer.

One Telekom rider who hadn't been impressed was the Italian domestique Giuseppe Guerini. 'What Armstrong did was a clown show,' Guerini says now. 'He took the piss out of us, out of the specta-tors and the whole of cycling.'

With the hubris long since faded and another mask having fallen, Armstrong sounds almost remorseful about the episode today. The idea that he set out not just to beat Ullrich but to crush and embar-rass him is one that causes him to squirm.

'The whole "Look" thing wasn't all that it was cracked up to be. It was a hot day, and I was good but not great, and Jan was good – or I thought he was good – and I was looking back thinking that, when this failed, I needed to get bailed out. I was looking to see who was going to bail me out.

'Anyway,' Armstrong continues, 'I would never have trash-talked Jan. Never. He was too kind and I liked him too much. I didn't really know him too much but I just liked him.'

I ask Armstrong whether his frequent praise of Ullrich wasn't also a mind game, a tactic to put him under pressure.

'No,' he says firmly. 'I didn't do that for anybody. If I praised someone, it was because I cared about them and respected them. I didn't praise anybody if I didn't mean it.'

That may be true, but, when he wasn't flattering his rival, Arm-strong could sound as frustrated with Ullrich as everyone else. As his former teammate Frankie Andreu says, 'Lance thrived on, lived off confrontation' – and there were times in the 2001 Tour when Arm-strong seemed to lust for a stiffer, fiercer test. Ullrich had prepared better than in 1998 and 2000, but was still falling short. Armstrong would go on to beat him by a minute at Chamrousse and drop him again in each of the next two stages in the Pyrenees. They then rode in side by side on the final mountain stage to Luz Ardiden, with Ullrich stretching out his hand as they crossed the line – he said to congratulate Armstrong and 'and thank him for the fair contest'. Armstrong obliged but truly it had been a mismatch. He thrashed Ullrich again in the final time trial in Saint-Amand-Montrond, on a course that Ullrich hadn't even bothered to recce in full. That night, to a gathering of journalists in the garden of his manor house hotel, Armstrong argued that it wasn't talent that had given him the edge over Ullrich – and it sure as hell wasn't doping. No, he said, the reporters and Ullrich should all ask themselves, 'Where was Jan Ullrich when I was here in April in the pissing rain, riding the time-trial course?'

For Armstrong, whose dangerous liaisons with Michele Ferrari had been revealed by David Walsh of the *Sunday Times* at the start of the Tour, Ullrich's laziness thus became an effective shield. Another one, like the cancer which had, he said at least, given him perspective and a community of sufferers and survivors he would never think of betraying.

Nowadays, he is less scathing of Ullrich's professionalism, perhaps because there are no more torch lights to deflect. Or maybe out of loyalty and affection.

'We didn't view [Telekom] as haphazard or amateurish,' he says. 'They may not have been as successful as us, but they didn't have a Johan and they didn't have a Ferrari. And, true, Jan wasn't me when it came to the details. We had Jan and Riis's old mechanic, Jean-Marc Vandenberghe, and he would say that the difference between me and Jan was that you could move my saddle a millimetre and I'd know instantly, whereas you could move Jan's a centimetre and he wouldn't know. Which is kind of cool. People like that. I even like that . . . but I just wasn't wired that way. So, yeah, we were a tighter outfit in that sense.

'Rudy was probably good on the road, I guess, but that's the last little piece,' Armstrong continues. 'You've got to get that crew, plan out their year, motivate them . . . Bruyneel was a thousand times better. Just so I'm on the record about this, Johan Bruyneel was the greatest coach in the history of sports. Yes. Fact. Based on how he

could motivate and inspire. He was smart, tactically very astute, and
he didn't just do it with me: he did it with Contador, with a bunch
of other guys later. He's just special. I know that's not going to be
popular but I don't care.

'So, no, going back to Jan, I would never say he didn't do anything with his talent, or that he wasted it. I would speak of him in
terms of how much I respected him, and how much potential he
had . . . Because it's purely potential. But that narrative as you
described it just became the narrative. That's what you guys took out
of it, that's what the public took out of it, and, you know, in those
situations, the guy who gets chunky in the winter, the guy who
doesn't live up to his potential and makes these mistakes that human
beings make, those ultimately endeared him to the people. He was
much more popular on the road than I was. But Poulidor was always
popular too – and he always finished second. And Merckx wasn't. So
there you go . . .'

Armstrong coasted into Paris with an advantage of nearly seven minutes over Ullrich on the overall standings and an even bigger margin
in a different competition. The Tour's photographers had awarded
him their annual Prix Citron, or Lemon Trophy, for the bitterest, most
obnoxious rider in the field. The presentation of a basket of lemons
was made on the final morning. Armstrong's reaction was acidic and
expletive-laden.

Jan Ullrich pondered his third runners-up finish in four Tours
over a glass or three of red wine on a boat on the River Seine. The
memorable, water-bound venue for their post-race party seemed
befitting of Telekom's fine Tour overall. The team's dedication to
Ullrich had not stopped Erik Zabel from claiming three stage wins
and his sixth green jersey. Ullrich had never truly threatened Armstrong but seemed reconciled, like Rudy Pevenage and Walter
Godefroot, to the American's invincibility, at least in this edition. The
Telekom bigwigs in Bonn were also satisfied. At a homecoming
reception at corporate HQ in Bonn a couple of days later, Telekom
board member Heinz Klinkhammer introduced Ullrich as 'not the
first loser of the Tour but the second winner'. All present responded
with rapturous applause.

Klinkhammer's plaudits echoed Ullrich's own feelings about how
he had performed. For the first time in years he had finished a Tour

free of regret. He had overcome the travails of his early spring and Armstrong's comments in Saint-Amand-Montrond seemed not to have shaken his own belief that his way was the right way – at least for him. Besides, Armstrong might well ask where he was in April, but Ullrich could equally turn the question around and ask where Armstrong had disappeared to in August. The answer was a schmooze-cruise of American talk shows, receptions and festivities, followed by a long holiday. Meanwhile, Ullrich took his post-Tour form into a series of lesser races and demonstrated what cycling would look like without Armstrong. Which is to say, with Ullrich ruling the world.

After his world championship time trial victory in Treviso in 1999, two years on, he targeted a historic double in Lisbon – victory in both the time trial and the road race. Ullrich had been the first German to complete the first half of the 'rainbow slam', and now he hoped to end a thirty-five-year road-race drought since Rudi Altig's victory on the Nürburgring.

He would justify his pre-race favourite's billing by winning the time trial, but the margin of victory over Britain's David Millar was gossamer thin – a mere six seconds. Many in the German camp already had visions of Ullrich uncorking champagne on Sunday night. But fears that he needed a tougher test than the Lisbon course proved well-founded. Terrorized by his performances in hilly one-day races like the Championship of Zürich and Giro dell'Emilia in August and September, rival teams now built their entire game plan around thwarting Ullrich – and ultimately succeeded despite his three thunderous attacks. This left Erik Zabel to forage for crumbs of consolation for the German team, but Zabel could only manage fifth in the bunch sprint won by Oscar Freire. Walter Godefroot, for one, was unimpressed. 'Jan goes on the climb but doesn't get enough of a gap, then he doesn't bother leading Erik out in the sprint. If he had, Erik would be world champion.'

Regardless, Ullrich was signing off for 2001 and doing so with a telling closing remark: 'I have no desire to keep finishing second in the Tour de France.' For all that the season had ended with another Indian summer, apparently being labelled as a perennial nearly man or, worse, loser had begun to grind Ullrich down.

Too few sympathized, but among those who did was Ullrich's first cycling hero, Greg LeMond. The two hadn't met, and indeed the

three-time American Tour champion had got to know Ullrich the
same way that Ullrich had got to know him – by admiring him
through a TV screen. LeMond had drifted away from professional
cycling after his retirement in 1994, disillusioned by what he
believed was the sport's escalating EPO problem. He had been back
in the news in the summer of 2001 – but that, too, was to do with
drugs or his suspicions about who was using them. LeMond's
response to the revelation by *Sunday Times* journalist David Walsh
that Armstrong was being coached by Michele Ferrari had read – and
perhaps been intended – as the pre-emptive epitaph for Armstrong's
career: 'If Lance's story is true, it's the greatest comeback in the history of sports. If it's not, it's the greatest fraud.'

These sentiments had started a war with Armstrong. Parallel to
that, LeMond also found himself feeling for Ullrich. LeMond had
heard many of the same judgements now levelled at Ullrich when,
in the dying embers of his own career, he was struggling to keep up
with a turbo-charged peloton. 'I can only imagine his frustration at
not being able to win again after 1997,' LeMond told me some years
later. 'There's always a human side to this, as well; he was a kid from
East Germany, with a different background. People were calling him
a fat pig, lazy, criticizing him, and I can only imagine how it felt to
him. He was finishing second in the biggest bike race in the world
yet it still wasn't good enough for anyone.'

Jens Heppner, Ullrich's friend and mentor at Telekom, had witnessed Ullrich's first, lopsided duels with Armstrong at much closer
quarters. Heppner now thinks that 2001 marked a watershed – or at
least the beginnings of hope's decay into resignation, of Ullrich's
already fragile passion paling into apathy. Heppner thinks it might
even have been the beginning of the end.

'I think at a certain point, maybe around that time, he lost his
love for cycling. Everyone had said here's this massive talent who's
going to win the Tour seven or eight times, then Armstrong appears
out of nowhere – and we knew Armstrong before; he was good going
uphill for five kilometres and no more. But now suddenly he's so
superior. Jan's problem then was that the idea that he should be winning somehow persisted, and yet he knew implicitly that he had
absolutely no chance. Zero. There was that contradiction. Yet the
journalists wanted to know why, how come he was only finishing
second again. He would say that Armstrong was just better, but at

the same time something didn't quite add up. That was where I think he stopped enjoying it.

'The problem wasn't so much that Armstrong had come back or how he'd done it. It was the air from Armstrong that "I'm the best and you're nothing." That was the aura he gave off to everyone. And Jan felt it.'

14

LOVE AND OTHER DRUGS

'One of the most famous people in Germany was walking
alongside me, a millionaire, and yet he was helpless'

—*Sylvia Schenk*

Telekom had finished the 2001 season as the 'best team in the world'
according to Walter Godefroot (the official rankings placed them
behind Fassa Bortolo) and the venue for their annual post-Christmas
training camp was also one for social climbers. The one star who
owned a villa over the road from the Dorint golf resort on Mallorca's
south-west coast, Claudia Schiffer, arguably said even more about
the prestige of where Telekom had made their base than the five on
the wrought-iron gate.

Godefroot, though, had other things on his mind besides the
valet service and fluffy towels. The Telekom boss was giving himself
a guided tour of the spa one day when he wandered into the gym
and saw something alarming. 'I come into the gym and Jan's not
gone training but there he is lifting heavy weights,' he remembers. 'I
say to myself, *Well, I'm not a coach, but that can't be good for him*. No
one on the team could push the weights that Jan did. I called everyone together – Doctor Heinrich, [Ullrich's masseur] Eule, Becker and
Rudy – and asked them whether they approved. I'm paying a doctor,
a coach and a soigneur yet there's Jan doing whatever the hell he
wants. It's not normal . . . I tell Rudy we have to talk to Jan but Rudy
says that we mustn't say anything because Jan's already threatening
to retire. It was the same with his food: people would be watching

him stuffing his face and they'd say nothing. Not Kindervater, not Becker, not Strohband, not Rudy. No one. I'm the only one – and even I don't say much.'

In South Africa before Christmas, Peter Becker had surprised Ullrich by reading him a letter he had penned a few weeks earlier, less a message than an oath, a manifesto for how, together, he and Ullrich would finally defeat Lance Armstrong at the Tour de France. Ullrich's main takeaway from South Africa, though, had been a stubborn pain in his right knee. Rumours later circulated that Ullrich had forgotten to pack his shoes, and that a new or borrowed pair had caused a painful misalignment further up his leg. Later, in his autobiography, Ullrich said only that he had felt good on the first day on the Cape and had ended up extending what was supposed to be a gentle limb-loosener ride to a full 120 kilometres. The following day he began to feel discomfort after a couple of hours. Then, on ride number three, the pain was so acute that Ullrich couldn't go more than half an hour without pausing on the side of the road. Finally, he was able to clock up around 2,000 kilometres for the whole trip, but only thanks to painkilling injections that he would later regret.

Those treatments allowed him to soft-tap through training rides at Telekom's Mallorca training camp and even to compete at the Tour of Qatar at the end of January. But the pain returned on a second trip to South Africa in early February, with scans showing inflammation in the tendons of the right knee. He returned early to Germany and underwent further tests in Freiburg. They confirmed that the knee had been damaged, overstressed. The only remedy would be rest and recovery.

Yet again, for the fifth year in a row, Ullrich's first race of the season was against the calendar. Each attempt to resume training was followed shortly afterwards by another enforced break, a further summons to Freiburg, more tests and another delay. Finally it was decided that the only way to break the pattern was for Ullrich to commit to three weeks of in-patient rehab at a clinic in Badenweiler, the Black Forest spa town where Anton Chekhov died in 1904, famously toasting the moment with a glass of champagne.

While present days consisted of aqua-jogging and physiotherapy, Ullrich's past excesses were again on the agenda as the court of Ullrich met for crisis talks. And, by excesses, Ullrich's coaches and doctors meant on the bike as well as off it – specifically his penchant for turning huge gears. Team doctors Lothar Heinrich and Andreas Schmid put it to Ullrich that pushing huge loads while he was overweight created a double jeopardy for which he was now paying the price. Peter Becker nodded in agreement. 'It was the usual business of, "I'm going to do it and I'll show everyone." And he ruined his knee with that bullshit,' Becker says now.

Nevertheless, when the inflammation visible on the earlier scans had disappeared, Becker would be driving from Berlin to Merdingen as he had done countless times before to take up temporary residence in the guest house belonging to Ullrich's friend, Erich Keller. This one, though, would be different from the training binges that Becker had overseen before; an old acquaintance from Becker's SV Dynamo days, the track sprinter, Eyk Pokorny, helped him to turn Ullrich's garage into an altitude chamber, where Ullrich would be able to train at high aerobic intensities while spinning small gears.

Ullrich now spent mornings on the indoor trainer, wheezing on oxygen-starved air, and afternoons on the Black Forest roads, with Becker observing from his car. So it went until 29 April, when Becker had to leave Merdingen and return to Berlin for his wife's birthday. And left Ullrich with the warning: 'Nothing stupid while I'm gone.'

The next morning, Ullrich woke as usual, trained for three hours on his indoor trainer, as usual, then met with Andreas Klöden for what was supposed to be a leisurely ride through the vineyards encircling Merdingen. Rainclouds had huddled in the valley but Ullrich announced that they would simply ride through them, past them, over them – whatever it took to clock up kilometres. They started slowly but as the second hour became the third and the third the fourth, Klöden noticed that Ullrich was picking up the pace – until Klöden was corkscrewing out of his slipstream. They were around 20 kilometres from home, now flying down the Rhine Valley, when suddenly Ullrich felt the familiar stabbing pain in his right knee. A couple of hours later, Lothar Heinrich arrived at Ullrich's house for a routine progress check – and Ullrich said nothing, even when Heinrich began to download the data off Ullrich's power meter onto his laptop and the doctor's posture stiffened. At first Heinrich thought one or the other device must be broken. Ullrich told him that, no, he had 'felt just great' and his knee was 'absolutely fine'. Which were lies.

The following day, Becker was back behind the wheel, back

behind Ullrich and Klöden as they rode towards the Glottertal, the valley north-west of Freiburg which acts as a gateway to the best cycling routes in the Black Forest. 'Look out, Klödi. I've had enough,' Ullrich announced at one point. 'I'm going to ride to the Glottertal, up this mountain, as hard and fast as I can. Either the knee holds together or it smashes to pieces.'

It was, Ullrich admitted later, 'total madness'.

They hadn't got far before Klöden was again struggling to hold the wheel and Becker was pulling alongside Ullrich with his window down, screaming at him to slow down. Soon Becker was barking at Ullrich to get off his bike and into Becker's car, which headed straight for the university clinic in Freiburg.

Ullrich could generally count on a more sympathetic audience from Andreas Schmid, but the doctor did the necessary scans and now also reviewed the data from Ullrich's power meter that had troubled Lothar Heinrich. Schmid told Ullrich that the previous day's session had been equivalent to a Tour de France stage.

Schmid promptly made an appointment for Ullrich to see one of Germany's leading knee specialists, Albert Güßbacher, at his clinic in Bavaria the following morning. Meanwhile, Ullrich decided to console himself with a night out in Freiburg with Eyk Pokorny, the track sprinter who had installed Ullrich's altitude chamber a few weeks earlier.

By the end of their meal, Ullrich and Pokorny had dispatched three bottles of wine, after which they headed to one of Ullrich's frequent haunts, Kagan, and drank more. It was gone three in the morning and they were finally about to head home when, on the way to their cars, the pair got chatting to two girls. Minutes later one of the new acquaintances found herself in the passenger seat of Ullrich's Porsche as he pulled out, wheelspun into a U-turn, misjudged speed and angles and smashed into a bike rack. The scene was witnessed by too many people for Ullrich to count and also too many for him not to be recognized. No sooner had he turned down a side street and got out to inspect the damage than police were approaching.

Having for a moment considered using Pokorny's name, Ullrich finally gave his own – and even had to hitch up his trousers to show the police his legs and prove he really was *the* Jan Ullrich, the cyclist. He then blew into a breathalyser. The reading was 1.4 milligrams of alcohol per millilitre of blood – almost three times the legal limit.

Ullrich would end up losing his driving licence for nine months. It had been coming: a few months earlier he had burst a tyre on the autobahn while doing over 250 kph. Now he was in danger of losing something more valuable than a car – his relationship with his partner of seven years, Gaby. The fact that another woman had at least a walk-on part in his nocturnal escapade made it even harder to explain away. Whatever soul-searching Ullrich did privately would be followed by another mea culpa in his autobiography a couple of years later: 'In the first part of the year I'd been far too wrapped up in myself to realize how much I was hurting Gaby. I could have saved myself a lot of trouble if I'd been a bit more attentive. Gaby realized much more quickly and clearly than me that something was going very wrong in my life.'[21]

Peter Becker had got a call from Gaby at around about the time he and Ullrich should have been leaving for their appointment with Albert Güßbacher. He was angry with Ullrich but furious at Pokorny, telling him he was a 'hobo'. Becker still becomes animated when the incident is mentioned now. 'Ulli betrayed himself, he betrayed me and everyone else. I told him, "Right, now there are going to be some consequences. First, you call your manager and he can sort this whole thing out." And he said: "What do you mean? Nothing's happened. No one knows about it." The naivety. He thought it was no big deal!

'How far is he really aware of his responsibilities, and where's his social conscience? I can see one cause for it and I'm partly to blame – for him winning the DDR road race championships at such a young age, fourteen going on fifteen, and, later, also winning the Tour de France so young. His development, morally and socially, is out of proportion with his success. That's one cause. He hasn't understood who he is in the world and he wasn't ready to step forward and really give something of himself. In interviews it was always: "OK, mate, bye." He has to work on his image.'

Becker's choice of words alone – the talk of 'social conscience', 'giving something of oneself' and 'social development' – carries faint echoes of one of the seminal documents of the DDR, 'The Ten Commandments for the New Socialist Personality'. These edicts came from Party Secretary Walter Ulbricht himself, and were diffused not only through the media but also on concertina-shaped cards with which DDR citizens were called to adorn their mantelpieces. The

Ullrichs may not have even had or displayed one of the leaflets in their living room – but, at least for a while, they were beholden to a patriarchal figure, Werner Ullrich, whose violent tendencies and alcoholism may have had a significant influence on the personalities of a fledgling family. Becker may, then, be underestimating how many of Ullrich's problems had their root in his DNA, or in the neural rewiring caused by early traumas. Ullrich's mother confided at the time of the drink-driving charge that her son's most recent antics reminded her of his father. Ullrich admitted that this also crossed his mind when he went to Rostock to 'surprise' Marianne two weeks after the Freiburg incident. Perhaps jolted by Gaby's admonishments, he decided that his impromptu visit should be followed by a second, bigger gift: the promise to buy – or build – his mother a house in Papendorf, the village outside Rostock where they had spent the happiest years of Jan's youth.

As some serenity returned to his private life, professionally the outlook remained somewhat bleaker. At his manager Wolfgang Strohband's urging, Ullrich turned to the knee specialist Bernd Kabelka, whose client list included tennis stars Pete Sampras and Ivan Lendl and world-famous boxers Vladimir and Vitali Klitschko. Kabelka told Ullrich he needed an operation to remove an inflamed fold, or 'plica', in the tissue lining his right knee – and a few days later carried out the surgery. Doctor Lothar Heinrich was present at the operation but sceptical as to whether it was the best course of action, not least because none of the other experts who had seen scans of Ullrich's knee – 'all manner of doctors, therapists and even dubious alternative healers,' as Ullrich put it later – had mentioned the plica. Ullrich had also initially consulted Kabelka without Heinrich's and Andreas Schmid's permission.

Kabelka declared the operation a success, but there would be no miracle. Ullrich promptly announced that he would now miss the Tour de France at a press conference in Umkirch bei Freiburg, a few minutes' drive from his house and even closer to the spot where his Porsche had obliterated a bike rack. Soon he'd be checking into a lakeside Bavarian clinic owned by a multi-millionaire friend for residential rehab. Bad Wiessee is infamous in German history as the scene of key events in 'The Night of the Long Knives' – Hitler's 1934 purge on the Nazi's own SA and the execution of their leader, Ernst Röhm. The resort is also known and prized for its idyllic setting on the Tegernsee lake, in the heart of the Bavarian Alps – and for its proximity to central Munich.

Which, for Jan Ullrich, would quickly become synonymous with temptation.

Possibly because Telekom had also begun sponsoring Bayern Munich's football club, word of Ullrich's newly flourishing social life and frequent visits to some of Bayern's players habitual nightspots would quickly get back to Telekom HQ in Bonn. Jürgen Kindervater travelled to Bad Wiessee to issue a gentle call to order. It did not have the desired effect, for a few days later, Ullrich was spotted in the early hours in the company of an unidentified blonde and a vodka and Red Bull at Munich's Milch Bar nightclub.

Tabloid reporters speculated later that this could even have been when and where it had happened. Or it could equally have been the following night. *It* was Ullrich swallowing two white pills given to him by a friend he has never publicly named, to 'make him feel better'. And *it* would have disastrous consequences.

At the time, Ullrich felt nothing. No euphoria, no hallucinations – just numb anti-climax. He wouldn't even say where it had happened, either because he wasn't sure or to protect one of the venues where he partied that night, Pasha, whose proud door policy had given rise to a slogan: 'Music is the only drug'. Ultimately, the wheres also didn't matter, not to him. Ullrich knew for a fact that he had returned to Bad Wiessee some time around dawn, fallen asleep, then been woken at around noon the following day by a knock and a voice: 'National Anti-Doping Agency, Mr Ullrich.' When he opened the door, he was greeted by an unfamiliar face – not the guy the agency 'usually' sent. When Wolfgang Strohband heard this later, he became suspicious. 'We also always said someone must be with him when he got tested. But that day it was just him,' Strohband says.

Woozily, Ullrich asked whether or why he still qualified for testing given that he probably wouldn't race again before 2003. But the tester seemed nice enough and, having complied with protocol, Ullrich even sent him away with an autograph.

It would be seven days before consequence caught up with action. First there was a text message from Lothar Heinrich with the instruction to call him immediately. Then, when Ullrich did, Heinrich ordered him to get to Freiburg as soon as possible. Why, Heinrich wouldn't say.

The next morning he told Ullrich, 'Jan, we have bad news. You've got a positive test. There were traces of amphetamine in your urine.'

It had been one week since the fateful night in Munich and it would be one more before the news was made public. Ullrich assured Heinrich and Schmid that he had no idea what had happened, whether something he'd eaten or taken could have been contaminated. It finally dawned just as he and Gaby pulled into their drive in Merdingen: the two pills he had taken in Munich. He immediately called the friend who had supplied them, demanded to know what they were and wrote the name on a note. Four letters: MDMA. Ecstasy, amphetamine – it all added up to the same cataclysmic outcome. People would hear 'drugs' and think doping, he told Gaby. The only way out was to say that his knee had forced him to retire. She told him not to be ridiculous.

But nothing was off the table as long as only a handful of people knew. The new German Cycling Federation (BDR) president, Sylvia Schenk, was one of them. By chance, the German national championships were taking place that weekend in Bühl, not far from Merdingen, and Schenk was due to attend. She and Ullrich agreed to meet on the day of the race at a service station just off the Number 5 Autobahn.

In her first few months in the job, the cosiness of Telekom's relationship with the BDR had alarmed Schenk. She had competed for West Germany in the 800 metres at the 1972 Olympics before building a successful career as a lawyer and politician and also a reputation for uncompromising integrity. In a world more accustomed to tracksuits than trouser suits and where the only academics were men wielding syringes, Schenk's clipped tones and businesslike demeanour had immediately marked her out from the rank and file. When I meet her in Berlin in 2016, she describes her immersion in cycling's arcane social norms and idiosyncrasies as 'a culture shock'. She points to the fact that Olaf Ludwig managed a Telekom feeder squad and performed PR duties for the main team while simultaneously sitting on the BDR board and working as the German national team selector. She had finally reconciled herself to the fact that, whatever the conflicts of interest, Telekom's success had elevated the entire German cycling movement – and their influence still dwarfed all others. To her regret, Schenk had realized 'you cannot operate in the same way in sport and anti-corruption.'

She would demonstrate this new pragmatism by showing Ullrich her human touch. She suggested that Wolfgang Strohband wait at the service station while she and Ullrich went for a walk. She had decided that she would be sympathetic but not blur lines. Hence she made a point of calling Ullrich 'Sie', the polite German form of 'you', and not 'du', the more informal register that in cycling was also the common parlance.

'There were meadows behind the service station so we just left Strohband and walked for about forty-five minutes in the fields,' Schenk remembers. 'I asked Jan what he was thinking about it and he said, "Well, I'd better retire." At that time, of course, it wasn't in the public domain yet. Only about five people knew. So he said this and my reply was, "OK, well, what will you do for the next three months, then the next three years? Because you know cycling and nothing else." My view was that he had to go public with it, say he'd made a mistake. Then I talked to Strohband – we had a coffee in the service station, all of us together – and I said that he mustn't stop cycling and not say anything. That would be crazy. They were suggesting that one way out was to say that it was his knee and he simply couldn't ride any more. They finally agreed with me and the following day Olaf Ludwig, who was on our board, convinced Jürgen Kindervater. We were going to prepare for the announcement by making calls to all of our regional committees, some sponsors and journalists, just telling them what was going to happen and to be ready for it. This was the Monday, I think. Then, on the Wednesday, we found out that *Bild Zeitung* knew, so we had three or four hours to make all the calls and brief everyone.'

On her drive home from the Black Forest, Schenk had been able to reflect on Ullrich and his predicament. Lothar Heinrich had told her that he and Andreas Schmid were already worried before the positive test when they could barely get hold of him in Bad Wiessee. He had looked to her, too, like someone for whom it was all too much – especially now.

'To me, him saying that he wanted to quit was just him running away and not wanting to take responsibility,' Schenk says. 'Generally, he was not someone who was really thinking about things in great detail, I would say. He was always surrounded by people telling him what to do. We had one situation where he won the time trial in Lisbon the year before. I had a meeting that day for the UCI management committee, and when I came into the hotel they were celebrating the title. Jan had a finger of red wine in his glass, then he ordered a second glass. Everyone was there: Kindervater, the German national under-23 coach Peter Weibel, everyone. And no one said anything, except me. I said, "Er, do you really think you should be having another glass?" But he didn't think it was an issue and neither did anyone else. I think it was kind of the same thing with him putting on weight. In 2002, after the positive test, I had a phone conversation with Strohband. I told him I thought Jan had an eating disorder. Strohband asked me what an eating disorder was. I explained it to him, then said that, from my perspective, what was happening with Jan was more than just the usual weight gain that most athletes experienced in the winter. It sounded to me more like an addiction.

'But on that day in Bühl, I was thinking to myself that one of the most famous people in Germany was walking alongside me, a millionaire, and yet he was helpless. Totally helpless. He didn't know how to manage himself or the situation.'

Ullrich could at least count on the support of his employer. His problem was also Telekom's and, in particular, Jürgen Kindervater's. For over a decade, this fifty-seven-year-old from the Harz mountains in the centre of Germany had been the company's fire fighter extraordinaire.

Kindervater now swung into action by instructing Ullrich to leave Merdingen and head towards Kufstein, just beyond the Austrian border, where he would be met by a representative of another sponsor, Adidas. Gaby, naturally, would have to drive, since Ullrich was banned.

The Adidas intermediary, Otto Wiedemann, met Ullrich and Gaby at a petrol station at the border and told them to follow him to their destination – an alpine guesthouse at the foot of the Hintertux glacier, 1,500 metres above sea level in the Tyrolean Alps. They would end up staying there for three days, with Ullrich only ever leaving their room well after the sun had dipped below the encircling peaks. Daylight hours were spent pacing around his room, on the phone to Wolfgang Strohband, his lawyers or Kindervater. Between them, they agreed that Ullrich would comment on what was already three-day-old news at a press conference in Frankfurt on Saturday 6 July.

So it was that, mere hours before Lance Armstrong began his defence of the Tour de France in Luxembourg, and less than three hours' drive from the start line, Jan Ullrich finally came out of hiding. He sat flanked by Sylvia Schenk, Olaf Ludwig and the director of Bad Wiessee clinic, Hubert Hörterer. The underarms of Ullrich's grey Telekom polo shirt were soaked in sweat from the moment he took off his leather jacket.

'*Eine Dummheit*' – 'an act of stupidity' – was what it had been. Ullrich explained that he had been in a kind of crisis due to his knee injury and looking for distractions, some relief, anything to lift his *Weltschmerz*, his melancholy. It wasn't doping and neither did he have a drug or alcohol problem. Telekom had suspended him pending the outcome of disciplinary proceedings, which he considered 'perfectly justified'. Whatever happened, whatever he'd felt and said to his inner circle in the initial panic, Ullrich 'didn't want to finish his career like this'.

Jürgen Kindervater stood at the back of the room, tense and watchful. A few days earlier he had told journalists that Ullrich's was a 'human tragedy', perhaps hoping to drum up sympathy or hinting that Ullrich's issues were deeper than some imagined.

Meanwhile conspiracy theories flourished. One went that Telekom were fed up with Ullrich and wanted him off the books. Had they arranged for someone to slip Ullrich the pills and for the dope test the next day? It seemed unlikely, given Kindervater's repeated pronouncements about helping him out of the mire. Sylvia Schenk is also sceptical. 'In cycling at that time, I think everything was possible so I have no idea. But the doctors really took care of him, so I think it's unlikely.'

If Ullrich felt betrayed by anyone, Schenk says, it was by her and the German Cycling Federation. On 23 July, the BDR's disciplinary commission announced that he would receive a six-month ban, bumped to seven to account for the off-season, and be eligible to race again on 23 March 2003. Ullrich wrote in his autobiography that, although he hoped not to be banned, he found the punishment 'fair'. But a mutual acquaintance later told Schenk otherwise. 'Someone told me that Jan was angry with me because he expected not to be punished.'

By the time he learned of his sentence, Jan Ullrich was already living in therapeutic exile on the other side of the world. Officially, the contract between Telekom and Ullrich that ran to the end of 2003 had been voided by his positive test, but Telekom had made good on a verbal promise not to 'drop him like a hot potato'. They wondered whether a period of mutual 'cooling off' might be followed by a resumption of the relationship with different results. To that end, they came up with a plan to take him out of the fire.

Bob Stapleton had become a member of the Telekom 'family' by selling them his VoiceStream Wireless company for nearly $50 billion in 2000. One day, the softly spoken, hard-bargaining Californian businessman would take over Telekom's cycling team and oversee Jan Ullrich's sacking on his first afternoon in charge.

In July 2002, though, Stapleton was given the unlikely brief of Samaritan and travel agent.

'I'd first come across Jan in 2001, when our deal had just gone through and Telekom invited us to the Tour,' Stapleton explains. 'It was the day Armstrong bluffed at Alpe d'Huez. There were two Americans, the CEO Don Guthrie and me, and these forty German VIPs in hospitality, and they're all cheering when Lance is dropping back. Then the tables turn and Don and I are cheering, but we look behind us and it's like a funeral. We're thinking, *We'd better sit down here.*

'Later, we're invited into the room where the team was having dinner. I was just so shocked at how beaten to shit Jan was, frankly. He was eating – I'll never forget it – a bowl of simple pasta and, next to it, a long, tall glass, like a sundae glass, full of muesli, with warm water, not milk in it. I was thinking, man, this is one disciplined operation. Anyway, we met him briefly, and he's a very likeable guy. Very sympathetic, very empathetic. He can really connect to people, even without the vocabulary. Such a contrast to Lance in that people really liked him. An everyman guy. Liked his beer, liked his food – he had normal guy problems . . . whereas Lance, from my impression, unlikeable from the start. Super aggressive, paranoid, and you couldn't feel at ease around him. They couldn't have been more different in their emotional presentation. My wife is a great barometer – and she took an instant dislike to Lance. I met him for the first time at an event in California years later. We'd just bought this tiny puppy and we took it down with us. My wife is in the hotel with this puppy, and Lance just glares at her, like, *What the fuck are you doing with a dog in my hotel?* I mean, it was kind of a strange reaction to a cute little puppy.'

Stapleton digresses. Back to 2002 . . .

'Yes, so one of the guys in Germany just called me up and said, "We need to get Jan out of this environment, to somewhere where he can really focus on himself. He'd really like to go to the US. Have you got any ideas?" I just whipped up a spreadsheet of kind of nice places to go where no one would know him – places like Whistler. They got the list then said they wanted to discuss it on a call. So they set up this conference call, with, like, twenty people online, and I start to go through the options for them. I get to Whistler and they say, "Yes! Canada! Jan wants to go to Whistler!" So that's what happened.'

Memories return to Stapleton in flickers – of him picking Ullrich and Gaby up at the airport, of Jan giddily interrogating Stapleton about the capabilities of his Audi sportscar, of Gaby being 'very together, quite impressive', and of their dinner that night at Snoqualmie Falls Lodge, a famous filming location for the cult US drama *Twin Peaks*.

'I think they ended up staying in Whistler for over a month,' Stapleton goes on. 'People just kept arriving. It became this big posse, this whole entourage. I think they had a couple of motivational people come in to try and rebuild his psyche. But who knows what was going on up there. A big party. The guy from Adidas [Otto Wiedemann] was super intense. He was hammering away at all of Jan's defects, like this tough love, sports psychology spiel . . . It was clear from the reports I got later that it wasn't much of a therapeutic experience.'

The financial cost of the *Dummheit* would soon begin to bite, but initially in Canada all Ullrich had wanted to do was to drown his sorrows. His first night in exile was toasted with a bottle of 1982 Château Haut-Brion – a wine for 'people with fuck-you money', as the wine collection expert Maureen Downey puts it in the documentary *Sour Grapes*. Ullrich kept the label as a souvenir. He decorated it with a signature, the date and a battle cry: 'Now we go again!'

Back in Germany, reporters scrambled to reveal his location, but Ullrich, Stapleton and Telekom had outfoxed them. *Bild* claimed he was in the Caribbean, even offering photo evidence, but the picture was from a previous holiday. Other newspapers reported that he was in Florida. Meanwhile, Telekom were enduring a wretched Tour de France. The conspicuous lack of success, even from the usually reliable Erik Zabel, increased both the frequency and pertinence of questions about Ullrich's future. 'I don't even know if Jan is still bike rider,' Walter Godefroot snapped one day.

The reality was that, in Canada, Ullrich was slowly rediscovering a lust for his old life. Or some of it. Never an early riser, he made a daily exception to tune in to live broadcasts from France and the Tour. Afternoons were spent walking through the forest with Gaby, mountain-biking or riding a tandem with Otto Wiedemann. Walter Möbius, a newly retired doctor who counted former German chancellor Helmut Kohl among his patients, had been hand-picked by Jürgen Kindervater to help restore not only Ullrich's knee but also his spirit. On both fronts, things were looking up.

Gaby, too, was seeing the old Jan re-emerge. After months of unreturned calls and dubious new acquaintances, he was becoming attentive and sensible once more. On one of their walks, she confronted him about his drinking and he promised to change. She also asked him whether he would consider becoming a father. He responded without hesitation, in the affirmative.[22]

On reflection, in the late summer of 1997, there had been one better gauge of Jan Ullrich's standing in the national sporting pantheon than *Der Spiegel*'s poll ordaining him as the greatest ever. It had come not in the form of a vote, a trophy or accolade, but a meeting that took place in the head office of a company whose name had been, since its creation in 1924, a byword for German sporting royalty: Adidas.

From Steffi Graf to Franz Beckenbauer and the German football team, nearly all of the true greats had been as synonymous with the famous 'three stripes' of their Bavarian apparel supplier as they were with the black, red and yellow bands of the *Flagge Deutschlands*.

Having single-handedly awoken Germany's passion for cycling and the Tour de France, Jan Ullrich, naturally, had to be inducted into the kingdom.

'After the Tour in 1997 we were invited to Munich,' Wolfgang Strohband remembers. 'I was there having my meeting with the head of sponsorship when Robert Louis-Dreyfus, the CEO of the company, suddenly came in. He said, "Hello, what are you talking about here then?" So I, half jokingly, told him, "A new contract . . . and I'd really like five years." His reply was that I should go away for a while so that he could talk to the head of department. I came back a couple of hours later and Dreyfus said to me, "Listen, we don't want five years. We'll make it ten." The bonuses were no issue, either. Dreyfus was very laidback. He lived in Switzerland in a house with a fabulous view, except that it was partly blocked by a tree. I remember him telling us that he couldn't move the tree because of a conservation order, but he was thinking about moving the house a few metres. A few months later I read in the paper that that's what he's done – just moved the house!'

In the summer of 2002, after a positive test for amphetamines that represented a flagrant breach of his contract, Jan Ullrich's 300,000 euros a year retainer proved a much more easily moveable object from Adidas's payroll. A further, temporary casualty of this, his most expensive indiscretion, would come to light only years later: a highly controversial agreement between Ullrich and German state broadcaster ARD, worth up to 195,000 euros a year, which gave the TV channel special access and Ullrich performance-based bonuses, was now also canned.

Of course, his most lucrative and important commercial association had always been with Telekom – and, in the end, it would be Ullrich, not Telekom, who decided to take a chainsaw to that umbilical cord. His existing contract had officially been suspended with the confirmation of his doping ban, but within weeks Telekom were asking Wolfgang Strohband to put together a proposal for a new agreement. These weren't the only mixed messages. One minute Jürgen Kindervater was taking Ullrich to meet the new consorts under Telekom's sponsorship umbrella, Bayern Munich's footballers. The next, he was agreeing with Walter Godefroot at a meeting in Cologne that Telekom really ought to start planning for a future without Ullrich.

Rudy Pevenage remembers Godefroot in particular feeling 'betrayed'. 'With Jan you needed a lot of patience. He was very stubborn. But Walter had been putting up with the same thing for years, Even I was a bit sick of it.'

Pevenage says the discussion in Cologne ended with everyone agreeing that, regardless of what Ullrich decided or proposed, they, Ullrich's old minders, would all stay with Telekom. Godefroot had no idea that the next betrayal was just around the corner.

Godefroot tells me he 'couldn't wrap his head around' Ullrich's original sin, but 'didn't want to kick him out'. In the end, Ullrich simply didn't give him or Telekom a choice.

Wolfgang Strohband had in fact begun sounding out potential suitors during the Tour de France. One team – and one team manager – particularly piqued the German press's interest. Ullrich had flourished as Bjarne Riis's apprentice at the 1996 Tour de France, and now Riis was keen to 'relaunch' him in the team he managed, CSC-Tiscali. Strohband had secretly met Riis during the Tour. Soon they were making plans to reboot not only Ullrich but also Riis's team with another household German brand name on the jersey – Deutsche Post i.e. another hatchling from the privatization deal that had produced Telekom in 1995.

'The idea with Deutsche Post was that DHL, their parcel service, would be the name on the jersey,' Strohband remembers. 'They told me DHL did more deliveries by bike than anyone else in the world. They had a motor-racing driver, Heinz-Harald Frentzen, on their books, but they wanted out, they wanted to put their money into cycling. They wanted to hang a 70-metre long banner on their new building, right opposite Telekom's. The jersey was designed and everything was agreed in principal, but then they came along one day and said, "We'll have to break the whole thing off. We have to close such and such a number of post offices and save money." Bjarne was very disappointed. For me, the idea of Jan with him had been a real ray of hope.'

Throughout his courtship of Ullrich, Riis had given little away – and nothing of his three trips to Deutsche Post HQ in Bonn. In late September, Ullrich confirmed via his website that he would not be returning to Telekom in 2003, and Riis reacted with the tart remark that he had 'perhaps taken a decision alone for the first time in his life'. For the umpteenth time, here was someone who knew and had ridden with Ullrich highlighting his lack of autonomy – apparently in contradiction to the widespread view that he could also be infuriatingly set in his ways. Brian Holm says that, in fact, Ullrich's stubbornness sometimes manifested itself as a blind, deaf and if not dumb then minimally argumentative faith in – or loyalty towards – false prophets. 'He had his guys and not ten horses could have changed Jan's mind. Forget about it.'

Pevenage had been one such confidant for almost a decade, but even he now admitted, 'the Ullrich chapter is closed'. As summer turned to autumn, the German press suggested Ullrich's signature on a two-year contract with Riis was a fait accompli, just days away – only to report later, after Deutsche Post's withdrawal, that Ullrich's wage demands were the ultimate deal-breaker. The asking price was around two million euros – a princely sum for a rider who had undergone a second knee operation in August, this one carried out by Ernst-Otto Münch, who had previously rebuilt the knees of several top German skiers. While Ullrich called it a 'resounding success', Münch offered no guarantees that he would regain full movement and power.

When we speak in 2021, Riis doesn't mention money when I ask him now why the reunion with Ullrich didn't come to pass. 'I said, "Jan, I'm going to take you if you want, but it's going to be on my terms." Because I knew that's what he needed – to change his environment. That was my demand, but in the end he couldn't agree to it. The weight was only part of the problem. If you put the whole focus on that, you make it a bigger problem than it is. I was going to change the whole foundation of what he was doing, how he was thinking. But he wasn't able to do that. He knew I could help him, he knew he maybe needed me, but to do it a hundred per cent? He didn't want to take that step.'

Ullrich attended the Tour de France route presentation in October still without a team. The 2003 edition of the Tour would mark the race's centenary, and the Société du Tour de France had invited every living champion to its unveiling. Having previously said that, in his second coming, he wished to broaden his horizons and focus on other races besides the Tour, Ullrich looked and sounded spellbound by the race that had given him everything yet also sapped so much of his life force. In a group photo, he stood between Armstrong and the 1959 winner, Federico Bahamontes, and a few places down from Eddy Merckx and his first Tour heroes, Greg LeMond and Laurent Fignon. Before leaving for Merdingen, he walked Gaby through the gathering of old greats, collecting autographs for the first time in his life.

On his return from Canada, he had spent a few days in Switzerland, at the home of an old friend from the German under-23 team, Tobias Steinhauser. They talked about training and teams for the following year, given that Steinhauser too was out of contract. Steinhauser subtly planted a seed, an idea, that continued to germinate over the autumn: maybe one of Jan's problems was Merdingen.

Perhaps he would feel freer, less harassed, less vulnerable to assorted temptations if he could relocate to somewhere like, well, the sanctuary that Steinhauser had created on the shores of Lake Constance.

Gaby had been reticent at first but eventually Ullrich talked her round. There would be less tax to pay in Switzerland, but, most importantly, this was Ullrich proving that he'd meant what he'd said about breaking with the past. They had been together for seven years and spent them mainly on or around the corner from her parents' winery. She had her job in Freiburg, but surely she too would be happier knowing that her partner was well away from whomever or whatever had led him astray over the previous few months. Besides, just as they had planned in the summer, there would soon be a baby on the way. What better excuse for a fresh start?

In his book, *Wieder im Rennen*, Andreas Burkert quotes Ullrich's mum, Marianne, as saying that he would have left Merdingen even if Gaby had stayed – 'as harsh as it sounds'. Luckily, she didn't make him choose. As Wolfgang Strohband observes, 'Jan has always been very lucky with the women in his life.'

Ullrich told the press that moving to Switzerland would also help his cycling. More mountains, easier access to Tuscany, where he intended to train with Steinhauser over the winter. These advantages were marginal (a saving of fifteen minutes on a seven-hour car journey to Tuscany) but the remaining members of Ullrich's diminishing inner circle still welcomed his uncharacteristic decisiveness. In no time at all he had set his heart on a five-bedroom, 430-square-metre villa with lake views – and insisted on signing a contract to buy, not rent. Soon, for the first time, he would also seem suddenly interested in what money was going into and leaving his accounts. The quarterly balance sheets prepared and given to Ullrich by Wolfgang Strohband had previously remained unread.

He had admitted to the media in September that cycling had felt like his true passion until about three years earlier. Since then he had 'only ridden because [he] had to'. He had finally come to this realization and to one of those points in life's journey where change doesn't so much present as impose itself, not as unconscious transition but as a series of jolts – bracing, uncomfortable but necessary.

If Telekom had indeed been his 'golden cage', it was time, on the cusp of his thirtieth year, to find the door and tear it from its hinges.

*

Jan Ullrich had not been the only or indeed even the most important Telekom figurehead to be taken off the payroll in the summer of 2002. The weeks and months either side of Ullrich's ill-fated visit to a Munich nightclub had been traumatic ones at corporate HQ in Bonn, as German Chancellor Gerhard Schröder and his finance minister began to lose patience with the downward trajectory of a company that was still 43 per cent state-owned. The share price was plummeting and the CEO of the last seven years, Ron Sommer, had been castigated for splurging $46.5 billion on the purchase of Bob Stapleton's VoiceStream Wireless. Things were predicted to come to a head at a board meeting on 16 July – a rest day for the 2002 Tour de France and, as it turned out, time for Sommer to leave on an indefinite vacation, having duly been given the boot.

He had grown up in Israel and Austria, studied maths at university and known next to nothing about cycling when he arrived at Telekom from Sony in 1995. But from that point on, Sommer, Ullrich, the team and company had risen and fallen together, tracing the same parabola to giddy success followed by their swan-dive back to earth. In 1995, Ullrich took his first pro win at the German national time trial championship and Telekom monopolized the first seven positions in the road race, only for Sommer to ruin the party; literally interrupting the celebrations to tell them he would pull Telekom's funding if they didn't also succeed at the Tour de France. Erik Zabel's two stages saved them – and then, in 1996 and 1997, had come Riis and Ullrich.

Sommer has invited me to his home in Meerbusch just outside Düsseldorf to share his Telekom story. Known locally and now even nationally as the *'Stadt der Millionäre'* or 'Millionaire's Town', at the last check Meerbusch counted one seven-figure earner for every 580 residents – the highest density of anywhere in Germany's most populous state, Nordrhein-Westfalen.

Were it not hidden behind a high wall, even here Sommer's lair would stand out for its futuristic cubic design in a town that wears its wealth unostentatiously. Those expecting a cat-stroking cliché, though, would be disappointed upon meeting the man of the house. Years after the event, the *Süddeutsche Zeitung* described his arrival at Deutsche Telekom in 1995 in the following terms: 'Telekom and with it the whole of Germany wanted to be a bit like Ron Sommer: international, suntanned, sexy. Ron Sommer became Mr Germany.'

Sitting in his squash-court-sized home office, his straight-point collar unbuttoned and his black Oxfords glistening, Sommer appears greyer than in his cover-star years but in no way diminished. Now in his late sixties, he still treasures many of his memories from Telekom – and one important legacy the company left to his family: multiple summers as the cycling team's schoolboy cheerleader infected Ken, his son, with a passion that became a career. He is now an agent to some of the world's leading riders.

Even Ron eventually caught the bug, to the point where he is nodding in agreement when I relate what Rolf Aldag has told me about cycling and Deutsche Telekom in the mid-1990s: 'Deutsche Telekom were just a company you called up when you'd been over-charged on your phone bill . . . then all of a sudden, thanks to the cycling team, it became this great source of national pride.'

'Deutsche Telekom was originally part of the Bundespost, which was a government provider of postal services, banking and telecom-munications,' Sommer explains. 'It was a public administration, so hugely bureaucratic. My team didn't call a customer a customer – they called them an applicant. Remember, it was not only pre-internet but pre-anything. The network was analogue and completely use-less.

'Considering the total communications budget of the company, the cycling team cost us a tiny amount. Of course the main expense was general communication, to build the market for us in Germany and prepare the IPO. So it was never something that gave us finan-cial concerns and we enjoyed it when they started to give us huge success and become a German national team . . . The key for us was: do they win the hearts of the people? And you don't have to win the Tour to do that. The guy who wins is not always the guy everybody loves the most. From a corporate standpoint, it was more a case of, are they a real team?'

If the answer to these questions was yes, Sommer concedes that there was just one other key proviso: 'Then, of course, the question was being clean. If I had thought they were not clean, that day we would have stopped. But we were totally convinced.'

Over the two hours that I spend with Sommer, there will be plenty of time to discuss how trust and confidence can be the siblings of naivety or, worse, gullibility. But that is all part of the postscript. In the then and there, Sommer says, seen from his watchtower in Bonn, his team, the united Germany's team, and especially Jan Ullrich were the jolly bike-couriers of a corporate message and magenta-tinged dreams – a loose-change antidote to the higher-stakes stresses both company and customer faced every day.

'From the point of view of a huge organization like Deutsche Telekom, it's not a big issue: it's the fun part,' Sommer says. 'You're not making billion-dollar decisions and the risk of technology is not there.

'When the team came home from a race, win or lose, it didn't matter – we celebrated. We invited them to the HQ, there were thousands of employees with magenta flags. When they were winning we took them to the Marktplatz in Bonn to see the mayor, had a reception with 10,000 people outside, public and employees, a sea of magenta. I took them once to see the Chancellor in Berlin, for fun, because it was also fun for the Chancellor to meet the team and not some government head on serious business . . . So, anyway, at the end of the day, your concerns as a CEO are totally different.

'But I did like Jan. I only met him a few times but I understood – it was not difficult to understand the issues. When I told him in the bus one day it didn't matter if he won or not, that he only had to win hearts, I meant it. Did I dwell on it and wonder whether there was a danger anyway? No, because I felt that, if my guys felt comfortable, it was OK. In such a huge organization you'd better not spend your time thinking about sports sponsorship or advertising . . . If you have to cut 15,000 jobs in a year, that's a big issue you spend a lot of time on. So, no, you don't spend a lot of time on Jan . . .'

Sommer's voice trails off. In the traumatic summer of 2002, he had too much on his mind to contemplate the poignancy of his and Ullrich's parallel fairy tales with Telekom souring and then ending in perfect synchronicity, but since then he has often thought about Ullrich. A self-made mogul so committed he once slept with a fax machine on his bedside table and peppered interviews with mottos like 'there's no place for emotions in business', Sommer would appear to have little in common with a faltering sporting prodigy from the DDR. But it is perhaps because of their differences that he can see what Ullrich lacked in such stark relief.

'I had lunch once with my son, Ken, and Lance Armstrong, after the Telekom time, and I think Lance said something like, "If Jan had the character of Erik Zabel, I could never beat him." So there was a

clear weakness in Jan that wasn't compensated by the team supporting him,' Sommer says finally. 'It's like if you have a child and the
child has a weakness; yes it's the weakness of the child but you as a
parent didn't do your job properly: teaching, educating, supporting,
whatever. And if you look at the life of Jan, you find a lot of signals
like this . . . which is a shame.'

15

LITTLE MAN OF DREAMS

'Cycling's like cocaine: once you've tried it you want it again and again'

—*Luigi Cecchini*

It was the undignified end, if not of a beautiful relationship, then at least of a mutually convenient one. Not Telekom and Jan Ullrich but Walter Godefroot and Rudy Pevenage, the front office and the fore-man of 'Germany's team'. Pevenage's promise in Cologne to stick with Telekom, the spiel about the Ullrich chapter being closed – it all turned to sugar dust on the yule log one day between Christmas and New Year. 'Walter was going on holiday to Tenerife and coming back just before Christmas. I didn't want to tell him before his holiday, and I didn't want to ruin his Christmas either . . .'

Pevenage says he was trying to be considerate. Only that's not how Godefroot saw it.

'I was really angry and upset,' Godefroot tells me. 'He parks up in front of my house in Drongen, comes inside and tells me the kind of things you only tell a friend. Friend is a big word . . . but, anyway, he starts talking to me about private issues, things you only tell a friend. And the punchline is that he wants to quit. I said, "OK, but you know how much you earn with me. Do you want to go with Jan? Is that it?" "No, no, it's family stuff . . ." And so on and so on. That sort of thing. He says he's not going to stay in cycling, that's for sure. This is when he's been going around in a car that I've paid for, making calls on a phone that I'm also paying for, trying to arrange his new job. I call Kindervater and his reaction is, "What a way to pay you back!" I said that, no, it wasn't like that, it was for family reasons . . . but then I speak to Bjarne Riis. "Do you not know, Walter?" Bjarne had found out [Rudy was leaving] when he was talking to potential sponsors, because they were telling Bjarne that they were talking to Rudy too.'

Godefroot looks sternly at me over his spectacles.

'There are lines you don't cross.'

Pevenage says he understands why Godefroot never really got over it. He also looks remorseful when trying to explain why he went back on his word. He finally took the decision when he travelled to Scherzingen to retrieve Ullrich's T-Mobile team bikes and, over dinner, Ullrich made an offer Pevenage was never likely to refuse. Pevenage hemmed, hawed, phoned his wife and finally told her he would follow his heart. 'Ultimately, winning the Tour with Jan was a big personal ambition for me. We were going it alone – it was me and Jan, not the big Telekom machine. Somehow I couldn't imagine being a directeur sportif without Jan.'

Brian Holm had seen enough in his five years riding for Telekom to know what was coming Godefroot's way. 'When I left the team in 1998, I'd said to Walter, "Thanks for everything, but your good friend Rudy is gonna fuck you eventually. Don't trust him. Always look over your shoulder." So then Walter calls me at the end of 2002: "What you said about Rudy . . . you were right." I said, "I fucking told you, Walter."'

'You didn't have to be Einstein to see it coming. It was obvious Rudy would do that one day,' Rolf Aldag concurs.

Godefroot finally agreed – the warning signs had always been there. 'Rudy was a good directeur, but too crafty,' he says. 'Always wheeling and dealing . . . And being known as a schemer is not a good thing. I'll give you an example: we're at Milan–Sanremo and the Mapei team car drives up. I'm in the car next to Rudy. Mapei had already put a couple of riders on the front to bring back a break, and now they wanted to know whether we would too. But Rudy wasn't even winding down his window. He just stepped on the accelerator and drove away. He thought he was being clever but that'll come back to bite you. I always used to assume that others were at least as clever as me, whereas Rudy always wanted to prove that he was the smartest.'

The bad news for Godefroot was, of course, a positive

development for Jan Ullrich. He had locked down the services of his most trusted directeur sportif despite the fact that neither of them yet had a team for the 2003 season. That, though, was about to change. It wasn't US Postal, although, remarkably, they did try. 'I was at Johan Bruyneel's house three times, there were calls with Lance, but Jan and I agreed that wasn't the way to go,' Wolfgang Strohband confirms.

No, Ullrich would find his saviour much closer to home. He had been the fuse and fireworks for an explosion of interest in professional cycling in Germany that had produced two new teams, Gerolsteiner and Coast. It was therefore logical and somehow fitting that he would end up at one of them. In Ullrich's current spirit of self-revolution, Coast would also represent the sharpest pivot: from a national behemoth counting 250,000 employees and a net revenue of 50 billion euros to an upstart, mid-range high-street fashion retailer with 50 million euros in annual sales and sixteen stores, all of them in the industrial Rhine-Ruhr region unaffectionately known in Germany as the *Kohlenpott* – 'the Coal Scuttle'.

The road less travelled had been sold to Ullrich and Wolfgang Strohband by Coast's owner, Günther Dahms. Unremarkable in appearance, with his centrally parted brown hair finishing just above his rimless glasses and the physique of a forty-something more used to watching sport than doing it, Dahms was anything but ordinary in ambition. He had stood among the million Germans pressed against the barriers when the Tour de France crossed the Rhine for two days in 2000, and had an epiphany. Years earlier he had paid millions to get his name on a tiny panel of Michael Schumacher's racing overalls; now, he realized, he could spend the same money on a cycling team that would win the Tour de France. Within months he had his team and, in it, the riders who in the 1999 Tour had finished second and third behind Lance Armstrong, Alex Zülle and Fernando Escartín. The team presentation took place in the rooftop restaurant of the Reichstag in Berlin.

'A strange bird', according to Wolfgang Strohband, Dahms himself delighted in telling journalists he was 'a little bit of a chaos monster'. As *Der Spiegel* would observe later, 'With Dahms the line between passion and calculation becomes blurry, and he's more enthusiastic about how to shave a couple of grams off the spokes of a wheel than he is about accurate bookkeeping.' This much had been clear at the end of the 2002 season – a wildly successful one on the road, with Coast finishing fifth in the world rankings, and a precarious one off it. The Swiss rider, Mauro Gianetti, was in dispute with Dahms over unpaid bonuses, while the team's sizeable Spanish contingent had all lost a large slice of their salary due to Dahms's misunderstanding of German tax laws. When the Société du Tour de France confirmed in autumn 2002 that Coast were on their 2003 guest list, and Dahms also revealed that he was negotiating with Ullrich, his dream suddenly inched closer – and yet so did oblivion. The UCI announced they were withholding the team's racing licence for 2003 until Dahms got the team's finances in order.

Marcel Wüst had long since ceased to find the chaos endearing. One of the best German sprinters of the late 1990s, Wüst had retired in 2001 after a horrifying crash cost him his right eye. He was Coast's manager in 2002, but had eventually become weary of Günther Dahms's freewheeling management style. In 2003, he told Dahms, he would stay at the team but in a different role, as their communications chief. Still, Dahms wanted Wüst's input on what could be a game-changing decision. 'I was cycling down the Rhine one day in the autumn and Günther called to say he was considering signing Jan Ullrich. What did I think? I said, "Günther, if you have the money in the bank to pay Jan Ullrich and you can get everything organized, there's no better deal than signing Jan Ullrich. But if you don't have the money and think that by signing Jan Ullrich you're going to get a co-sponsor, do not do it."'

Dahms reassured Wüst that all was in hand. Which meant that, no, he didn't have the money, and, yes, he was doing exactly what Wüst had cautioned against – leveraging Ullrich's name to entice new commercial partners. Negotiations were soon underway with Coca-Cola, Vodafone and RWE, Germany's second biggest electricity supplier. 'There were contracts waiting to be signed – I think three million euros with RWE,' Wolfgang Strohband recalls. Dahms, though, had already said in interviews that he was 'a glutton for risk'. As Marcel Wüst puts it: 'Dahms wasn't a criminal. He was just buying shoes that were a size too big for him.'

In December, Jan Ullrich still had three months to wait until his ban would expire and he could race again, but he was growing impatient. Ullrich wanted the deal done when he, Strohband and Pevenage met Dahms at Strohband's Hamburg office on

20 December. There was still no co-sponsor, but Dahms promised them one would be in place by 15 January. They discussed clauses and contingencies deep into the early hours, until, at around 3.30 a.m., pens were passed around and signatures added to dotted lines. Ullrich stood to earn around 2.56 million euros a season. He had also secured jobs for Pevenage, his friend Tobias Steinhauser, the physiotherapist Birgit Krohme and his younger brother, Thomas, who had previously worked as a mechanic at Telekom.

There would be no official announcement before Coast's team presentation in Essen on 15 January, but word soon got out. While Bjarne Riis accused Ullrich of following the money, Lance Armstrong damned his supposed arch-rival with faux-fatherly career advice: 'It's his affair, but I don't think that's the best way. Was it the money? That's not the attitude of a champ. I'm disappointed. I would have accepted Bjarne Riis's offer. At CSC he would have been forced to take responsibility.'

Touché.

If Telekom to Team Coast was one journey to the other end of the pro cycling universe, Jan Ullrich was about to embark on another as he set out to make 2003 the year of his reinvention.

Point of departure this time: Peter Becker's back porch in Prenzlauer Berg, Berlin. At least, this is where Becker is explaining to me how, without warning, he and Ullrich reached the end of the line, this time for good.

'So, sixth of January 2003. The training plan was done and dusted and I say to Ulli: "This year we're really going for it. I want to see more from you. You haven't won the Tour of Flanders, Paris–Roubaix, the Giro and you also want to join the really greats and become the world road race champion. These four things, that's what we're going for. Obviously, to achieve all of this, you're really going to have to focus." To that, he says, "Ach, Trainer, I can't suffer from January to December. I'm not like Armstrong." And I reply, "You know what – you've suffered a lot more over the years because of the way you go about things. You could have it so easy. There's really no need to stuff your face like you're training to become a sumo wrestler. You only have to stay at a decent weight and continually keep on top of that, keep watching what you eat." He says maybe I should just help him to put the finishing touches to things and, that way, I wouldn't have to travel so much. I say, "Ulli, I'm your coach.

That's my role from dawn till dusk and now I want us to get after it . . ." But what he was getting at was that it was all over. It wasn't the last time we spoke but, as far as training was concerned, that was the end.'

Sixteen years they had worked together. Becker didn't know, certainly couldn't understand, but Ullrich had been seduced under the Tuscan sun. The training paradise that Tobias Steinhauser had raved to Ullrich about the previous summer had proven to be just that. They had gone there in the autumn and Ullrich had fallen under the spell of the region and of a man known to some in cycling as a genius and to others as an enigma.

The Via del Cimitero in Vicopelago is a procession of towering Renaissance villas nestled between olive groves and topaz swimming pools a few kilometres to the south west of Lucca, the 'City of One Hundred Churches' and birthplace of Puccini. House numbers seem to follow no logical sequence, as though picked on a whim, to confound visitors. After 395, a hundred metres or so later, the next plaque is 275. And here, behind ancient stone walls, a wrought-iron gate and thick pine-tree canopy, is the Villa Talenti Cecchini, Luigi Cecchini's palatial hideaway.

'Cecco' has told me to call him when I reach the tiny piazzetta opposite his gate, outside the eighteenth-century baroque chapel which also belongs to him. I duly park in its courtyard and dial Cecchini's number.

The seventy-year-old gentleman who a few moments later shuffles into view must be one of the least-photographed famous people on the planet. An internet search produces around half a dozen images taken at irregular intervals over twenty-five years. In most of them, the recession of Cecchini's wisps of grey hair is the only marker of time, while, in others, we see him in an office cum improvised lab with the rider he helped to turn from a journeyman into a Tour de France winner, Bjarne Riis. Cecchini will confirm to me later that he hasn't sat down for a 'proper' interview in seventeen years. He has accepted my request, albeit hesitantly, 'because I'm old now and thought, *Why not?*' But also, mainly, because I, he and Riis have a common friend, the former Orica-GreenEDGE team's communications chief Brian Nygaard, who lived for years in nearby Pisa.

I follow him around the side of an old stable block and up a stone staircase. In a thick, melodic Tuscan accent, with its barely audible 'C's and 'G's, and intonation that suggests a sneeze could come at any second, he apologizes for the slow progress: for a few days now an old back problem has kept him not only housebound but mostly horizontal.

Finally, he hobbles through a doorway and into a corridor, at the end of which I glimpse the office where he was once photographed with Riis. The room looks almost unchanged from those pictures – same or similar bike perched upon an ergometer in front of his glass desk, magazines and books stacked on top as they were then, same signed jerseys on the wall. We turn right into a different room, this one a disorderly man cave littered with antique furniture, sports equipment and, most curiously, a decrepit pinball machine. Cecchini apologizes that he'll have to lie down, for his back, and he duly lowers himself onto a blue chaise longue. A copy of today's *La Gazzetta dello Sport* lies between us on the floor, under a coffee table scattered with cycling magazines and beside a Swiss ball almost obscuring the doctor from view.

Finally, Cecchini holds his phone up in front of his glasses, stabs the off button with his index finger, and places it face down next to him.

'*Allora*,' he begins, 'a book about Jan? *Gentilissimo*, Jan. So let me tell you a few things . . .'

Luigi Cecchini always thought he was destined to be a surveyor. He had done the training and was ready to look for his first job when he succumbed to an old Italian curse and fell into the family business. In the Cecchinis' case it was textiles, shirts to be precise, and from the age of seventeen until he was thirty-two, Luigi more or less ran the show. 'I thought that was me,' he says, 'but then, one day, I picked up a book on medicine and I couldn't put it down.' At age thirty-two, he would enrol in medical school partly because two of his five-a-side football teammates were already undergraduates. Six years later, Cecchini got his degree *summa cum laude*.

At thirty-eight, Cecchini says, he was too old to work in hospitals or even set up practice as a GP. Instead, he turned to his old love of sports.

'I'd been a decent footballer and tennis player, then an Italian champion in car racing, and had also won things in skiing, so I decided to become a sports doctor. The first cycling team that I worked with was Ivano Fanini's here in Lucca, then I gradually moved through different teams. I'd started cycling myself mainly because I'd put on some weight when I was studying and I had high blood pressure. The director of the cardiology department said that I shouldn't be taking pills for it and should start cycling instead. So I did and, you know, cycling's like cocaine: once you've tried it you want it again and again.'

Cecchini's 'addiction' took him into the cycling big leagues when he accepted a job as Ariostea's team doctor. It was there, in 1990, that he also met and briefly worked alongside Michele Ferrari, a few years before Ferrari linked up with Lance Armstrong. By the mid-1990s, they would both be mainly 'freelancing', Cecchini after Ariostea's disappearance and Ferrari after Gewiss-Ballan had fired him in the spring of 1994, following an infamous comment reported by *L'Équipe*: 'EPO is not dangerous, it's the abuse that is. It's also dangerous to drink ten litres of orange juice.'

Soon, between them, Cecchini and Ferrari were carving up cycling's most prestigious races. In 1996, the last season before the UCI tried to stem the EPO plague by introducing blood tests, Cecchini coached the winner of the Tour de France and the gold, silver and bronze medallists in the Olympic road race. Meanwhile, Ferrari's clients took the Giro, Liège–Bastogne–Liège and the Tour of Lombardy. The Italian media hyped up a rivalry that acquired further mystique thanks to both coaches' reticence about giving interviews. Besides their similarities, the two *preparatori* also offered a succulent dichotomy: Ferrari scheming out of his hideout in Ferrara on one side of the Apennine mountains, Cecchini serenading champions in Lucca on the other; Ferrari who, according to one former charge, Filippo Simeoni, 'treated you like a number', Cecchini for whom you were 'one of the family, like a son', as former client Dario Pieri tells me; Ferrari, known as 'il Mito' – 'The Myth' – to many of his clients, Cecchini, who to everyone, regardless of status, would forever remain simply 'Cecco'.

When I remind Cecchini of how it was all spun at the time, he tuts and shakes his head. 'The Cold War between me and Ferrari . . . that was another *cazzata clamorosa*. Complete balls,' he says. 'Ferrari's a friend. He's someone I was with at Ariostea. I still consider him the number one coach in the world. I learned a lot from him in terms of training . . . But I must have spoken to Michele three times in ten years.'

Listening to him, one could be forgiven for thinking that Cecchini's Achilles heel over the years was that he kept mixing with – or getting mixed up with – the wrong crowd. In 1998, for example, a magistrate wire-tapped his phone and that of a pharmacist in Bologna and caught them discussing the banned hormone DHEA. In conversations with a supplier, the pharmacist was also heard describing Cecchini as 'a bloke who prescribes a lot, if he gets into it' and saying that Ferrari had 'cleaned out the chemist!'

Both doctors' houses were subsequently raided in the summer of 1998. It was the last such experience for Cecchini, but not for Ferrari. The former has never been charged with any doping-related offences, either by sporting authorities or the judiciary, unlike the latter.

'They took away all of the paperwork they could find – all my old notes and my computers,' Cecchini remembers. 'I hired a lawyer but no one ever questioned me. My lawyer wanted to go and see the magistrate, but, then, after two years, the case was closed.'

Then there is Francesco Conconi, Ferrari's mentor and his forerunner as cycling's most infamous 'EPO doctor'.[23] A multitude of online sources describe Cecchini as one of Conconi's pupils at the University of Ferrara, like Ferrari.

This has Cecchini risking another slipped disc by swivelling to face me.

'I'll tell you the truth . . . I don't even know Conconi. I've seen him at a couple of conferences . . . and he was great: he can explain difficult concepts in a way that everyone understands. But I've never studied at Ferrara! I studied in Pisa. If you go onto Wikipedia, it calls me a pupil of Conconi. Don't even know the guy.'

All of which leaves Cecchini with one final name in his address book to account for. In 2001, the Kelme team doctor, Eufemiano Fuentes, was a familiar figure within the sanctum of pro cycling's travelling circus but largely unknown to the sport's wider audience. That began to change when, after the Vuelta a España won by the Spanish rider Ángel Casero, a Spanish magazine obtained telephone messages sent to Casero by Fuentes on the morning of the final mountain stage of the race, telling Casero that he would be in Madrid 'with you know what'.

This was bizarre: Casero didn't even ride for Fuentes's team, unlike his rival for overall victory Oscar Sevilla. Fuentes's explanation also sounded unconvincing: he claimed the 'you know what' were pedal cranks that Cecchini, an old friend, wanted him to pass on to Casero.

Casero later sued the magazine for violating his privacy and implying that the Fuentes–Cecchini axis was his doping supply line. Casero says now, 'The damage that leak caused me was inestimable.' He insists that Cecchini was his coach in 2001 but that he never worked with Fuentes, contrary to what Fuentes later told the press. 'Fuentes said he worked with me . . . and with Bush and with Bin Laden,' Casero says. 'It was bravado. Bullshit.'

Lying on his flea-bitten old couch in the stables of his villa in Vicopelago, eyes now fixed back on the ceiling, Luigi Cecchini doesn't so much as twitch when pressed for the truth about his connection to Eufemiano Fuentes. 'Fuente [sic], I'll tell you straight away . . .'

'Fuentes.'

'Yes, him. Fuentes. It's true that I was a friend of Fuentes. Because Fuentes is the nicest bloke in the world. I don't know if you know him, but he's exceptional. And there was this problem – he'd had an issue with his little girl. She had a cancerous eye. And because there's a group in Siena who specialized in those tumours, we were in contact a lot for a while. I'd met him in 1991 or 1992, when he was doctor for Javier Mínguez's team and I was at Ariostea. Mínguez introduced us. Then I used to see him at the Tour, the Giro, and we'd talk, as you do at races. But we never worked with the same rider. Besides, Fuentes wasn't a coach. There was only one rider – the guy who once won the Vuelta . . .'

'Casero.'

'Casero, that's him. Fuentes treated him in Spain, and Casero used to come here four or five times a year to do tests.'

Which should settle things, but of course does not. Lance Armstrong can't recall exactly when he found out that Jan Ullrich was being coached by Luigi Cecchini, but he thinks Michele Ferrari probably told him. Armstrong can also remember or at least imagine his reaction. 'Cecchini is Fuentes, right? I made that association straight away. Cecchini didn't want to run the medical side of things, so he just handled the training side. Right?'

Right, halfway right, or completely wrong. Having let him have his say on Fuentes, I cut to the chase and ask Cecchini what service exactly he was offering Ullrich.

'I'd already stopped working for teams at that point, by the time the police raided the house,' he says. 'In 1995, I was still the team doctor at MG-Technogym, but I had other riders coming to see me and creating a right old mess, with a conflict of interests. The Mapei team's owner, Giorgio Squinzi, didn't like it and neither did my team's boss, Giancarlo Ferretti. I was also sick of breaking my balls, travelling a hundred days a year. I preferred just training guys. Then, after the raids in 1998, I even completely stopped looking at all blood values. A rider who wanted to be trained by me just had to bring his medical certificate to say he was fit to ride a bike – because, if a guy has a heart attack when he's doing a test, it's a mess. I have a defibrillator but you never know; something like that goes wrong in Italy and you'll be under investigation for twenty years. The second point is that the teams always knew when I was training their guys. I'd say, "Look, you get your directeur sportif to contact me and tell me you've got his consent." I didn't want guys coming in secret, with a fake moustache or beard. You laugh but it would have happened . . .

'In any case,' he continues, 'half of the riders came for a month then I never saw them again. They would come at the end of November, do a test, then I'd draw up a programme for three weeks in December on the basis of that test. I would tell them to do that programme then decide if they wanted to carry on. I would do December free of charge. But then so many guys would say, "Cecco, this is great, but your training's too hard for me." Or "I don't want to have to send you files every day." If that was the case, there'd be no hard feelings. The guys who liked it, though, would carry on. And Ullrich was one of those who stuck around.'

A few kilometres to the east of Lucca, on a road rising steeply towards the village of Montecarlo, lies the Fattoria Borgo La Torre. Its cluster of primrose-coloured farmhouses and converted barns don't particularly command the traveller's attention – the Tuscan hills are scattered with rural hotels, *agriturismi*, like this one, many of them more handsomely situated, opulently decorated and expensive to visit. For Jan Ullrich, though, for several weeks in 2003 and three seasons thereafter, La Torre became home from home.

On an electric-blue May day in 2015, middle-aged tourists amble between pottery shops or wrestle with their fold-out maps on Montecarlo's cafe terraces. Back down the hill, silence reigns at Fattoria Borgo La Torre but for the chatter of the cleaning staff. In reception, the owner smiles in vague recognition when I mention Jan Ullrich. 'Ah, yes, I remember him. Them,' she says. 'They used to come here for a few weeks in the spring. The boys in the kitchen, the chef, I think he had more contact with them . . .'

The chef. Of course. Unfortunately his shift won't begin for a few hours.

Even without sampling the *bistecca fiorentina* or speculating about what was on Luigi Cecchini's menu of training programmes, it's easy to see why Ullrich felt that he'd located his promised land in La Bella Toscana. Thomas Dekker, Tyler Hamilton and Jörg Jaksche have all spoken or written openly about their doping, about Eufemiano Fuentes supplying the drugs and also about being coached by Cecchini – and all of them tell more or less the same story: the Fuentes–Cecchini link is a red herring, a disservice to Cecchini, his genius and the soul-nourishing, strength-giving magic of training in this region of Italy.

Dario Pieri, an Italian classics rider with weight problems worse than Ullrich's, tells me he called Cecchini '*l'omino dei sogni*' – 'the little man of dreams'. 'He would make you dream, not by forcing you, but by saying, "If you do this, this and this, you'll achieve this." But he was against doping . . .'

Likewise, it was Jörg Jaksche's impression that Cecchini had been traumatized by the police search of his home in 1998 and 'didn't want anything to do with doping'. 'When Cecchini trained me, he charged me barely a token fee, 800 euros a month,' says Jaksche. 'He did it for passion. He just loved riding his bike and coaching bike riders. He said that coaching young guys kept him feeling young, that he always wanted to feel thirty.'

Thomas Dekker has a similar memory. Dekker says that doping was never taboo with Cecchini, but he 'never supported it, never got involved with it'. Echoing what Tyler Hamilton wrote in his 2012 book *The Secret Race*, Dekker explains, 'Cecco would tell you: the only thing that really works is increasing red cells with blood transfusions or EPO. He said that with all the other stuff that people did – cortisone, testosterone, insulin, growth hormone – you were just poisoning your body and not getting much of an advantage.'

Dekker has his own theory about why Ullrich, in particular, found Cecchini's charisma irresistible.

'I think everyone knows when they go to Cecco that this guy has coached the best riders in the world. I mean, growing up, I was more an Ullrich guy than an Armstrong guy, so the thought of being coached by the same trainer as Jan was pretty attractive. And then Tuscany is just beautiful for riding your bike. It doesn't matter if you were Jörg Jaksche or Juan Antonio Flecha or Kim Kirchen – everyone was coming from less beautiful places, and the training went easily over there. You're always with really nice people with the same goals, who have also travelled to be there to work with the same guy, so you get a bit of a community. And Cecco is like the Pope to everyone. Then in the evening, it's like a whole family: his wife has a beautiful clothes shop in the centre of Lucca, they invite you to their beautiful villa, the food is amazing . . . It's *la dolce vita.*'

Dekker goes on: 'You also need to think, a guy like Ulle, not the best childhood, and a guy like Cecco – laidback, warm, wealthy Italian – and he puts his arm around you, knows what he's talking about. He's one of the first guys in the world to work with SRM power meters, he's won the Tour with Riis . . . There's this whole mythology around him. And Ullrich was not a happy cyclist. Didn't seem to love the sport. He was just a product of East Germany, finding this guy who treated him like a human . . . But also, probably no one else could get through to Jan. Maybe he would tell Pevenage and Steinhauser that he wanted to go home after four hours behind a motorbike, but he probably didn't have the balls to tell Cecco that if Cecco wanted him to do six. He was probably so indoctrinated when he was young, and he was probably so good when he came to Telekom, that he never had a guy who was pressing the right buttons. If he'd spent his whole career in Italy, just training with Cecco, Jan would probably have won the Tour more times than Lance Armstrong. Because I think everyone knows that Jan had the bigger engine.'

Cecchini only vaguely remembers his first encounter with Ullrich, but is fairly sure that it followed his usual formula. 'I would always get the rider to do a test on the stationary bike there,' he says, waving a hand towards the adjacent room. 'That was a Conconi test, or what people now call a lactate threshold test. Generally, I preferred the tests outdoors.'

One stretch of road, in particular, had become synonymous with Cecchini and how he assessed his riders: a 6.1-kilometre drag from the village of Buti up to a small dimple on the eastern flank of the Monte Serra, the mountain overlooking Lucca. The climb almost never featured in Italy's national tour, the Giro d'Italia, or indeed any other professional race. And yet, thanks to Cecchini, performances there were the subject of feverish speculation among the world's top professionals. Ullrich's first ascents, together with what Cecchini had observed in his lab, left the doctor in no doubt. As he says now, 'Jan had a huge engine. One of the two or three biggest I've seen. Maybe only he and Fabian Cancellara would ever get to 510 watts in my lactate tests.'

But no one had questioned Ullrich's physiological capabilities. The difficulty was getting him to channel them on a consistent basis. Could Cecchini succeed where Peter Becker, Rudy Pevenage and an assortment of Telekom 'babysitters' had failed?

'I don't really consider myself a psychologist,' Cecchini sets out straight away. 'To be honest, if I'd sent Jan to a psychologist it would have been the shrink needing help after a fortnight, with the character that Jan had . . .'

Meaning he was stubborn?

'Yes. I don't think a psychologist could have influenced him. There are also riders, though, who need someone, if not a psychologist, then at least someone who could take away all of the fears they have. There are some riders who are finished in a race the moment they attack, turn around and see that there are still guys on their wheel. But this wasn't Jan's problem. He wasn't one of those riders who are afraid of their own shadow . . .'

Ullrich's much bigger issue, most believed, was his weight.

'Well, obviously Jan knew better than anyone that he had a big problem with that,' Cecchini says. 'But in two months he could get down maybe not to his ideal weight – I think he only got to his ideal weight in the year that he won the Tour – but he always came down a lot. Even with me, he'd get very skinny, in my opinion, but still be three or four kilos heavier than when he won the Tour. He was a rider who, when he decided to train and came here, really trained: he'd do his six hours, then an hour on the rollers when he finished. He was also quite careful about his food when he wanted to be, but he was also the kind of guy who, if you put a bottle of wine in front of him . . . well, you understand? That was the issue. I think he always gave away two or three kilos to Armstrong, and that was just fat.

'I'm not a dietician, so I'd say to him, "Look, this is your form weight, and dieticians recommend that you eat a little and often, avoid alcohol . . ." Just general rules like that. He was also an adult, and it's really something that has to click in the rider's head, that makes him want to make those sacrifices. If you break a rider's balls, stress him, you also tend to have the opposite effect, and he ends up eating a lot. You can't hold a pistol to his head. If you'd done that with Jan, his head would have exploded first. He was unlucky as well, in that where he stayed in Montecarlo they had an excellent restaurant. If he was doing seven hours on the bike, then getting back there for his evening meal . . . Sometimes he would be able to resist, other times he cracked.'

Cecchini laughs, but the point, the reason why I've come to Tuscany looking for answers, is that something, in the weeks before his return to racing in March 2003, did finally seem to flick the dopamine switch, open the motivation tap in Jan Ullrich's brain. There were other ingredients, no doubt, but Cecchini's influence was undeniable.

'I think there were two main reasons for 2003 being so good,' Cecchini says. 'One was that he was really motivated because he'd changed teams. The other point was that he's a very respectful and polite boy and he saw this old man getting on the Vespa every day to spend six hours motor-pacing with him, tying his back in knots, ruining his spine, and I think he somehow wanted to show that he was grateful for that. He didn't want to let me down.'

At home in Berlin, even had he known how and with whom Jan Ullrich had replaced him, Peter Becker is adamant he would not have cared. 'I'd heard of Cecchini, the name, but that's all,' he says. 'Cecchini this, Ferrari that . . . From 2003 on, I wasn't interested any more.'

Which, of course, does not mean that Becker looks back without regret – or recrimination.

'Pevenage engineered that whole thing. He wasn't a coach, but Ulli's biggest fan. He only wanted to keep me at arm's length while he made Ullrich great. Fine. I just wanted the kid to be where he belonged, achieve everything he could achieve. He's a once-in-a-generation talent. I just wanted him to achieve those four things – Flanders, Roubaix, the Giro and then, on the day when he becomes the world champion, to say, "Dear friends, that's me done." Everyone would have celebrated him. He would have gone with a status, an image that would have guaranteed him everyone's lifelong admiration.'

16

REBOOT, REINVENTION

'He does the strict minimum until he starts to realize that it's working, and then this kind of euphoria kicks in'

—*Raphael Schweda*

It didn't take a handshake, a smile and 'a welcome back' from Lance Armstrong at the Circuit de la Sarthe in north-west France the first week of April for Jan Ullrich to finally feel like a cyclist again. At his Team Coast unveiling in Essen in mid-January, Ullrich had surprised some of the assembled journalists with his slenderness after so many months off the bike. Gone, apparently, were the days when, according to his old teammate Brian Holm, the Telekom riders would have official photos taken for supporter autograph cards in November or December, and Ullrich would put his shoot off until the spring because, says Holm, 'He looked like a fucking Christmas turkey – and he hated being heavy.' Gone, too, were the wardrobe malfunctions – perhaps the effect of signing for a team sponsored by a fashion brand: this time Ullrich did not take off his black jacket, so there would be no snarky remarks in the papers about sweat patches under his arms.

There would be enough perspiration over the next few weeks, for better and for worse, on and off the bike. Ullrich spent much of February in Tuscany with Tobias Steinhauser, following Luigi Cecchini's training plans and sometimes Cecchini himself on the back of his Vespa. His right knee occasionally still swelled after long rides and Ullrich didn't want to take any chances. Consequently, for once, he stuck to small gears and high cadences. Progress was relatively slow until mid-March, when suddenly Steinhauser experienced something like what Rolf Aldag had seen in the Black Forest in the late spring of 1995: from one day to the next, Ullrich suddenly seemed to burst from his chrysalis and take flight. 'I had to be careful then that he didn't finish me off,' Steinhauser reported later. Before packing him off for his comeback race, Luigi Cecchini decided that it was time for his truth serum – the timed ascent of Monte Serra from Buti. Ullrich stopped the clock at just under sixteen minutes, the best time Cecchini had ever seen – 'plus he was still overweight,' Cecchini notes.

Throughout the spring, Ullrich had kept his focus while Günther Dahms, his new boss, seemed to be losing control. Coast's Spanish riders were still arguing with Dahms about their German taxes, and Dahms had also failed in his search for a second sponsor. Riders complained publicly about wages arriving late or not at all, and in the first week of March the UCI suspended Team Coast's licence to compete. Two weeks later, on the eve of Milan–Sanremo and three days before the end of Jan Ullrich's doping ban, the licence was restored – unlike most people's faith in the future of Dahms's project.

Ullrich and Tobias Steinhauser set off for the Circuit de la Sarthe on 6 April unsure of whether they would even be allowed to start the race. As they waited for a connecting flight in Paris and a phone call from Wolfgang Strohband to confirm that the team would stagger onwards, Steinhauser suggested that he and Ullrich abort their journey. It was literally a 'sliding doors' moment – and they had shut a split-second before Ullrich and Steinhauser agreed they should get off the airport shuttle bus and head back to Zürich. Having been forced to board their flight and land in Nantes, they waited another four hours and had already booked a return via Paris for the same afternoon when finally the phone rang and Strohband informed them that the team's bike sponsor, Bianchi, had released enough cash to keep Coast afloat.

Ullrich finished comfortably in the peloton on stage one to Fontenay-le-Comte and felt truly welcomed back into the bosom of the bunch. Armstrong greeted him with a smile and handshake. Ullrich had recently made a happy announcement – Gaby was expecting their first child – and Armstrong took the opportunity to wish them both well. Others, like Jens Voigt, saw the definition in Ullrich's legs and made flattering remarks about how hard he must have been training. A sizeable delegation of German journalists had made the trip, and at a press gathering on the first night they, too, found Ullrich to be more relaxed than in his Telekom days, when he would be shuffling in his seat and looking at his watch during similar affairs. Some credit for this was due to Marcel Wüst, Coast's Head of Communications since the start of the year, who had found the Telekom riders to be 'guarded, scared of speaking their mind' when Wüst raced against them during his career. At one of Coast's winter training camps, Wüst had told Ullrich that breaking with the past also meant showing a more mature approach to media relations. 'At Telekom it had been King Jan,' Wüst explains. 'There, if Jan didn't want to give the interview, it didn't happen. Basically, I told him that, if I decided it was important, he had to speak to the press and, if he didn't like it, he had to speak to them anyway and not give the impression he didn't like it. I think this was the first time he saw the difference between everything being rolled out for him and needing to take responsibility for other people.'

The week continued in the same heartening vein, but Ullrich wasn't getting ahead of himself. As he had said the previous autumn, the first year of his comeback would be a slow re-immersion with no other measurable goal than 'not looking terrible' in the Tour de France. He finally finished the week twentieth on general classification, while Armstrong quit with a virus on the second day.

After cruising through four stages of the Vuelta a Aragón, Ullrich pulled out on the final day to fly to Cologne for the Rund um Köln. It was Easter Monday, not Sunday, but otherwise the scriptwriters were spoon-fed a perfect tale of resurrection: racing for the first time in Germany since September 2001, Jan Ullrich, the redeemed sinner, powered away with 53 kilometres to go and was already celebrating by the time he swept underneath the twin towers of Cologne's gothic cathedral and into the last kilometre. Banked five or six deep on either side of the road, the hordes gave Ullrich a Messiah's ovation – and he responded by riding alongside the barriers and collecting their high-fives. It would be almost two minutes before they saw another rider.

A glorious spring afternoon had, then, ended with the home fans finally basking once again in the afterglow of a Jan Ullrich victory. Meanwhile, Sylvia Schenk, the German Cycling Federation president who had talked Ullrich out of retirement at a motorway service station the previous summer, felt torn – between her happiness for Ullrich and concern at something she'd been told while standing at the roadside witnessing his exhibition. It had come from Ullrich's former Telekom doctor, Lothar Heinrich. A single cryptic sentence: that Ullrich had 'surrounded himself with the wrong people'.

'The way he said it to me, I took it to mean Jan was doping,' Schenk says. 'Now, I actually think what Lothar was saying was that Jan would be better off with *his* dope, not someone else's.'

Had Jan Ullrich carried on through the finish line in Cologne and ridden about another forty minutes up the Rhine, he could have pulled up outside Günther Dahms's front door in Essen and demanded answers to two questions that reporters kept putting to Ullrich: were Coast's financial problems resolved and would the team survive?

Rudy Pevenage had already taken matters into his own hands and contacted an old friend, the former Dutch rider Jacques Hanegraaf, who for years had also worked on commercial projects at Team Telekom. Hanegraaf had sat in board meetings the previous summer and been 'in the minority' who believed that Ullrich should finish his career at Telekom – but now he had an altogether different problem to fix. The issue was Günther Dahms, who had left a first impression on Hanegraaf that foretold Team Coast's recent woes. 'The first time I visited him, he offered me a very, very expensive bottle of wine from his cellar,' Hanegraaf recalls. 'A 3,000-dollar bottle of wine, the kind of bottle that even a collector would keep. I said to myself that he was trying to impress me. Unfortunately, he didn't have enough money to pay for the team. He was like an ostrich, sticking his head in the sand and telling me that it'd turn out all right.'

Hanegraaf, Pevenage and Wolfgang Strohband had finally decided they wanted Dahms out of the picture, and so began working on a plan to move forward without him. On 8 May, Team Coast's licence was suspended for a second time, bringing matters to a head. It was now not about ousting Dahms but simply saving the team and Ullrich's season. Bike manufacturer Bianchi had already kept them on the road in April. Now, Hanegraaf went to the Swedish holding group that owned Bianchi, Cycleurope, with a proposal – that the brand associated with the legendary Italian rider Fausto Coppi in the

1940s and 1950s could reclaim its iconic status with Jan Ullrich in the twenty-first century.

'I arranged a meeting with the president of Cycleurope, Tony Grimaldi, in Italy, and I made a very nice PowerPoint presentation on the early days of the Bianchi brand in cycling, basically saying they ought to revive the historic image of the brand. I even took a picture of Jan Ullrich and photoshopped an old Bianchi jersey onto him. Grimaldi was so impressed with my presentation that after half an hour he suspended the meeting and told me to get into my car and that we were going for dinner in Bergamo, near the Bianchi head-quarters. As soon as I got into the car, he stretched out his hand and said, "Are you sure you can do this?" I said that we were and that was the deal done – Tony said they were in for the next few months.'

Within days, Hanegraaf had travelled to the UCI headquarters in Switzerland to get rider contracts transferred and the new 'Team Bianchi' fully registered. He bought two lorries from the recently disbanded Mapei team and had them driven to Holland. A new team bus would be laid on by the tyre manufacturer Vittoria and there would be no repeat of the costly debacle of previous seasons, when Dahms had failed to secure a car supplier and instead hired Mer-cedes for every race, incurring massive charges when they were (frequently) damaged; instead, Rudy Pevenage and Team Bianchi's other directeurs would drive sponsored Renaults. The team's jersey would be a shade greener than the mock-up in Jacques Hanegraaf's presentation and the colours worn by Coast to date in 2003, a touch bluer than the Bianchi bikes. Ullrich reckoned it was 'on the old-school side'. That, he noted, 'is quite in at the moment'.

He had been the last of the eighteen riders formerly under con-tract with Dahms to sign their new deal with Bianchi. There were rumours of the Phonak, Quickstep and Cofidis teams making a late move, and Hanegraaf had started to get edgy. He didn't trust Wolf-gang Strohband, whom he considered to be 'opportunistic' and makes a point of mentioning that he was a 'second-hand car sales-man'. In the end, Hanegraaf had issued Strohband with an ultimatum and a signed contract worth nearly a million euros a year less than the one Ullrich had inked with Dahms came through with minutes to spare. Hanegraaf got the impression that Ullrich had finally, uncharacteristically, overruled his entourage. 'It was also one of the best decisions he ever made,' Hanegraaf says.

Ullrich raced for the first time in his new, old-fashioned Bianchi jersey at the Rund um die Hainleite on 31 May. The next day, he attended his second team presentation in six months in Dresden, where the Deutschland Tour was about to start. Günther Dahms, naturally, was nowhere to be seen. Just as well, said Ullrich, since 'Dahms really took the piss out of us.'

There was one Bianchi rider in Dresden who didn't care whether his new jersey was sky blue, celeste, spearmint or however else the press would describe it the following day. Before their presentation to the media, Raphael Schweda had noticed something else: for the first time all season, the riders in the team all had matching tracksuits and trainers.

Schweda has invited me to his home in Potsdam to discuss the many things he had in common with Jan Ullrich and the even more that he didn't. Both were born in Rostock, both were coached by Peter Becker and both had ended up at Bianchi in 2003, but there the similarities ended. After that season as, in his words, a 'token German' at Bianchi, Schweda quit pro cycling at the age of just twenty-seven. He went on to take up a management position in the Wiesenhof team before stepping successfully out of cycling and into Berlin's booming start-up scene. We sit at the kitchen table in the house he now shares with his wife, young child and dog in one of the vast, glorious forests that fan out of Potsdam. Schweda says he remembers the 'euphoria' of Bianchi's arrival in the late spring of 2003 – and something else that occurred at a race around that time. Although the team had survived, one of their riders still wasn't happy: he complained to another teammate and compatriot that he wanted to embark on a programme of blood-doping but the doctor who could administer it wouldn't let him into the gang. 'At the time I didn't know the name of the doctor, but I knew there was a guy at Kelme that everyone wanted to treat them. I found out later he was called Fuentes.'

Schweda was intrigued rather than surprised or morally offended. He had doped with EPO himself, 'twice a year for two weeks at a time'. He informed his parents, 'because my mum's a biology teacher and she knew how the business worked'. He had been given a crash course in blood transfusions by a Bianchi rider with whom he had shared a room at races. This individual circumvented the costly, risky

process of extracting, storing and re-injecting his own blood by refill-
ing with his brother's. The teammate told Schweda that he could
compete with the best one-day racers in the world if he also got with
the programme. Schweda says he promptly went to see to Rudy
Pevenage with half an idea to try it out, but that Pevenage 'immediately shut the conversation down'.

Over the previous few months as teammates, Schweda had
gained an insight into Jan Ullrich beyond what he had gleaned when
they had first ridden together for Germany at the world championships in 1999. If then Ullrich had struck him as a 'normal,
down-to-earth guy who liked fast cars and didn't pretend to be something that he wasn't', four years later Schweda realized that Ullrich
had grown older but not necessarily matured. Once, says Schweda,
the pairing of Ullrich's emotional fragility and Peter Becker's 'dominant personality' had suited Ullrich perfectly; now, with his old coach
out of the picture and the Telekom comfort blanket cast away, Ullrich
finally had the chance to 'emancipate himself', yet was still struggling
to truly set himself free. 'Part of Jan's problem was that he surrounded
himself with the wrong people. Becker had loads of passion, could
motivate a young rider but his scientific knowledge was basic. Then
Rudy was someone who would go around wiping Jan's arse, but not
the kind of guy who would tell him, "Ulle, that's not on."'

Still, Schweda had observed Ullrich enough over the years to see
his momentum building ahead of the 2003 Tour. The perennial spiral
of lethargy, weight gain and low self-esteem had somehow been
reversed, and Ullrich looked unstoppable.

'I think he loved it at those moments,' Schweda says. 'What he
didn't love was all the work for him to get to that point. Because, in
the nicest possible way, he is basically a lazy little pig. He does the
strict minimum until he starts to realize that it's working, and then
this kind of euphoria kicks in. That was how it worked at the training
camps: at first you had to practically drag him along, then suddenly
he started going OK and his talent did the rest. After that it just
became a virtuous cycle, and he absolutely loved that.'

Given what Ullrich had said all spring about his limited ambitions for
the Tour, the question of whether he could defeat Lance Armstrong
was scarcely being broached. One role reversal had, though, already
occurred, unbeknownst to almost everyone outside Armstrong and

US Postal's closed cache. Early in the year, Armstrong had rented a house in Santa Barbara, California with his wife of seven years and mother of their three children, Kristin. Armstrong was in California for work – appearing in a TV commercial – but ended up taking care of some other urgent business: one day when they were strolling on the beach, Armstrong turned to Kristin and told her that, after several rocky months, their relationship was done.

He had regrouped since the Circuit de la Sarthe but in his last tune-up race before the Tour, the Critérium du Dauphiné Libéré, Armstrong toiled. The week started with the unlikely victory of a scrawny climber, Iban Mayo, in the prologue time trial. Armstrong restored order by winning the next, much longer time trial, but Mayo continued to get under his skin. As he told the journalist Richard Moore years later: 'He was attacking me all the time. And, let me tell you, I was not a fan. I was not a fan of Mayo. I thought he was a little punk. We were all sort of . . . dirty, but I viewed him as being a lot dirtier than us.'

A crash three days from the end of the race left Armstrong more battered and groggy. He finally held on to win but knew the bill would land on his table sometime during the Tour. In interviews, he conceded that he couldn't remember a Dauphiné ever being so hard. Then again, he'd 'never faced a rival of Iban Mayo's calibre'. 'I like him . . .' Armstrong added by way of an unsolicited footnote, and blatant lie.

Armstrong admits now that, as had been the case with Marco Pantani in the 2000 Tour, his battle of egos with another rider stood to benefit Jan Ullrich. Johan Bruyneel sums it up when he says, 'Lance was being Lance – Mayo kept attacking and attacking, and Lance was just killing himself.'

'Ferrari just couldn't fucking understand why I was staying there. But, as usual, I had a guy in front of me and wouldn't let go,' Armstrong picks up. 'Mayo was just a small engine. I mean, I knew that was a small engine running on high-octane gas. I could see that, just looking at the guy. You look at a guy's amateur career, his career arc. These guys come up from nowhere . . .

'That year had also just been stressful,' he continues, sighing. 'Kristin and I got back together for the summer, but then split up for good in the August. We were together in the Tour. But the whole process had started in the winter. That was stressful, just dealing with that, as it would be for anybody. I started maybe drinking some more. I'd have like a glass or two at dinner, which was a departure from what I'd done before. It used to be nothing from February to July twenty-fifth. I mean, if Ferrari was at dinner, obviously I'd have nothing. Alcohol? I mean, if he saw alcohol, oh my God . . . he'd ground me.'

Ferrari's concerns deepened when Armstrong's pre-Tour blood test revealed a haematocrit of 38 per cent – a number more indicative of an anaemia diagnosis than impending victory over riders turbo-charged with EPO or blood transfusions to within sneezing range of the 50 limit. 'I mean, you know you're in trouble then,' Armstrong says. 'In theory you can go higher, but it's already pre-determined that you're going to have two bags of blood.'

Two blood transfusions, which was . . . par for the course in a Tour de France?

'I mean, it's not like I was looking at people's arms for the needle marks. These guys would know, though. Guy number eight or nine on the team would go up to guy number eight on another team . . . I mean, dude, there were no secrets. Jörg Jaksche was always a good source. He wasn't at Telekom that long, but, when he was there, he talked. And Ferrari would know. If they were going from two to three bags, Ferrari would know. I don't know how he'd know. But he would.'

As to whether Ullrich had his own Ferrari in 2003, Armstrong shrugs as if to say it's not that he didn't know, but more that it scarcely mattered.

'I was very aware of Fuentes back in 2003 and what he was like. But even knowing that Jan was with [Fuentes], it's not like we thought, *Shit's about to get real* . . . I always assumed it was about to get real with Jan. It doesn't matter if it's Fuentes or someone else: he's going to be there. That year was also interesting because he was kind of desperate. Coast went away, then it was Team Bianchi, and all of a sudden those guys are going, *Fuck, we're riding for our livelihood, no one's paying us a gazillion bucks, or a ten million bonus if I win; I've got to make a name for myself again.*'

At times, Armstrong's understanding with his directeur sportif, Johan Bruyneel, could seem telepathic, but their accounts occasionally veer apart. Bruyneel maintains that he and Armstrong had heard nothing of a potential connection between Ullrich and Eufemiano

Fuentes in 2003. Had they done so, whatever fears they were taking into the Tour may well have multiplied.

'It would have been an extra fear factor for us, definitely,' Bruyneel confirms. 'You'd seen some things with riders with Fuentes that were just unbelievable . . . And we'd known about Fuentes since the nineties. I had one rider who came to the team, who was with Fuentes, and I told him he had to stop but he wouldn't. This guy swore by Fuentes. And it was definitely a different level with him.'

17

SLIDING DOORS

'Ullrich and his story make him the kind of hero whose defeats we easily forgive because, with him, the difference between victory and defeat disappears'

—*Burkhard Spinnen,* Frankfurter Allgemeine Zeitung

As births go, they were both scary, somewhat gruelling but ultimately joyous. At just gone a quarter past three on 1 July 1903, sixty trailblazers on bikes set out from the Réveil Matin cafe in southern Paris, bound for Lyon and the finish line of the first ever stage of the Tour de France, 467 kilometres away. One hundred years to the day and in fact almost to the minute later, in Freiburg, Gaby Weis gave birth to a 2.5-kilogram baby daughter who would take her father's surname. Her dad's were also some of the first words Sarah Maria Ullrich ever heard: 'If you're good, I'll buy you a cabriolet on your eighteenth birthday.' Hearing this, the little girl stopped wailing and fell silent.

For its centenary edition, the Tour would begin where it usually ended, in Paris, and Jan Ullrich felt as though his race was already won. Rudy Pevenage had never seen him so happy. Only a couple of days in, Ullrich said that fatherhood had already changed his perspective on life, more even than the tribulations of the previous summer. For the first time since 1996 he was also coming into the Tour with only modest ambitions: nominally, he would be Bianchi's joint leader with the Spaniard Ángel Casero, but would be thrilled with 'a nice stage win', he said. Pevenage told the press a podium place was almost out of the question.

Ullrich did finish fourth in the prologue, only two seconds behind winner Bradley McGee. The result was significant; Ullrich had beaten Armstrong in a Tour prologue for the first time, and by a decent margin of five seconds.

The next major test was a time trial, this one ridden in teams between Joinville and Saint-Dizier. At Coast's training camp in Gandia in Spain in the winter, Ullrich had organized a team dinner to smooth his integration into the group, and riders and staff had eaten, drunk and bonded until three in the morning. Since then, the money issues with Coast and ensuing suspensions, plus the difficulty of mixing Ullrich's German clique with a large Spanish contingent, had stifled any sense of developing camaraderie. The switch from Coast to Bianchi had also created assorted logistical problems – including with the riders' time-trial bikes. By the time they were assembled, checked and polished – and the mechanics could finally go to bed – daylight was already bleaching out the darkness over the Marne river.

When Bianchi rolled off the ramp a few hours later, Ullrich produced a performance that his teammates that day have never forgotten. 'It's very simple: Ullrich went like a bullet,' says Ángel Casero, who had the invidious honour of following Ullrich in the Bianchi paceline. An effective team time trial is generally one in which everyone takes regular turns on the front to ensure a steady pace. 'But that day it was almost impossible for me to come around him,' says Casero. 'There were riders in the team who didn't take a single pull.'

Another of Bianchi's Spaniards, Félix García Casas, says simply that it was 'pure Ullrich . . . I think the last 20 kilometres were practically all him.'

The afternoon ended with Armstrong and Johan Bruyneel hailing US Postal's best ever team time trial, and yet Ullrich had conceded only forty seconds. For Bianchi it had been a triumph – or would have been had Ullrich not started to feel unwell that evening, shortly after receiving a legal, intravenous infusion of amino-acids and vitamins, he said. When he woke the next day with diarrhoea and a temperature in the high thirties, the Bianchi team doctor deduced the previous night's 'treatment' had somehow been contaminated.

Had the terrain been hillier, the racing more aggressive, he would never have made it through the next two stages, Ullrich said later. As it was, he endured a silent, private torture – some of the worst hours he had ever spent on a bike.

That he was able to hide his suffering owed in part to paranoia; their fear of US Postal listening in led Pevenage, Ullrich and Tobias Steinhauser to devise a method whereby Steinhauser would drop back to the race doctor's car to ask for paracetamol or other remedies on Ullrich's behalf. Pevenage also said nothing to the other Bianchi riders, lest they let on to friends in other teams. 'There were two days when he didn't even come down to dinner with us, which we thought was odd,' says García Casas. 'He'd always gone around the rooms to thank us for our help every evening – he was a fantastic guy, not cold as you'd expect a German to be – yet all of a sudden the guy was invisible. We found out later that he had acute diarrhoea and Rudy didn't even want us to know. We were going back to the team car the whole time to get bottles . . . but it turned out they were to rinse his shorts, not to drink. After he'd made it through that, I said to myself that he was mentally and physically ready to win the Tour. You could also tell what condition he was in when he took his top off in the bus: I'll never forget how you could see the vein running up his shoulder.'

Although recovering, Ullrich conceded just over a minute to Armstrong on the first mountain stage to Alpe d'Huez. He got through 'on grit alone', according to Pevenage. Armstrong 'completely sucked', he says now. But he was less preoccupied with Ullrich than with who had won: that punk Iban Mayo.

The 2003 summer was the hottest on record in France. Three months of temperatures edging 40 degrees Celsius killed 14,802 people by the French National Institute of Health's estimates. On 14 July, Bastille Day, the Tour de France headed south, even deeper into the furnace. It was the very definition of *Ulli Wetter*, as the Germans called it – and exactly the conditions Armstrong despised. Soon the American would be glad to still be in the race, never mind the yellow jersey; when Joseba Beloki's back wheel slid through a patch of melting tarmac on the descent of the Col de Manse, Armstrong swerved around the Spaniard and off the road. His ensuing detour across a ploughed field, over a ditch and back onto the race route was and would remain the most astonishing, perhaps the defining moment of his reign.

But in the 47-kilometre time trial between Gaillac and Cap Découverte four days later, Ullrich didn't so much beat Armstrong as incinerate him. Armstrong would say later that at one point he'd thought about climbing off his bike and quitting. He was dehydrated, burned up, wrung dry by two torrid weeks. Meanwhile, in hellish heat, Ullrich had become the devil: his margin of victory, his first in a Tour stage since 1998, was one minute, thirty-six seconds. Of the other riders, only Alexander Vinokourov, Ullrich's old teammate and his replacement as Telekom's leader, came within two and a half minutes. Armstrong still led the Tour but his advantage had been cut to thirty-four seconds over Ullrich and fifty-one over Vinokourov.

At home, six million Germans had tuned in to watch what was described in *L'Équipe* the next day as '*Le Retour du Wunderkind*'.

Ullrich now had three Pyrenean stages to land his coup de grâce. He was the strongest rider in the race but the margins were too fine for that to suffice. He would also need to outmanoeuvre or outthink Armstrong, and herein lay his problem. As Ángel Casero reflects, 'When he was strong, that was when he lacked the ability to read the race. He thought he could smash everyone to pieces – he lost his cool.'

During act one, the mountaintop finish at Ax 3 Domaines, Ullrich looked at times to playing it too safe. He finally launched a violent attack two kilometres from the line, moments after Vinokourov, reducing Armstrong's usually effervescent cadence to a leaden clunk. 'Everything felt so fragile,' Johan Bruyneel admits now. 'We were just hanging on, even in the car. We thought Lance could crack at any moment. There was no strategy: just hang on.'

Armstrong eventually conceded only seven seconds, to which was added Ullrich's bonus for finishing second on the stage: twelve more. Pevenage hadn't been certain bonus seconds were on offer, and – somewhat embarrassingly – had to check with the mechanic in the back of the Bianchi team car. Armstrong was still in yellow but now only fifteen seconds ahead. Vinokourov had burned bright and faded fast, coming in ten seconds behind Armstrong.

One opportunity down, two to go.

When I mention the second Pyrenean stage to Loudenvielle, even nearly a decade and a half later, Rudy Pevenage bows his lead. This one was on him. As he tells me, 'There, it was me who messed up. *Allez* . . . I made a mistake that I wouldn't usually have made.'

Vinokourov and Telekom drew the error, given that, parallel to his battle of wits with Johan Bruyneel, Pevenage was desperate to get one over on his and Ullrich's old employer. In their three years together at Telekom, Ullrich and Vinokourov had built a close friendship, and it also now made sense for them to unite against a common enemy in Armstrong. However, when Vinokourov countered Ullrich's attack on the last climb of the day, the Col de Peyresourde, Pevenage ignored one of the most elementary rules in the Tour de France instruction manual – that you always make the yellow jersey chase. Especially when he's going for his fifth win. Instead, it was Ullrich who went to the front and Armstrong who enjoyed an armchair ride.

'We had left Telekom and it was still war with them,' Pevenage explains sheepishly. 'Vino was my friend, Jan's friend . . . but he was the captain of Telekom. Maybe we got our priorities wrong and thought too much about Vino. The plan in the morning was to race really hard and set Jan up for an attack on the Peyresourde, but we hadn't recced that stage. The stress had also been too much from the start of the Tour. Getting the bus ready, the time trial bikes arriving with hours to spare . . . I still don't know how we got it all together. Anyway, I'd got my timings wrong a bit on the Peyresourde. Our Spaniards should also all have been there, but they'd already gone out of the back – David Plaza, Aitor Garmendia, Casero. The Peyresourde was right into the wind, and Jan attacked too early. Lance jumped right onto his wheel, then Vino countered and went away. I should have stayed calm because Armstrong needed to win the race too. But I didn't want Telekom to win the stage or the Tour, and I knew Vino was strong. I didn't want to take the risk of Vino getting two minutes, so I told Jan to ride. Maybe there we should have gone for broke and seen what Armstrong could do . . .'

No maybes. Not according to Johan Bruyneel. 'The Peyresourde was their big chance.'

Armstrong isn't sure. Or doesn't remember. Or doesn't care. One of the three. He's trying to decide. 'I think there are probably guys who sit around and think about this shit all of the time. But if you don't ask me these questions . . . I mean, to think about Loudenda-dee-da in 2003 . . . I mean, I haven't thought about that in five years. I don't care. I'm more worried about where I'm playing golf tomorrow. Or what legal bullshit I have to deal with. Or what time my kid's game is tomorrow. I just don't think about it. Is that weird? Or maybe not.'

Never mind. Vinokourov, who said later that Ullrich and Pevenage had committed a 'big mistake' had taken back forty-three
seconds.

Two chances down, one to go.

Jacques Hanegraaf, the man who had struck the deal with Bianchi
and salvaged Ullrich's Tour, makes a good point years later: Jan Ullrich's whole career had been a continuous, at times exhausting tussle
with the same opponent – himself. He had never really paid much
attention to anyone else. Every spring, in every race, his single preoccupation had been to inch closer to that physiological sweet spot at
which he knew that he had once atomized the world's best, at the
1997 Tour. As such, Ullrich had been a professional for eight seasons
but had raced, truly *competed*, relatively sparingly. And that would
show in a three-way fight that was now also a tactical puzzle.

Moreover, Rudy Pevenage could sense that Armstrong, the sleeping dragon, was beginning to stir. In their pre-race briefing in
Bagnères-de-Bigorre, Pevenage instructed his men and Ullrich to be
on their guard. Regardless, one of the Bianchi riders, Fabrizio Guidi,
stepped off the team bus and told an Italian reporter that Ullrich was
going to 'smash' Armstrong.

But Johan Bruyneel had bad news for Guidi, Ullrich and his Geraardsbergen neighbour Pevenage. 'If we wanted to win the race,
there was no way we could go into the last TT with fifteen seconds,
but I could see in the bus that, mentally, Lance was really ready. It
was like, *OK, this has to happen now.*'

For its final day in the Pyrenees – the last mountain stage in what
some pundits were calling the most thrilling edition in memory – the
Tour would be blessed with a grandiose setting on its journey from
Bagnères-de-Bigorre to Luz Ardiden. There were six kilometres to go
to the summit of the Col du Tourmalet and forty-two to the finish
line when Ullrich kicked. Armstrong followed for a few seconds then
let go, as had Vinokourov. Suddenly everything Ullrich had done the
previous day made sense: he had let Vinokourov cook himself in the
sun while marinating Armstrong for the last supper. Now he stuck a
fork in the American and would soon be licking the plate.

Only that's not quite what happened. The gap grew to ten seconds, peaked at twelve, then Armstrong slowly, coolly clawed his
way back. By the end of the descent, at the foot of the final climb,
even Vinokourov would be back with them.

Why had Ullrich made such an early move? Rudy Pevenage couldn't work it out; the plan he had laid out in the morning was that they would wait until the last climb. Félix García Casas wondered whether something had changed, for on the approach to the Tourmalet Pevenage had called him back to the team car and handed him a paper note. 'Give it to Jan and don't let anyone see,' Pevenage said. Minutes later, Ullrich was attacking and García Casas was 'flipping out, because that wasn't the plan'. Indeed, according to Ullrich, the initiative had come from him, only him, and had been an attempt to give Armstrong a dose of his own mind medicine. 'I wanted to show him that I could hurt him,' he said later.

Johan Bruyneel remembers Ullrich trying again on the way down the Tourmalet. 'Lance was getting a gel or something from the car at the time and he just put his head inside the window and said, "Well, that's stupid . . ."'

For years, the spectre of what Ullrich could theoretically achieve had teased the best out of Armstrong without ever making him draw from that crimson, flaming pool of fuck-you determination that he could access when faced with adversaries that were also antagonists – chumps and punks like Iban Mayo or Marco Pantani. It was an impulse that had its roots in Armstrong's childhood, though where exactly, Armstrong tells me he doesn't understand. He has also never really dwelled on why, given that they were both the sons of abusive and absent fathers, raised by devoted single mothers, Jan Ullrich turned out so different. 'I'm sure the whole single-parent thing is somewhere, has some influence on my story . . . I mean it must have been part of my make-up early on, because I was born to somebody that I had no contact with, was raised for ten years by someone who I ended up really not caring for or having any contact with, so a true critic or cynic would say that when I attacked I was thinking, *OK, Fuck Terry Armstrong! Fuck Eddie Gunderson!** But that stuff never even crossed my mind. Did it, though, from those primitive years into middle school and high school, was it forming me? I'm sure. But I don't think Jan ever leaned over his bike and said, "I'm going to show my dad, the guy who walked out on me." Or maybe he did, but I had my own little fictitious rivalries to rile me up.'

A day or two before what was now clearly turning into the

---

*   Lance Armstrong's adoptive father and biological father, respectively.

decisive stage, one of Armstrong's teammates had seen a quote from Pevenage to the effect that Ullrich taking the jersey off Armstrong was only a matter a time. The US Postal rider had shown it to Armstrong, who had read it and snarled back, 'They will never have that jersey.'

Now, on the climb to Luz Ardiden, for the first time in the Tour, Armstrong felt a surge of the old power, the muscular electricity for which he and teammate George Hincapie had coined their own jockish codewords – 'No chain, baby!' Iban Mayo was his on-switch: when the Spaniard attacked, Armstrong cranked harder on the pedals and roared past. Ullrich gasped but hung on until Armstrong sped up again, hugged the inside of a slight right-hand bend . . . and tangled with the yellow cotton bag of a young spectator. Suddenly Armstrong had crashed, also bringing down Mayo. Ahead of Ullrich was only open road.

A few years later, a similar incident would give rise to one of the Tour's strangest ever incidents and images – of Chris Froome, the two-time champion, running up Mont Ventoux having lost his bike in a collision with a motorcycle. The following day, in L'Équipe, Philippe Brunel meditated on the question of whether the race jury had been right to neutralize the race from the moment of Froome's mishap. Brunel's conclusion was that trying to divorce the race from 'imponderables to which the Tour is fatally exposed in the mountains, in the middle of a fervid crowd' was to rip out its soul – that of 'an open-air theatre, playing out in a heedless natural world, both beautiful and cruel, grandiose and threatening, where anything can happen.'

That 'anything' in 2003 had been a spectator's cotton bag. One could well espouse Brunel's romantic image of the Tour and its cosmos, or more mundanely point out that Armstrong should not have been riding so close to the crowd. But neither of these notions could distract Jan Ullrich from an unwritten cycling diktat – that, when a rival crashes or punctures, you wait, particularly if he's in the yellow jersey. Armstrong had also slowed for him when Ullrich had crashed on the descent of the Peyresourde in 2001.

Ullrich said later it had been an easy choice because 'fairness is everything in sport'. In the spur of the moment, Rudy Pevenage didn't agree. He grabbed his intercom receiver and screamed in Ullrich's ear: 'It's only once, the Tour de France. Just ride!'

Armstrong initially panicked – his foot slipping out of his pedal, nearly bringing him down again – before a huge, thermonuclear jolt of adrenaline brought him back to the lead group and, after another attack, straight past them. Ullrich also now looked like his old self – the spluttering diesel engine left behind. He sprinted at the top of the mountain to take third place and eight bonus seconds but by then Armstrong was towelling himself down beside the podium. The time gap now: one minute, seven seconds.

Ullrich headed down the mountain in a Bianchi team car. Usually he communicated with his Spanish teammates through Pevenage's translations, sign language and his tiny but expanding Italian vocabulary. But now, with teammate Félix García Casas sitting along-side him, Ullrich stayed silent. 'He was devastated. We all felt that night that the Tour had slipped from our grasp,' says García Casas.

The first Tour that Ullrich had seen, the seed of the dream he'd realized in 1997, was the 1989 edition won by Greg LeMond. That year, a time trial had turned the race on its head and the same would have to happen here. But Ullrich didn't need a miracle – a repeat of Cap Découverte would do. There he had gained on Armstrong at a rate of just over two seconds per kilometre. Do the same again between Pornic and Nantes and he would win easily – never mind that Armstrong had won the final time trial in every Tour since 1999.

Rudy Pevenage was still hopeful until, on the morning of the time trial, he woke to torrential rain. He and Jacques Hanegraaf then set off on a route recce . . . without Ullrich.

'He'd really impressed me the whole Tour with his mentality, but there, suddenly, his mentality changed and he really disappointed me,' says Hanegraaf. 'In the morning, we're there thinking this is it, we have to go for it, really study this course and get everything right and all of a sudden he decided not to get out of bed. It was very frustrating. I said to Rudy, "He has to go. This is the day." But Rudy defended him. Rudy said that Jan must have a good reason. And he ended up staying in bed. I mean, how naive can you be? Thinking that a video could be the same preparation as doing the circuit? Then, when we're on the course, we have a guy leaning out of the car to film it, and what's the first thing we see? Lance Armstrong in his yellow rain jacket, doing the circuit. And of course that's what Jan saw in his bedroom two hours later. It was not good.'

Ullrich told a Belgian documentary years later that he had

decided to lie-in because the course was 'so simple'. 'There were a couple of roundabouts and that was it. Why go out in the rain just to see that?'

Having looked unusually tense and fidgety on the start ramp, he soon found his groove out on the road. At the 32-kilometre time check Ullrich set the fastest time . . . but it was only three seconds quicker than Armstrong. He pushed harder, forced a little more, tilted his front wheel a little more sharply into the wet corners. Pevenage yelled instructions through his intercom radio – 'Right here! Left in 200 metres!' – but he and Hanegraaf had spotted a problem with the notes they had made in the morning. 'We'd used the odometer in the car to make notes about when the corners and roundabouts were coming, but the time trial started and there were discrepancies,' Hanegraaf says. 'It seemed like we had a different car from the one we'd used in the morning. Rudy panicked a bit, started saying, 'Oh, it's not correct. It's not correct. The roundabout's going to be later now . . .'

It was just as well that, as Ullrich said, the course was so simple, with just those 'couple of roundabouts'. So simple that messages had been sent to Hanegraaf and Pevenage's mobile phones to tell them two Bianchi riders had already crashed at one of them, 13 kilometres from the line. 'But we made mistakes there,' Hanegraaf concedes now. 'I still recall that on this roundabout the message in [Jan's] ear wasn't that he needed to slow down.'

The result: a skid, a crash, a slide across the tarmac, and the end of whatever hope remained – at least in this Tour de France.

Ullrich at least hadn't lost his sense of humour. 'I skated better than Katarina Witt,' he told his teammates. He would later insist the Tour had 'felt like a victory'.

The 2003 Tour had been a different experience for Wolfgang Strohband. For years Telekom had asked him to make arrangements for their VIP guests on the last day of the Tour, and Strohband had felt too embarrassed to tell friends and acquaintances that he – like CEO Ron Sommer and Jürgen Kindervater – was staying in the Crillon. 'Of course I wouldn't be paying, but I'd sneak a look at the price for a suite. It was borderline excessive,' Strohband tells me. In 2003, he followed the last week of the race but felt somehow marginalized, which was how Jacques Hanegraaf wanted it. 'Strohband was following us everywhere. He was always in the hotel next door,' Hanegraaf says. 'I didn't want him with us so I wasn't booking his rooms. And I didn't really realize what he was doing.'

There may have been no ulterior motive, but Strohband was well aware that, having crashed the previous summer, Ullrich's stock was suddenly soaring. Just over nine million Germans tuned in to the Nantes time trial and an average of just over six million watched the Tour every day. This eclipsed even the figures from 1997.

But it was more than just numbers. The Ullrich of 1997 had personified the exhilaration and promise of youth, of a Germany struggling to reconcile its broken pieces, and the fragments of a society that still felt betrayed, alienated or ambivalent – whereas now he seemed to stand for something even more universal and relatable. As Rolf Aldag and Lance Armstrong have already told me, Ullrich was the fallible Everyman who everyone wished they could somehow shake out of mediocrity and into the kind of excellence he had nearly, so nearly produced at the 2003 Tour. It was a paradigm that could be applied to athletes, lawyers, milkmen – and resonated even with novelists like Burkhard Spinnen, writing in the *Frankfurter Allgemeine Zeitung*. For Spinnen, for Germany, 'Ullrich and his story make him the kind of hero whose defeats we easily forgive because, with him, the difference between victory and defeat disappears.' Even in Ullrich's decision to wait for Armstrong on Luz Ardiden, Spinnen saw not adherence to an unwritten code but a common paradox – the fear and loneliness of approaching success, and the magnetic force that sucks us back towards our enemies, demons and, yes, defeat.

The inspirational value of a message like that was clear to René Obermann, who had been appointed the CEO of Telekom's mobile division – T-Mobile – late in 2002. Obermann didn't offer Wolfgang Strohband a suite at the Crillon but he did suggest that they meet in Paris 'to talk about Jan'. Strohband knew immediately what it would be about: Telekom wanted Ullrich back for the rebranded team.

Soon, their legal team would be presenting Strohband with a contract. As Strohband remembers: 'The lawyer from T-Mobile drew up this contract that was 108 or 109 pages long. We started negotiating – me and my lawyer, them with theirs – and I went away saying to myself, *I can't talk to people who have no idea what they're on about*. There were clauses like Jan never being allowed to go into a restaurant and drink a glass of water because there could be something in it. He had to go to the tap and pour it himself, or open the bottle himself. You couldn't believe some of the stuff in there.'

They also didn't sign – yet. A further meeting took place in Strohband's Hamburg office on 1 September, followed by another one in Berlin. They finally settled on a 'signing-on' fee of two million euros and a salary that would rise from 2.76 million euros in 2004 to 3.26 million euros in 2005. Ullrich would also receive three payments of 500,000 euros for contributions to T-Mobile ad campaigns. And, of course, there were handsome results-related bonuses.

Jacques Hanegraaf and Bianchi were party to none of this. They had also met Strohband in Paris and believed that they, too, had an agreement: Tony Grimaldi of Bianchi would look for co-sponsors to secure the team's future on the understanding that Ullrich was central to it. Over the next few weeks, Grimaldi and Hanegraaf sounded out multiple major companies, including Samsung and Deutsche Post, who had wanted Ullrich in a Bjarne Riis-led team a few months earlier. 'Deutsche Post were willing to get involved . . . but only with Jan Ullrich,' Hanegraaf remembers. 'I got into a kind of triangle then: I couldn't convince Jan Ullrich to sign up, and no sponsor would sign without him.'

Volkswagen was another lead: they were apparently ready to commit 30 million euros a year, almost double Team Telekom's annual budget, to fund a team to promote a newly released minivan. Strohband was leading those talks, but they also ran aground, perhaps partly because Telekom had Ullrich on the hook and now wouldn't let go. As Hanegraaf reflects now, 'We'd talked about a figure of two million euros a year, but I got the feeling later that when Strohband had mentioned a number to Obermann, he'd just added a million on top.'

As September turned to October, Hanegraaf believed there was still one last chance. He and Tony Grimaldi would meet Strohband and Ullrich and tell him that sponsors were waiting, money was available. But first Ullrich would have to make a pledge.

'We called this meeting in Switzerland, with Jan, Rudy and Strohband. We wanted Jan to give us a final green light, because the money was all there for the future. All that wasn't there was Jan Ullrich. His behaviour had also changed a lot after I think he'd taken the decision. We'd had a lot of contact with Jan and especially Rudy, but after the Tour it was total silence for a week. And this was very strange to us. So, anyway, we decided to have this meeting in the Mövenpick hotel at Zürich and cut to the chase. And that's where he told us he was going to another team. He didn't say T-Mobile – but in fact the day before he had already had a meeting and posed for pictures in a T-Mobile jersey. Those pictures got released a few hours after our meeting. So that was very bitter. They told us, then Strohband got up, Ullrich got up and Rudy followed them, and we were left sitting there, me and Tony. Tony turned to me and said three words: "Let's get drunk."'

A couple of weeks after the Tour, Ullrich had welcomed German celebrity magazine *Bunte* into his villa in Scherzingen, posed for pictures with Gaby and Sarah Maria, and opened up about his wonderful new life in Switzerland. Had he won the Tour, Ullrich revealed, he might have 'given up straight away'. It was perhaps better that he hadn't because now he had 'one place left to aim at'. Regardless, no one could be happier than he was at that moment, 'with success in every area of my life, a relationship that's working well and the baby'.

There was similar talk of family bonds when, finally, T-Mobile unveiled Ullrich at a press conference in Bonn on 4 October. René Obermann said Ullrich was like a 'lost son' from whom Telekom had had to distance itself in order to appreciate, and perhaps vice versa. It should nonetheless not be seen as a comeback or a reunion, more a new beginning.

Ullrich also spoke about having returned to his roots. And maybe having turned back time. Whether this was a good thing or not was hard to say. He stopped mid-sentence in his answer to one journalist's question, unable to remember what it was or where he was going. A bead of sweat glistened on his brow. 'I'm a bit stressed,' he told the reporters, smiling meekly. 'I haven't slept for days.'

18

AFTER THE LOVE HAS GONE

'I think maybe 2003 sort of broke Jan. After that he wasn't even close'

—*Johan Bruyneel*

Like Jan Ullrich, Brian Holm had known and raced for Telekom before the team's first Tour win in 1996, he'd known the team afterwards, and after a short hiatus a little like Ullrich's, he knew the environment into which Der Kaiser would be returning in 2004.

Holm had rejoined the team as a directeur sportif at the start of 2003. And it's fair to say the Dane had not been impressed.

'You had the Spanish division on one side, then Matthias Kessler and Andreas Klöden and those guys on the other. The Germans didn't speak one word of Spanish and the Spanish didn't give a shit about the Germans and probably didn't like them. Fucking weird team. It was the biggest team there has ever been in cycling and for sure the worst.'

The world of magenta and white again revolved around Ullrich, but he wasn't the callow, wide-eyed lamb who had sung Cranberries songs in the hotel room he shared with Holm at the Classique des Alpes in 1995.

'Everything about the young unspoiled Ullrich that I'd known had changed,' Holm confirms. 'He was still a nice kid but to me it looked like he fucking hated his life. He'd gone away for a year, then came back with Rudy . . . and he wasn't that unspoiled kid any more. He liked a glass of wine, for sure. I got the impression – of course I could be wrong – but he hated every second of standing there every day in front of the media. It had become big, big, big. He had become that superstar. Bjarne could handle it, Lance could definitely handle it, but Ulle didn't like it. He wasn't cut out for that stuff. I think, you know, if you have two or three glasses of wine maybe things start to look a bit brighter, a bit more optimistic, then you sleep and you get up and go through the same cycle. Unfortunately, there was no one with the balls to stop him. There was not one person who had the balls to say, "OK, if you do this or that, I'm fucking sending you home." Because he was too big. And another problem was that he was such a nice guy: you didn't want to hurt him, and you would never start a conflict just to make him look silly.'

One of the few constants throughout the Telekom life cycle had been Walter Godefroot. The wise but increasingly jaded old owl had nurtured his baby through its first growing pains, seen the team mature and prosper and was now presiding over its age of bourgeois opulence. 'And the dimensions it took . . . I didn't like,' Godefroot notes, referring to the year-by-year increase in both the team's budget and its fetishization by a certain cadre of rich and influential Germans. One man in particular, the politician, Rudolf Scharping, had become Telekom's most prominent fan and a frequent visitor to races and training camps. Gregarious and controversial, Scharping became a popular figure of fun in the German media when the celebrity magazine, *Bunte*, published photos of him frolicking in a Mallorcan swimming pool with his girlfriend, a countess, in 2001. Scharping, the defence minister at the time, had stepped out of a meeting about imminent German military deployment in Macedonia and straight onto an army plane, which had flown him to the Balearic Islands at a cost of over 100,000 euros. The proximity of another Mallorcan tryst to the 9/11 terrorist attacks earned him an invidious nickname: 'Bin Baden'. 'Baden' being the German verb 'to swim or bathe'.

'Scharping was no gift for me,' Godefroot says now of the politician's close affiliation with the team. 'When I first met him he was standing for German Chancellor as Helmut Kohl's opponent. He came with two bodyguards, an armoured vehicle – and we drank too many beers. We were drunk, and I said to him that he could come in the second team car the next day. One of the bodyguards says, no, they couldn't leave the armoured car, to which I responded that we'd be fine because one of our soigneurs, Eule Reutenberg, was an old Stasi man . . .'

Wolfgang Strohband remembers another of Scharping's visits when he was standing for the German Chancellorship, another boozy evening ending with Scharping going to bed and his bodyguard announcing to the gathering he'd left, 'If they make him the Chancellor, I'm leaving the country.'

At the time, Godefroot saw the glad-handing as a necessary evil – a reasonable quid pro quo for Telekom's financial largesse. He did, though, occasionally draw the line. Like when Telekom's marketing men informed him they had done a deal with Audi that would see Ullrich, Bjarne Riis and Erik Zabel given A8 models, the rest of the team A6s and Telekom's under-23 riders A4s. 'There I put my foot down,' Godefroot says. 'Jürgen Kindervater told me about it and I went silent. He asked whether I didn't think it was a good deal. I said, well, one, it'll go to their heads, and two, what happens when we suddenly don't have a sponsor who can give us that?'

In the autumn of 2003, Godefroot had also had to be firm on another point: just because Jan Ullrich was 'coming home' to T-Mobile, that did not mean Rudy Pevenage was forgiven or welcome to return. Godefroot made that clear as soon as Ullrich's return was mooted in the summer.

'I was happy to have Jan back, of course. Jan's a good rider. You always want good riders. He's also a nice guy. You can't say he's an arsehole. But as for Rudy, there's a phone call, not from Obermann but the guy under Obermann who's in charge of the team, Martin Knauer – 'We have to talk.' I think it was a Friday morning. I said OK, but he should call me Monday. No, it was too urgent for that – I had to go to Bonn. I had a few things to do but in the afternoon I was there. 300 kilometres to Bonn. I go into the office and there's a huge photo of Jan in the yellow jersey. Then I knew what was going on. The reason they've brought me there is to ask me whether I'll work with Jan . . . and Pevenage. I say I don't trust Rudy, and once the trust is gone, it's gone forever. So I refuse. But Knauer . . . There were a few of these guys. One of them had been in the car at the Tour the previous year. I'd had to drive the second car for a day so that I could entertain this guy from T-Mobile. I'd told him how it all worked – the race director's car, the commissaires, how the peloton worked, the feed zone – and he was shocked because he thought the riders got off their bikes to eat. That was the level. And now here I was with this guy telling me I had to work with Pevenage.'

Eventually a compromise was struck whereby T-Mobile and Godefroot would tolerate Pevenage working privately with Ullrich, but he would not be allowed to stay in their hotels at races. Godefroot tells me he would occasionally see Pevenage and mumble a hello, no more. 'It was strange, yes. Rudy himself said he was the best-paid bag carrier in the peloton. But the bottom line was that I didn't trust him.'

Pevenage, for his part, felt that in 2003 he and Ullrich had been liberated – and they were returning to the golden cage.

'We'd felt free of the big Telekom machine in 2003, so it was a weird situation. Jan said that he'd draw up a personal contract for me, that he didn't want to leave me in the shit. But only seeing him in the evening – that wasn't what I was good at. I could go to the hotel in the evening and see Jan at the start, but I couldn't have any other contact with the team. It wasn't good for me or Jan.'

The factory reset seemed from the outside to be working out well enough for Jan Ullrich in the final months of 2003 and the period that had typically been his Bermuda Triangle, between Christmas and the season's start. Before that, he had been reminded once more of how far and how loudly his exploits the previous summer had resonated when Mikhail Gorbachev presented him with the 'World Connection Award' at a gala in Hamburg for having waited for Lance Armstrong at Luz Ardiden – a supposedly exceptional contribution to international relations. Which was curious and a little awkward, given that Armstrong was about to bring out a second autobiography with a new take on what had occurred – namely that Ullrich hadn't slowed down at all.

Hearing this, Ullrich laughed, and there was further merriment on a visit to Kazakhstan to see his friend, rival in 2003 and now teammate again, Alexander Vinokourov. A *L'Équipe* journalist, Philippe Le Gars, was also on the trip, and Le Gars came to feel later that it was the first time that Ullrich had truly opened up to members of the press. Later in the year, on the eve of the Tour de France, Ullrich would call Le Gars with an idea: he wanted to assemble a collection of wines, all from 2003 and produced in regions that the race would visit in the forthcoming edition, to gift to his daughter

Sarah Maria, born the previous year, on her twentieth birthday. When Le Gars enquired about a budget, Ullrich replied with one word: 'Unlimited!'

To other members of the media, and particularly those who attended T-Mobile's team launch in Mallorca in January, changes were harder to discern. Some even thought there had been a regression. At T-Mobile HQ in Bonn, he was no longer just Jan Ullrich but, internal memos said, 'Premium Product Jan Ullrich', an ambitious new PR-strategy having been elaborated to 'leverage the asset'. Jürgen Kindervater, Telekom's old communications chief and a sort of spiritual father for the cycling team, had left not long after CEO Ron Sommer in 2002, and Wolfgang Strohband thought some of the team's soul had departed with Kindervater. 'I wouldn't say going back was a mistake. We just thought that it would be the same as at Telekom. But it was totally different. At Telekom everything came from Kindervater and Sommer. It was more human. At T-Mobile it all started with the 108-page contract which, admittedly, we later got down to forty pages. It all smacked of an approach that was all about putting business first, the athletes second.'

Some saw just the escalation of a process that had begun with Ullrich's Tour win in 1997, or even the year before with Bjarne Riis's. Ullrich had occasionally faltered, often fell short of expectations, but the cake kept rising and everyone wanted their slice. Another major German team, Gerolsteiner, had got richer and more ambitious every season, and in 2004 the German calendar would feature a total of ninety-nine days of UCI-ratified racing, compared with forty-seven in 1996. Stuttgart was also about to win its bid to host the UCI Road World Championships in 2007. The German economy may have been struggling, so much so that French and British analysts gloated that Germany was now the 'sick man of Europe' with its record unemployment, but there was one sport and one sportsman who could still get the moneymen pulling out their wallets.

And if Ullrich was the Sun, Telekom and everything else in his orbit was the Earth, basking in a golden glow. This was certainly how it felt to riders like Rolf Aldag, who soaked up the rays while also wondering about the long-term effects. 'The Belgians go to the Tour of Flanders and if one of their riders wins they're happy, but they'll go anyway because they went there with their granddad, with their dad, and they'll go with their son. That never existed in Germany. So that's why it was a little bit strange. I'm not sure everyone knew how to handle it. And then in my opinion it was also a bit overdone, with two German television stations coming to the Tour with more people there than the host broadcasters, the people who send everything up in the air. It was like the Germans had occupied the Tour de France. It was a little bit of a weird feeling, not always the right feeling, because you always think, like, we lost two World Wars, now we try it with cycling, with power, with money.'

The analogy is a little overblown, Aldag knows, but that's also his point.

'It was over the top, but we also enjoyed it a lot,' he picks up. 'If you went to a hotel and they gave you a better room because of who you were, that was also nice.'

Brian Holm simply felt that the team which had reabsorbed Ullrich in 2004 was choking on its own hubris.

'Even Team Sky would look like a village team compared to that. That was another level. I mean, which team has racing caps in different sizes? The Audis . . . At the team meetings, if they wanted to take us to play ice hockey, there'd be an ice-hockey kit in Telekom colours with our name on the back. If they took us go-karting, we'd have a full, personalized go-karting suit waiting for us. Fucking biggest hotel I've seen in my life. We were as spoiled as hell. I mean, who wouldn't like that? But basically the riders were overpaid, with no results. That was T-Mobile. They really lost it. Too much red wine and too little ambition.'

Ullrich was at least used to fighting for elbow room with Erik Zabel – and the hierarchy had been re-established at the T-Mobile team presentation in January, when the riders all filed onto the stage in alphabetical order with one exception – Ullrich coming after Zabel. It didn't appear to unduly fluster Ullrich that in interviews Zabel kept offering the team's assorted successes in 2003 as proof that it was perhaps a good idea to pursue other goals besides the Tour.

A bigger concern for Ullrich was the glut of talent that Godefroot had assembled in T-Mobile's stage-race division. The Australian phenom Cadel Evans and the Colombian Santiago Botero, a double stage winner in the 2002 Tour, had already been signed to partially fill the Ullrich-shaped void in 2003. For 2004, Godefroot had also added the 2002 Giro d'Italia champion Paolo Savoldelli. The aggressive recruitment drive, together with Vinokourov's rising stock, prompted speculation about internal rivalries that Ullrich found unsettling. The various language barriers and quirks of some of the characters involved, particularly Evans – whom Andreas Klöden said later was 'a peculiar character who didn't fit in' – provided rich material for stories like the one in Belgian newspaper *Het Nieuwsblad* calling the team 'a snake pit'.

Not that any of this was an excuse for Ullrich to again start slipping into bad old habits. Page after page in his new contract was dedicated to anti-doping clauses and protocols, but there was still little, it seemed, that Walter Godefroot could make Ullrich do about his weight and fitness early in the season. His various colds and flus between January and March were, this year too, either cause, effect or aggravator of his excess kilos and shortage of form. In January, it had been Lance Armstrong justifying dietary choices after his new girlfriend, the pop star Sheryl Crow, made an offhand comment to a reporter at an LA Lakers game – 'I'm a bad influence: I always head for the Krispy Kremes.' But when Armstrong and Ullrich clashed for the first time in 2004 at Vuelta a Murcia in March, Armstrong looked taut and ready while Ullrich's belly drooped. A few weeks later, Ullrich was abandoning La Flèche Wallonne and admitting that he had 'overestimated his body'. Meanwhile, Rudy Pevenage and Walter Godefroot now sat at either side of a farcical, Kafkaesque impasse – with Godefroot blaming Pevenage for Ullrich's lack of application while at the same time refusing to let him in from the cold. Pevenage felt as though he had seen and tried it all before with Ullrich. 'If T-Mobile come along and offer you that much money, like they did in 2004, you have to maybe change your life to make sure you give them back what they want. But Jan never could,' Pevenage says now.

Luigi Cecchini had appeared to crack the code the previous year, but he now claims to have only casually advised Ullrich after 2003, explaining, 'He would come to dinner and occasionally ask me to get the Vespa out and motor-pace him, but that was all, because he was back at Telekom.' This contradicts what Ullrich would tell Philippe Le Gars on the eve of the 2004 Tour, in a story clearly planted to head off another journalist who was about to 'unmask' Cecchini as Ullrich's coach. Walter Godefroot said at the time he was 'flabbergasted' by that news. But no one should have been, because *La*

Gazzetta dello Sport had already linked Cecchini to Ullrich in October 2003.

Regardless, Cecchini's charisma could accomplish many things but had not provided a lasting solution to the brain-twister of Ullrich's weight. 'When he came here he'd still have the odd glass of wine, but he wasn't out of control like I've heard he could be at other times,' the doctor says. Cecchini also disapproved of the extreme springtime diets that had previously wowed teammates and fast-tracked Ullrich to something like his target weight but done so at a price. 'The problem comes when you don't eat much, you do six hours, then you get home and you could eat a horse. You're not replenishing your glycogen stores, and suddenly you can't train as well. Jan's problem was that he started off six or seven kilos overweight or more. I always tell them that six or seven kilos is too much to put on, that they have to control themselves when they stop racing in the winter. Many listen but most don't.'

Lance Armstrong's coach, Michele Ferrari, was reputed to be an even bigger stickler for calorie control than Cecchini. After years of observing Ullrich's struggles from afar, Armstrong was also mystified as to why, almost a decade into his career, his rival hadn't yet found a way to exercise more self-control. 'The weight thing has to be food,' Armstrong says. 'I mean, you'd hear stories about ice cream . . . just bad habits.'

Speculation about new-fangled diet pills and obesity drugs like Xenical also lit up the peloton switchboards, especially when Ullrich suddenly seemed to transform himself in the spring months. Those rumours also reached Armstrong. 'I'd hear that and be like, *Man, just push the plate away in the winter*,' he says.

At the same time, the Ullrich method also included remarkable feats of endurance and sacrifice – brutal two- or three-month purges as the Tour approached that left teammates open-mouthed. Beppe Guerini, Ullrich's mountain sherpa for many years, says that no one else could have extracted so much from their body in such short periods, or even contemplated trying. 'There were years when he got through races like the Tour of Switzerland in June eating practically nothing because he still had so much weight to lose. On the first day he'd barely be holding on and by the end of the week he'd be climbing with the best guys.'

Another of T-Mobile's Italians, Daniele Nardello, agrees: Ullrich's starvation-on-demand springtime ritual was remarkable – but also unsustainable. 'You can't train for a Tour de France on a bowl of muesli,' Nardello says. 'You might be OK for a week or so, or two weeks, but you can't compete with Lance Armstrong like that.'

The other question was whether years of the same, self-imposed feast-to-famine pattern hadn't mentally ground Ullrich down. Since turning thirty in December 2003, he had already noticed that his body was reacting differently. Teammates and friends could also easily imagine how years in the same spiral had built layer upon layer of mental scar tissue. Beppe Guerini rejects the idea that it was a disillusioned, listless Ullrich who had rejoined his old team in 2004, but occasionally he did give that impression. On one occasion, Guerini thinks at the start of 2004 or 2005, Ullrich punctured 50 kilometres from the team hotel at their Mallorca training camp and hurled his bike into a field, muttering that he felt like giving up.

Jan Schaffrath had spent his whole career at Telekom. Primarily a Classics rider, he didn't often ride the same races as Ullrich, but an experience in 2005 did leave him wondering about the burdens that his fellow East German was carrying.

'I think the last two or three months before the Tour every year took a lot out of him. When he had to train so intensively, live so seriously . . . somewhere you also need an escape valve, and Jan's escape valve perhaps got bigger every year. That was my impression. I base that mainly on something I did in 2005. I'd had a really bad spring, and we decided that I'd do the Giro, mainly to lose weight. In a grand tour you always feel that you're eating too little anyway – but there I really restricted myself, ate no desserts, and was going to bed hungry every night. Well, I lost weight . . . but mentally I was completely dead at the end of the Giro. And it pretty much finished me off as a pro bike rider. It cost me so much energy, mentally, to be that disciplined every day. I came home from the Giro, went to a Hofbräu house in Berlin and just stuffed myself up with food and beer. My girlfriend said that it simply wasn't possible to eat that much.

'So then, thinking about Jan,' Schaffrath continues, 'you add the weight issue to the general pressure of being a general classification rider, and it's so extreme. Jan had battered himself for months to get himself down to the right weight, then he went in knowing that he couldn't afford a crash or a lapse in concentration. You're on a knife edge the whole time. All you can think about is food . . . then you have the added pressure of knowing that your season begins and ends with the Tour. I could really understand Jan and why certain things happened after that experience at the Giro. I also thought about other people who had experienced the same thing. For example, the East German swimmer, Franziska Van Almsick, had the same stuff thrown at her. They called her fat too. You start to think about what effect that can have on a young person. You also know how some people react to the stress: by eating and drinking. It becomes a vicious circle.'

However strong the vortex into which Jan Ullrich had fallen in early 2004, by June he was, as usual, finally swimming with the current and back in his flow. Having roared into the Tour of Switzerland with his first win of the season on stage one, Ullrich rounded the race off with victory in the final-day time trial. He later said he had been inspired by the presence of partner Gaby and daughter Sarah Maria, and especially the photos that Gaby had sent him moments before he left the start ramp. Ullrich looked in magnificent shape. 'He is just gliding through the other riders. It's awesome to watch,' swooned Bradley Wiggins.

Lance Armstrong's form offered Ullrich further encouragement. Armstrong had been thrashed by Iban Mayo and his old teammate Tyler Hamilton at the Dauphiné Libéré, most notably on the mountain time trial up Mont Ventoux. According to his US Postal teammate, Floyd Landis, no sooner had Armstrong towelled himself down and checked the time gaps than he was calling the UCI president, Hein Verbruggen, to forcefully suggest that the drug testers keep a closer eye on Mayo and Hamilton. Hamilton claimed in his autobiography *The Secret Race* that, the same evening, he received a summons to Switzerland from the UCI. Their subsequent meeting amounted to a warning, Hamilton believed, or possibly a threat that he could soon be cut down to size.

Armstrong perhaps felt doubly sensitive, extra paranoid because of concerns about how he was going to 'optimize' his own performances at the 2004 Tour. A few months earlier US Postal had fired one of their doctors, Luis Del Moral – and in so doing lost his expertise in the delicate art of blood transfusions. The team had also been put on edge by the release of David Walsh and Pierre Ballester's book, *L. A. Confidentiel*, which contained a litany of doping allegations against Armstrong, just days before the Tour. 'Extraordinary allegations require extraordinary proof,' would be the take-home line of Armstrong's pre-Tour press conference in Liège, and the death stare he shot at Walsh the most abiding image. As far as many were concerned, the Irish journalist and his French colleague had assembled by far the most compelling case to date for Armstrong being a cheat.

The narrow margin of his victory over Ullrich in 2003 had also unsettled Armstrong to the point that, in the winter, he had called all of his equipment suppliers to a fancy Los Angeles hotel to demand better from them in 2004. Everything he would use at the Tour had to be lighter, more aerodynamic, more badass. Between them, Mayo, Hamilton, Ballester and Walsh had also now done their bit, stirring in the final ingredient to Armstrong's motivational soup – not just opponents but enemies, people to fuck with and destroy. Armstrong would boil down his recipe into a single, four-word mantra later in the Tour: 'No gifts this year.'

Ullrich claimed in Liège that he was the lightest he'd been at the start of a Tour since 1997. For once, he had also done even more route recces than Armstrong, the American having stayed in the USA with his kids in April. On the subject of fatherhood, one of the German tabloids, *Bild Zeitung*, had responded to the release of Ullrich's own memoir in June by diving deeper into his family life. A *Bild* reporter had located Ullrich's estranged dad, Werner, in a village in the far north of Germany. Werner Ullrich said that he would be happy to finally reconnect with his son, twenty years after walking out on his family and just over a decade after last seeing Jan, fleetingly, at a race in Berlin. He was living 'alone and forlorn' in Schleswig-Holstein, close to the Danish border.*

'Forlorn' would unfortunately also describe Jan Ullrich's mood halfway through the Tour. After a lacklustre prologue and team time trial, he flopped in the first Pyrenean stage to La Mongie. His friend and domestique, Andreas Klöden, was even ordered to leave Ullrich behind and went on to finish the stage third, twenty seconds behind Armstrong and Ivan Basso. Ullrich conceded nearly two and a half minutes.

---

* Werner Ullrich would die in 2013, having never been reconciled with Jan.

No one in the team let on that Ullrich had fallen ill a few days before the Tour and been put on a course of antibiotics, and neither did Godefroot consider these mitigating circumstances. In the past he had questioned Ullrich's professionalism; now he said he wasn't sure whether Ullrich even had the will to fight. It was left to one of the T-Mobile directeurs sportifs, Mario Kummer, to leap to Ullrich's defence, observing that in his position many riders would already have given up. 'Sometimes we had to lie, or at least keep things private,' Kummer admits to me in 2016. 'In my opinion the press sometimes praised him to the skies when things were going well but then lost touch with reality and put an incredible amount of pressure on him. And when it didn't go well, they really hammered him.'

There was some truth to that, but it would also have been disingenuous to talk about an outbreak of *Schadenfreude*. One German media outlet, ARD, would even face allegations of an unhealthy pro-Ullrich bias when their pundits criticized Jens Voigt for chasing him down on the first Alpine stage – despite the fact it made perfect tactical sense given that Voigt's team leader, Ivan Basso, was a rival for the podium places. The harshest criticism had been levelled at Voigt by ARD host Hagen Boßdorf, who just happened to be the ghost-writer for Ullrich's autobiography. Moreover, ARD were a co-sponsor of the T-Mobile team and, personally, of Ullrich. The following day, Voigt finished the mountain time trial to Alpe d'Huez close to tears, having been booed and called 'Judas' or worse by German fans all the way up the climb.

Armstrong, too, was spat at and abused on the Alpe, but almost seemed to relish the hostile atmosphere. Without Ullrich to seriously challenge him, he cruised through the three weeks, meting out summary justice whenever and to whomever he pleased. By stage eighteen, with the Tour as good as won, there was still one antagonist left to crush: the journeyman Italian, Filippo Simeoni, who two years earlier had testified against Michele Ferrari in a trial that would end years later with Ferrari overturning a one-year prison sentence for 'sporting fraud' i.e. doping athletes including Simeoni. Armstrong's response to Simeoni's accusations had been to call him a 'liar', prompting Simeoni to sue Armstrong for defamation. Now, two days before the end of the Tour, Armstrong hunted Simeoni down as the Italian tagged onto the back of an innocuous breakaway on the road to Lons-le-Saunier. 'I have a lot of money and I'll destroy you,'

Armstrong allegedly told him. Later in the stage, while Simeoni wept at the back of the peloton, Armstrong could be seen giggling with Ullrich as they rode side by side, before turning to the TV camera and zipping his lips in mime. One of Ullrich's teammates, Beppe Guerini, was later disciplined by the Italian Cycling Federation for also having verbally abused Simeoni.

The incident would cause further, lasting damage to Armstrong's credibility and popularity, in spite of him wrapping up his record sixth straight Tour win three days later. Ullrich's Tour, meanwhile, had been the worst of his career and the first he had finished as neither the winner nor runner-up. He had not even been the best rider in T-Mobile colours, Klöden taking second and Ullrich a further two minutes back in fourth. He was proud to have finished the Tour but angry with Walter Godefroot, who had spent much of the last week bemoaning Ullrich's mental fragility. 'Mr Godefroot doesn't even really know me,' Ullrich snapped in a post-Tour appearance on Germany's most popular TV chat show, *Beckmann*.

In truth, Godefroot wasn't the only one who thought Ullrich had looked like a permanently beaten man in July 2004. Johan Bruyneel had reached more or less the same conclusion.

'You know, Lance and Jan never really spoke that much. They basically didn't speak, but I'll always remember being with Lance at the doping control after he'd won the final time trial in 2004, and Ullrich coming over and giving Lance a hug. He said, "Ach, come on, Lance, it's only a bike race." And we all commented on that afterwards. We said, you see, it's only a bike race for him – it's not the most important thing. Which is what it was for us at the time.

'I think maybe 2003 sort of broke Jan,' Bruyneel says. 'After that he wasn't even close. He wasn't even that out of shape in the winter any more – he got better at that – but I think mentally he was just broken in 2003.'

Broken, resigned or just happy enough with the status quo. Peter Becker had watched the Tour from his home in Berlin and reached the latter conclusion. 'He simply thought that what he was doing was enough. Like, he's won the Tour once and that's enough – what else do people still want from him? "I'm up there, fighting for the Tour." That was how he saw things – he was satisfied and fulfilled. He simply wasn't prepared to invest any more.'

The question seems gratuitous, almost rhetorical, but I put it to

Becker anyway: would Ullrich have won the Tour, say, five times, if the approach taken to talent incubation and development that he'd known in the DDR could have been frozen in time and transposed to a reunified Germany?

'I think so,' Becker says. 'Back then they all wanted to go abroad, they all wanted to do the Peace Race, they all wanted to go to the Olympics, and there were also financial implications for everything. There was this pressure on them all back then that forced them forwards. So, no, Armstrong could have shown up in whatever condition he wanted . . .'

A couple of weeks after the end of the 2004 Tour de France, on a restaurant terrace in Sezze, his home town in central Italy, Filippo Simeoni offered me his postscript to a race that had brought him worldwide notoriety but no peace of mind. 'Time is a gentleman' Italians are wont to tell each other in times of crisis, but from Simeoni's point of view Armstrong's actions in France hurt just as much a fortnight later as they had at the time. As bad, if not worse, was the behaviour of the other riders, for more gestures or messages of solidarity had come Armstrong's way than Simeoni's. 'I don't know how much the punter who waits for hours at the roadside wants to see a doped athlete. But there's no solidarity, no medium through which to deliver this message,' Simeoni lamented.

It had been a bruising year all round for cycling and its reputation. The latest and perhaps until-then worst in a conga line of dismal seasons for the sport's credibility began with the Cofidis team all but imploding after a series of doping-related raids and arrests. In February, the man who in 1998 had halted all talk of an extended Jan Ullrich reign in the Tour de France, Marco Pantani, had died in Rimini not from performance-enhancing drug use but an overdose of cocaine. Pantani had fought an addiction to the recreational drug after failing a blood test at the 1999 Giro d'Italia that strongly indicated the use of EPO, thereafter spiralling into a pit of depression, shame and self-loathing. His death came just weeks after the eerily similar demise of another once-brilliant climber, the Spaniard José María Jiménez.

If those tragedies united the cycling world in grief, a previously little-known Spanish rider named Jesús Manzano was soon shaking the sport to its gangrened core and laying bare exactly the kind of hypocrisy Filippo Simeoni decried later in the summer. In a series of interviews with the Spanish newspaper *AS*, Manzano delivered the grisliest exposé of doping practices within the pro peloton to date. Perhaps most shocking was Manzano's account of how, on the first Alpine stage of the 2003 Tour, while riding for the Kelme team, he had fallen off his bike and, moments later, into a coma after attacking on a climb. Manzano claimed the blackout had been caused by an injection of an experimental blood substitute. He alleged his team doctor had administered the drug and that his team manager had also ordered him to refuse all follow-up tests when he was rushed to hospital, lest his poison be discovered.

Kelme rubbished Manzano's claims and publicly received the widespread backing of their peers and the authorities, despite their invitation to the Tour de France being withdrawn.[24] Privately, though, for many riders and directeurs sportifs, the *AS* stories were confirmation of what they had been hearing about certain Kelme riders for years: if nearly everyone in pro cycling played with fire, some of the boys in green, blue and white were pyromaniacs who would light, fan and eat roaring flames. They were reckless, feckless and, for the unwitting spectator, sensational to watch. Their doctors, Walter Virú and, until the end of 2002, one Eufemiano Fuentes, were believed to possess or dispense magic powers – in Fuentes's case, as Jan Ullrich's ex-Bianchi teammate Félix García Casas says, 'the ability to turn a very average rider into a very good one'.

The repercussions of the Manzano scandal would play out way beyond 2004, in ways neither Jan Ullrich nor anyone else could foresee. Jörg Jaksche was also destined to end up in the crosshairs, but in the summer of 2004, Jaksche says, his fears and paranoias had mainly been triggered by a news flash from Switzerland. The Swiss 1998 world champion Oscar Camenzind's positive test for EPO was extraordinary in that testers from the national Olympic Committee had identified and stopped him in the middle of a training ride and demanded a urine sample on the spot. To fans, it sounded like just another cheat getting his comeuppance; to riders up to the same tricks, like Jaksche, it looked like a shot across their bows.

'There was a broad spectrum of how people dealt with the stress of cheating and hiding it,' Jaksche remembers. 'In 2004, there was this Camenzind story and everyone was suddenly frightened about going to those alpine resorts that had always been popular for altitude training, St. Moritz in Switzerland or Livigno just over the Italian border. Suddenly everyone started dressing in black [to remain inconspicuous on training rides]. I was riding for CSC at the time. It was like, "Problem! We have a problem!" And straight away I went to a bike shop to buy some black kit. I took it to the till and the guy was like, "Oh, it's funny, you're the fifth pro I've had in here buying black stuff. Don't you not get that from your team or what?" So people got stressed. This was also the reason some guys got caught; when you're stressed you make mistakes.'

A mistake was what it would usually take for someone to get busted, according to Jaksche. Out-of-competition testing was infrequent and, says Jaksche, sometimes circumvented by hiding behind drawn curtains or a rider pretending he was, say, the brother of the pro cyclist who was out on his bike and uncontactable. Only in 2005 would the World Anti-Doping Agency (WADA) roll out ADAMS – the Anti-Doping Administration and Management System obliging athletes to provide their whereabouts for an hour every day. It would be a game-changer. Certainly for riders who, until that point, had found it harder to hide their doping from partners and family members than from the testers and their own conscience.

'I got EPO in Spain from a pharmacy when we were at training camp,' Jaksche recalls. 'You can buy like 2,000, 5,000 and 10,000, so I bought like 40,000 units of EPO, which was enough to do it up to Paris–Nice [in March]. I had this crazy girlfriend at the time and she stressed me out so much that I just kept crashing, so my season was pretty much done after Paris–Nice anyway. I broke my elbow, my vertebrae. I was living in her place in Innsbruck and I was always hiding stuff in her fridge. For example, this was a typical trick: you would get a Toblerone, drill a hole in the middle of it and the syringe would fit perfectly. Someone had come up with this because hotel minibars pretty much always had a Toblerone in them. So with our criminal minds, we thought of that straight away.'

There were elements of pantomime, like this, but also moments when the sport seemed not so much to have mislaid its moral compass as lost contact with Earth's magnetic field. In September 2004, Tyler Hamilton offered a further window into the beckoning dystopia when he tested positive for a homologous blood transfusion – injecting the blood of a different person – and initially offered a jaw-dropping defence: that he may have absorbed, in utero, DNA from a deceased embryonic twin – a genetic condition known as chimerism. If this sounded like gallows humour, it was nothing compared to the jokes allegedly tickling some of the Kelme riders who had been incriminated by Jesús Manzano. Sometimes, Manzano said later, they would moo or bark at each other as they left team hotels depending on whether they had taken Oxyglobin, a medicine used to treat anaemia in dogs, or Actovegin, an extract of calves' blood.

The Italian rider Danilo Di Luca had also been barred from the 2004 Tour due to his involvement in a doping investigation. Years later, Di Luca described the peloton's prevailing worldview thus: 'The cyclist thinks that if fifteen drops are good then thirty are better. He's used to giving everything of himself, as a man and an athlete, because this is a sport which demands that. There's no other way to see or live it . . . There's a huge dose of unconsciousness, of arrogance and of egotism . . . If you finish the stage alive you've already won and you don't care about the consequences.'

While the 2004 and 2005 seasons would shatter many myths, T-Mobile and Jan Ullrich kept themselves largely above suspicion – except among a well-connected few. Sylvia Schenk tells me that worrying noises about the University of Freiburg and their work with the team reached the German Cycling Federation at the end of 2003. 'Someone told me at the end of 2003 that stuff was going on at Freiburg, but we had no witnesses on the record, so no proof. It was someone important in the federation. They said to me Telekom were doing stuff, just enough not to get caught. I said to them that we had to do something. But this person wouldn't speak publicly and I knew they would deny it all if I tried to say something. From that point on I tried to look more closely and dig around, but I couldn't find anything.'

Not only did Schenk fail to uncover any evidence of wrongdoing, she also praised T-Mobile in an interview with the *Frankfurter Allgemeine Zeitung* in September 2004. They had 'given [her] hope . . . by reacting so determinedly to the 1998 Festina scandal.' Schenk was referring mainly to the people in the boardrooms in Bonn and particularly the way they had dealt with Ullrich's positive test for ecstasy in 2002. But the uninitiated among the German public almost certainly didn't make the distinction – T-Mobile was Ullrich and here was another figure in authority vouching for both team and star rider. Among Spanish desperados, Italian mafiosi and American

gangsters, T-Mobile – like other great German brands – had successfully harnessed all the tropes of modern Germany's self-flattery and
its positive traits as seen by the rest of the world: its efficiency, its
high morals and, yes, in certain respects and arenas, perhaps an
intrinsic superiority over neighbours and enemies.

In 'After The Catastrophe', his essay about the burden of guilt in
post-war Germany, the Swiss psychiatrist Carl Gustav Jung said that
the Germans' centuries-old obsession with their own prestige had
always truly come from insecurity. Jung recalled Frederik Nietzsche's
conception of the 'pale criminal', who 'will stoop to every kind of
self-deception if only he can escape the sight of himself'. He
continued:

> Nowhere does [this] appear to be such a national characteristic
> as in Germany. This condition can easily lead to an hysterical
> dissociation of the personality, which consists essentially . . . in
> wanting to jump over one's own shadow, and in looking for
> everything dark, inferior, and culpable in others. Hence the hys-
> teric always complains of being surrounded by people who are
> incapable of appreciating him and who are activated only by
> bad motives; by . . . a crowd of submen who should be exter-
> minated neck and crop so that the Superman can live on his
> high level of perfection.[25]

Even in a wider context of worsening decay, surrounded by scandal, somehow 'Germany's team' and its own Superman, Jan Ullrich,
had wriggled clear of every accuser and kept burnishing their halo.
Released in June 2004, a fly-on-the-wall documentary focusing on
Erik Zabel and Rolf Aldag at the 2003 Tour provided a saccharine,
technicolour ode to the yeomen on bikes and their honest toil. The
subject of doping was conspicuous by its absence – because the director said he'd seen none and, besides, he was a 'filmic storyteller
and not an investigative journalist'. When asked, Rolf Aldag said it
was more simple than that: there was no need to establish ground
rules about whether and how the subject was broached because 'at
T-Mobile there's no doping'.

Not in 2003, 2004 or any other year.

Throughout the highs, lows and assorted vicissitudes of Jan Ullrich's
decade as a professional cyclist, one person had remained at his side

and in his heart. Rarely interviewed by the German media and hence little-known, Gaby Weis deviated far enough from the stereotype of the trophy blonde to enhance Ullrich's homespun, boy-next-door schtick but not far enough to arouse genuine curiosity. Profile pieces afforded her a short paragraph and epithets that were neither inaccurate nor uncomplimentary, though could seem patronizingly blasé. 'The winemakers' daughter from the little village on the Rhine,' she would read – and feel her insides stiffen.

The release of Ullrich's book in June 2004, with its long passages about how Gaby's support had seen him through his darkest hours, had caused a ripple of new interest. That, though, only made it more painful when, just three months later, Gaby found out that Jan had fallen for Sara Steinhauser, the sister of his teammate and training partner Tobias.

When Gaby confronted Ullrich, he didn't try to lie. For weeks that ran into months over the late summer and autumn of 2004, they talked about saving the relationship while knowing that Ullrich's love already resided with another woman. In February 2005, Gaby still hoped things could be salvaged, particularly when she was in hospital getting treatment for an abscess and Jan interrupted his training in Tuscany to visit her. Gaby and Sarah Maria went back with him to Italy, but by then the whole thing had started to feel doomed. Mother and daughter would soon be returning to Germany and the realization that Jan – 'the man of my life, with all his little flaws', as Gaby later told *Bunte* – wasn't coming back. It was 'official' when Ullrich told *Bild am Sonntag* that he and Gaby were no longer together. He had never been that categorical in conversations with Gaby. Reading it in a newspaper, she said, felt like a 'slap in the face'.

Ullrich swore that there was no one else involved, but the *Berliner Zeitung* was soon reporting a possible liaison with his physio-therapist Birgit Krohme. And at a training camp in Mallorca, he was sighted in the disco of the Robinson Club, where T-Mobile were gathered, in the company of a woman with whom he seemed 'intim-ately acquainted', according to *Bunte*. The mystery female wasn't named or identified at the time. But then almost exactly a month after Ullrich announced his new single status, he wanted to set the record straight, this time to *Bild*: his new girlfriend was Sara Stein-hauser, whom he now called 'the love of my life'.

Rudy Pevenage surmises bluntly that 'for a while Gaby suited him, then there came a point when another woman suited him better'. That was no doubt true, but Ullrich's handling of the situation struck many as clumsy. Wolfgang Strohband, Ullrich's manager, is maybe stating the obvious when he says, 'Gaby suffered but I don't think Jan did'.

Gaby's friends and family would indeed confirm that every mention of Ullrich's new romance by newspapers layered a further insult on top of the injury; whether it was Ullrich announcing in November 2005 that he wanted a child with Sara or the news that he had moved her into the house in Scherzingen, bought her a new Audi and persuaded her to give up her job in the marketing department of Munich-based ski manufacturers Elan. For months, Gaby couldn't stand the sound of his voice when he called every two days to speak to Sarah Maria. Jan hoped they could one day be friends, but Gaby told *Bunte* she was 'too wounded' and thought he still hadn't realized he'd done anything wrong. Luckily, she still had her sense of humour: on the day she rounded up her things and left Scherzingen for good, she joked to friends that she was leaving her VIP status at the border.

Meanwhile, Wolfgang Strohband advised Ullrich against throwing himself too wholeheartedly into his new relationship. Strohband was worried that Ullrich's naivety, or gullibility, could make him vulnerable – not that Strohband particularly suspected Sara of impure motives. Nonetheless, one Sunday in December 2005, Strohband took a break from jet-washing the oak leaves off his apartment terrace in Hamburg to give Ullrich a lengthy pep talk over the phone – or, as he called it, 'some fatherly guidance'. He had nothing against Sara, he stressed, but maybe Jan should just, well, be careful how much he said about certain subjects and how much he put on display. It was sound advice that might have served Ullrich well. Just not in the way that Strohband intended.

With the exception of the 1999 and 2002 seasons in which misfortune and misadventure had kept him out of the Tour, and his 1998 *annus obesus*, Ullrich's 2004 campaign had been his worst since 1995 – but he could still salvage it by defending his Olympic road race title in Athens. On a course that didn't suit him, in forty-degree temperatures, Ullrich rode creditably to finish nineteenth, but the German team's race was maybe most remarkable for something Jens Voigt blurted to journalist Klaus Blume after crossing the line: 'I'll never ride another Olympics or world championships . . . or at least not with Jan Ullrich!' Voigt evidently believed his spade work had deserved better from his team leader. Ullrich was still expected to win a medal in the individual time trial, but slumped to sixth place. 'Weißbier-Jan' (Wheat-beer Jan), as *Bild* called him, was then 'welcomed back' to Germany by the newspaper's unflattering pictures of him drowning his sorrows – a Photoshop stitch-up according to Wolfgang Strohband. Ullrich himself didn't have the energy to cry foul. He noted only that, 'Last year I was the golden king of hearts, whereas now suddenly I'm just Beer-Ulle.'

A final flourish in the end-of-season Italian races, including victory in the Coppa Sabatini, wasn't enough to alter the storyline of the winter. Again, the German media asked what Ullrich needed to change – his coach, his diet, his race programme or his mental approach. Walter Godefroot had announced that he was going to retire as T-Mobile's manager at the end of 2005 and pass the reins to Olaf Ludwig. Godefroot was winding down – but not about to climb down from his position vis-à-vis Rudy Pevenage, however much it had affected Ullrich in 2004. 'David Beckham doesn't sign for Real Madrid and say I want to bring my coach with me,' Godefroot sniffed. At a press event in Amsterdam, Ullrich spoke about wanting a more relaxed atmosphere in the team, more like what he had at Coast/Bianchi, and not putting too much pressure on himself. These were more than just the idle musings of someone who was broadly happy with life in his new, old team. Soon murmurs had reached the German press that Ullrich was trying to wriggle out of his contract and sign for one of the big Spanish outfits – Liberty Seguros or Illes Balears.

He ended up staying but, for all the talk of fostering better team spirit, the harmony that reigned at T-Mobile team gatherings early in 2005 was at best fragile, at worst an illusion. Andreas Klöden and Erik Zabel had clashed over the former's comments in an interview to the effect that T-Mobile would have more chance of winning the Tour without Zabel. Tension between the two dominant cabals in the team – one beholden to Ullrich and the other to Zabel – simmered closer than ever to boiling point. Klöden and Matthias Kessler, a precocious youngster from a wealthy family in Bavaria, were Ullrich's closest allies and also increasingly viewed as troublemakers.

Brian Holm remembers a team-building exercise at the end of the

2005 season which, he says, did more to highlight who and what was wrong in the ranks than put it right. 'We did this army camp, you know, the big T-Mobile happy family going off, climbing up a rope then having to count down and jump to conquer their fear. The soldier was counting down, "Ten, nine . . ." and then Kessler starts, *"Neun-undneunzig, achtundneunzig . . ."* ['Ninety-nine, ninety-eight . . . '] You know, just starting shit. And that was the team. It looked great from the outside but it was a total mess.'

Years later, a serious accident when he was training in Mallorca left Kessler severely handicapped, which makes Brian Holm reluctant to dwell on the negative influence he had at T-Mobile. After leaving the team, Kessler would also apologize to certain members of staff for how he had behaved. Nonetheless, Holm is not alone in suggesting that he exemplified much of what had become dysfunctional at T-Mobile – Ullrich's 'being a mastermind at picking the wrong friends', a growing sense of entitlement among riders, how they were indulged and the dwindling returns. Mario Kummer, another of the directeurs sportifs at the time, counters that, 'Jan was the one who complained the least.' But others saw a culture of excuses that poisoned the general ambiance. The first four months of the 2005 season were a disaster. The team registered not a single victory until Alexander Vinokourov saved the spring by winning Liège–Bastogne–Liège.

Jan Schaffrath, one of the team's elder statesmen, pined for the more modest and more successful Deutsche Telekom of the early years.

'Once upon a time you could win a stage of the Bayern Rundfahrt then celebrate with a beer afterwards, which everyone thought was fun, but later, when the team got bigger, you weren't allowed to do that any more. And of course, as the boundaries got tighter, the excesses got greater – which was a response to dissatisfaction in the team. A reaction to the pressure as well. And there were excuses. We're not winning because of the bikes or because we don't have a big enough bus. Things that you never considered before. I remember when all the discussions about Jan's weight were going on at the Robinson Club in Mallorca, at the training camp. We ate in the buffet with everyone else, but at a certain point a decision was taken that we needed healthier food, more "sporty" meals, and a separate room was found for us downstairs. Then, though, that wasn't OK either, and it was finally decided that we could eat upstairs on the day before the rest day. These were huge discussions that, when you look back, were a massive waste of energy. Everyone had become so caught up in that artificial world. Only when it all fell apart did you really get things in proportion again. I can remember sitting with Matthias Kessler and Andreas Klöden years later, and them saying, "What the hell were we complaining about?" But that culture had set in and it became hard to change. It was just a consequence of the whole thing getting huge.'

Walter Godefroot had overseen the whole metamorphosis, from five-million-deutsche-mark-a-year minnows that were Germany's first team at the Tour de France for nineteen years in 1992, to the 15 million-euro fat cats of the international peloton. The only thing that hadn't really changed was Godefroot – the drill sergeant with the smile of an antiquarian bookseller, who would tell riders that cancer was the only good excuse for abandoning races and almost mean it.

'Klöden is particular, but not a bad lad,' he says now, responding to a direct question about Klöden, Kessler and their effect on Ullrich. 'With Kessler it was more difficult. He was a bit of a skinhead. He had piercings and a shaved head when I first met him. He's from a rich family. Dad had a lot of property in Munich. He would go on and on about lightweight bikes, so one day I said to him, "What's the point of you having a lightweight bike? Get rid of all that other metal first, then we can talk." Then, in fairness, he took out the piercings.'

Whatever other burdens were weighing Ullrich down in the early months of 2005 – be it guilt he secretly harboured over Gaby, the pain of missing Sarah Maria, problems in his team or, literally, the excess body weight he had carried into this season as well – he could at least be confident that one load was about to be lifted for good. After keeping everyone guessing throughout the winter or, as Ullrich said, 'playing a little poker game', Lance Armstrong confirmed that he would compete in the 2005 Tour de France after all. Then he would ride off the Champs-Élysées into the Parisian sunset and out of the sport.

Armstrong would be a young retiree at thirty-three, but he appeared to have had enough, bombarded by doping allegations, hounded by trolls and surrounded by lawyers. The runaway success of the yellow Livestrong bracelets that Nike had launched in 2004 to raise money for his cancer foundation, the 80 million people who eventually bought one, also suggested that he had outgrown the sport. Among colleagues, a prevailing *omertà* or law of silence perhaps helped preserve a force field of impunity, but it didn't make him any more popular. One of the more notable reactions to his announcement about the 2005 Tour came from the Italian rider Franco Pellizotti: 'I'm curious to see him go for a seventh Tour, although I much prefer Ullrich as a guy. Ivan Basso's the only person in the peloton who likes Armstrong.'

Ullrich's principle of non-aggression, by contrast, would continue until Armstrong's very last pedal stroke. He reserved his resentment for critics who failed to grasp the sheer bad luck of his and Armstrong's careers having coincided, not the nemesis himself, and indeed Ullrich said he was happy that Armstrong was going for number seven. Without him, the challenge wouldn't quite feel the same. T-Mobile's hype machine continued to push the idea of a fearsome, three-pronged Ullrich–Klöden–Vinokourov attack, but justifiable doubts persisted about how that configuration could work. In 2003, at Team Coast, Jacques Hanegraaf had come to the conclusion that Ullrich lacked any real tactical nous because of a preoccupation with merely getting and staying fit, after which he had come to believe his talent would look after the rest. Bjarne Riis, his old teammate and now team manager to Ivan Basso, said much the same in the Tour build-up: 'Jan loses because he only concentrates on his own race and doesn't look around. He doesn't look at Armstrong and see what he's doing.'

Meanwhile, perversely, it was the guy who kept winning who remained obsessed with his age-old rival, and with keeping Ullrich in the corner. Sometimes, for Armstrong and US Postal, it was less about getting a genuine edge than the feeling that they had outsmarted Telekom. Thus, three years after orchestrating Armstrong's famous 'coup de bluff' over the radiowaves at Alpe d'Huez, Johan Bruyneel was delighted to discover that one of the team's new sponsors, electronics company AMD, could supply them with scramblers for their intercom devices. This meant Bruyneel could continue to eavesdrop on T-Mobile's in-race tactics while his counterparts tried to do the same and heard only crackles. 'I suppose they could have figured out eventually what was going on, but then you're not always talking in scrambled, so it confuses them and keeps them wondering,' Bruyneel fairly chortles.

In a mismatched physiological war, Ullrich had long since been defeated, but Armstrong and Bruyneel weren't about to let up. 'It was May of 2005 and we were in the Pyrenees with Chechu Rubiera and Roberto Heras to recce the Pla d'Adet stage,' Bruyneel recalls. 'Generally on recons we wouldn't do the whole stage because it was too long, so we'd maybe do the first 50 kilometres in the car. And on this day, on the drive, we saw three T-Mobile riders who happened to be looking at the same stage. It was Ullrich, Botero and Sevilla, I think. We didn't want to be riding too close to them, so we passed them, and of course they saw us. We decided then that we didn't want them to catch us, but we'd have to stop for a drink and a piss . . . so it was going to be a kind of race. We knew they would "chase" us and consequently our guys ended up riding a bit faster than they should have. Anyway, we finally got to the bottom of Pla d'Adet and went up, knowing that we'd see them on the way down. But we came down, didn't see them and we thought we'd have some fun. On the first hairpin of the climb to Pla d'Adet there's a spot where you can see right down into the village below, and we decided that we'd stop there and wait for them; we'd descend past them just as they were starting the climb, then we'd turn around at the bottom and pretty much race them back up the climb – and also show them they were doing it twice. But the thing was – and we couldn't believe this – they never showed up. Later we found out that they didn't do Pla d'Adet because they were going to miss their flight. So that was another little victory. You know, they'd rather catch their plane than do the last climb of a Tour stage. Meanwhile we were going to do it twice.'

Ullrich naturally didn't mention any of this in his traditional pre-Tour briefings with the German press. He stressed that he wasn't fixating on finally toppling Armstrong, no matter how hard journalists banged that drum. When Rainer Seele of the *Frankfurter Allgemeine Zeitung* asked whether recent turbulence in his private life had been a distraction, he answered like a man who didn't know what it was to be thrown off course. 'I'm a positive-thinking person and I can always motivate myself. I'll think, right, now I'll concentrate more on my sport and then I'll figure out my life in the winter.'

Ullrich's results in preparatory stage-races had also been better than in any season since 1997. In the Tour of Switzerland, where he so often stirred from his spring torpor, he won a long time trial and finished third overall. Armstrong told the press Ullrich looked better, more menacing than ever.

That was also Rudy Pevenage's profound conviction a week before the Tour. Then, to Pevenage's bafflement, something went awry. 'He must have put on two kilos in that week. I think it was always the same problem – in his head,' Pevenage says, shaking his.

The countdown to the Grand Départ on the island of Noirmoutier off the Atlantic coast was typical Telekom, quintessential Ullrich: a costly private plane journey from Freiburg, boasts about the unpredictably of their Ullrich–Klöden–Vinokourov triumvirate, followed by calamity in the final hours before it was time to race. Ullrich got too close to directeur sportif Mario Kummer's team car on his recce of the opening-stage time-trial course and, when Kummer had to brake behind a lorry, Ullrich flew headlong through the rear windscreen. The location of Ullrich's wounds, all up the left side of his neck, suggested that he'd been fortunate not to slice off his head. From a critic's point of view it was a moment of pure Ullrich slapstick that, Kummer says sternly, 'could have been very, very serious'.

If the injuries were 'superficial', their effect was clearly not. Armstrong has already described to me his mixed feelings at setting off a minute behind Ullrich in the time trial the next day, catching and passing him four kilometres from the line, and thinking, 'I can't go by this guy, I'm going to beat him over the next three weeks, but I can't go by him here.' Likewise, Johan Bruyneel almost squirms at the memory. 'Oh God,' he says. 'That was terrible. The poor guy. I mean the crash the day before seemed like typical Jan . . . but actually that was sad. It was a sad sight.'

Mario Kummer scoffs when I relay these comments. 'Armstrong says he didn't enjoy it? I think that's a lie. He's a beast, is what I think, and he wanted to land a psychological blow there.'

Regardless, Ullrich had already conceded over a minute and the tone was set. Armstrong's coach, Michele Ferrari, would tell the documentary filmmaker Alex Gibney in *The Armstrong Lie* years later that his protégé was never stronger before a Tour than in 2005. 'He won the Tour like this,' Ferrari said, putting two fingers to his lips as though smoking a cigarette. 'Lance took it easy because if you win too much, then everybody blah, blah, blah.'

Armstrong is surprised to hear this. 'I thought 2001 was the best Tour I ever did, but 2005 was probably the easiest, the least stress.

It's funny – you telling me that makes me want to see that scene. I should see that documentary. He said my watts per kilo were my highest ever? Huh. Because they would have been high in 1999 . . .'

Ullrich and T-Mobile did give him one nervous moment early in the race. On stage eight through the Vosges mountains, US Postal disintegrated around Armstrong under modest pressure. Armstrong finished the stage in the yellow jersey but angry, not least because Klöden had gained half a minute – and he was one T-Mobile rider whom Armstrong definitely did not like.

Soon, though, the procession had resumed for its seventh straight year. Ullrich, Klöden and Vinokourov all did poorly in the first alpine stage, the trident supposedly made of tungsten made to look like a chocolate fork in a microwave. Vinokourov went on to take a consolatory stage win in Briançon, but the dream of denying Armstrong his perfect send-off had by now all but gone.

'As usual it wasn't so much the way he was riding as the way it was spun, as a big failure, that irritated Jan,' says Beppe Guerini. Indeed, in interviews, Ullrich started to sound unusually tetchy. One day, the T-Mobile press officer even had to apologize for his snappiness and explain that he was just 'letting off steam'. One writer, Klaus Blume, reported later that Ullrich had told friends he wanted to 'get into bed and cry under the duvet'.

He rallied in the Pyrenees, justifying what Mario Kummer had said with an unfortunate turn of phrase: 'Jan will fight until the last drop of blood'. The image would certainly have raised a smirk from the Dane Michael Rasmussen of the Rabobank team. A stage winner in the Vosges, Rasmussen planned to 'refill' with his second blood transfusion of the Tour ahead of the Pyrenean stages, only for his Rabobank team to veto it. Having looked like the strongest climber in the race and a potential threat to Armstrong in the Alps, Rasmussen suddenly found himself going backwards. 'You can see it. You can feel it,' he says. 'I mean, you're competing against the same guys every day. In 2005, from being able to ride to the top of Courchevel with Armstrong, they just dumped me five days later. Lance and Ullrich just went away. I assumed they probably just had another bag, like I had . . . only Rabobank wouldn't let me use it.'

Rasmussen typified the peloton's prevailing esprit de corps by railing not against the rivals he believed were doping but team management who stopped him from doing the same. Ullrich dropped him on the stage to Ax 3 Domaines, and again at Pla d'Adet before making a final attempt to bury the Dane's podium hopes on the last big mountain of the Tour, the Col d'Aubisque. 'Then, just on the little plateau after we'd gone over the summit, he rode alongside me, sort of shrugged and said, "Look, I'm sorry about that but I had to try." I thought that was pretty nice of him.'

Even today, Rasmussen is still charmed, and slightly bewildered by the memory.

'Jan was just an amazing athlete who never really fulfilled his potential,' he goes on. 'If you had the engine of Jan and the head of Lance you would have won the Tour ten years in a row.'

As it was, Ullrich finished third in Paris, just over six minutes behind Armstrong and nearly two adrift of Basso. The Italian and not Ullrich now looked the likeliest heir to the throne Armstrong was about to vacate. Ullrich nonetheless claimed he was proud to stand alongside Armstrong on his final Tour podium. He positively beamed as, in what became an infamous parting message, Armstrong took the microphone and told the thousands massed on the Champs-Élysées and millions watching at home that they should believe in Basso, Ullrich and the Tour. 'This is a hard sporting event and hard work wins it. So *Vive le Tour* . . . forever,' were his final words, to some ears a valedictory middle finger.

Ullrich would return the homage later that night. The speech that was still jerking at Lance Armstrong's tear-ducts a decade later was delivered at 1.10 a.m., from the foot of a staircase in the restaurant at the Ritz Hotel. Ullrich's hands were buried deep in the pockets of the pinstripe suit that suddenly drowned him, his white shirt was untucked and his smile was wide. When Armstrong passed the mic, he bashfully rolled his head around his shoulders and then finally spoke.

'Congratulations for you,' he said. 'Seven times to win the Tour de France is unbelievable, so *chapeau* for this. I try all but you were too strong for me.'

It would have seemed self-evident on that long, emotional Parisian night in July 2005 that one of Jan Ullrich and Lance Armstrong had ridden their last Tour de France and one had not. Most – including Armstrong and Ullrich – would just have had it the wrong way around.

Armstrong was certain that he'd pulled off his last heist and left no fingerprints, but only a few weeks later the case for his prosecution as a cheat rather than champion was handed a smoking gun. *L'Équipe* journalist Damien Ressiot had got wind of the French Anti-Doping Agency's experimental, retrospective tests on urine samples from the 1999 Tour, when EPO wasn't detectable, and discovered that some of the new analyses had come back positive. Ressiot had then tricked Armstrong into giving away the reference numbers which identified his samples and found that six of them had contained EPO. 'Le Mensonge Armstrong' – 'The Armstrong Lie' was *L'Équipe*'s headline as they broke the story in late August. At the time, in the United States, the scoop received little airplay and was easily spun as a French conspiracy. 'They don't mind us when we're buying their wine or storming German pillboxes. But aside from that, they don't really care for us,' said Mike Lopresti of *USA Today*.

Jan Ullrich and T-Mobile were noticeably cagey in their response. Even today, more than a decade on, after all that has happened, all that was revealed, doping is a taboo word even if then it wasn't a taboo deed. 'The *system*. I won't use the word "doping". I'll say the system as it was then,' Rudy Pevenage immediately set out when we established parameters for our interview in Geraardsbergen.

Pevenage was one of those who was neither surprised nor felt cheated after *L'Équipe*'s 2005 claims – much like Ullrich. Where they perhaps differed, Pevenage suspects, was how he and Ullrich felt about the 'system' in 2005.

'He won't agree, but I think that all of these stories – Festina and so on, the whole situation – I don't think Jan liked it. The *system*, I mean. In winter I think he ate as a response to the stress. I think he was afraid of the system. Maybe afraid for his health. I think Jan was innocent when he got into professional cycling. He had been world champion in Oslo in 1993, third in Sicily the next year, and he came into a world where there was a different attitude . . .'

Pevenage's voice is quiet, every word carefully measured. The roundness of his face and his garland of white hair give it an almost babyish outline, but the creases across his freckled brow are also scars. We are talking about a time, 2005, just before his whole career, his life, the way he saw the world and how it regarded him, turned irrevocably.

'Jan will never tell everything. Never. And me neither,' he picks up, softly, defiantly. 'If I did say everything, it'd hurt a lot of people. Whereas Jan never hurt anyone. He arrived in a period when that's just the way it worked. And I'll say it again: if you put Lance Armstrong and Jan Ullrich in quarantine before a Tour de France, it's Jan Ullrich who wins . . .'

19

A MESSAGE TO YOU, RUDY

'What great news! What's sure is that it's unfair you've been caught up in this game of politics . . . someone who's always been on the cyclists' side. They are compromising your work and the way you share an ideal – improving, excelling and trying to be the best . . . a guy who's always been in the battlefield, eating dust, getting behind us and listening to their "sensations" so you can look for whatever remedy it is that will ease the fatigue, the pain, the injuries, the fears, the pressure . . . pulling your end of the rope, rowing in the same boat as us, looking out for our health . . . because that's the way it is, Eufe, and it's not right. I'm sending you my very best and I hope people don't forget you . . . Whatever happens, there'll only ever be one genius'

—*Text message to Eufemiano Fuentes from an unidentified sender, 20.47, 29 May 2006 (translated from the original Spanish by the author)*

At lunchtime on the day after the 2017 Vuelta a España's grand finale a few streets away, the rustle of beech leaves and rhythmic to-and-fro of the Chamberí district's well-healed residents give the Calle Alonso Cano in Madrid an ambiance at odds with dark secrets from the neighbourhood's recent past.

Of late, Chamberí has become one of the Spanish capital's most sought-after barrios – a haven of authentic or *castizo* charm dotted with the buds of gentrification. Fancy burger joints have sprung up alongside family-run ironmongers; traditional tabernas with blackboards advertising their *cocido madrileño* flank ateliers and boutique hotels. The apartments have pastel facades and wrought-iron balconies. Number 53's much more utilitarian, grey breeze-block construction therefore draws the eye. So, too, given the context, does the name of the restaurant I notice directly opposite: 'La Fuente'.

It's close enough.

At half past three on the afternoon of 12 May 2006, a Friday, a gynaecologist from the Canary Islands named Eufemiano Fuentes shuffled down the marble-floored corridors and under the yellow-beamed canopy roof of Madrid Barajas airport's Terminal 4, as he had done countless times before. The difference on this day was that Fuentes was not only being watched by airport CCTV cameras but also listened to by Spanish police on two of the half dozen mobile handsets, most of them blue and silver Nokia 6310s, with which he would regularly contact friends, family, some of the world's best cyclists and their advisors.

Two days earlier, permission had been granted for the Guardia Civil to begin tapping Fuentes's phones as part of an investigation into possible crimes against public health that they were calling Operación Puerto – Operation Mountain Pass. They had been conducting video surveillance on Fuentes and a few of his presumed accomplices since the middle of March, with immediate results: at 8.30 p.m. on the very first day, José Luis Merino Batres, an ageing cardiologist with suspected links to Fuentes, left Number 53 Calle Alonso Cano carrying a white plastic bag then dumped it in a bin in a parallel street. The Guardia Civil recovered the bag, examined the contents and found remnants and residues that pointed towards the manipulation of blood and transfusions. They had also established that Fuentes was renting the apartment.

Now, on the phone, the investigators were plunged immediately into the doctor's wild, wild world. Within two hours of landing in Madrid, Fuentes had thanked Merino Batres for 'saving his life'. A miscalculation in their planning the previous winter – or perhaps just them underestimating demand for their services – had led to a short-age in their stock of SAG-Mannitol, an additive solution that helped to preserve frozen red blood cells. It was just as well Merino Batres had a contingency plan, because Fuentes reminded his friend that 'this weekend is important, because you know it's the one with the . . . the thing with the . . .'

Soon Fuentes would be telling Merino Batres that 'Birillo' had called to say that he 'wanted more', as did 'the other one'. The more they listened, the more the Guardia Civil began to make sense of Fuentes's coded language – a patois punctuated with ellipses and innuendos suggesting first, that something sinister was afoot, and second, that the protagonists either knew or feared that they were being spied on. Later the strange names – the Birillos, the Zapateros, the Hijos de Rudicio – would also have to be decrypted. Eventually, the Spanish press would give the Lingua Fuentes – its numbers, symbols and pseudonyms – its own appellation: 'The Sanskrit of Eufemiano'.

For now, the Guardia Civil just listened.

'This one is for Siberia. It's the one Ali Baba took to send to Siberia . . .'

'Go to the pizzeria. As you'll understand, this is done at the pizzeria . . .'

'I want to save the weekend, because, boy, people are coming from abroad . . .'

In a call at 6.30 in the evening, Fuentes told Merino Batres, 'So I think that with that, at least the urgent things, the one that's coming from . . . abroad, German and Italian, I'll see them . . . but the rest can fuck off and I'll tell them that I'm very sorry, and that . . . there have been problems with supply.'

For Eufemiano Fuentes this frantic day ended long into the next one, after a text message to an Italian telephone number, in Italian: 'I need to know what time you're arriving tomorrow.' In conversations the following day, Fuentes told anyone who called that he had been up all night.

More than once, the neighbours above and below the apartment in the Calle Alonso Cano had complained to the housekeeper, Ignacio, that a strange, mechanical whirring noise rattled the walls and shook the floorboards.

For Jan Ullrich, the sixth day of the 2006 Giro d'Italia would be an easy one. It began in the central Italian town of Busseto, where Giuseppe Verdi was born and the locals are equally proud of their famous *salame* – culatello. Ullrich had started the race overweight but now he was beginning to look the part. According to his team-mate Serhiy Gonchar, Ullrich had been flying in the team time trial the previous day. In fact, he had fairly vacuumed the Ukrainian into the race leader's pink jersey.

As the peloton beelined across the plains of Emilia-Romagna, it was noticeable how nimbly Ullrich's legs twiddled astride his Giant bike – his 120 revs per minute cadence exceeding even Armstrong's in his egg-beating pomp. It was a big change for Ullrich, whose speed of rotation sometime resembled that of a railway turntable.

Neither Ullrich nor Rudy Pevenage had mentioned anything in public, but in fact there had been a change. At his annual training camp in South Africa in the winter, Ullrich had felt a familiar pain in his right knee that got worse over several days. Eventually, his physiotherapist, Birgit Krohme, decided that they needed to get help. Krohme had been coming to South Africa since long before she met Ullrich, and had contacts at the Sport Science Institute of South Africa (SSISA). When Krohme called, Jeroen Swart, the head of the cycling division, and the physiologist Ross Tucker said that they would be happy to examine Ullrich and see what they found.

Swart remembers Ullrich being 'one of the most pleasant, professional guys I've ever worked with'. He also recalls an athlete who had an obvious problem with an even clearer cause. In the right knee that Ullrich had damaged in 2002, an MRI scan showed patellar tendinopathy, a common overuse injury sometimes referred to as 'jumper's knee'. Isokinetic and ergometer tests also gave strong indications as to how the issues had started; Ullrich's pedalling stroke was lopsided, with a pronounced right-leg, right-hip bias. His mechanical efficiency – what his bike got out compared to what Ullrich put in – was poor for an elite cyclist, and very poor at low cadences. When Swart and Tucker reviewed clips of Ullrich from the previous Tours de France, pennies dropped like dimes in a Vegas casino: Ullrich's gears had got bigger and his cadence lower as the years had gone by. And the harder he ground the pedal cranks, the more crooked he had become, and the more he may also have gained weight.

'What we saw was that over the years he'd gradually lowered his cadence from typically above 80 revs per minute to below seventy,' says Swart. 'The lower the cadence, the more asymmetrical he was, the more he relied on his quadriceps, and, also, the less able he was to respond to accelerations, because he couldn't generate the torque. He wasn't fat when we saw him – his bodyfat was about 10 per cent. It was all muscle because these big gears were basically resistance training and they'd made him heavier.'

For years, Ullrich had argued that smaller gears didn't suit him, while others, like Peter Becker, thought either ego or laziness were getting in the way. Now, over the weeks and months that followed, Ullrich finally made a smooth transition to the 85 rpm can-can Swart and Tucker prescribed – and saw immediate improvements in both his knee and key performance markers.

At the Giro, Ullrich hadn't had time for a look around Busseto and he also may not have known much about Giuseppe Verdi. Parallels with one of Verdi's most famous operas, *La Traviata*, and a finale in which Violetta suddenly, miraculously rises from her deathbed exclaiming 'Oh joy!', apparently cured of disease, would therefore be pure operatic licence.

Then again, no sooner does Violetta get up than she falls again, this time never to stir.

From where the Guardia Civil were sitting in Madrid, the mid-May days of Eufemiano Fuentes seemed to fall into a predictable rhythm. Which is in no way to say that they were dull. The doctor himself was getting more and more agitated, his anxiety levels foreshadowing the synchronized crescendos of the Giro and the cycling spring – or some dark premonition. On the fifteenth, there was more talk of late nights, of stress and of the glycerol 57.1 per cent solution for which he and Merino Batres were searching high and low, from Seville to Valencia to Germany. Fuentes was also now damned sure they were being watched or listened to. He could hear a strange humming noise on two of his phones.

A new, central character in the Operación Puerto mini-drama was also about to enter the fray. '*El Gordo*' – 'The Fatty' – Fuentes called him. Whoever he was, Fuentes had arranged to meet him in Madrid on the afternoon of 15 May, and their rendezvous was piquing the curiosity of Fuentes's co-conspirators. Fuentes, it seemed from a conversation with the Kelme team's directeur sportif, Ignacio Labarta, was not readying himself for a joyous reunion with an old friend. 'I don't want any kind of compromise – I just want to see money,' Fuentes said. The pair speculated about whether El Gordo would use the meeting to fish for information. He already seemed desperate to suss out whether Fuentes and 'Birillo' were somehow linked, given how well the latter was performing in Italy. They also expected Fatty to forage for intel about 'his own guys'.

What Fuentes wouldn't do, he told Labarta, was pull any

punches. He intended to tell El Gordo, 'You didn't pay me and I ended up without the rider and without the money.'

Fuentes's paranoia was hindering the investigation – but it also clearly went against his nature to exercise caution. Every now and then there would be a slip. The investigators only had to wait. It was hard to know at this point who or what were 'El Artista', or 'The Artist; 'Manos Pequeñas', or 'Little Hands'; 'El Bigotés', or 'Whiskers'. But on 14 May a few cats had scampered out of bags as Labarta and Fuentes briefly discussed the results from the day's stage of the Giro d'Italia.

Fuentes seemed pleasantly surprised to hear El Búfalo had finished fourth. Labarta added that Birillo had come in sixteen seconds down. Among the riders who had lost twenty seconds was Zapatero.

The investigators scanned the results. In fourth place was the stoutly built José Enrique Gutiérrez, surely 'El Búfalo'. Birillo could only be one of three riders: Serhiy Gonchar, Davide Rebellin or Ivan Basso. And of the trio of possible Zapateros, the clear frontrunner was the Italian whose name, Scarponi, meant 'boots' in English . . . and zapateros in Spanish. There was no mention of the thirty-sixth rider across the line, Jan Ullrich, or any nom de guerre that might point in his direction.

Yet.

The next day brought further worries, notably about 'an old bottle at the back of the freezer' that Merino Batres was sure could still be used. 'If it goes wrong, I'm going to be fucked – I mean we'll all be fucked but it will be my fault,' Fuentes told Merino Batres.

There was at least more good news from Italy, delivered in a text message from a Swiss number, congratulating Fuentes on events at the Giro. Fuentes had watched the race on TV and later spoke to Labarta about the victory of 'a strange one, the CSC [rider], Basso, a certain Ivan Basso.'

'A certain Ivan Basso,' Labarta echoed approvingly.

'Fuck, yeah,' Fuentes purred.

Having seen Verdi's birthplace, it was time for Jan Ullrich to go to the home of another iconic Italian 'V' – the Vespa. The famous scooters were invented in 1946 in Pontedera, near Pisa, and now Ullrich summoned all of his horsepower in the Giro time trial heading out of and back to the town on 18 May. These were roads that Ullrich

Above: Ullrich and Marco Pantani (*left, with yellow sunglasses*) moments before Pantani's decisive attack on the Galibier in the 1998 Tour.

Right: En route to victory in the 1999 world time trial championship in Treviso, Italy.

Ullrich leads Abraham Olano on the Alto de l'Angliru in the 1999 Vuelta a España.

Ullrich on his way to winning
the 2000 Olympic Games road
race in Sydney.

Telekom's clean sweep of the
podium positions in the same race:
(*from left*) Alexander Vinokourov,
Ullrich and Andreas Klöden.

Ullrich (*right*) and
Lance Armstrong show
their mutual respect on
stage fourteen of the
2001 Tour de France.

Looking a long way from
his Tour de France weight
at a training camp in
Mallorca in January 2002.

Doctor Luigi Cecchini outside
his home near Lucca, Italy.

Jörg Jaksche (*right*) and the journalist Andreas Burkert in Munich in 2015.

(*From left*) Walter Godefroot, Telekom doctor Lothar Heinrich and Ullrich at a press briefing in 1999.

Ullrich leaving the press conference called to address his 2002 positive drugs test.

Armstrong's dramatic crash at Luz Ardiden on stage fifteen of the 2003 Tour de France. Armstrong went on to win the stage.

Above right and right: German fans watch Ullrich fall on stage nineteen of the 2003 Tour de France.

Jan Ullrich at the 2004 Tour de France, with Walter Godefroot looking on.

Ullrich with Rudy Pevenage at the team presentation for the 2006 Tour de France, hours before T-Mobile sent them home in disgrace.

Ullrich leaves the 2006 tour. Wolfgang Strohband is in the foreground.

Team doctor Andreas Schmid.

Ullrich announcing his retirement in 2007.

Ullrich with his wife Sara at their friend Boris Becker's wedding in St. Moritz, Switzerland, in 2009.

Above left: Doctor Eufemiano Fuentes (*right*) arrives at a court house in Madrid in 2013. *Above right*: Ullrich in handcuffs in Mallorca in 2018, after his unsolicited drop-in to Til Schweiger's property.

Below: Mike Baldinger and Ullrich pictured in Merdingen in March 2022.

knew as well as any, from all the time he'd spent in Tuscany at Fattoria Borgo La Torre. While there, he also still occasionally trained
behind Luigi Cecchini's Vespa.

By the evening there would be plenty of talk of Ullrich 'going like
a motorbike'. He blitzed the 51-kilometre course in just under 59
minutes. 'I wasn't even firing on all cylinders at the start,' Ullrich
bragged later. He was only in Italy for training, he repeated; his priority was the Tour.

Ivan Basso had also ridden brilliantly in the pink jersey to finish
second.

The best day of Jan Ullrich's Giro also turned out to be a fruitful one
for Guardia Civil in Madrid. On 17 May they had heard more about
'Ali Baba' and confirmed that Fuentes knew they were listening to his
conversations when he told one caller that they should 'speak on the
other phone because this one is tapped'. Bafflingly, two hours later
Fuentes was talking on the same device, with the same number, to
the Colombian cyclist Santiago Botero. Botero had ridden a poor
time trial at the Volta a Catalunya, and Fuentes wished to reassure
him. 'The artist Botero will paint amazing landscapes when he starts
painting with Colombian felt-tip pens,' he said. Whatever that meant.

Fuentes had later phoned Iberia airlines to book a flight to
Madrid for the following day, the eighteenth, returning to the Canaries on the nineteenth. He was especially insistent about one thing:
that his seat be near the emergency exit.

At 11.27 p.m. a text landed from a number the investigators
hadn't previously seen. The dialling code was Belgian, the message in
Italian. It said, 'Friend when can we speak for a minute. Rudicio.'

The next day, the day of Ullrich's time trial tour de force, there
was a call from the same Belgian number at twenty past midday.
Fuentes was busy, couldn't really speak. Later in the afternoon didn't
work for 'Rudicio' because, as he told Fuentes, 'it's the time trial'. It
would have to be that evening. It was urgent, Rudicio said. Good,
because they needed to 'sort the dates for June', Fuentes agreed.

Then came a long conversation with Labarta at 16.40, with the
race still on. The pink jersey was going well, Fuentes said. He was
the 'only one who can take victory from the guy leading at the
moment who's German, this . . . Ullrich.'

*

As the Giro had edged closer to the Alps, on the third weekend, slowly the German press pack started to swell. Ullrich's victory in Pontedera had caused flurries of interest in newsrooms which usually only had eyes, ears and correspondents for the Tour. A handful of reporters had been dispatched to Italy to get their audience with Der Kaiser.

One writer, Klaus Blume, believed that he'd landed his big Ullrich scoop a couple of months earlier. In his 2011 book, *Des Radsports Letzter Kaiser*, Blume wrote that in March 2006 he had got a tip-off from a good source that Jan Ullrich was about to get busted for doping. The source didn't know exactly when, how, or by whom, but Ullrich would soon be exposed. Over the next few weeks, Blume heard the same rumour from at least one other contact.

Eufemiano Fuentes had a hundred things to do and 'a thousand things in my head', he breathlessly told an unidentified caller on 19 May. The stress was exacerbated by Fuentes sensing that he was a marked man. 'Just remember, this phone's being tapped,' he told his sister, the Kelme team doctor Yolanda.*

The next day, 20 May, at 10.44 a.m., the Italian-speaker with the Belgian number, 'Rudicio', phoned to announce that he had spoken to a 'third person' on the bus and he 'perhaps wanted to do something'.

At 11.32 came a text from the same number: 'Franciacorta near Brescia.'

Among the many unsolved mysteries was why Fuentes kept talking, kept texting, kept feeding the Guardia Civil. It was hard, indeed, for the investigators to know whether this was simply his *modus vivendi*, pinging between contradictory states of agitation and recklessness, or whether the outlaw had started to glimpse the outline of an endgame. On 21 May, he prefaced one seemingly coded exchange about diluting yoghurts in water with 'a greeting to those who are listening to us'. Was he taunting them, certain that the various decoys, euphemisms and nicknames were enough of a smokescreen? Or was Fuentes so used to living on the edge that he had become desensitized?

The Guardia Civil had heard him mention a flight booking from

---

* Yolanda was a co-defendant in Operación Puerto but was acquitted.

Las Palmas to Madrid on the evening of 22 May and a room reservation at the hotel Tryp Diana ahead of a proposed meeting with 'Fatty' in Madrid the following morning. They had also heard Merino Batres agree to go with him. There was more talk of debts, and Fuentes wanting to prove to Merino Batres that he had acted in good faith – 'because of the friendship between us'. Fatty owed them all, Fuentes reminded Merino Batres, including 'Little Hands, Whiskers and Ali Baba'.

'Fatty' also had a name, a real one: he was called 'Manolo'. The Guardia Civil had by now also figured out his last one: Saiz.

And his position: the manager of the Liberty Seguros cycling team.*

Extending from Brescia to the southern shores of the Lago d'Iseo, the emerald vineyards of the Franciacorta region produce small quantities of the most refined sparkling wine in Italy. Not that Jan Ullrich would have much opportunity to indulge his burgeoning oenological interests on his one-night stay on 22 May.

One T-Mobile staff member had also been too busy for cantina visits despite not attending the race in the afternoon. As one of the team's soigneurs, it was Johan Van Impe's job to drive ahead to the team's evening billet, put luggage in rooms and generally prepare for the riders' arrival. On this particular day, Rudy Pevenage had also told him that a package would be delivered to the hotel. Van Impe should collect it.

Van Impe was still en route, behind the wheel of one of the team vehicles, when his mobile phone rang and he picked up to hear what he thought was a Spanish voice gabbling words he couldn't understand. Van Impe hung up, only for the same caller to ring again. This time he worked out that the man was a friend of Rudy's. Confirmation came in a text message from a number with a Spanish dialling code a few minutes later: 'Soy el amigo de Rudy estoy en el hotel' – 'I'm Rudy's friend and I'm in the hotel.'

When Van Impe pulled up in the hotel car park not long later, a middle-aged man he didn't know, had never seen before, was already waiting for him. Moments later, the man was wheeling a

---

* Saiz was tried but acquitted in Operación Puerto.

small, Samsonite trolley bag across the tarmac, leaving it at Van Impe's feet and gesturing that it should go straight to Rudy's room in the hotel.

The man got back into his car and left, and Van Impe did what he was told. Van Impe didn't know then and never found out what was in the trolley bag.*

Once again, on 23 May, Eufemiano Fuentes's day didn't so much start as spill over from the previous night. 'Tutto OK. Rudicio' – 'All OK. Rudicio' – said a text message to Fuentes's mobile late on the 22nd. Only when the sun was rising at around five a.m. did he finally climb into bed in his Madrid hotel room.

The meeting with Manolo Saiz – aka Fatty, the one they had all been talking about for days – would happen in the bar of the Hotel Pio XII at 11 a.m. sharp. Merino Batres and Saiz joked about Fuentes's abysmal time-keeping as they sat waiting and the minute-hand ticked through the hour and towards ten past. Exactly 11.10 was in fact the time at which Fuentes hurried out of the front door at another nearby address, number 20 on the Calle Caidos de la División Azul, carrying a green plastic bag. He turned right. Right again at some traffic lights, took a call on one phone, hung up and then started talking on a different one. Finally he walked through the reception doors at the Hotel Pio XII and to where Merino Batres and Saiz were sitting.

The Guardia Civil knew because they were watching – this time not on video screens but from a position outside the window.

There were no listening devices in the hotel but at one point Fuentes handed the green bag that he had brought with him to Saiz.

At 11.50, their meeting over, Saiz and Fuentes stepped outside and were met by agents in Guardia Civil uniforms. By now, as per a warrant signed the previous day by the Madrid judge Antonio Serrano, officers had also poured into four Madrid properties owned or rented by Fuentes and Merino Batres, who was about to be apprehended inside the Hotel Pio XII.

---

* Pevenage admitted orchestrating Ullrich's doping in his autobiography, *Der Rudy* (Uitgeverij, 2020).

Ignacio Labarta and Alberto León, a former mountain biker the Guardia Civil believed to be the 'Ali Baba' in Fuentes's pantomime of forty or probably many more thieves, had also been arrested at their homes in Zaragoza and San Lorenzo de El Escorial respectively.

Throughout the afternoon, the black Nokia the Guardia Civil had taken off Eufemiano Fuentes kept ringing. Dozens of calls and a steady stream of text messages, including one at half past two from someone who identified themselves as 'the wife of Serrano'. She wanted to talk to Fuentes. She hoped he could explain something about 'Marcos'.

Marcos Serrano, a thirty-three-year-old former Tour de France stage winner, had been riding the Giro d'Italia for Manolo Saiz's Liberty Seguros team. Had been, because Serrano fell ill in the evening after stage twelve and was rushed to a hospital in Tortona. He stayed there for four days, after which he would spend another ten in a ward in Vigo, north-west Spain, receiving treatment for what Italian investigators believed was drug poisoning.

Serrano subsequently claimed that it had been a normal virus and that his wife was calling Fuentes because the Spanish Embassy wasn't aiding their efforts to repatriate him and they needed Fuentes to help translate.

Eufemiano Fuentes sat waiting for his lawyer to arrive at the Guardia Civil's main police station in the Calle de Guzmán el Bueno, making a mental inventory of what they could have found and its possible repercussions. At the Calle Alonso Cano apartment that they presumed to be the hub, the nerve centre of Fuentes's operations – and the place he and Merino Batres referred to as 'la pizzeria' – the Guardia Civil had discovered sixty-eight bags of blood and forty-five of plasma. A further ninety 450 ml packets of blood had been removed from fridges in the apartment in the Calle Caidos de la División Azul.

There were also hundreds of pages of documents from various drawers and files – from calendars to invoices and even post-it notes. In Fuentes's wallet alone, there were seven SIM cards to go with the three Nokia phones that he'd been carrying – the black one, a blue one and another that was silver.

There was also no telling what compromising evidence had been

found on Merino Batres, or 'the old man', as Fuentes had unflatter-
ingly called him in discussions with other members of their network.
Had he known, Fuentes would probably have been relieved to find
out that Merino Batres had at least been trying to keep track of who
was who in their portfolio of clients – although perhaps not thrilled
with his lack of discretion; in the cardiologist's wallet, the Guardia
Civil had found the business card for a seafood restaurant, the RAFA,
with a handy key on the back.

It read '1. HIJORUDICIO 2. BIRILLO . . .' all the way down to
'33. CLASICOMANO'.

At the Giro, it was one of those days when just stepping outside of
the press room felt like a dereliction of duty. The action was happening not at the finish line but on laptop screens and phones in the
marquee filled with journalists. The news went around after the
stage had already turned into a non-event, with Ivan Basso proving
so superior on the climb to Monte Bondone that, as I wrote in my
piece later, to the rest of the field he had become a 'pink-tinted irrele-
vance'. I had covered enough Grand Tours by then, in the post-Festina
era, to recognize and guiltily relish the buzz of a breaking scandal –
the rustle of papers, the pitter-patter of keyboards, the hushed
excitement. A trouble as much as a specific noise. It was happening
now, as colleagues either sat staring at their screens or sprang out of
their chairs. 'Manolo Saiz arrested?!' 'And Eufemi– Eufemian—. . .
Ah, yes, him.'

When he heard the news, at home in Texas, the newly retired
Lance Armstrong seemed to immediately appreciate the magnitude
of what had happened, and to whom. 'What?! They caught Eufe?!'
Armstrong was said to have spluttered.

Basso gave his post-race press-conference in a poorly lit room
which must have been the only available space up on the mountain,
in the clouds swirling around the Bondone's summit. But there was
nothing noticeably shifty or nervous about his demeanour. Most
reporters present knew one thing about Fuentes – that they had
covered some murky story about the doctor, Ángel Casero and a message to Luigi Cecchini during the 2001 Vuelta. That was one link to
Basso – Cecchini once having been his coach as well as Ullrich's. But
for now no one broached it.

The first hint that this went way beyond Saiz's Liberty Seguros team came that night from a Spanish radio station, Cadena Ser. They claimed that Basso and Ullrich could both be on a list of 200 cyclists that Fuentes may have been treating. The following morning, Basso was put on the spot and said that he didn't know Fuentes, had never met him. Jan Ullrich stepped out of the T-Mobile team bus and rode past the microphones, straight to the start line. This left Lothar Heinrich, T-Mobile's pejoratively nicknamed 'TV Doctor', to tell the media, 'There's no truth to any of it.'

By late afternoon on the day of his arrest, more voicemails and text messages were arriving on Eufemiano Fuentes's phones. Nothing like Clara Serrano's, but rather expressions of support, solidarity, a shared sense of consternation.

A voicemail from his wife at 21.13 said that there were bigger problems in the world than what sportsmen do or don't take and, anyway, it was the cyclists who came looking for him and not the other way around.

Text messages that would continue to arrive throughout the next day, most of them wishing him strength and, yes, justice.

In the meantime, the Guardia Civil had taken their first statements. Fuentes had told them the meeting with Saiz was about his daughter's rare and serious eye condition, for Saiz had previously run a team sponsored by the blindness charity ONCE and still had contacts there; Saiz also said it was a 'private matter', although he admitted that Fuentes had previously treated some of his team's riders, including Roberto Heras; Merino Batres confirmed that he had performed blood transfusions for elite athletes but always and only at Fuentes's behest; León told them he was 'Ali Baba' and that Labarta was 'Little Hands'; and Labarta said the drugs they had found in his home were for strictly personal use.

León, Labarta and Saiz were all released on the day of their arrest. For Merino Batres and Fuentes, it took three more days and bail of 120,000 euros each.

The Giro finished in Milan on 28 May with Ivan Basso winning by an enormous margin of nine minutes from the surprise runner-up, José Enrique Gutiérrez. On the evening of the 29th, Fuentes answered a phone call for the first time since his arrest, from his mother, and warned her they might have to wipe or swap a particular SIM card. Three hours later, he texted 'Birillo' to ask for his 'other' number, since 'they' had taken his address book. A few minutes later, there had been no reply, so Fuentes messaged a different Italian number. 'Excuse me, madame, I'm the friend from [sic] Birillo and I need him to call me before to see me. Please tell your husband. He knows what to do. A thousand thank-yous.'

Jan Ullrich hadn't made it to Milan – or even the summit of the Passo San Pellegrino and the end of stage nineteen on 26 May. At the bottom of the climb, Ullrich pulled off the road and into the car park of the Hotel Stella Alpina in Falcade, where T-Mobile were due to stay that night. He told a handful of journalists T-Mobile invited to the hotel that he had planned not to start the stage, but that would have looked 'strange' in light of the stories that had come out of Spain over the previous forty-eight hours. Those headlines linking him to Eufemiano Fuentes were just 'sad', Ullrich said.

It was put to him that, if the rumours intensified, the Tour de France organizers might ban him from starting their race.

Impossible, Ullrich said. 'Someone who has nothing to hide also has nothing to fear.'

20

THE VANISHING

'I've got nothing to do with this. I'm just a victim'

—*Jan Ullrich*

Although the setting seemed incongruous, it was somehow also fitting that Jörg Jaksche, a professional cyclist, had his first conversation with Eufemiano Fuentes in a destination that has become notorious among skiers. The '*Streif*' or 'Stripe' run down the Hahnenkamm mountain, above Kitzbühel in Austria, is one sport's synonym for risk, speed and lethal danger, and Jaksche stood in its shadow as he made the acquaintance of an individual many associated with the same things in cycling. It was New Year's Eve 2004, and Jaksche's new team's manager, Manolo Saiz, had told him to expect Fuentes's call. Speaking English and a little German – for Fuentes would later tell Jaksche that he had learned much of what he knew in the DDR – they made plans for what would be their first meeting in person in Gran Canaria. They then wished each other a goodnight and *Guten Rutsch* into 2005. After which, Jaksche stomped through the snow and back indoors to where his friends were celebrating.

A year and a half later, Jaksche was at a Liberty Seguros training camp in northern Spain when he learned that Manolo Saiz and Eufemiano Fuentes had been arrested.[26] Jaksche booked the first flight out of Bilbao the next day, fearing that he too could soon be in handcuffs.

Instead, within days, in the second week of June, Jaksche was lining up at the Tour of Switzerland oblivious to the fact that he was in the same or a similar bind to his former teammate, Jan Ullrich. Meaning that they were both clients of Eufemiano Fuentes and, so, dead men riding. Jaksche had his suspicions about CSC's Ivan Basso and knew for sure that his own Liberty Seguros teammates weren't the only riders for whom Fuentes had provided a bespoke blood-swapping service. Fuentes had rather given this away one day when they were making arrangements for Jaksche's 'refills' at the 2005 Tour de France. 'He pulled out this route map of the Tour,' Jaksche remembers, 'and he'd written so many numbers on it that you couldn't even see France. He was like, "Ah, here's the third stage . . ." and I was squinting to even see it. I think there were fifty-one different numbers on it, and I knew we didn't have fifty-one riders in our team. At that moment I was sure it wasn't only Liberty.'

In Switzerland, Jaksche looked for clues that Ullrich was also fretting, also feeling, like Jaksche, that 'the shit had hit the fan'. But he saw and heard none. 'I even chatted to him at the race and he was just completely cool about the whole subject. Like, "Nope, it's not an issue for me." I took from that that he definitely wasn't involved with Fuentes. Now, I think that he was sure they couldn't catch him because they never had any telephone contact; it was Pevenage who arranged everything. There was that and the fact that, in those days, we really didn't think we were cheating. Attacking when the yellow jersey had stopped for a piss was cheating, but not blood transfusions. You didn't really like doping, but you also didn't want to stop, because, even if everyone else said they'd stopped too, you wouldn't trust them.'

Jaksche had realized he was probably doomed when he watched Spanish TV news footage of the 23 May raids and saw one Guardia Civil officer removing a blood bag labelled with his code name, Bella, from Fuentes's freezer. After that, he went to Switzerland assuming that performances there might offer pointers as to who else's wings had been clipped. Instead, he says, it was like the last days of Rome, with five riders who were later confirmed as Fuentes clients finishing in the top ten on general classification.[*]

---

[*]   Ullrich, Jaksche, Schleck, Vicioso and Caruso. Schleck was later suspended by his team for making a 7,000-euro payment to Fuentes for 'training advice' but cleared of doping by his national federation. Vicioso denied using blood transfusions and said he had seen Fuentes only for 'sporadic medical consultations'.

Ullrich was the best of the lot. Aggressive in the mountain stages and superlative in the final-day time trial, he had sent out the clear message that he was heading into the Tour in his best form since 1997. There were ten days to go until the Tour's Grand Départ and he spent them hammering up the steepest, toughest climbs he could find near Scherzingen, and even some over the border in Austria. Andreas Klöden sometimes trained with him. Klöden's coach, Thomas Schedewie, told acquaintances later that he had never seen Ullrich looking so strong, so motivated, with such fire in his eyes and his legs. Ullrich had also never been so happy: he told *Bild Zeitung* that Sara Steinhauser had just accepted his marriage proposal.

He even seemed unfazed when, shortly after his final training session before leaving for France, Ullrich learned that *El País* had presented the most damning evidence against him to date. The newspaper knew about the business card for the RAFA restaurant that the Guardia Civil had found in Merino Batres's wallet – and what was written on the back. The paper alleged that the code names scrawled in biro were Fuentes's clients and Ullrich surely had to be 'Hijo de Rudicio' – 'the son of Rudy'. Ullrich promised T-Mobile's Head of Communications, Christian Frommert, that he had nothing to do with any of it – and repeated the denial twice for emphasis.

It was at roughly this point, however, that Rudy Pevenage started to think that their game was up. 'I knew a few days before the Tour that something was going to happen, I just wasn't sure what,' he tells me quietly. 'I told Jan we were in trouble, but he replied that everyone was in the same boat.'

Pevenage has one major regret. He knows that it may not have mattered, but one mistake still gnaws at him.

'I always used to use public phones with Fuentes, whereas the others were obviously using their mobile phones,' he explains. 'I told Fuentes I wouldn't take the risk and he said I was being stupid, that they were free in Spain, but I was paranoid about getting caught. It was very stressful. We were at the Giro, Jan had won the time trial . . . I didn't have contact with Fuentes every day. From time to time, we'd speak – "Ah, it's going OK . . ." and so on – but, there, Jan wins the time trial and I decide to call Fuentes. The problem is that my Italian pre-pay card has run out and I can't recharge it. Anyone in Belgium can buy a pre-pay card, but not in Italy; you need a passport. A friend of mine had bought this one for me. But she wasn't around on this day, so I called Fuentes on my Belgian phone to tell him Jan had won, that we'd see how things went in the mountains and so on. They had my number then. Maybe they would have rumbled us anyway, but now they had proof.'

As well as text messages and calls that led them directly to Pevenage and Ullrich, the Guardia Civil also had multiple bags of Ullrich's blood. According to a calendar found in one of Fuentes's apartments, Ullrich had been due to have two bags removed and two put back in on 20 June, two days after the end of the Tour of Switzerland. That blood was now in the Guardia Civil's DNA storage bank in Madrid, so Ullrich had presumably had to make alternative arrangements.

Fuentes had at least offered Jörg Jaksche an apology. The doctor called him one day to say he was sorry for everything, that he hoped it would all end well. That now seemed unlikely, given that Jaksche's team sponsor, insurer Liberty Seguros, had pulled out within forty-eight hours of Manolo Saiz's arrest. Alexander Vinokourov, their star, had saved the team by securing funding from the city of Astana in his native Kazakhstan, but the prospects of the Tour organizers letting them race looked bleak.

Jaksche had also started to think that Fuentes's service may not be the slick, boutique operation his premium prices implied. Long-held doubts now crystallized. Many of them focused not on Fuentes but his assistant, the kindly but creaking Merino Batres. When Operación Puerto finally came to trial in 2013, Merino Batres was excused from taking the stand and the charges against him dropped on the grounds that he was suffering from Alzheimer's. Jaksche wondered whether the cardiologist's first symptoms hadn't started to manifest themselves years earlier, when he was in his early sixties.

'Merino Batres never went to races. He was too old,' Jaksche says. 'I probably saw him six to eight times, and every single time he said, "My friend, where are you coming from today?" I'd say, "Austria, Innsbruck." To which he'd reply, "Ah, I was there for skiing in 1968." Every. Single. Time. I eventually said to Fuentes, "Are you sure this is the right guy for this job?"'

Forgetting someone's travel arrangements or nationality was one thing. Mixing up two clients' code names and their blood bags would be another, with potentially deadly consequences. This was presumably why Merino Batres always kept a list of code names in his pocket – or that could have been a relatively new innovation.

Fuentes client Tyler Hamilton's 2004 positive test for a homologous blood transfusion – essentially having traces of someone else's blood in his system – was a first for the sport. But only a few weeks later, Hamilton's teammate and fellow Fuentes patient Santi Pérez tested positive for the same thing. It was never proven or even widely suggested that Merino Batres gave Hamilton's blood to Pérez and vice versa, but, today, Hamilton tells me this or some form of sabotage remain his 'two best guesses as to what happened'.

Unlike Jaksche, Hamilton received no mea culpa from Fuentes. 'If I met him today I'm sure we'd have an, er, interesting conversation. There are certainly some questions I'd like to ask him,' the American says.

Jörg Jaksche stops short of Luigi Cecchini's 'Fuentes is the nicest bloke in the world', but he also can't help but embroider a romantic, almost chivalresque mythology that has grown around the doctor. From the moment Fuentes collected him at Las Palmas airport in January 2005 and they tore through the city streets in his choked-out Toyota, with Fuentes talking Jaksche through his complete catalogue of steroids and hormones as they went, Fuentes fully lived up to the image of the caddish, thrill-seeking outlaw – a lab-coated Robin Hood toting his syringe in place of a bow and arrow.

'He was a fun guy,' Jaksche confirms. 'He also wasn't super strict about the money; the most important thing was that one of his riders won. He was the engineer. I always described his behaviour in terms of . . . he would jump a red light just to see what happened. For example, one day we met in this bar in Calle Zurbano, where he had one of his offices. He came in, looked at me, and I thought, *Ah, it might be Eufemiano but it might not*. Because he had these fake glasses on and a beret. I didn't really know if I should say hello or not. But he came over and was like, "Hola, amigo!" I asked him why he was in disguise and he explained that he'd been at the presentation of some new blood bag made by Baxter [a major healthcare company]. This one lasted longer in the fridge or something like that. Anyway, then he does the fake trumpet sound, "Da-da-ddaaaaa!", and pulls one of these bags or a prototype out of his briefcase. "How the hell did you get that?" I said. He told me he'd been sitting in the last row at this convention, the last seat on the right-hand side, and the guys presenting had passed one of these prototypes around and told everyone to pass it to the person on their right. "And there wasn't anyone on my right, so I put it in my bag!" Fuentes said, grinning at me. He was a funny guy. If he was here, we'd be having a lot of fun . . . but you also never forget what he did.'

Indeed – whether it was the shameless profiteering, the law-breaking, the lying and the recklessness that Hamilton has described at length, and which Jaksche saw in glimpses.

'I never really had bad experiences with him, but sometimes he would forget you were coming, forget to take the blood out of the freezer, and he'd have to immerse the bag in hot water to defrost it . . . but it'd still be freezing cold when it got injected and you'd be close to collapsing. One time he had an Italian rider, and this Italian rider came with a friend who had the same blood group. Normally it should have worked out because they were the same blood group, but when they did the re-injection he got like an allergic reaction and couldn't breathe. I just know from this guy that Fuentes was like, "Ach, stop being a pussy!"'

'I don't care. Tomorrow I'm riding the Tour de France.'

At around lunchtime on 30 June 2006, Christian Frommert had heard these words and let their empty conviction dissolve into the huge sweat cloud filling Jan Ullrich's bedroom in the Hôtel au Boeuf in Blaesheim, near Strasbourg, with Ullrich at its centre. Frommert's efforts to make Ullrich understand the allegations in the morning papers and explain their implications had come to nothing. Jan had simply carried on hammering the pedals on his turbo trainer. He was in the form of his life – 'Bombenform', as he kept telling teammates. Frommert now surveyed the ropes of bluey-green veins protruding out of his calf muscles and decided that these might have been the only true words that Ullrich had spoken all week.

A few metres away, Ullrich's directeur sportif, mentor and friend, Rudy Pevenage, sat on Ullrich's bed, staring at the floor. The previous Monday, the team management had confronted the Belgian with reports in Spanish newspaper El País claiming that Pevenage – and by association Ullrich – was dishonourably mentioned in the files seized from Eufemiano Fuentes in May. Pevenage's initial denial had been unconvincing, so they asked again. 'I've got nothing to do with it,' Pevenage repeated.

'I've got nothing to do with it,' he told Frommert for a third time now.

Frommert made a curious candidate for a pivotal role in what was turning, minute by minute, into one of the greatest scandals of Tour de France history. Just a week or two earlier, he had been only an entry in journalists' address books, a business card in their wallet, or a nameless face under a thick canopy of jet-black hair whom they occasionally saw at races, almost invariably with a cigarette dangling from his lips. His official title was T-Mobile's 'Director of Sports Communications'.

That morning, he had stood with three colleagues staring at a fax machine in a greenkeeper's shed at the back of the Kempferhof golf resort, waiting for lights to flash. There were flags, shovels, spades, and barely enough elbow room for four to stand. The Amaury Sport Organisation (ASO), the media group that runs the Tour de France, had promised to send over everything they would receive that morning from the Spanish police on Ullrich, Pevenage and their involvement in the Operación Puerto. Finally, at precisely 9.35, the machine started spitting its truths. Luuc Eisenga, the team's multi-lingual press chief, took the pages and translated as he read, his expression darkening with every line. Pevenage was heavily incriminated. Worse, Ullrich could also be identified from various code names and numbers used by Fuentes.

At this exact moment, Ullrich and the other T-Mobile riders were on their way to the Kempferhof in the team bus. T-Mobile had organized what they were calling a 'Grand Déjeuner' for the day before the Grand Départ. The canapés were arrayed, champagne was on ice. Microphones had been checked. The riders' late arrival didn't seem to bother the reporters; the nibbles tasted good, the wine already flowed, plus, hey, not even the Germans are punctual all of the time.

What the journalists couldn't know was that the T-Mobile team bus had parked up outside the entrance to the golf club, awaiting further instructions from Frommert. After Eisenga's translation and a quick brainstorm, Frommert called and gave the order to turn the bus around and return to the team hotel in Blaesheim.

Frommert then went to inform the media that there was a problem.

A couple of hundred kilometres away, over the German border in Stuttgart, Ullrich's manager, Wolfgang Strohband, had stepped off a plane and picked up his hire car. Strohband was approaching the Rhine Valley when then the first item on the 11 a.m. radio news bulletin almost sent him off the road: 'Jan Ullrich suspended and out of the Tour de France.'

Strohband grabbed his mobile phone.

'Jan, where are you?'

'On the rollers, in my room.'

'What about the presentation?'

'We turned around.'

'So what now?'

'Just get here.'

At around midday, Strohband was pulling up in Blaesheim, hurrying inside and asking for Ullrich's room number. On his way through the corridor, he passed a sobbing Oscar Sevilla, Ullrich's Spanish teammate and a fellow Fuentes client. When Strohband finally found Ullrich, he, in contrast, was defiant. 'I want to ride. I'm in . . . *Bombenform.*'

Only Strohband and two or three others knew that this was supposed to be more than just another Tour de France, Ullrich's ninth. All being well, it would also be his triumphant last. Ever since 1999, there had been repeated threats to quit cycling, to leave behind a world that sometimes felt to Ullrich like a prison. These had been fits of pique, but they also revealed a cumulative fatigue that had brought Ullrich to a resolution: he would put everything into winning the 2006 Tour de France, then bid the sport adieu at the Deutschland Tour in late August.

While Strohband and Ullrich now considered desperate measures, sometime in the early afternoon, Frommert invited Bob Stapleton to join him for an impromptu meeting. Since selling Voice-Stream Wireless to Deutsche Telekom in 2000, Stapleton had followed his passion for cycling on a meandering path over the next four years. In 2006, he had combined his position as the manager of T-Mobile's women's team with a consultancy role that now required him to be with the men's team in Strasbourg.

All year, on his trips to see the team, Stapleton had got 'bad vibes'. The riders he didn't know seemed secretive, shifty, even allowing for their mistrust of anything or anyone from outside of their inner sanctum. The ones he did know had told him they were well paid but miserable. Their mood seemed even to have spread to the wives and girlfriends. 'They just had a bad feel, all round,' he says now.

Frommert invited Stapleton to take a seat in the Hôtel au Boeuf's closed, deserted bar. He then laid out what would be the T-Mobile strategy: they would stay at the Tour without Ullrich and Sevilla; the company would honour its sponsorship for the time being; and, finally, they wanted Stapleton to take over the team.

Stapleton let Frommert's proposition sink in, then replied that, yes, he'd be open to the idea of helping in any way that he could.

This was good, Frommert told him, because now Stapleton would have to send Ullrich home.

'Er, I'll tell him *with* you . . .' Stapleton replied.

Soon Ullrich sat before them in the same empty hotel bar. Frommert did most of the talking, in German. Stapleton picked up what he could, which wasn't a lot. Ullrich didn't flinch, didn't protest, and generally displayed the body language of a man who had accepted his fate. Frommert finally told him that there were press waiting in front of the hotel and that they would have to make a statement. They discussed what he should say and went outside. Ullrich let out a deep, eloquent sigh, thrust his hands into the pockets of his jogging bottoms and stepped into the huddle of journalists. 'I've got nothing to do with this. I'm just a victim. I'd prepared for this Tour de France like never before . . . This is the worst thing that's ever happened in my career.'

Questions were neither invited nor answered. Instead, Ullrich turned and went back to his room. His best friend, Andreas Klöden, was one of several riders who argued that the whole team should pull out, in solidarity. Ullrich told him not to be so stupid.

His manager, Strohband, had spent nearly the whole afternoon with his phone pressed to his ear and clinging to a frail chance. Strohband's lawyer had ordered him to ask Frommert for the evidence incriminating Ullrich, whereupon Frommert showed him the three sheets of paper that he had pulled out of the fax machine at the Kempferhof that morning. There was plenty in that to incriminate Pevenage, much less pointing to Ullrich. OK, Frommert said, but the Tour was going through Spain, and if Ullrich didn't leave now he could be yanked out of the race, maybe in handcuffs, when they got to the Pyrenees. Strohband called his lawyer again. The lawyer said that he would phone a judge in Aachen, where the team's holding company was based. The judge's verdict: Ullrich may still be able to challenge the decision, but they would need the second and third opinion of two colleagues. Unfortunately, neither of them would be available before Monday.

And with that, Ullrich packed his bags, said his goodbyes, and followed his brother Stefan, one of the team's mechanics and now his getaway driver, across the car park and into a black Audi.

Throughout an unusually cold, snowy winter, and even more so during the early spring of 2006, the German media had raised and repeatedly returned to the same two questions: would home support galvanize Die Mannschaft to victory in the football World Cup; and, perhaps of greater significance, could hosting the tournament that summer somehow crystallize a common identity, a sense of German-ness that had eluded the unified nation since 1990 and Die Wende?

The first signs had not been good. A reminder of Germany's sheepish, strained relationship with its own past was served mere hours before kick-off, when the city of Berlin formally acknowledged the location of Hitler's bunker for the first time. A lonely information board, rising out of a car park a few blocks down from the Branden-burg Gate – inconspicuous enough not to encourage ghoulish tourism – was the capital's sombre, tentative nod to this, one of its many embarrassing recesses.

Next had come the opening ceremony in Munich. Some hailed it as a masterpiece of involuntary symbolism – not of what it repre-sented to be German but of the beer-swilling, bratwurst-guzzling, oompah-playing caricature already embedded in the world's collect-ive imagination. More than that, the whole half-hour confirmed what the social commentators had been saying for months: the amalga-mated Germany had no idea who or what it was, and was about to embark upon a gruelling month on the psychoanalyst's couch with the world watching on.

'Foreigners know precisely what Germany's identity is,' wrote Dirk Kurbjuweit in *Der Spiegel*. 'To be German means to wear Leder-hosen and dance around slapping one's knees. This is exactly what they saw in the opening ceremony of the World Cup . . . If you were German and not from Bavaria, though, you didn't feel represented by any of the commotion happening on the pitch. It was quite absurd.

'Identity and Germany are contradictions. Indefinite and forever changing populations and borders have seen to that. The Holocaust is another major obstacle. Germany can't create an identity with it, but certainly can't without it. Any attempt to do that in the foreseeable future will be doomed to fail.'

The general sense of disorientation continued when, after their Costa Rican opponents, the German players lined up for their national anthem. The song itself is controversial, the first two of its three verses having been culled in 1990 on grounds of political incorrectness and historical inaccuracies. Long before that, Friedrich Nietzsche had declared perhaps the most infamous lyric, 'Deutschland über alles' – 'Germany above all' – the 'most stupid words in the world'.

As the players lip-synced, the soporific, barely audible dirge of the one surviving stanza groaned around the Allianz Arena.

Despite the less-than rousing send-off, Germany went on to win 4–2.

Further victories followed against Poland, Ecuador and Sweden, setting up a quarter-final with Argentina on 30 June.

The change in the national mood could now be measured in the decibel level of the 'Deutschlandlied' before every match, and in the number of national flags flapping from car or bedroom windows, or displayed in shops and schools. 'If you had hung a German flag outside your house before the 2006 World Cup, people would have assumed you were a Nazi. Now, suddenly, everyone was doing it,' the journalist Andreas Burkert says today.

The Patriotismus-Pegel, the subjective 'Patriotism Gauge', as the media had christened it, was about to surge again as the Germans faced Argentina. 72,000 packed into the stadium. One million turned the 'Fans' Mile' between the Brandenburg Gate and the Victory Column, where nine giant screens had been erected, into a roaring river of noise and emotion.

German were heading for defeat until Miroslav Klose equalized with ten minutes to go. Extra-time ended goalless, meaning a penalty shootout would decide the result. But, of course, to paraphrase a famous line from the former England player Gary Lineker, football is a simple game: twenty-two men chase a ball for ninety minutes – or 120, if absolutely necessary – and, at the end, the Germans always win.

The English-based Süddeutsche Zeitung and Guardian reporter, Raphael Honigstein, admits now that it was hard, as a German watching these joyous outpourings, not to get swept along. In his book, Das Reboot – How German Football Reinvented Itself and

Conquered the World, Honigstein quotes one of the German substitutes against Argentina, Thomas Hitzlsperger: 'The summer of 2006 was Germany's Summer of Love, our generation's Woodstock.'

'It was just this huge snowball that kept getting bigger,' Honigstein says now. 'For the first time that I or pretty much anyone else could remember, people just started to feel relaxed about being German. For the first time, we presented ourselves to the world as fun-loving, hospitable, the kind of people you wanted to be around. I don't think that had happened since the war. There was nothing aggressive or unwelcoming about it; it was our party and everyone was invited. Like Oktoberfest in Munich, but on a huge scale. The team itself also came across as nice guys, good winners, good ambassadors for Germany. Whether that was the reality or not didn't matter; that was the impression. It also didn't matter whether you were from the East or the West. If there was a divide, it was between those who were and weren't proud to be German, and it just felt as though everyone was piling over the top to be with those who were.

'On the day of that game against Argentina, life just stopped. It was utterly overwhelming, almost too much to take in. You could have robbed two banks that day and got away with it.'

Honigstein's memories, like those of many others, are plasma-sharp.

He admits that he has clean forgotten just one thing: that, on the same giddy evening as Germany reached the semi-final, an athlete responsible for another moment that had enraptured and briefly reconciled the same, disconnected people nine years earlier, exited the stage of his intended virtuoso performance without playing a note. Not only that, he left with his head bowed, never to reappear.

To be precise: at 18.42 Central European Time, just one minute after Klose's equalizer and twelve before the full-time whistle in Berlin, Jan Ullrich climbed into a car and was driven away from Strasbourg, out of the Tour de France and out of cycling.

It was indeed a good time to rob a bank . . . or to vanish.

21

CHECKMATE

'I don't want to talk about the Fuentes period. I met him when I was riding myself. I met him, we talked, and voilà . . .'

—*Rudy Pevenage*

Long before Eufemiano Fuentes became a vampiric scourge of professional cycling, his family's bloodline had already left an indelible, sanguinary mark in the chronicles of the Canary Islands.

Born in 1911, the doctor's uncle, also called Eufemiano, created his own tobacco empire and helped build a football club, Unión Deportiva Las Palmas, which now plays in the Spanish Second Division and whose stadium once bore his name. Eufemiano senior is better known in the Canaries, however, for the events of 2 June 1976. In the middle of that night, a masked man broke into the Fuentes family villa, hauled its pyjama-clad owner out of his bed, into Fuentes's own Cadillac, and sped off into the darkness. Months later, thanks to a tip-off from a relative of the presumed culprit, a seasoned local villain nicknamed 'El Rubio' or 'The Blonde', police found Fuentes's mutilated body at the bottom of a well twenty minutes' drive from Las Palmas. Twenty-two years would pass before they could finally track down, arrest and convict El Rubio.

Another Eufemiano Fuentes, the doctor's cousin, later put the family back in the news, in similarly grisly circumstances, in 1994. When a Las Palmas prostitute named Carmen Diepa Pérez refused to stub out his cigarette on her chest, Fuentes flew into a rage and killed her. He then hacked apart Pérez's dead body with a chainsaw and scattered the body parts in various skips around his home city.

By the mid-1990s, of course, the Eufemiano who would one day become the most talked about member of the Fuentes clan was cannily forging a career in sports medicine. He had been the first member of his family to go to university, studying medicine at the University of Navarra. On the day of his uncle's kidnapping, he was sitting a gynaecology exam. Described by classmates and his tutors as a brilliant and curious student, Eufemiano also excelled as an athlete, winning the Spanish Universities 400-metre hurdles title in 1976. According to an article in Pamplona newspaper *Diario de Noticias de Navarra*, 'Eufemiano Fuentes caught the attention of 1970s Pamplona from behind the wheel of his Alfa Romeo, and those who knew him say that, with his well-bred airs, his intelligence and his gift of the gab, he had plenty of success in the art of seducing members of the opposite sex.'

It wasn't only women who fell under Fuentes's charm. José Luis Pascua was as well known in Spanish athletics for his coaching as for the rebellious streak that had earned him a three-year ban for defying Franco's institutions in the mid-1970s. After the General's death, the Spanish athletics federation appointed Pascua to head up their quest for medal success at the LA Olympics in 1984 – and Pascua enlisted the help of a kindred spirit studying at the Spanish National Institute of Physical Education in Madrid, one Eufemiano Fuentes. An Argentine named Guillermo Laich, whose clients later included Diego Maradona, completed a formidable brain trust. In the run-up to Los Angeles, Laich set up a 'cultural exchange' with Eastern Bloc counterparts and the athletes whom they were training, often in the Canary Islands, with methods that he, Fuentes and Pascua considered to be state-of-the-art. After Czech athletes' remarkable performances in 1984, Laich told *El País*, 'If you ever published a photo of a Czech athlete on the eve of a competition, anyone would think that it was an intensive care unit, with all the vials of serum going straight into the veins.'

What Fuentes, Laich and Pascua called their system of 'biological preparation', others called doping. There were rumours of Spanish athletes following the lead of Finnish runners and American track cyclists by experimenting with blood transfusions. It was also alleged that Fuentes et al were carrying out their own dope tests to ensure their athletes sailed through the official controls, as was common practice in East Germany. Embarrassingly, the method didn't save Fuentes's wife, the 400-metre runner Cristina Pérez, who tested positive for a banned amphetamine in 1987, although her conviction was later overturned.

Luckily, Fuentes had by then found his calling in a different sport. Before the 1985 cycling season, Pascua's brother, Manuel, had recommended Fuentes for the job as team doctor to the SEAT-Orbea squad, whose riders included the future Tour de France winner Pedro Delgado. Fuentes arrived with his usual flourish, pulling up to his first training camp at Font Romeu in the Pyrenees in his Porsche, then guiding Delgado to victory in the Vuelta a España the following May. The team's directeur sportif, Txomin Perurena, recalled him fondly years later: 'He was a lovely guy, very good at his job – and extremely funny. He wasn't a morning person, let's say, and every time he showed up late he'd tell us with a big smile that his grandmother had died. I don't know how many grandmothers he had . . .'

One of SEAT-Orbea's star riders, Pello Ruiz Cabestany, also recalls a sharp, compassionate operator who respected the conditions laid down in their first meeting, namely that Cabestany wanted only legal treatment. '[Later] I think he lost his head,' Cabestany told the journalist Ander Izagirre.

By 1990, such was Fuentes's reputation that, when the ONCE team manager Manolo Saiz asked his riders to suggest candidates for the role of team doctor, calls for Fuentes rang back in a resounding chorus. One day, Saiz proclaimed the doctor 'the best psychologist that ever existed'. Whether because of his magic words, hands or potions, in Fuentes's two seasons at ONCE, the team soared. When journalists recognized Fuentes on their flight to Mallorca for the decisive time trial of the 1991 Vuelta, the doctor nodded towards a package on the seat next to him. 'In there is the key to the Vuelta,' he grinned.[27]

Fuentes eventually left ONCE, claiming to be worn out by the stress of frequent travel to and from races. He enjoyed more relaxed schedules at Amaya first, then Kelme, yet was still able to produce similarly transformative results. In 1995, the owners of Kelme, a sportswear company, begged him to give their hometown football team, Elche, a final push in their bid for promotion to the Spanish second division. Fuentes's efforts proved vain, but Barcelona still made him a handsome offer, with perks including a beachside villa, in 1996. Fuentes declined – so he told *Stern* magazine in 2008 – and waited four years before his next flirtation with the beautiful game with the club of his native city, UD Las Palmas. There, Fuentes's methods were 'shrouded in mystery' and kept largely hidden from the medical staff upon whom he had been 'imposed', as they later told the press. He reported for work only once a week and administered all treatments behind the closed door of his office in the bowels of the Estadio Insular. He frequently promised players that he could make them '300 per cent better'. Not long after his arrival, Las Palmas made a quick getaway after an away match at Rayo Vallecano – and left ampoules and pills strewn across the dressing-room floor, according to a cleaner who found them. The leftovers were never analysed, but Las Palmas still felt compelled to call a press conference the following day. The syringes had contained only vitamins, Fuentes said. One player had even refused an injection when he was told that it would do nothing for his receding hairline.

Las Palmas enjoyed their best season since the late 1970s, finishing eleventh in Spain's top division – and yet the doctor didn't return for a second campaign. Asked years later if it was true that Barcelona had made him a second offer in 2002, he said that he would rather not comment. In one interview with Cadena SER in 2006, he bragged that he had worked for another football team, 'almost winning the league, and the next year, when I was gone, they nearly got relegated'. If that was one clue, the initials RSOC on documents seized by the Guardia Civil in their Puerto raids in 2006 was another. The former Real Sociedad president claimed in 2013 that an internal investigation had uncovered years of substantial payments to Fuentes for 'strange medicines'.

On the evolutionary timeline of professional cycling and its credibility, as we have noted already, Jan Ullrich's ride to Arcalís in 1997 had marked a significant moment. While Ullrich swept Germany off its feet, he was also, unbeknownst to himself and the wider audience, giving cycling its last experience of unquestioning, untainted awe on its grandest stage. After the following year and the Festina scandal, there could never again be the same swoons without suspicion or caveats.

On 30 June 2006, the ensuing age of well-founded cynicism was also reaching its acme, or its nadir, with Ullrich. My own fifth Tour de France began that morning, on the steps of Strasbourg's Palais des Congrès, where I chewed over the rumours of Ullrich and Ivan Basso's imminent banishment with Luigi Perna of *La Gazzetta dello Sport*. Luigi, like me, had previously interviewed Basso at his home and been introduced to the family dog: Birillo. 'Birillo' was also the second name on the business card in Merino Batres's wallet, just underneath 'Hijo de Rudicio'. Three hours later we were squashed into the doorway of the local Holiday Inn with more of our colleagues than could fit, while the CSC team manager Bjarne Riis read a statement to create a diversion, and Basso snuck out the rear exit and out of the Tour.

The Spaniard Paco Mancebo had also been sent home, as had Jörg Jaksche's entire team. Five of their riders, including Jaksche, were implicated, meaning they were too short on numbers to even start. Soon it would be the turn of the two T-Mobile riders, Oscar Sevilla and Jan Ullrich. Wolfgang Strohband, Ullrich's manager, followed the Audi driven by Stefan, Ullrich's brother, and with Jan in the passenger seat. Strohband remembers a scene like a Hollywood car chase, filmed on an eerily silent set beside the Rhine river, as events in Berlin – where Die Mannschaft were knocking Argentina out of the World Cup – had drained the German roads of traffic. 'There were eight motorbikes following us with paparazzi on them. I almost rode one of them into a car coming the other way because we were on a little country road and he was trying to overtake to get his picture.'

T-Mobile and Christian Frommert had in fact pulled off a minor PR masterstroke by suspending Ullrich and Sevilla at 9.45 in the morning, before other teams acted and before the Tour organizers ASO had even had time to nudge them towards that decision. As then ASO boss Patrice Clerc tells me, 'If the teams had refused to send the riders home, we couldn't have forced them to do that from a legal standpoint.'

Frommert, though, was a shrewd operator who had quickly shifted into crisis management mode. The man T-Mobile were about to install as the team boss, Bob Stapleton, describes him as a 'hard bastard' and a 'real talent who single-handedly kept T-Mobile in the sport'. In an autobiography published later and largely dedicated to his lifelong battle with anorexia, Frommert wrote about another gruelling struggle – to get Jan Ullrich to realize that 'communication isn't everything but without communication there is nothing'.[28] In the days before and weeks that followed Strasbourg, Frommert would see Ullrich languish in a state of infuriating inertia.

As Frommert wrote, 'Jan doesn't and can't hurt anyone. He wants to be loved, by anyone and everyone . . . a guy who craves harmony and wants above all to be seen as down to earth. A lot of people describe him as naive, perhaps because he was never really aware of his star status in this country.'

Despite opening a trapdoor under Ullrich, Frommert initially gave the impression of looking for the softest landing both for him and T-Mobile. There was talk of a televised confession on the first rest day of the Tour. Ullrich didn't initially reject this idea, and on 12 July his fiancée Sara even emailed Wolfgang Strohband two draft statements: one still dismissing the allegations as speculation yet also announcing Ullrich's retirement; the other admitting that Ullrich and Pevenage had 'gone down a route that we didn't think constituted doping' and which led to Ullrich having blood extracted by Fuentes but never re-injected – i.e. that he had only 'attempted to dope'. The latter would have been identical to the defence employed by Ivan Basso the following spring.

Frommert was never going to sanction either statement, even if it looked to Ullrich like a way out. Their lines of communication were cut for good when Ullrich sent Frommert a message withdrawing the invitation to his wedding.

'Frommert was perfect for T-Mobile – they came out of it smelling of roses,' says Wolfgang Strohband. Strohband's calls to T-Mobile's HQ in Bonn were soon also ringing out and going unreturned.

'Jan didn't seem to have fully understood the dimensions of the whole thing,' Strohband says. 'He didn't think they could stop him from riding the Tour. Why would they? How could they? I don't know if he fell apart – but I had never heard him scream before that moment in his room in the hotel. I simply hadn't experienced that from him before. It could be that he's someone who just bottles everything up and never lets it out.'

Processing what had happened was made harder by Ullrich's sense of betrayal. He swam endless lengths of his pool in Scherzingen, feeling the muscles sculpted by months of graft straining at their sinews, his lungs billowing under his ribcage and dark thoughts thumping inside his skull. In time, the extent to which T-Mobile, the management and even Ullrich's teammates could and should have been aware of his trips to Madrid would reveal itself – but for now it was bad enough or maybe worse that T-Mobile were turning the whole thing to their advantage. For years, Ullrich, the sponsor and the media had maintained an unholy, unspoken alliance whereby access was granted in return for positive coverage. Now T-Mobile and Christian Frommert in particular found a way to maintain the same cosy arrangement, at least temporarily, while cutting Ullrich adrift.

Michael Ostermann, who was covering the 2006 Tour for television network ZDF, could see what was happening. Ostermann knew that Frommert was a master of strategically planting stories, particularly in *Der Spiegel* and the *Süddeutsche Zeitung* – coincidentally or not the two outlets with the most comprehensive stories about Ullrich and Fuentes. On the day after Ullrich's exclusion from the Tour, Ostermann could hardly believe his eyes when he opened the *Süddeutsche* to see a long article outlining Frommert's plan to clean up T-Mobile. Then he twigged. 'Christian Frommert was a T-Mobile guy, and as soon as they learned that Ullrich and Pevenage were dealing with Fuentes, it was clear they had to save T-Mobile. I realized that he'd been the *Süddeutsche*'s source all along because they seemed to have all the information that Frommert was getting. Frommert really knew what he was doing. I mean, look at it from the T-Mobile side. The day after Ullrich got kicked out, Frommert had managed to give everyone the impression that Telekom were the good guys and they would clean up the mess. From a PR point of view, that's perfect. Your team is going down the drain and there you are telling everyone you're going to save the sport.'

The more Frommert talked, the more it seemed as though, with Ullrich gone, T-Mobile had completed its own *Wende*, similar to Germany's in 1989. In reality, says Ostermann, his first instincts in Strasbourg had been correct. 'I think in the first thing I wrote I said that whatever came out of it, it was going to be a massive blow from which German cycling would probably not recover. And I think that's what happened. It wasn't because I was so clever. Ullrich was simply the axis on which cycling in Germany turned. With him gone, it was obvious everything would fall apart.'

An editorial in the *Frankfurter Allgemeine Zeitung* said much the same thing: 'With Jan Ullrich cycling became a mainstream sport in Germany. And with Jan Ullrich it will fall at least halfway back down again. People will still ride bikes, if that's what they enjoy. But why should they still be interested in events like the Tour de France or the Giro d'Italia? It's high time everyone woke up. The dream is over, not only for Jan Ullrich.'

WADA chief Dick Pound said that cycling's image was 'in the toilet'. Three weeks later, Floyd Landis won the show that did go on, the 2006 Tour, only to test positive and lose his title soon afterwards.

Without specifying exactly how and when, Rudy Pevenage is sure about one thing: he wanted and even urged Jan Ullrich to tell the truth about Eufemiano Fuentes. 'We never argued . . . The only problem we had was that I wanted it all to come out. I can't bear the hypocrisy in cycling any more. But Jan didn't want it to come out.'

Two or three days before leaving for the Tour, Pevenage had received a call from the former UCI president, Hein Verbruggen, forewarning him of what would occur when they got to France. Verbruggen urged Pevenage to stop Ullrich travelling to France, to make him stage a fall down some stairs and break his arm. But Pevenage knew that wouldn't fly, certainly not with Ullrich in *Bombenform*. He hoped and prayed that somehow they would slip through a crack, even when the Quickstep team manager, Patrick Lefevere, saw him in the car park outside the press room in Strasbourg and called out an ominous greeting: 'Hey, Rudy, you're famous today and you'll be even more famous tomorrow.'

Pevenage concedes that, after his careless text messages to Fuentes during the Giro, he would do one other thing differently if he had his time again. 'If I regret one thing, it's not getting a lawyer and staying in Strasbourg. There were riders who were with Fuentes who still started that Tour . . . But the hardest thing for me was the trip to the airport. Sneaking out of the hotel by the back door, driving to Basel, knowing that I was finished as a directeur. Frommert and Luuc Eisenga broke the news to me . . .' Pevenage makes the motion of someone twisting a knife. Then adds a rueful footnote: 'Jan wanted to do the Tour, then the Deutschland Tour as a farewell. Leave cycling. He was young but he was sick of it.'

It was of course obvious that Pevenage had led Ullrich to Fuentes.

While he at first denied it, the 'Hijo de Rudicio' nickname pointed clearly to that conclusion. Eventually, in 2010, Pevenage would admit it in an interview with Philippe Le Gars of *L'Équipe*.

By this time, what documentary evidence may previously have been lacking also lay in the hands or on the hard drives of the German federal police (BKA) in Bonn. Ullrich had barely unpacked the unworn clothes from his Tour suitcase before, on 7 July 2006, a former athlete turned criminology professor named Britta Bannenberg was filing a criminal complaint against him for alleged fraud and infringing the German medicines act. At nine a.m. on 13 September, officers carried out simultaneous searches of Ullrich's residence in Scherzingen, Rudy Pevenage's in Geraardsbergen, Walter Godefroot's in Sint-Martens-Latem and the offices of Wolfgang Strohband in Hamburg and T-Mobile in Bonn. For Ullrich it was an unwelcome wedding present, four days after he and Sara had tied the knot in front of a hundred of their friends in St. Nikolaus von Lech in the Austrian Alps. After the 'happiest day of [his] life', he returned to one of the most traumatic. The same went for Pevenage, whose home office contained all the documentation the BKA needed to prove beyond doubt that he was the conduit between Ullrich and Fuentes. During the search, Pevenage had whispered to his wife to stuff a bag filled with incriminating paperwork into the suitcase of their visiting granddaughter; they were foiled when one of the police officers demanded they unzip the little girl's luggage.

In total, the BKA determined that Pevenage had made at least fifteen trips to Madrid between December 2003 and the spring of 2006. Ullrich was usually if not always with him. Some receipts for flight bookings, room reservations and drinks at hotel bars were still lying around Pevenage's office in plastic folders. Others were stored on his computer. Several had been deleted but were discovered by the BKA's data-recovery experts. On some trips, like the one on 21 February 2005, Ullrich was in Madrid for only a couple of hours before he boarded a plane back to Zürich, while Pevenage went home via Brussels. Their preferred hotel, or Fuentes's, was the Tryp Diana, less than a kilometre from the arrivals lounge at Barajas airport. The BKA presumed Ullrich, Fuentes and Pevenage gave themselves just enough time for a 'fly-thru' refill – mere minutes to reach the hotel, less than an hour for Fuentes to do his work, then a mad dash to make it back to Barajas in time for the gate closing.

They found no direct evidence to suggest that anyone else could have been in the loop – except an email from Pevenage to Ullrich's then fiancée Sara in November 2005 asking about flights for Jan's forthcoming trip to Madrid. On the days when he was in the Spanish capital, the calendars of T-Mobile manager Olaf Ludwig and Wolfgang Strohband indicated that Ullrich was training at home in Switzerland as far as they were aware. Strohband admits that he knew about at least one flight to Madrid – but thought perhaps Ullrich had met a Spanish girl and was having an affair. He didn't pry. 'He never said anything to me . . . A lot of it, including the medical stuff, passed me by,' Strohband concedes sheepishly.

The BKA, though, also gained access to Ullrich's bank statements. His payments to Fuentes had left a paper trail. Strohband admits that on one occasion, he believes in 2002 or 2003, Ullrich asked Strohband's daughter, his bookkeeper, to transfer money to a Spanish account registered to the surname Fuentes – 'who I didn't know from Adam'. Strohband says the payment had escaped his notice until the BKA went through his files. Regardless, when Ullrich made requests, generally they would be granted without further questions. Perhaps significantly, 2003 was also when Strohband noticed that Ullrich had suddenly started showing a little more interest in his finances.

Between the fruits of their searches and what the Guardia Civil had sent over from Spain, the BKA were able to assemble a comprehensive picture of the Fuentes–Ullrich–Pevenage ménage à trois, how it functioned, when and where. Calendars taken from Fuentes's apartments and annotated with numbers, code names and symbols – the 'Sanskrit of Eufemiano' – were paired with travel bookings and bank transfers to determine exactly what Ullrich had done and what it had cost. Thus, they were able to establish how repeated trips to Madrid in the winters of 2004, 2005 and 2006 had served to build a blood bank from which Ullrich would draw at important moments of the season. In total, the BKA believed they had found evidence for two Madrid appointments in 2003, five in 2004, twelve in 2005 and five up to the moment when Fuentes was arrested in 2006. At Ullrich's home they had found a Compur Mikrospin centrifuge used to measure haematocrit in blood.

The Fuentes method itself had become more sophisticated in 2004 when he acquired a deep-freeze he and his collaborators referred to as 'Siberia'. Frozen blood bags could be preserved for years, but the process of storing and re-injecting them was delicate, time-consuming and costly. Fuentes told one of his star clients, Tyler Hamilton, he would offer the use of Siberia to only top-tier riders – meaning Ullrich, Basso and a couple of others. These were also the only ones who could afford what Fuentes was touting as his club-class service. The BKA identified two payments to Fuentes from Ullrich's Credit Suisse account, one for 25,003.20 euros on 4 February 2004 and one for 55,000 euros on 9 January 2006. The Guardia Civil also believed this was only a fraction of what Fuentes had received from or was owed by Ullrich. On a sheet of paper found in his apartment at the Calle Caídos de la División Azul, Fuentes had scribbled a breakdown of his expected income from various clients in 2006. Next to the number one, thought to denote Ullrich, Fuentes had scribbled down a 50,000-euro basic fee and a further 10,000 euros for the use of 'Siberia'. In the same table were letters and symbols which, based on what Jesús Manzano had told the Guardia Civil, indicated that he expected to supply Ullrich with the banned hormones EPO, testosterone and human growth hormone. On a further sheet Fuentes had jotted 70,000 euros alongside '1. Nibelungo', another of Ullrich's presumed code names, and also noted bonuses of 50,000 euros for a Tour de France win and 30,000 euros for first place in the Giro or Vuelta. Ivan Basso evidently had exactly the same arrangement. One well-placed source claims that Basso didn't know that Fuentes was treating Ullrich. By the time he got to Strasbourg before the 2006 Tour, Basso was certainly in the picture – hence why, at the team presentation on the eve of the race, he approached Pevenage in a panic and asked what Pevenage thought would happen to them the following day.

The transfusions themselves seemed to follow a well-established cadence, with one generally occurring a day or two before a grand tour and another on the first rest day. Certain anomalies could be explained only by someone well-versed in the Fuentes method – like Jörg Jaksche. Before his arrest, Fuentes had Ullrich booked in for what the BKA believed was going to be the re-injection of two bags of blood and the extraction of the same number, both on 20 June, ten days before the Grand Départ in Strasbourg. Jaksche believes this could have been because Fuentes sometimes had riders acting as their own 'blood mule', as Jaksche had also done in the past. As he explains: 'To avoid transporting the blood across an international border during the race, Fuentes would get you to carry it to France, probably Paris, in your own body. He'd have someone in Paris waiting to take the blood out again as soon as you landed, and then the blood would be in France, ready to inject again straight after the pre-Tour medical checks when they would test you.'

Whatever exactly it consisted of, the Guardia Civil could see that some kind of last, pre-Tour tango in Paris had been scheduled for that third week in June. Two hotel rooms, one at the Holiday Inn and one at the AGIL 7, were reserved for five and six nights respectively. Per their airline tickets, Fuentes and Alberto León – aka Ali Baba – had been due to arrive in the French capital on the sixteenth and seventeenth of June. As it turned out, by that point, they were under arrest and there was no blood left in the bank.

Between them, the Guardia Civil and the BKA assembled thousands of pages of evidence, and there were also the nine bags of blood presumed to be Ullrich's seized from Madrid and now stored by the Guardia Civil at the Municipal Institute of Medical Research in Barcelona. But they couldn't know everything. For the purposes of their respective cases it also didn't matter to the BKA when exactly Ullrich had first turned to Fuentes – although many were still curious. Günther Dahms, the man who had signed Ullrich for Team Coast in 2003, certainly had a vested interest. When in 2008 Ullrich sued Dahms for around 500,000 euros in unpaid wages from his four months with Coast in 2003, Dahms retaliated with the allegation that Ullrich's doping in that period breached his contract. One of the year planners found in Fuentes's apartments indeed showed an appointment with '1. Nibelungo' on 14 April 2003, three days after the end of the Circuit de la Sarthe, Ullrich's comeback race after his ecstasy ban. But how could it be proved that Ullrich took illegal drugs that day, as opposed, to say, just having Fuentes talk him through his menu? Even if Fuentes had performed a first extraction during their meeting, demonstrating Ullrich's intention to cheat at an indefinite point in the future, Dahms's case looked weak and was defeated.

In none of his subsequent legal proceedings was Ullrich ever called to pinpoint exactly when he and Fuentes had their 'first date' – but, privately, he did tell a reliable source that it had been in late April 2003, when he and Pevenage were on their way to a race in

Spain, possibly the Vuelta a Aragon. Ullrich had heard Spanish team-mates at Coast raving about Fuentes in conversations earlier in 2003, and it was at around the same time that Pevenage dialled the doctor's number. In their first encounter in Madrid, speaking English, Fuentes immediately talked Ullrich through his list of available treatments. He then asked Ullrich to imagine driving to a traffic light: did he want to wait for green, go through on amber or run the red? Green – in fact 'light green', was apparently Ullrich's reply. At this moment and at others, the words of his first and in some ways only spiritual guide, his grandfather, perhaps echoed through his conscience: 'Better to give up than carry on riding and take drugs.' Ullrich cared about his health and his future – but had also convinced himself, like many of his peers, that anything that didn't take him above the UCI's 50 per cent haematocrit limit was not doping.

The second entry in Fuentes's 2003 diary suspected by the BKA to relate to Ullrich was not until 29 May – after he had officially left Team Coast for Bianchi and all ties with Dahms were cut. Again, though, as long as Ullrich, Fuentes, Pevenage and other interested parties would not put it on the record, the only calendars available were the ones retrieved from Fuentes's apartments in Madrid. The doctor's home and clinic in Gran Canaria were never searched.

Another unsolved puzzle was whether Ullrich's performances were enhanced and his blood enriched by other banned substances. Multiple signs and annotations in Fuentes's files suggested this was the case, and synthetic testosterone had also been found during the search of Ullrich's house in Scherzingen in September 2006. A few months after that, the BKA also requested samples from the nine bags of blood stored in Barcelona. They were analysed by world-renowned expert Wilhelm Schänzer in Cologne – but none were shown to contain banned substances. It was also impossible to prove whether Ullrich had ever used a Fuentes *especialidad de la casa* – the substance others referred to as 'the powder of the Madre Celestina'. By covering one's hands with this 'magic' red dust and then urinating over them in a dope test, a rider could apparently cleanse his sample of EPO and escape detection. The BKA thought it likely, based on papers found at Number 53 Calle Alonso Cano, that Ullrich had bought tubes of the substance from Fuentes on multiple occasions. TV and newspaper reports by Swiss media in October 2006 also alleged that three urine samples collected from Ullrich in recent

months had been 'suspiciously' free of EPO – even the naturally produced variety. But evidence like this enabled only a very educated
guess.

What could be verified, eventually, was that the nine bags of
blood in Barcelona were indeed Ullrich's. Immediately after Strasbourg, both he and Pevenage indicated that he would be willing in
principle to give a DNA sample to cross-reference with the bags now
being kept in Barcelona. Ullrich finally had to provide Swiss police
with a saliva sample during the September 2006 house search. That
couldn't be used by the BKA but, eventually, pressure from them led
to Ullrich giving a further sample on 1 February 2007. Two millilitres
of blood from each of the nine bags in Spain were duly sent to Düsseldorf for a comparative analysis, the results of which were expected
to be announced in March.

At which point, it surely would be game over.

In the many appraisals of Eufemiano Fuentes's customer service and
his bedside manner, one thing that crops up repeatedly, on and off
the record, is his talent for making patients feel at ease. There were
occasional slips, appalling punctuality, the permanent air of someone
who had left a cooker on or a tap running, plus clients like Thomas
Dekker who felt he was 'just hungry for money and attention'. But,
in the eyes of most who met him, Fuentes's charisma cast a spell as
powerful as any of his potions.

'I don't want to talk about the Fuentes period. I met him when I
was riding myself. I met him, we talked, and voilà . . .' Rudy Pevenage tells me. When the BKA interviewed Pevenage in October 2008,
he was marginally more forthcoming, explaining that he had struck
up a friendship with Fuentes when he began his career as a directeur
sportif with Histor in 1989 and Fuentes was working for Kelme. Later
still, Pevenage revealed that he and Fuentes got talking about blood
transfusions – then something of which Pevenage was only vaguely
aware – one evening at the Vuelta a España, when both men were
several glasses of wine deep, possibly in 2000.

To me, Pevenage continues to offer only tempting crumbs – such
as, 'Fuentes wasn't involved for the 2003 Tour' – but for the most
part he wants to avoid any more bother. As he says, '2006, 2007 and
2008 were awful for me.'

For all his languid charm, the way he makes dreary postulates of endocrinology sing like delicious verses crafted by Dante or Boccaccio, even Luigi Cecchini sounds in a hurry when I press him on Fuentes. 'Per favore,' he says, 'don't ask me to judge Fuentes.' Later, he wearily acquiesces, 'There are bad things happening in all sports. It's true that there are lots of positive tests in cycling but that's because there are so many tests. If you tried to do that many tests in football . . . but, per favore, don't make me say any more.'

I turn to Tyler Hamilton, who – like Thomas Dekker, Jörg Jaksche and Ullrich – was coached by Cecchini and treated by Fuentes. Surely, I put to Hamilton, Cecchini must have at least known that Fuentes was supplying medical 'care' to his riders. The BKA logged multiple occasions when Ullrich flew directly from Madrid to Cecchini's local airport in Pisa, or vice versa.

'With me, Luigi knew [I was with Fuentes],' Hamilton says. 'He didn't push it on me, he knew it was all crazy but he also understood there were other riders doing the same thing. But he wasn't doing blood tests so he wouldn't have seen the evidence of what I was doing.'

In 2007, one Italian newspaper reported that two Fuentes clients, Basso and Michele Scarponi, had told Italian Olympic Committee prosecutor Ettore Torri that Cecchini had put them in contact with Fuentes.[29] Cecchini firmly rebuts this and Torri tells me on the phone in September 2015 that he can't remember what the riders told him. Despite Torri's blessing, the Italian Olympic Committee declines permission for me to see the transcripts of the two riders' statements.

Whatever misgivings or embarrassment prevent Cecchini or Pevenage from saying more, there is, or was, one man for whom the topic was even harder to broach: Jan Ullrich.

As the weeks passed in the summer then autumn and winter of 2006, Ullrich's silence became ever more awkward and more incriminating. Another of Ullrich's grandfather's favourite sayings had been that 'words are silver and silence is golden' – a policy at the antipodes of what Christian Frommert had advocated. But Frommert and T-Mobile were out of the picture from 20 July 2006, the date on which Ullrich's contract was officially terminated. Remarkably in the circumstances, T-Mobile had paid Ullrich a severance fee of 250,000 euros. The T-Mobile marketing chief Ulrich Gritzuhn told the BKA that the company didn't want to wait around to see whether Ullrich was cleared – they simply preferred to get him off the books.

Ullrich was 'no backstabber', said one email between the T-Mobile executives – and indeed any worries about what he might disclose in public would have been misplaced. In October 2006, the possibility of a full confession still hadn't been completely discarded when Strohband made an appointment with the hotshot defence lawyer Johann Schwenn in Hamburg. Schwenn insisted on speaking to Ullrich alone before any strategy was decided upon. After an hour and a half, they called Strohband into the room . . . only for Ullrich to announce that he was no longer allowed to say anything, not even to his manager of the previous fifteen years.

Ullrich fed his fans and the entire cycling community in Germany the same message. And many let him know that he had lost their confidence. The Deutschland Tour had been rescued from oblivion and turned into one of the richest, most attractive races on the international calendar on the back of Ullrich's success. The 2006 edition in September was therefore a good place to test the mood of the nation – and the *Süddeutsche Zeitung*'s headline on the first day, 'Threat of Apocalypse', captured it succinctly. State TV channel ARD had already given the organizers an ice-cold shower by saying that it was fifty-fifty whether they would show the race in future years. ARD's now head of sport, their former Tour de France presenter and Ullrich's one-time ghostwriter, Hagen Boßdorf, had been portrayed in some quarters as the worst of Ullrich's media facilitators – and it now looked as though Boßdorf and ARD wished to atone by building a bonfire. A young fan called onto the stage before the roll-out in Düsseldorf knew who should be the burning guy. 'Who's your favourite rider?' boomed the MC, to which the boy replied, 'Not Jan Ullrich.' A matter of weeks later, a Hamburg magistrate would open an investigation into private, financial agreements between Ullrich and ARD – which Hagen Boßdorf still defends. 'These contracts are very normal. RTL had one with Michael Schumacher for years,' Boßdorf says when I meet him in Berlin.

By the autumn, Ullrich had given up his Swiss racing licence and was officially ineligible to race – though not retired or even officially suspended, he was at pains to point out. There were rumours of negotiations with various teams and of him competing in 2007. He also announced he still wanted to win the Tour. A Russian beer and banking magnate with designs on precisely that prize, Oleg Tinkov, was among the suitors, as were a second-tier Austrian team,

Volksbank. Meanwhile, at home in Scherzingen, Ullrich felt hunted, stressed, cheated – including by T-Mobile. His last communication with them had been the fax he received to say he was sacked. Eleven seasons, a Tour de France, gold medals, unquantifiable media exposure, dissatisfied customers who became infatuated fans – all signed away with an adieu, an '*Auf Nimmerwiedersehen*' or good riddance. 'I didn't feel they'd treated me well. Whatever mistake you've made, to be fired by fax – to basically be told you're so toxic we can't even call you – that's not a very human way of doing things,' Ullrich said later.

It felt less like a goodbye than a lobotomy. Not surprisingly, Ullrich also seemed to want to obliterate all memories of his fifteen years with the team. One surviving connection was the car on his drive, one of the latest models from long-time T-Mobile partner Audi. On the last day of October, a classified ad for the vehicle appeared on a Swiss second-hand car website, urging readers to contact the 'well-known owner'. The contact address was Ullrich's in Scherzingen.

Sara would one day open up how 'pressures from the outside' had caused 'lots of arguments, misunderstanding and lots of tears'. Ullrich's mum Marianne had to seek treatment for the mental strain. Two of her sons had lost their jobs – Stefan, the mechanic, having left T-Mobile at the same time as Jan. But the BKA investigation, triggered by Britta Bannenberg's criminal complaint, had been the final insult. 'No company in Europe got as much publicity out of cycling as T-Mobile and Telekom,' seethed Marianne Kaatz. Ullrich's mum wasn't the only one horrified by Bannenberg's apparent vendetta: soon various letters threatening violence led to Bannenberg being given police protection.

For Ullrich, the final hope of clearing his name would dissolve with the Spanish court ruling early in 2007 that allowed the Bonn prosecutors access to blood samples from the Fuentes stock. In the last week of March the bags would finally arrive from Barcelona and be cross-checked against the saliva sample Ullrich provided in Düsseldorf on the first day of February. Before that point, he had stayed fit and even honoured an annual tradition – his winter training camp in Mallorca. Upon his return to Switzerland, he mulled over his options with his lawyer, Johan Schwenn – or rather the lack thereof. A scene from a few weeks earlier was also lodged in his memory: his three-year-old daughter, Sarah Maria, had told Ullrich that all she wanted for Christmas was to spend more time with her dad.

An email sent to journalists one Friday in February 2007 said that Jan Ullrich had an announcement to make at the Intercontinental Hotel in Hamburg the following Monday. It added that he would take no questions. This cryptic message was enough for many of the main German networks and newspapers to correctly guess that Ullrich had decided to retire.

The substance may not have been a surprise, but the style in which Ullrich delivered it was to many. Overlooked by a giant picture of himself celebrating in the yellow jersey at the 1997 Tour, he appeared slimmer than in other years in late February, and oddly upbeat – or at least belligerent. Upon taking his seat he welcomed the journalists who had come from all over Europe – as Ullrich said, 'Some I'm pleased to see for the first time in a while and others who don't fill my heart with the same joy, black sheep who, I'm not going to lie, are tolerated rather than welcome.'

If that made one or two sit up straighter, they were soon gulping as, working his way through a pile of prompt cards, Ullrich took aim: at everyone who had contributed to an 'overreaction' in Strasbourg; at the federations which weren't helping him to prove his innocence; at the German media not covering any of his grievances; at Werner Franke, the Heidelberg professor who had turned exposing Ullrich into a personal crusade; at Britta Bannenberg; and at Rudolf Scharping – aka 'Bin Baden' – the former German defence minister who, the German tabloids said, spent more time splashing around in Mallorca swimming pools with his girlfriend than fighting terrorists, and who, having become the president of the German Cycling Federation in 2005, Ullrich thought had duly turned his back on an old friend.

Occasionally he would smile defiantly, or season his monologue with black comedy, like when he asked whether everyone had fallen asleep ten minutes in. Then he would catch himself, mutter that, 'the past is the past now anyway', yet still reveal his wounds through a veil of faux matter-of-factness. 'Ach, well, we're still alive, eh, darling?' he said at one point, turning to meet Sara's gaze in the front row.

There were indisputable truths, like when he noted how few German journalists in the room had followed cycling pre-1997. But this neither endeared him to the gallery nor lessened their frustration. They had come for answers, mainly, and not to hear Ullrich confirm that he would now work as an advisor to Team Volksbank, a clothing company and a manufacturer of puncture repair kits.

The adjectives 'sad' and 'embarrassing' would pepper comment pieces the next day. Not all of the journalists, though, saw it like that. Michael Ostermann had first met Ullrich when he was an amateur living in a bedsit in Hamburg. Ostermann had also covered Ullrich's rise and fall over the next decade and a half, and seen fortunes and his superstar status wax, wane and finally wear him down.

'I was there and I got asked by a German media magazine – *Zapp* – what I thought,' Ostermann recalls. 'I said that I thought he was really authentic, that we'd seen Jan Ullrich unfiltered. It was bizarre but it was him. For the first time in a long, long time, I think he did something the way he wanted. He decided not to listen to any advice. He hasn't done that very often. When I met him for the first time there in Hamburg he was himself, but later on he was in that Telekom system and there was always a press officer who gave him advice. I used to do some work for the T-Mobile website, and a lot of the time journalists had to send in their questions in writing and they'd get them answered in writing. And it wasn't Jan who was writing them – it was someone in the press department. So with the retirement press conference, if you watch it again and keep in mind that it was his choice to do it that way, you see it a bit differently.'

Wolfgang Strohband had seen the whole choreography of the event take shape, and hadn't agreed with the advice from Ullrich's new media advisor, Michael Lang, about not taking questions. It was, though, the second act of Ullrich's staged farewell that would cause both Ullrich and Strohband the sharpest regrets. Reinhold Beckmann is Germany's best-known talk show host, so when he offered Ullrich the chance to say a more informal farewell to millions of German TV viewers, there appeared to be everything to gain and nothing to lose. Given that he would go straight from his press conference to Beckmann's studio, it would also be the perfect opportunity to smother any negative feedback already coming Ullrich's way.

This was the idea. What ensued was a PR catastrophe that not only eclipsed whatever he had said in the Intercontinental Hotel that morning but is still, over a decade on, many Germans' abiding, unflattering image of Ullrich – that of an inarticulate, deluded former athlete who had sold them fantasies disguised as dreams, and who could now safely be consigned to the same scrapheap as other fallen national idols. Asked first to define 'doping', Ullrich first stammered and let out a deep sigh while looking heavenward. He then fell silent for several, excruciating seconds before offering, 'It's when . . . you're trying to get an advantage over your rivals with medicine and stuff like that. An unfair advantage . . .' The comic Mathias Richling's later skit on the grilling, including such gems as, 'I've always ridden with my own DNA, even at the Tour de France, never without', confirmed that most watching Germans had not known whether to laugh or cry.

Little did the viewers realize that the entire *mise en scène* of the Beckmann interview was itself possibly an exercise in double-dealing and dissimulation.

'Beckmann came to my office to talk through how it was going to work,' Wolfgang Strohband remembers. 'I knew Beckmann before this – and now I don't want to know him. In my office it was Sara, Jan, Beckmann, his producer and me. We went through it all and I said to him, "Just ask Jan two or three questions about doping, then stop there, OK? The lawyer has said Jan can't talk about it." We were going to be able to watch the whole interview back before it was broadcast and cut out what we wanted. No problem, they said. I'm still glad that Sara and Jan were there because otherwise they might have thought I'd agreed something else with Beckmann.

'Anyway, in the morning we did the press conference, which Jan had only partly talked through with Sara and not at all with me, and then we went to Beckmann with Lang, the press advisor Jan had hired, and one of our legal representatives. Beckmann took Jan into the studio and we were allowed to watch the recording in the next room. We had agreed that they would also play pre-recorded interviews with Rudolf Scharping and [T-Mobile's CEO] René Obermann. We sat there for a quarter of an hour and it was all fine. Then suddenly: "And now to our anti-doping expert Hajo Seppelt." He was evidently standing by in another room or building. I was absolutely beside myself and ready to force my way into the studio, but the producer told me that I had to stay where I was and calm down. I told him you could see Jan's mood changing, that this wasn't what we agreed and so on. He said again that we could cut what we didn't like. But then the programme finished and Beckmann suddenly vanished.

'We wanted to watch it all back but suddenly we weren't allowed to. Finally they let us see it, but when we started telling them what needed to be taken out, a woman from the network came along and said the programme had been made and nothing was getting cut. The lawyers said we'd get an injunction to stop it being broadcast – but they had recorded at six and it was going out at nine thirty. There was no time. Sara and Jan went back to their hotel, watched and couldn't believe what they were seeing. The whole thing angered me so much . . . although the bottom line is, if Jan had opened up about everything then, I really don't think he'd have come out of the whole thing as badly as he did. And he wouldn't be perceived the way he still is now.'

22

STORMING FORT KNOX

*'People want to make cycling an island of purity
in a dirty world. It's not possible'*

—*Walter Godefroot*

On the morning of Sunday, 2 July 2006, I stood in a car park in
Strasbourg mulling over the events of the previous forty-eight hours
with an old acquaintance. I hadn't needed to look for an ice-breaker
or even mention Jan Ullrich's name – the T-Mobile doctor, Lothar
Heinrich, had seen me approaching the team bus, smiled and sighed.
What else would there be to talk about except the Armageddon that
had befallen them with Ullrich's banishment from the Tour?

Of course, Heinrich had known nothing about Ullrich's trips to
Madrid, he said. There was no way for even the UCI to detect autolo-
gous transfusions – i.e. re-injecting one's own blood – let alone
Heinrich and his colleagues at the University of Freiburg, though
good news was also on its way: a professor in northern Bavaria was
devising a test method using carbon monoxide. T-Mobile would start
using it for internal controls before it was even approved by WADA.

As ever, the doctor spoke differently from and looked unlike his
counterparts on other teams. They were middle-aged, standoffish
and had legacies of malpractice recorded in court archives in towns
up and down Italy, France and Belgium. Heinrich could have been a
recently retired athlete – a skier or rugby player. From the Adidas
stripes on his fresh white polos to his stern, bass monotone, he
seemed to epitomize typically German traits, values and virtues that

belonged more to the sales pitch of 'Germany's team' than its reality – at least while Ullrich's waywardness was the dominant storyline.

Bob Stapleton, the American multi-millionaire whom T-Mobile now wanted to save the team, was also quite taken with Heinrich. 'He was shovelling you shit the whole time. These big brown eyes, just feeding you shit. He was quite clever. He fooled me too,' Stapleton says.

It should have come as no surprise that a practitioner known uncharitably as 'Doc Hollywood' would be a good actor, but Heinrich's performance that weekend in Strasbourg was still remarkable. In the morning, he was telling me that Jan Ullrich had betrayed his team and his sport. The same evening, according to a sworn testimony by T-Mobile rider Patrik Sinkewitz, Sinkewitz's girlfriend was driving him, Andreas Klöden and Matthias Kessler from their team hotel to the sports medicine department at Freiburg's Uniklinik. There, Heinrich's fellow team doctor, Andreas Schmid, was allegedly waiting to administer the illegal blood transfusions prepared before the Tour. The riders then returned to France and the next day took their place on the start line of stage two of the race. Only 'happy circumstances' prevented Sinkewitz suffering serious damage to his health, so sloppily was the procedure carried out, the Freiburg magistrate investigating the claims would say later.

When he learned of Sinkewitz's claims, Stapleton's thoughts raced back to the moment when Ullrich had exited the team hotel, the Tour and as it turned out his career. 'The management called a rider meeting, and there are a lot of unhappy people in the room. They're shocked, they're upset, they're talking about pulling out of the race en masse, just fuck it, all go home. I can remember Klöden being really worked up, shouting and swearing. Everyone else is sitting there with arms folded and legs crossed, stone-faced. This goes on for more than half an hour. The whole time I'm asking people what's going on, but I think it finally starts to turn, and the meeting ends with them all being undecided as to whether or not they'll race. Klöden was very loyal to Jan. He could have been the biggest single benefactor, but he was the one saying, "Fuck this." But they decide to hash it out on a ride, and while they're out on the ride they decide they're going to start the Tour. Which, ultimately, I suppose, meant that they were going to go down the Rhine to Freiburg.'

Stapleton is looking out over the Pacific Ocean from our table in a cafe in Avila Beach, a few miles from his home in San Luis Obispo on the central Californian coast. When he agreed to step in as T-Mobile's firefighter during the 2006 Tour, he hoped that Ullrich's departure would signal a new dawn for the team – and for several months he thought that was what he had overseen. One of his first, significant steps had been to pick Lothar Heinrich's brains about how T-Mobile could make sure they were different in a sport clearly riddled with charlatans and cheating. Heinrich had fixed him with those hypnotic hazel eyes and suggested a raft of measures, from a purge on external coaches like Ullrich's old guru – Luigi Cecchini – to a renewed commitment to internal testing. It was everything he wanted to hear, and came from a doctor at one of Germany's most prestigious universities. Telekom's former CEO Ron Sommer has talked to me about Telekom's ironclad trust in Freiburg in the team's early years – that 'having this medical team, for us . . . it was like having your money in Fort Knox. Safer than safe.' Stapleton wasn't as confident as that, but he also didn't have much choice: the T-Mobile chiefs in Bonn were adamant that Freiburg should be the cornerstone of T-Mobile 2.0.

Heinrich and I would speak again about the reboot early in 2007. He even admitted that he had considered his position in the wake of Strasbourg but that, in the end, he had seen it as an 'opportunity to look back and be critical of what I had and hadn't done in terms of prevention'. His next chance to confront past mistakes would follow shortly afterwards – for Jef D'Hont, a Belgian soigneur who had worked for Team Telekom between 1992 and 1996, was about to publish his memoirs. D'Hont's book hit the shelves in April 2007 – and it had the effect of a tornado through the scaffold of T-Mobile's reconstruction. D'Hont wrote that he had been instrumental in a team-wide doping conspiracy that partly accounted for Telekom's rise from minnows to Tour de France winners in 1996 and 1997. The allegations were itemized with names, dates, places and products. Lothar Heinrich was not spared and neither was Jan Ullrich. Journalists at *Der Spiegel* had known D'Hont for years, having approached him about being a source for their Telekom doping exposé in 1999. He had been unwilling to go on the record then, and his son Steven had been taken on by Telekom, also as a masseur, shortly thereafter. But, with Steven now working for another team, the pre-existing relationship ensured the book and its claims got maximum airplay in Germany's biggest news magazine. In an interview, they asked him to be more specific about Ullrich and his first Tour de France, the 1996 edition, where he was second behind Bjarne Riis. Was Ullrich among the Telekom riders who took EPO in that race? D'Hont said he was and that Ullrich had also taken growth hormone. D'Hont had brought the EPO himself on a nervous journey home from the Tour of Switzerland: at a border check, one customs officer searched his boot and was about to find Telekom's portable pharmacy when his colleague noticed that D'Hont's car had no toll sticker on the windscreen. D'Hont was sent on his way with a fine.

When it was time to administer the drug, D'Hont said Ullrich needed only small doses, because 'he was in a class of his own, physically . . . he would have beaten them all for years if no one had doped.' But dope he also did. With the knowledge, blessing and direct input of Lothar Heinrich and the team's other University of Freiburg doctor, Andreas Schmid, the soigneur alleged.

It would have been easy to dismiss D'Hont as an embittered former employee, but the detail of the accusations and the context in which they were made – the spring after Strasbourg – made them impossible to shrug off. Stapleton and his new regime had also made a very public pledge of transparency. One of the long-term stalwarts of the team in his riding career, Rolf Aldag, was now Stapleton's team manager. Aldag urged Heinrich, Schmid and Freiburg to 'explain themselves' while stressing that he had never doped himself. But that was a lie with short legs: on 1 May, after the Rund um den Henninger Turm one-day race, Aldag and Erik Zabel, who was now riding for Milram, stood propped against a cigarette machine in a quiet corner of the hotel their teams were sharing, slowly persuading each other that a public confession was the only available course of action. Stapleton had already suspended Schmid and Heinrich after other riders came forward, most notably Bert Dietz. Dietz said on Reinhold Beckmann's chat show that the Freiburg doctors had given him EPO in 1995 – Beckmann's second cycling scoop in a few weeks after Ullrich's car-crash farewell interview.

That was on a Monday. On the Tuesday, former Telekom rider Christian Henn came clean. On Wednesday, Udo Bölts told ARD that he regretted having earlier called D'Hont's allegations 'utter rubbish', because they were true. Then, on Thursday, it was Aldag and Zabel's turn at a press conference in Bonn. On Friday, Brian Holm joined the club. As did Bjarne Riis, finally, after years of denials.

As the *Rheinische Post* put it, the snowball had become an avalanche. And yet Jan Ullrich stood frozen once again. Frozen speechless.

Bob Stapleton could now fully grasp what he had inherited.

'We were obligated to use the University of Freiburg in our sponsorship contract,' Stapleton explains. 'That had me and T-Mobile convinced that they were the good guys and that they were the right people to oversee the anti-doping programme and the training programme. And their position was that what Jan had done, he'd done on his own, and that was Fuentes. It turned out to be a pretty remarkable history of misconduct. It was well financed, well organized, and a doctor-overseen programme. And Lothar was central to that. I had put a lot of confidence into him and Schmid. You, know, Schmid, this solid, trustworthy guy, who apparently started to give riders information for their own safety when EPO came into the team, for their own health. But then that just spun out of control into some spectacularly organized programme. However well-intentioned it was when it started – however true that was – it became something that was quite over the top. Lothar's "Doc Hollywood" thing was also central to that. He'd love the limelight, being at press conferences, and that just corrupted it even further. I think once you start doing crazy shit like that, the moral boundaries are gone. You can't pull back. All judgement is out the window, and all alternatives are pretty bad. I think it just got pretty wild.'

Stapleton would be grateful to T-Mobile at the time for reaffirming their faith in him and in the team to reinvent itself. Equally, in what had occurred over the previous few months and what Aldag in particular had told him, he could see a textbook tale of corruption fed by money, egos and dishonesty. All set against the backdrop of a sport so replete with foul play that it had long since become desensitized.

'There was also just so much money involved at that point,' Stapleton says. 'T-Mobile was putting north of 25 million euros into the team and its promotion. By the standards of that time it was a huge amount of money. They'd put cycling on the map in Germany, they were a proud German team, they had the best German athletes, they were celebrated. There was this cultural undertone to it – we're better at this, partly because we're German. There was a big aura of superiority that the whole thing carried. And I don't think that was just me. They were *Die Mannschaft*, and they kicked everyone's ass. They were bigger and badder than everyone else – and they wore that on their sleeve. The CEO, Ron Sommer, Kindervater . . . that was their pride and joy. They felt they'd created it. Zabel and Jan were regularly on the front page of the press with the CEO, or whoever it might be that day, so they had a role in the German mind and the German media that was far beyond what any other cycling team had. Far beyond what Lance had here in the US. As well known as Lance was, you heard about him around the Tour, whereas Jan was followed around the clock. He took the trash out in baggy sweatpants and the next day there was a photo in the tabloid press and a caption underneath, pointing out how fat his ass was. It was a remarkably visible sponsorship and affiliation with Telekom. And I think that was a ripe environment for all kinds of crazy things to happen.'

Ron Sommer, the Telekom CEO until 2002, had also been deceived by the Freiburg doctors. The question of how much Telekom did or should have known was hotly debated. But initially, Sommer says, his reaction was not one of self-reproach but disbelief.

'You're a newly privatized company, you float on the stock market, and you want to be cleaner than clean, whiter than white. The question was: is there a danger in sponsorship in general and sports sponsorship specifically? Our conclusion was that if we were supported by the Freiburg sports clinic, it was like being supported by the notary of the Bundesgericht or something . . . You know – if you wanted an organization to make sure you were clean, there wasn't anything better on Earth than going to that clinic – that turned out to be the centre of the dirty stuff. I met the doctors a few times because we went to visit the team at the training camps. We took customers. We felt totally safe. They were good guys, nice guys, great reputation. Perfect. We never had the slightest idea that anything was dirty there. Of course we knew that it was a high-risk sport but we thought that with guys like that taking care of them nothing could happen.'

To err is, of course, human. But is it understandable, or forgivable, when those slipping up had made fortunes for themselves and their corporations by being brilliant, thorough, faultless – certainly not naive? Ron Sommer sighs. As he has already told me, his and to a large extent the company's energies were focused elsewhere. Cycling was meant to be the fun part.

'I don't think we were in any way negligent,' he says. 'Freiburg, we could not even have investigated. I mean, can we investigate how clean the German police is? No, I have to trust that when they protect me, they are not corrupt. That when they protected my life at certain stages they aren't paid by some people who wanted to kill me. So there are certain things you just don't doubt unless you have a signal to be careful. And for Freiburg we didn't have this signal, at least not at that time.'

In October 2015, I travel to Nuremberg for a congress on anti-doping in the National Germanic Museum, but it is the attendees who resemble a living, breathing Madame Tussaud's of the field in East, West and now unified Germany.

Munching through a slice of cheesecake on one side of the green room is Brigitte Berendonk, the former discus thrower turned whistle-blower and heretical heroine of anti-doping in Germany. A few metres away, Berendonk's husband, the microbiologist and drugs cheats' bête noire for five decades, Werner Franke, has his huge paws clasped around Hajo Seppelt. Seppelt is the renowned journalist whose exposés on doping in Russian athletics have made headlines around the world – and whose impromptu appearance on Reinhold Beckmann's chat show so flustered Jan Ullrich in 2007.

I also recognize a stocky, balding man of around fifty who has the sleeves of his cable-knit jumper rolled up to reveal his thick forearms. They are the muscles of a shot-putter – in this case Andreas Krieger, or Heidi as he was called when winning a gold medal in the 1986 European championships. Heidi became Andreas after sex reassignment surgery in 1997. Andreas says today that he was confused about his gender even before his voice became deeper, hair started growing in strange places and he experienced other alarming side effects of the steroid Oral Turinabol. Nevertheless, even today Krieger will tell you 'they killed Heidi'. 'They' being both those 'little blue pills' that fuelled the most successful and notorious state doping system in sports history, and the doctors and coaches who imposed them.

The day's lectures will provide an aerial view of anti-doping in Germany in 2015 – much as two televised round tables on the same subject did on state channel ZDF in March 1977. Brigitte Berendonk and Werner Franke will never forget them, not only because they were protagonists but because many lives, including Jan Ullrich's, might have turned out differently if more people watching had paid more attention.

Before the first 1977 programme, Berendonk had written an article in the *Süddeutsche Zeitung* that one of the speakers in Nuremberg calls 'still the greatest achievement in the history of anti-doping'. In the piece, Berendonk had laid bare two co-existing cultures of rampant steroid abuse, in the East that she had escaped at the end of the 1950s and in the West that had adopted and feted her for her athletic achievements. A few days later, she was repeating the claims on national, West German television.

That was the cue for a slim gentleman with an outsized briar of white hair to introduce himself. 'Here I am, Frau Berendonk,' he said, 'one of the sports doctors you described as a criminal and ignorant.' This man's name was Joseph Keul, the director of the University of Freiburg's sports clinic – a position that he would hold right up to his death in 2000. The same man to whom the Telekom cycling team would effectively entrust its medical programme, with Lothar Heinrich and Andreas Schmid as his underlings, from the first day of its existence. And who would assure Jürgen Kindervater in 1998 that no one at the team could be using EPO.

Berendonk put it to Keul that the use of steroids had been endorsed at a recent sports congress in Freiburg. Keul responded that steroids needn't be dangerous if they were administered in the right doses.

Berendonk also asked the professor whether he had ever prescribed steroids to healthy people. Keul turned away indignantly without answering, then finally conceded that he had prescribed nandrolone.

Berendonk asked whether Keul was familiar with the banned list. He didn't respond.

The programme continued in the same, fractious vein. So fractious that it would end with Werner Franke, Berendonk's husband, rising from his seat on the front row of the audience, and striding across the studio floor to berate Keul. Franke now judges the very notion Telekom could have enlisted Freiburg and Keul to run a clean programme 'a joke'. While Keul was conducting experiments with steroids and weightlifters in the early 1970s, records show that in the second half of the decade the professor's Freiburg colleague, Armin Klümper, was plying cyclists with some of the same drugs, funded by the West German national cycling federation. With sporting competition a vital battleground for the East – given the DDR's limited ability to use trade and diplomacy to influence the world beyond its borders – the West had become increasingly aware of the need to keep pace, and how to do it. As a doctor to the German Olympic team for almost four decades, Keul received the explicit backing of West German government ministers. Another of the attendees of the Nuremberg congress, Professor Gerhard Treutlein, said of Keul: 'He was ambitious, great in public and his aim was to become more famous and the greatest. He needed doping for this. He knew that without doping you couldn't be among the very best.'

Statements like this are, we should add, counterbalanced by favourable memories of Keul. One sportsman who was treated by the professor, the tennis player Charly Steeb, later also became Ullrich's manager. Steeb assures me Keul was irreproachable as the doctor of the three German Davis Cup-winning teams in which Steeb played between 1988 and 1993.

Not even Werner Franke can say what Keul's precise role was in the genesis of Team Telekom's doping programme, but then, in Franke's eyes, there is plenty of blame to go around. Ten days after the Nuremberg congress, Franke invites me to visit him in beautiful Heidelberg, the jewel of Germany's south-west. On a cold November morning, the city that enchanted Goethe, Mark Twain and a generation of German Romantics wakes under a thick mist that chokes the valley of the Neckar and half-obscures Heidelberg's most famous landmark, the castle ruins. Franke has told me that he has 'six huge files' on Ullrich and his doping waiting for me in his office at the German Cancer Research Centre in Heidelberg University Hospital. The documents were the basis for Franke's defence when Ullrich tried to sue him for libel over allegations about Eufemiano Fuentes in 2007.

At the agreed hour, Franke appears at the end of a corridor, walking, as usual, with the gait and tortured air of an old bear battling through a rainstorm. A black canvas trolley bag scuttles behind him.

He instructs me to follow him to an empty conference room, where he proceeds to unzip the bag and wearily unload its contents – half a dozen huge folders – onto the table. After he's pulled up a chair, I ask him whether he doesn't feel pangs of sympathy for Ullrich, at least insofar as the 1997 Tour winner was the victim of multiple corrupt systems, both Eastern and Western in their creation. After all, Franke was one of the founding fathers of the Doping Opfer Hilfe organization that now offers support and financial compensation to survivors of DDR state doping – admittedly, many of them minors and non-consenting.

The professor nearly explodes out of his seat.

'Sympathy?! *Sympathy?!*' he booms. 'Why should we have sympathy?! These people are liars! Permanent liars! You say he may not be well educated, but to lie or not to lie – that doesn't need much education! Should we have sympathy for Armstrong next?!'

The bear's cage has been truly rattled.

'Read the statement of Jörg Jaksche! On the Tour de France they went over the border to Karlsruhe, into a hotel room, onto the bed and they got blood pumped back into them! Sympathy?!'

I have my answer.

Even without our twenty-twenty hindsight, in truth, there were many reasons to be concerned about Freiburg across Team Telekom's lifespan, not only or even mainly to do with Joseph Keul. In mid-May 2007, a fortnight after Heinrich and Schmid's suspension from their T-Mobile duties, an expert commission was appointed by the University of Freiburg to investigate what appeared to be a long, undistinguished history of doping by the department of sports medicine stretching back to long before reunification. The enquiry had barely begun before both Schmid and Heinrich had confirmed in written statements that they had both played an active role in Telekom riders' doping. Schmid added one caveat: he had never administered the drugs himself. Heinrich stated that he was merely 'integrated into an existing system' that he 'neither initiated, directed, nor controlled'.

Schmid was fresh out of medical school when he was taken on by Joseph Keul and the Uniklinik in 1989. One of his first responsibilities was the medical care of Team Stuttgart, an outfit too modest to compete in races like the Tour de France until Deutsche Telekom arrived as a title sponsor at the end of 1991. This was also when Walter Godefroot took over the team, bringing with him a posse of Belgian soigneurs, including Jef D'Hont.

Ahead of the 1992 season, D'Hont and Schmid discussed the medicine that they would take to races and, according to D'Hont talked about obtaining medical certificates for the riders to use the steroids betamethasone and prednisolone. D'Hont also sought permission to introduce his 'magic drink' – a mix of caffeine, persantin, a vasodilator, and alupent, a banned bronchodilator that he had been giving to bike riders since 1977. According to D'Hont, Schmid took plenty of persuading, but eventually agreed the drink could be used.

A bidon hadn't even been filled, a pedal not even turned, though, before Team Telekom had its first whistle-blower. Martina Wechsung told the commission set up to investigate the Freiburg Uniklinik that, in 1991, she worked on behalf of Telekom to identify existing teams that they could sponsor, and had been alarmed by the company's attitude. In particular, Wechsung objected to the decision to recruit Walter Godefroot as a team manager, given that the Belgian had tested positive three times in his riding career. Wechsung also claimed to have warned Telekom that Godefroot had a 'dirty' reputation as a team manager. She told the Freiburg commission that Telekom not only ignored her advice but relieved her of her duties. She also claimed to have felt intimidated to the point that she felt compelled to leave Germany.

Under Godefroot, results were underwhelming in the team's rookie season. Jef D'Hont told German federal police in June 2007 that, meanwhile, one of Telekom's star riders at the time, Uwe Ampler, had heard about the new wonder drug EPO from riders at the Dutch PDM team. Ampler also wanted to try the miracle potion – and, according to D'Hont, did just that. Andreas Schmid disapproved at first but could already tell that resistance would soon be futile. The Freiburg commission concluded that Schmid was soon helping to procure EPO for another of the team's star riders. The following spring, Erik Zabel was fined 2,000 euros and docked fifty UCI points for his unauthorized use of a steroid-based saddle cream.

The 1994 season was significant for another reason: Lothar Heinrich joined the Uniklinik on 1 July. Jef D'Hont told an SWR television documentary in 2008 that it took Heinrich just a few conversations with him, the riders and Schmid to familiarize himself with

Telekom's 'system'. 'After a week he'd got the hang of everything, and then we soigneurs did nothing. Lothar took on everything.'

On the same programme, D'Hont maintained that the impulse for Telekom's doping programme had originally come from one group of individuals: 'The riders wanted it. Then, later, the doctors and the directeurs sportifs too. The team simply won more afterwards. The riders also said that they couldn't even keep up with the bunch without EPO and growth hormone.'

Dozens of eyewitness accounts from other cyclists in other teams suggest the Telekom riders were not alone in believing they faced a dope-or-be-damned Hobson's choice. Also in 1994, the Italian athletics coach and researcher Sandro Donati presented his national Olympic Committee with a devastating exposé of how an EPO plague was tearing through professional cycling, estimating that 70–80 per cent of pro riders were using the drug. Designed as a call to arms, his report was ignored, he said buried, until *La Gazzetta dello Sport* leaked it in 1996.

Donati is also present at the Nuremberg congress in October 2015. Between lectures, over coffee, we speak about Telekom, Freiburg and Jan Ullrich, who was on the cusp of turning professional at the end of 1994. It was, Donati concedes, a deeply inopportune time for a young rider to receive his baptism.

'Everything could have changed, because that was a key moment in which the EPO plague was starting but it was being controlled on an international level by a few doctors,' Donati says. 'It was contained, so an intervention would have been possible. The problem was that my dossier showed that the institutions didn't want to act because they were totally compromised. I showed that Francesco Conconi was one of the biggest contributors to the problem taking hold – at a time when he was the president of the UCI's medical commission and a member of the International Olympic Committee. He claimed to be researching a detection method, and for seven years he carried on saying it was nearly ready, when in actual fact he was doping athletes with EPO. So, yes, action could have been taken then, but my dossier showed that the problem wasn't even Conconi or others like him – it was the institutions above them.'

Donati says that when the UCI finally acted, introducing blood tests and a haematocrit limit of 50 per cent in 1997, what they had effectively done was 'send out an open invitation to dope up to that limit'. He is adamant that, even if EPO couldn't be directly detected in urine until 2001, a version of the biological passport finally rolled out by the UCI in 2008 could have been implemented many years earlier.

After Donati, later in the day, I discuss some of the same themes with another Italian, Letizia Paoli. A criminologist with a rich pedigree of research into mafia-type organizations, Paoli was appointed to the chair of the Freiburg commission in 2009. Notwithstanding assorted disputes and repeated accusations that the University of Freiburg has obstructed the expert commission it set up to investigate its own sports medicine department, Paoli still holds that position when we speak in October 2015. She is therefore uniquely placed to evaluate the pressures that Ullrich would have faced upon his introduction into what some have called a 'system', and others liken to . . . a mafia.

'In both cases, mafia organizations and cycling at that time, there's a process of socialization over many, many years,' Paoli says. 'A lot of people who are born and grow up in certain areas of southern Italy – in parts of Palermo or Reggio Calabria or San Luca or the Aspromonte mountains – believe that what the Calabrian mafia, the 'Ndrangheta, does, and what the Sicilian mafia does, is completely legitimate. It's the same in cycling: past generations in particular grew up with the idea that it was absolutely normal and legitimate to dope, meaning it becomes the social norm.'

Over the course of their investigations, Paoli and the Freiburg commission heard multiple accounts to the effect that, by the time Telekom convened for their pre-season training camp in Mallorca in January 1995, on the eve of Jan Ullrich's rookie year, EPO doping was about to become the standard, the expectation, the societal norm in the team.

Rudy Pevenage had been recruited the previous season. When I ask Pevenage whether Ullrich was immediately presented with the choice or obligation to take EPO, he reacts uncomfortably but decisively. 'No, no, no. Don't ask me that. It's too difficult for me to talk about . . . but no is the answer.'

At this point one thing seems to be widely agreed upon by Pevenage, Walter Godefroot, ex-Telekom riders and Peter Becker, Ullrich's coach in 1995: it was certainly not Becker who introduced Ullrich to

EPO, either when he was a teenager in the DDR,[30] in Hamburg as an under-23 or when he joined Telekom.

Becker considers the very suggestion ludicrous. 'In 1995 and 1996 I didn't notice anything. In the time when I worked with him it also wouldn't have been possible. He would have had to inject the stuff himself. But he promised me that I had nothing to worry about, that he wasn't [taking EPO]. Word for word, he said, "Coach, at the end of my career I don't want to be sitting there, with money and whatever else, but having ruined my health and with big horse's teeth growing out of the front of my mouth." I told him that was all good but he had to be open with me. When it all came out later, I was disappointed beyond belief.'

Less plausibly, Becker assures me that Ullrich didn't need EPO even in a peloton hooked on the stuff.

'The kid was so trainable. His ability to recover was enormous. And I'll say it again: if he really did use EPO and whatever else, it simply wasn't necessary. He just had to train properly with me. The kid has a gift, he hits numbers that others can only dream about. If he's doping and Armstrong's still riding away from him, of course that's shit. But if what you're taking is still not enough, why take it?'

Becker's oversimplification will strike some as disingenuous, but it won't surprise many who were trained by him. Former 'pupil' Raphael Schweda remembers how Becker 'would get very angry if ever doping came up. It'd be, "Here, we don't dope. End of story!"'

Walter Godefroot is also willing to vouch for Becker's righteousness – or for his naivety. 'I think Peter Becker is a good coach, but he's like a horse – he just goes straight ahead and doesn't look left or right,' Godefroot says. 'Peter's not really up to speed with modern cycling, if you know what I mean.'

A smirk creeps across Godefroot's lips.

He'll elaborate: 'In Peter's head, EPO doesn't exist. He only knows what he's learned in East Germany. He also said silly things in the press . . . again, because he doesn't know what's happening in the team.'

Since Operación Puerto and the Freiburg affair, Godefroot has said almost nothing in the press about his years running Telekom. Late in 2015 he speaks to me in the Holiday Inn just outside Ghent in Belgium, a few kilometres from his home, only thanks to the intervention of a mutual friend, the journalist Guy Vermeiren. Vermeiren also sits in on our interview. At one point in our discussion, I'll ask Godefroot whether, more than Pevenage's arrival in 1995, it was the signing of Bjarne Riis the following year that really changed the team's culture vis-à-vis 'medical preparation', as others have told me, and as results on the road also suggested. Godefroot has already told me about the promise he made to Riis before the Dane signed – that the whole team would raise its game in order to assist him, and that there would be *Unterstützung* – 'support'. Again, when he says this, Godefroot smiles.

Now, he says that, yes, in answer to my question, 'Riis changed the culture of the team.' He then turns to Guy Vermeiren to ask in Flemish whether he can trust me. Vermeiren responds kindly, in the affirmative. And so Godefroot decides to loosen the lid a little more.

'Riis changes the culture of the team, but it's different from Armstrong: no one's pushed into doing anything. Someone putting pressure on teammates to dope . . . that never happened in my teams. It was always the individual's choice.'*

I push my luck by asking whether Pevenage had been hired primarily to coordinate Telekom's doping.

Godefroot laughs. 'Time out! Time out! Just because I've said "A" it doesn't mean you're going to get the whole alphabet!'

A different tack. Did he ever consider getting rid of Pevenage?

'We're getting into dangerous territory,' Godefroot responds. 'But, look, Jan eats out of Rudy's hands. It's Rudy who put him in touch with Fuentes later. And that works for me. Of course I also knew that Jan needed Rudy . . . but I can't tell too many stories about Pevenage. It wouldn't be fair. That's also why I don't write a book. I trust you, but I don't want to go into the story of when we started with the EPO and so on. That'd take several books.'

Godefroot is here on his terms. I am not the German federal police, nor the Freiburg commission, neither of which could force Godefroot to go on the record about how he and others contributed to Telekom's 'system' years ago. To my surprise, though, the more we talk, the more he opens up, beginning when I ask whether Ullrich could have beaten Riis in the 1996 Tour. I don't even need to broach one of Jef D'Hont's more lurid accusations – that Riis had doped to

---

* Johan Bruyneel and Lance Armstrong have denied that anyone was pressured or coerced into doping at US Postal.

excess, that his body was shutting down in the final week; Godefroot already assumes that's what I'm getting at.

'Yes, Jan was stronger,' he says. 'But I don't really know what's happening in my team there. I always say that when you're in charge of a team it's like with adultery: everyone knows except the wife or husband. Jef D'Hont was always doing things and telling people, "Don't tell Walter." I was always the last to know.'

So what percentage of D'Hont's allegations were truth, and what percentage invention?

'Hard to say. I mean, *ooof* . . .' Godefroot puffs out his cheeks. 'They're things that go on. Everything happens in the context of its time. That said, to sell a book like that you have to sex things up a bit. That's also why I won a lawsuit against him.

'But yes, after 1996 everyone came to me congratulating me, saying that we knew who was going to win the next five Tours, i.e. Jan. Then, one day, we were all together and I said to Jan, "You mustn't follow Bjarne's example. Bjarne's an American car which uses a lot of petrol and a lot of oil. You're a young Mercedes and you're clean and smooth. Be very careful." There is EPO but there's also cortisone, steroids . . . If we start talking about drugs, though, we could be here for hours.'

Yet, still, at least for a few more minutes before retreating to safer ground, Godefroot goes on.

'In 1996, when [the UCI president] Hein Verbruggen congratulated me for the Tour win, I told him that I wasn't proud, that it hurt a bit in my heart, because I wasn't sure but I thought things were happening that were dangerous for the health of riders. He replied, "Yes, I know he's doing this, and he's doing that" – I won't say the names – "but we still can't find the product, so what can we do?" That year there was a meeting in Geneva with all of the directeurs sportifs and all of the doctors. No one knew what the haematocrit limit should be: the Italians were saying fifty, others wanted fifty-two, the team doctors didn't know what to suggest. It was Verbruggen who finally took responsibility and made the decision. It ended up costing the UCI a lot of money, at a time when EPO was being used in all endurance sports. What could he do? All I could do was offer my resignation. But I always said that the only people who had any right to complain about EPO were the people who had never taken cortisone, steroids or caffeine either.'

Godefroot sounds unapologetic. In a way, he is – except to Telekom and in particular Jürgen Kindervater, Telekom's Head of
Communications from 1990 to 2002 and the team's biggest cheerleader at company headquarters in Bonn. The Freiburg commission
would devote considerable effort to finding out how much Telekom
knew about their team's doping. Their work eventually spawned two
published reports, one in 2009 and another in 2015, authored by the
researcher Andreas Singler. The latter was deeply critical of Kindervater personally, noting that 'the way that he publicly tried to
neutralize doping rumours at least partly and disturbingly mir-
rored . . . the typical reaction of the accused doper.' It was even more
scathing about Telekom and T-Mobile in general, asserting that it was
possible to 'sketch a picture of an unscrupulous sponsorship' and
referring repeatedly to their 'offshoring of responsibility' or, more
simply, a wilful ignorance if not outright, fully cognizant complicity.

All of which, Walter Godefroot tells me, is wildly inaccurate, an
unjust misconstrual.

'Telekom weren't naive but they didn't know anything. I said to
Kindervater later that I needed to apologize to one person: him. He
quizzed me on several occasions. He was the only one who deserved
an apology. He asked me directly several times: "There's no doping
in the team, though, is there?" No one in the Telekom management
knew. They weren't naive but they trusted us.

'Also, I have to say Telekom made a lot of money out of us,'
Godefroot continues. 'They floated on the stock market, then Riis
won the Tour and the share price rocketed. Everyone wanted to be
part of the success . . . But, no, there weren't that many people who
knew. Even I was the last person to know sometimes.'

There is a rugged realism – if it is not more honest to call it
cynicism – that seeps into the worldview of everyone who has
worked in professional cycling for a significant number of years. Certainly it seeped into the minds of people who were around in the
period when Godefroot was managing Telekom. This, maybe more
than the doping itself, was the real contagion in that process of
socialization: a numb acceptance that, whatever hopes and values
are projected onto a sport which styles itself as the pursuit of all that
is epic, noble and transcendental in humans and nature, the wheels
never truly leave the ground. There cannot be, or at least has never
been, any escape from the same venalities and vulnerabilities present

in other reaches of the human condition – only illusions of one. Reality, with its sinners and imperfections, will bite as surely as rubber meets the road.

In November 2015, Walter Godefroot's heart is still healing from a bypass operation and his nose and sinuses from a fall on his bike. His birth certificate says that he's seventy-two but Godefroot is sure he's 'aged years in the last twelve months'. He still feels disorientated, not quite himself – and yet he is also as sure as ever about one thing: when it comes to drugs and cycling, moralizing is a vain endeavour.

'Cycling is the working man's sport,' he says. 'It can't defend itself. After the war, there were a lot of amphetamines around, the amphetamines that the Japanese kamikaze pilots had been taking, for example. My mother worked in a textile factory where there were women doing twenty-four-hour shifts with earplugs in, taking thousands of painkillers . . . It's that kind of time. A lot of people were taking too many drugs everywhere. It was inevitable that would leak into an endurance sport where initially there were no doctors, just soigneurs, some good, some bad. And the bad ones were having more success than the good ones. Cycling isn't better than the other sports but it's certainly not worse. The BALCO scandal in athletics . . . that's only the start. Russia. Bribery in football. People want to make cycling an island of purity in a dirty world. It's not possible.'

One sub-section of the second Freiburg report, authored by Andreas Singler in 2015, poses the question of whether doctors Lothar Heinrich and Andreas Schmid may have doped Jan Ullrich before 1996. Singler's conclusion is that the possibility exists, but, between Jef D'Hont's claims and the findings of the German federal police, it seems more plausible that he began taking EPO, at least, in May or June 1996, in the build-up to his first Tour de France.

Rolf Aldag's description of Ullrich's almost overnight metamorphosis when they trained together in the Black Forest in the spring of 1995 might point to an earlier 'initiation'. Nonetheless, Aldag is inclined to believe what Rudy Pevenage has told me – Ullrich reached his fork in the road later.

'I think his early results were pretty fair and clean, then whoever realized this kid could go really far then, yeah, they probably convinced him,' Aldag says. 'I think it was after the training camp with me in the Black Forest. I don't really think he did anything in 1995. I don't think in 1995 Jan ever had that status where it was like, "Let's give him wings and he'll fly." I personally think that maybe in the second half of 1995, someone said, "Hang on, that's not so bad." Then in 1996 it maybe came to a point where it was like, "What do we do?"

'That's also the point: it's really not in Jan's nature,' Aldag continues. 'He's not an active guy. He's not active in terms of finding out about stuff, doing research. He was an absolute follower.'

Like other riders who saw Telekom's 'system' develop and escalate in the mid-1990s, Aldag says that it relied, if not on total secrecy, then at least on discretion. 'At the time, it also would have been dangerous to have other people knowing what was happening,' he explains. 'Why would you do it? Because let's say you're talking to Walter about a contract, about him giving you less money or more money. You don't want to give me a contract? OK, all the world will know tomorrow morning what you have done . . . If I ever started talking about medication with Walter Godefroot, after two sentences he'd shut me down. "You know what? I pay doctors for that. I'm not a doctor." And this is self-protection. It's clever.'

Jens Heppner, Ullrich's roommate for many years, concurs that, 'Everyone cooked their own broth.' Meaning that he didn't know what Ullrich was doing or taking; whether it was the soigneurs, Pevenage or the Freiburg doctors who were taking charge. Heppner himself was one of twenty-two riders including Ullrich whose urine samples from the 1998 Tour de France were re-tested six years later for research purposes and shown to contain EPO, according to a 2013 French Senate report.

Brian Holm definitely doped with EPO – but he too says that his blinkers came off slowly, belatedly, and even then not entirely. He hadn't even heard of the drug until April 1994, when Gewiss-Ballan's riders swept the Flèche Wallonne podium and that infamous article appeared in *L'Équipe* quoting the team's doctor, Michele Ferrari – 'It's also dangerous to drink ten litres of orange juice.' Holm soon moved with the times but, for him at least, 'the soigneurs dealt with it, not Schmid and Heinrich'. Holm informed Schmid only after his first, nervous phase of self-experimentation. 'The most difficult bit was knowing how much to take,' he says. 'No one knew at the start. You'd heard people were dying from it and you didn't have a clue. You didn't know whether to take 2,000 units a month, a day, or an hour. You'd take one ampoule, wait a week and think it'd give you magic powers, but then you raced again and thought, *What the fuck is this?* So then you would take more.'

It seems highly improbable that Ullrich lost his 'virginity' in the same dilettantish, ad hoc fashion. Rudy Pevenage has told me that he 'got close to Jan' at the 1995 Vuelta, and Walter Godefroot also wants me to understand that 'Lothar Heinrich is Rudy Pevenage.' Hence, the findings of the Freiburg commission indicating that Heinrich oversaw Ullrich's 'coming of age' before the 1996 Tour, together with what Godefroot has told me about Bjarne Riis's arrival 'changing the medical culture of the team' that year, begin to look like pieces in a more complete jigsaw. The commission also noted the coincidence, or not, of the German Olympic Committee being unable to locate Ullrich for any out-of-competition dope tests in 1996 before 11 August. The following year, after Ullrich had won the Tour de France, *La Gazzetta Dello Sport*'s Angelo Zomegnan wrote that the UCI had not submitted Ullrich to a single blood test in 1997.

Ensuring riders didn't test positive was at this point no doubt easier for Schmid and Heinrich than hiding their activities in Freiburg from prying eyes. One co-worker at the Uniklinik spoke to the commission about how the two doctors' 'Telekom life' was kept hidden behind the doors of their two private rooms, to which no else was allowed access. Hans-Hermann Dickhuth, the head of sports medicine at the Uniklinik from 2002, has also pointed out that most illicit procedures appear to have been carried out at weekends, in the evening or when the doctors were away at races. Nevertheless, the Freiburg commission assembled a catalogue of episodes and behaviours that should have raised red flags. There were multiple opportunities over the years to spy hidden agendas in comments like Schmid's on the eve of the 1997 Tour about the fallibility of the UCI's recently introduced blood tests, and spurned chances, like the time a colleague found a box of anabolic steroids in Schmid's office but kept quiet. Schmid was also visibly panicked after *Der Spiegel*'s allegations about Telekom's systematic doping in 1999, blurting to his friend, Walter Schmidt of the University of Bayreuth, 'Now a bomb's really going to go off!' He wore a general air of being conflicted, of having a heavy conscience, which at times of stress would spill over

into mutterings about 'going back to my disabled guys' – meaning
the para-sport athletes he had treated in the past. Then there was
the day early in 1996 when, amid rumours of an EPO test being
close to approval, Schmid approached a colleague in the Uniklinik's
blood transfusion department to enquire about extracting red cells
from a whole blood sample.

Blood transfusions also seemed to interest Lothar Heinrich in the
late 1990s. In Andreas Singler's 2015 Freiburg report, he lamented
'a perhaps unique opportunity to expose the Freiburg sports doctors
at an earlier date' that had arisen in 1998. An eyewitness working in
the Uniklinik's transfusion department at the time told the Freiburg
commission that, one day that year, they received an email from
Heinrich asking for information about how to get hold of blood storage bags. A fortnight or so later, on a Sunday morning, one of the
doctors in the department appeared with a knotted, half-filled bag of
blood that, he claimed, had come from Heinrich and needed to be
centrifuged. The doctor in question joked that it was perhaps Jan
Ullrich's blood. He waved away the witness's urgings to report the
incident.

Others who over the years tried to raise questions were treated
in the same offhand manner, notably by Joseph Keul. 'There's no
doping at Telekom,' Keul told an employee who raised questions
about the frequency of blood tests on the team riders – and over the
years that remained the party line. Lothar Heinrich trotted out similar platitudes whenever the subject came up, on TV or to newspaper
journalists. In the middle of the scandal-ravaged 1998 Tour, Rudy
Pevenage was caught retrieving empty ampoules from a dustbin outside the Telekom team hotel in the Pyrenees. 'The doctor had put our
ampoules in the bin and I went to fetch them, in case the police
looked through them. I fished them out and crushed them under my
feet,' Pevenage tells me. And yet, in Paris at the end of that Tour,
Telekom's communications director Jürgen Kindervater was parrot-
ing the old dictum – 'There is no doping at Telekom' – and believing
it. Hours later, Telekom were taking out those full-page adverts in
every major German newspaper: 'Well done, clean performance,
boys!'

This was also the point at which one of the most barefaced acts
of deception was being concocted in Freiburg – the doping-free sport
initiative proposed by Keul and funded by Telekom.

In his 2015 report, the Freiburg commission member Singler would conclude that *Dopingfreier Sport* was in fact more Trojan Horse than genuine attempt to combat illegal performance-enhancement. He compared it to the protocol employed in the old DDR, whereby athletes were systematically screened before going abroad to compete and withdrawn if they were in danger of testing positive. Singler noted that not once during the group's three-year mandate was a Telekom rider suspended, despite the numerous indicators of EPO use in their clinical files. Perhaps worst of all – simply 'embarrassing', as Singler put – was Keul's unsuccessful bid, days after the Festina scandal broke, to make the Uniklinik Germany's third UCI-accredited anti-doping laboratory.

Dopingfreier Sport ended up outliving Joseph Keul, who died in July 2000. By then, Lothar Heinrich had long since established himself as Keul's heir. The Freiburg commission alleged that in May 1999 Jörg Jaksche received a batch of EPO from Heinrich at the Herzogenhorn training centre in the Black Forest – where Heinrich was participating in a conference under the aegis of *Dopingfreier Sport*. The delivery fees for some of the drugs sent to riders were also included in *Dopingfreier Sport*'s running costs.

In 2007, Jaksche told the German federal police that Schmid and Heinrich seemed not to be motivated by money and were supplying the Telekom drugs 'because they thought that was better than us buying them from some gym in Timbuktu'.

In Munich in 2015, Jaksche describes Heinrich to me in less flattering terms.

'We called Lothar the television doctor. If someone crashed, for Lothar it was important to go on TV and tell them what had happened. Schmid was a super-good guy, and he didn't like having to dope people, but the athletes were like brothers and sons for him. He knew that he had to do it somehow, or that we had to do it, so he tried to keep it under control. He'd be like, "Don't use insulin, don't use that." Whereas Lothar was a nice guy, very well educated, but more freestyle.'

Where Heinrich's supposedly 'freestyle' approach situated Telekom and Ullrich in the medical arms race is hard to say. Jens Heppner scoffs at the idea that Heinrich was 'extreme', but robust evidence points to his growing influence as the years passed, particularly after Jef D'Hont's departure at the end of 1996. Christian

Frommert joined the T-Mobile staff in 2005 and was astonished to discover that 'the nice older guy' he assumed to be Heinrich's assistant was in fact Andreas Schmid, at least nominally Heinrich's superior, although it was 'Lothar who always acted like the boss'. Where Ullrich was concerned, Rudy Pevenage tells me that, in his second spell with the team, post-2003, he consulted the Freiburg doctors only for 'normal things' and Andreas Schmid specifically for 'private matters'. Meanwhile, Eufemiano Fuentes sourced the heavy artillery from Spain. But the Freiburg doctors could without doubt have seen the effects of Fuentes's treatments in their routine blood tests. The TV network ARD reported in 2009 that a professor who examined the Uniklinik patient files stored in Freiburg had seen 'implausible' variations in Ullrich's blood values only a few months before Fuentes's arrest. Prior to that, the haematocrit level recorded for a patient logged as 'Ulrich Maier' in Heinrich and Schmid's filing cabinet had dipped miraculously in the space of a few hours shortly before the 2005 Tour de France. Not that Maier would be winning bike races any time soon: he coincidentally shared a birthday with Jan Ullrich, 2 December, but was born not in 1973, like Ullrich . . . but 1937.

I re-establish contact with Lothar Heinrich in October 2015. An email. He replies: 'Good to hear from you. Yes, it's been a very, very long time. I am doing well, hope you too. Obviously you are still in cycling, I am not. I stopped in 2007 and after some time for orientation changed my focus completely.'

He went on to say that, no, unfortunately he couldn't agree to an interview because of medical confidentiality. My follow-up went unanswered.

In a final analysis, most would believe that Schmid and Heinrich got off lightly. The Freiburg commission heard detailed accounts of blood transfusions that were rushed and haphazard, and conduct that was seemingly in violation of their Hippocratic Oath. Not that this was how Schmid and Heinrich had seen it, in their certainty that riders would take drugs with or without them. As an utterly bereft Jürgen Kindervater told Der Spiegel in June 2007, he could only imagine that Schmid and Heinrich 'wanted to make sure, out of a sense of responsibility as doctors, that the riders didn't fall down dead off their bikes'. Better the devil, or the doping, they knew, in other words.

Heinrich earned a 100 per cent pay rise when, oblivious to his past and the revelations around the corner, Bob Stapleton put him in charge of T-Mobile's new anti-doping plan in 2007. Granted, Heinrich's 120,000-euro wage barely registered alongside the eight-figure sum that Jan Ullrich had amassed over the course of his career. Ullrich, though, was also left holding by far the biggest emotional and legal bills of all the old gang; Walter Godefroot lost his (new) job as an advisor to Team Astana but successfully sued Jef D'Hont for accusing him of financing Telekom's doping;[31] Andreas Schmid got a fine equal to ninety days' pay from a Freiburg magistrate but kept his medical licence; the same judge could do nothing against Lothar Heinrich, who declined to testify and had emigrated to the United States, but who was also spared because at the time there was no provision in the German Medicinal Act for blood transfusions, and the allegations about more conventional forms of doping were too broad. Three other Freiburg doctors outed by the commission for lesser offences simply got new jobs. Meanwhile, Ullrich's friend and training partner, Andreas Klöden, was also investigated by the federal police in Bonn, but they closed the case when Klöden made a substantial donation to charity; Klöden maintained that he was innocent and never made the trip down the Rhine on the opening weekend of the 2006 Tour, but had coughed up just to halt the investigation, 'to make sure this case wouldn't obstruct my career any longer'. Kessler issued a similar denial to Klöden but tested positive and was banned months later. Rudy Pevenage paid a five-figure sum to end his involvement in the federal investigation, but was at least spared the same excoriation as Ullrich.

At the Nuremberg conference in October 2015, Sandro Donati shrugs at a dynamic he has seen play out many times before.

'Individual responsibility is relative to age and experience, to upbringing and intelligence. That said, the athlete is always a victim and a beneficiary. That's one point. After which, the athlete is a victim and a victim only the moment he's found out and he becomes the target. On one hand that's right, on the other, when it goes beyond and he becomes a symbol of doping, the person is destroyed in their self-esteem. His character's assassinated. I can understand people being that severe when they judge athletes as long as they're just as severe in their judgement of the institutions. You also have to consider that athletes are around for six, seven, eight years, whereas the authorities and the coaches stick around, in this society of dinosaurs where people don't given up their positions – that's the source of corruption. It's a source that starts way back and remains.'

Telekom were the institution which had unwittingly funded Schmid and Heinrich's dirty work. But then, as they also pleaded to the Freiburg commission, the telecommunications giant's arrangement with the cycling team was no different from the one they had with Bayern Munich: they paid a pre-agreed fee and in return got their name on a jersey and, hopefully, success on the field or the road. This was also how nearly every team in the top tier of professional cycling functioned. Godefroot, and after him Olaf Ludwig, gave them a rough breakdown of how much money was needed and on what it would be spent, but itemized receipts and invoices were never sent to Bonn.

All of which made it easy for Telekom to act like the injured party, despite the justifiable charge that the reflected glory also came with responsibility. Their negligence, though, could be spun as a lesser sin than Ullrich's deception. Ullrich's was, after all, the main if not only face the lay public recognized, cared about or felt personally betrayed by, and that suited Telekom just fine.

'If we'd been smarter we would have discovered it earlier and the damage would have been smaller, but you know in sports it's even more emotional because millions of people consider you a hero,' says Ron Sommer. 'They admire you, they're all saying, "Woah, I want to be like this guy." But one thing that has not changed enough in any sport, and is still the weak link, is the quality of support around the sportsmen. If the people in the entourage were doing their work as well as the superstar was doing his part, wow – but in my time in cycling that was not the case. How do you protect and make sure this huge success in this one area does not kill him?'

By 2007, none of this was T-Mobile's concern. They had believed there was still something to be saved, or gained for them, from a team without Ullrich, but he had cut holes in the blindfold and the Freiburg revelations tore it from their face. Then came two successive punches in the nose – Patrik Sinkewitz's positive test midway through the 2007 Tour de France, which had prompted the ARD and

ZDF crews to pack up and leave the Tour, and Lorenzo Bernucci's in September. It was a point of no return – commercial returns or indeed anything remotely positive for the company image. They announced they were pulling out before the 2008 season had begun – even if it meant incurring a substantial kill fee. Having spent millions to get their name on the team jersey for a decade and a half, they were now effectively paying Bob Stapleton to take it off.

'From the spring of 2007 it was just blow after blow,' says Stapleton. 'I think it was extreme both ways: the hero worship was excessive, and then the public flogging was over the top too. But my impression is that Jan would have been forgiven if he'd played it differently. On the other hand, the German media is quite remarkable. There's a whole level of journalism that you just don't see in many other places. Super aggressive, super knowledgeable and quite relentless. It's also a very literate culture – newspapers are still very widely read. So you had numerous good, insightful reporters covering this, and just hammering away. That brought out Jef D'Hont and lots of other information. Then the Freiburg thing in the end was just overwhelming for T-Mobile and everyone.'

Five years after leaving the organization, Telekom's former CEO, Ron Sommer, and his old wingman, then communications chief Jürgen Kindervater, watched the whole thing unravel from afar, and with dismay. In time, Kindervater would find himself in the dock, among the main accusees: how could he, the team's midwife at its inception and a sort of doting godparent for years thereafter, not have known? Even if Walter Godefroot has assured me that was indeed the case.

Despite Kindervater's insistence, detailed in Chapter 9, that he had 'total confidence' in the clinic because its university status placed it 'above everything', he *was* aware of Keul's controversial comments about anabolic steroids on German national television in 1977. Over the next two decades, Keul became more circumspect in words if not actions, although his efforts to publicly minimize the prevalence, effect and danger of doping remained a recurring theme. Given that he specialized in rhetoric, it was perhaps not surprising that he found a way to sweet-talk the suits at Telekom. Their lack of due diligence seems startling nevertheless – although, equally, much of what we now know about Keul was only uncovered by a tenacious team of experts working for several years on the Freiburg commission.

As for the charge that Kindervater himself had known or even masterminded whatever was happening in Freiburg, he has no better defence than an appeal to our common sense.

'If someone suggested to me that I knew or in some way promoted doping, I'd have asked them whether they really thought I'd imperil my whole existence for the sake of that?' he says. 'I mean, to what end? I'd have been endangering my financial and my professional future to push sportsmen towards success that would bring me nothing personally. It would have been crazy. And, similarly, with Keul. Personally I think the same applied to him . . .'

This final claim is debatable, but there is no future in arguing the point, not today, years later. Meanwhile, enthroned in his space-age citadel in Meerbusch, Ron Sommer has made a career, his life, out of predicting upcoming events, but it's also an eternal source of frustration to him that more people don't learn lessons from the past. Equally, he may not have felt that Telekom deserved their slice of the blame for Ullrich, Fuentes, Freiburg et al, but he did believe it was in their interests, if not an obligation, for them to commit to cycling's reconstruction.

'I'm not sure I would have left the sport if I'd still been CEO when everything was discovered,' he says. 'You know, it's the same thing as being in a company and having a technical disaster. You don't run away; you fix it. You can fire the sports people because they didn't play by the rules, tell them we don't want their kind, but saying goodbye to the whole sport is pretty unfair in my opinion. Cycling was not bad to you; there were some specific people who did really bad stuff. They cheated, they cheated themselves, their families, the sponsor, the public, and the worst of it was that they thought they were right because they thought everyone was doing it. Maybe they were, I don't know, but if my neighbour kills someone that doesn't mean I have the right to kill someone.'

Sommer knows the analogy is a little forced, and pauses. There are no simple answers here. He purses his lips, gathers some closing thoughts.

'I really feel sorry for people like Jan. He could have been a superstar without necessarily winning a Tour. Jan is really a good guy. He doesn't want to hurt anybody. He was not calculating – that's why he didn't do well on the training side, gained too much weight, fell from one trap to the next. At the end of the day, everyone is responsible for himself, but it could have gone a different way with different support. A different manager, different doctors, a different masseur and so on . . . Maybe he would not have won the Tour de France but he would have been the clear winner of German hearts, and not only Germans.'

23

NADIR

'You know. You climb this tree. It's all you aim for. Right up there you see the fruit. I was climbing. Climbing. Ready to reach for the fruit. And then. Nothing. I sat in the car driving home from Strasbourg thinking: that was it. It is all over. And it was. I was right. For the next four years I sat in my house and looked out the window'

—*Jan Ullrich to* Rouleur *magazine, 2015*

One day in the early summer of 2008, Jan Ullrich momentarily broke free of the stresses that had enveloped him for the previous two years to poke fun at an old friend. Ullrich and Boris Becker had much in common – both red-headed *Wunderkinder* who had once captivated a nation, both now more frequently lampooned than celebrated in the land of their birth. Ullrich had been shamed for his doping, Becker for transitioning from tennis swashbuckler to tabloid editor's piñata, the self-parodying protagonist of bankruptcies, tax evasion, heartbreaks and, maybe most infamously, a 'five-second' tryst on the stairs of a London restaurant while his then pregnant wife was in hospital – which itself led to another child.

This, as he pointed Becker to the altitude chamber that he still kept in his cellar in Scherzingen, is presumably what inspired Ullrich's punchline: 'So, if you want to have sex at 5,000 metres above sea level . . .'

Three years later, incidentally, Becker would, true to form, declare his membership of the Mile High Club on a German TV game show.

The joke was one memorable takeaway of Ullrich's first public appearance in over a year, in an episode of *Boris Becker Meets . . .* on the ProSieben network. For all the staged bonhomie between the two friends – a speedboat trip across the Bodensee, a bike ride, their journey to meet Ullrich's mum in Rostock and finally Becker pronouncing Ullrich 'a really good guy' who was 'fully rehabilitated' – the programme met with a snooty reception among media commentators. Most now seemed to agree they made a perfect double act: two delusional has-beens with the same blind spots and tiresome gripes about 'Germans' and 'the media', both expats and exiles, as similar in their thud to earth as they had been on their meteoric rise. Once they had been poster boys, now they were kitsch embodiments of a Germany to be disowned. Ullrich's next notable public outing was also at Becker's invitation – to a charity event at Oktoberfest in Munich. Dressed in Lederhosen, swigging one-litre Steins of Spaten-Franziskaner, Ullrich now seemed to exist as Becker had for several years – as a dehumanized cliché, a court fool to comfort his mockers' sense of good taste and righteousness, so guileless that he laughed along with others laughing at him.

Out of the spotlight, though, there was nothing funny about some of the pressures that Ullrich was facing. Werner Franke, the Heidelberg microbiologist, had challenged the gag order banning him from alleging that Eufemiano Fuentes doped Ullrich – and Franke was a tenacious, brilliant opponent. Their legal battle would run for three years, from 2007 to 2010, during which Ullrich had tried but thus far failed to bed himself into a new identity. His feelings about cycling oscillated between pangs of longing and total repudiation. Rudy Pevenage had taken a job as the directeur sportif of the American team Rock Racing, a rogue's gallery of mavericks and Operación Puerto survivors whose owner had also courted Ullrich. Ullrich declined that offer, but, Lance Armstrong tells me, responded to Armstrong's comeback announcement in late 2008 with the suggestion they return to racing together – apparently not in jest. The revelation is hard to square with someone who, on other days, referred to pro cycling as 'that hell' and said he wouldn't go back for 'all the money in the world'. As it was, only one of them lined up for the 2009 Tour. Ullrich watched the key stages with the volume turned down, as always when cycling was on his TV.

In 2010, finally, the 'psychological crisis' to which his mother would later refer finally tipped Ullrich beyond his coping threshold. Ullrich himself talked about a 'knot' in his head that had become too big to untangle on his own. He needed professional help. He got it at a clinic in Zürich, not far from his home, along with a diagnosis of 'burnout' – often a vague description for a pot pourri of stress-induced symptoms, from anxiety to diminishing energy and self-worth.

His decision to open up about his illness – or at least publish a brief statement on his website announcing that he was undergoing treatment – was predictably greeted with sympathy by some, cynicism by others. The timing was certainly curious – on the same day that the Hamburg State Court officially lifted the gag order against Werner Franke. Ullrich didn't want to say whether the two things were linked. A couple of weeks later, he was flatly denying rumours that he was in fact battling alcoholism.

In truth, Ullrich was about to rediscover something that years, maybe decades earlier, had felt like an addiction – the pleasure of riding his bike. 'He'd hardly ridden for three years, but one of the doctors or nurses in the clinic said to him they'd love to ride with him. Sara then brought his bike and he slowly started up again,' Wolfgang Strohband recalls.

Soon, Ullrich would be riding for three hours every day, feeling the knot finally loosen. It was that simple – or at least sounded so in the only public accounts of the period Ullrich ever gave. 'I was there for two or three weeks,' he told the Danish journalist Morten Okbo. 'I talked with psychologists. And I learned that I needed to begin to train again. I realized that my head functions better on the bike. It got my spirits back.'

In another interview, he reflected on how and why he had hauled himself out of the mire whereas others from his generation found the climb too steep. Marco Pantani, for example, had seemingly never been able to cleanse the shame of his ejection from the 1999 Giro or clamber out of the legal quagmires of its aftermath. 'The same couldn't have happened to me. I never got to that point,' Ullrich said. 'I love life too much, and I also have a reason – with my life, and with my family now – to be really happy. I did end up in a state of burnout, but we soon realized that if I realigned body and soul somehow, and stayed active, and also let friends and family help me – and speak to a psychologist, as I did briefly then – it would quickly help me. I wouldn't be so stubborn to let no one help me. For a very long time I thought I only needed myself, because I was the Tour de France champion, I was strong . . . and that worked for a few years, but then I went kaput.'

Another of those 'reasons to be happy' was the news that Sara was to give birth to their second child, a boy named Benno. Their first son, Max, had been born in 2007. The atmosphere at their home had by Ullrich's admission been 'awful' before his treatment. Suddenly, his previously tortured, tired mind felt something that, after years of deprivation, it now barely recognized: the soft caress of hope.

Four years had passed since Operación Puerto. They had been cataclysmic for professional cycling in Germany, which had seen a nuclear meltdown of the races, teams and sponsors fertilized by Ullrich and Telekom's success. Now, the Milram team, sponsored by a large German dairy, had announced that they, like T-Mobile in 2007 and the equally scandal-ravaged Gerolsteiner in 2008, were also pulling down the shutters. Germany would hence have no major team in cycling's elite division in 2011 for the first time in twenty years. The UCI year planner made even more depressing reading: from a high watermark of fifty days of top-level racing in 2005 and 2006, Germany's calendar had shrivelled to a mere thirteen days in 2010. On one single 'Black Thursday' in October 2008, the national broadcaster ARD had announced that it would discontinue its coverage of the Tour de France, to be followed an hour or two later by the news that the Deutschland Tour, resuscitated in 1999, mid-magenta and golden age, would cease to exist – at least for now. The gangrene had set in at all levels, even in the most remote organs and orifices of the sport in Germany – like the venerable Six-Day scene. Ninety years after its inception, the Six Days of Stuttgart had perished in 2008, as had the Six Days of Dortmund; the following year saw the forty-sixth and final edition of the Six Days of Munich.

After their 2009 hiatus, the organizers of the Deutschland Tour briefly imagined reviving their race in 2010, only for that prospect to quickly vanish. The former race chief Kai Rapp spelled out why: 'Doping. It conditions everything – how attractive the race is to spectators, sponsors and host towns.'

Based on ratings from the 2005 edition (28 per cent audience share in Germany, 50 per cent in Belgium), where Ullrich had been the star attraction, Rapp had felt his race was well on course to become cycling's second biggest televisual event, on par with the Giro d'Italia and behind only the Tour de France. 'But then, unfortunately,' he told *Radsportnews*, 'there was a new development for cycling in Germany in 2006 . . .'

One day in May 2011, Jan Ullrich sat at the dining table in his villa in Scherzingen, surrounded by the faces and quotidian stage props of the last few years, with the Bodensee shimmering outside, and he began to describe how he imagined the next phase of his life.

Sitting next to Ullrich, smiling, nodding and chipping in their own ideas were Charly Steeb and Falk Nier. Both men were former tennis players, Steeb a three-time Davis Cup winner from the same golden generation as Boris Becker and Michael Stich and Nier a short-lived Challenger Tour hopeful who later became the German Davis Cup team manager. Now they worked together in a sports marketing agency, organizing events and managing athletes, including retired ones seeking self-reinvention. This was also why they had been summoned to Switzerland: after nearly five years and his recovery from burnout the previous summer, Jan had started to think about what could come next. Years later, Ullrich summed up his post-Puerto inertia thus to *Rouleur*: 'For the next four years I sat in my house and looked out of the window.'

As Nier now told Ullrich, they would never know how the German public might feel about a rapprochement, let alone redemption, unless they tried. It was about Jan finally taking control. Never mind that the UCI and the Swiss Cycling Federation were still debating whether they could officially punish Ullrich's doping, and that the Court of Arbitration for Sport (CAS) was poised to have the final say.

While the lawyers dealt with that, Ullrich called Nier and Steeb a week or two after their meeting to say that he liked their pitch. He had realized the previous year that he needed cycling for both his physical and mental health; their idea of him inching his way back into the public eye and the cycling marketplace with Gran Fondos – mass participation, non-competitive rides often modelled on major tour stages – made perfect sense.

Another former German sporting luminary was also looking out for Ullrich. With hair like a metal frontman and the hips of a samba-dancing Carioca, Frank Wörndl had become an overnight sensation after his 1987 world slalom championship victory – and fodder for the tabloids when, the following year, he had to leave his Olympic silver medal in a strip club in Calgary as a deposit, having burned through all of his cash. A few years later, Wörndl met and gave Ullrich skiing lessons in Sölden in Austria. Ullrich didn't wear a hat or gloves and blistered his feet to an icy pulp, which Wörndl found both horrifying and hilarious. They had become and remained good friends, and now Wörndl wanted to contribute to his chum's 'relaunch'. A friend in Sölden had challenged Wörndl to complete the infamous Gran Fondo finishing in the resort, the Ötztaler Radmarathon, in under eight hours. Wörndl took on the bet. And roped in Ullrich.

They decided to prepare by entering a multi-day event in the Italian Dolomites. Ullrich went 'incognito' under the name 'Max Kraft' – literally 'Max Power', with Max also, of course, being the name of his eldest son. 'The disguise didn't exactly work,' Falk Nier recalls. 'From the minute he got there people recognized him and wanted photos, but it was actually really good for him. He'd been out of the public eye for a long time, and people had built up this image of a guy hiding from the police or the authorities. We were also taking a first step with a view to him "coming out" in the long term, dealing with all of the questions so that he wouldn't have to deal with them in the future. Jan had been on the same level as Boris Becker, Franz Beckenbauer and Steffi Graf. We thought that him opening up could eventually take him back towards that level.'

Steeb and Nier recognized that Ullrich would need convincing. For years, he had been telling anyone who asked that he couldn't tell the truth about his doping for 'legal reasons', while friends and advisors cited the terms of his severance from T-Mobile. But Nier says these excuses were spurious: 'At most, he would have had to pay a small amount back to, for example, his old sunglasses manufacturer.'

No, as far as Nier and others could tell, there was one lingering, overwhelming worry – that admitting his guilt would result in him being stripped of his 1997 Tour victory. 'And in my opinion,' says Nier, 'it meant everything to Jan to be the only German Tour winner. If he loses that title, I think he loses everything in his mind.'

Others, like Ullrich's previous manager Wolfgang Strohband, would disagree. Strohband's partnership with Ullrich had petered out amicably post-2006 as Ullrich all but hid away and Strohband eased into retirement. In 2015, Strohband tells me, 'No one can take those wins away from Jan in his head; if they did officially, he wouldn't be a broken man.' Regardless, in the court of public opinion – insomuch as Ullrich experienced it on the road, via the pedalling brethren into which he was now re-immersing himself – he found unexpected comfort. As he reflected to Morten Okbo of *Rouleur* later, 'I couldn't understand it when the people turned against me. The media. I thought the media was the people. They're not. So when I came back out on the bike after those years, and when I met all the bike riders, I could see that they liked me.'

Ullrich's training rides with Wörndl were long, slow and full of laughter. They were followed by dinners where he could refill his plate or glass without a directeur sportif whispering into his ear and conscience. Even with only a few weeks of training before the Ötztaler, he managed to keep pace with the best riders on the Kühtai, the first monster climb on the route, before stopping to wait for Wörndl at the first feed station and again whenever anyone asked for an autograph. Despite these interruptions, he finished in a time of just over eight hours, only an hour after the winner.

Nier, Steeb and Ullrich slapped each other on the back and moved swiftly onto the next stage of operation relaunch, a provocative ad campaign for the shampoo brand Alpecin. Its slogan: 'Doping for the hair.'

The two topics – Ullrich and doping – remained indissociable, but the summer had confirmed to Nier and Steeb that leaning in was preferable to prolonging Ullrich's exile. The machinations of his legal case would rumble slowly on throughout the autumn and winter of 2011. The competent body in Ullrich's adoptive homeland, Swiss Olympic, ruled that their jurisdiction ended when he stopped racing, to which the UCI contended that in fact Operación Puerto was a second offence after his 2002 positive test, meaning he should be banned for life. Ullrich could do nothing – except finally start to take control of the narrative, tell his side of the story. Nier's gentlest of cajolements would turn into a long process of persuasion, with Ullrich finally agreeing to put himself through a series of mock interviews. Nier says the sessions revealed one thing: the TV interview they had in mind, possibly with either ZDF or ARD, would be another own goal, like his self-immolation on Reinhold Beckmann's talk show in 2007. 'I think he had also been scarred by that. He was authentic but it wasn't very polished or professional in some ways.'

So they would try a different tack. A print interview – but one that would be published this time, unlike the transcript of his meetings with the investigative journalist and TV personality Günter Wallraff in 2007. After allowing Sara to draft but never release a written confession in 2006, a few months later Ullrich had turned to Wallraff, who intended to document the 1997 Tour winner's come-to-Jesus moment in *Die Zeit*. The interviews were so secret that not even Wolfgang Strohband knew. 'One day Jan was supposed to be coming to see me in Hamburg, and I looked out of my office window and saw him getting out of Günter Wallraff's car. He told me they'd met three times. No idea what he'd told him.'

The result of their conversations also never made it to the news-stand, for Ullrich had got cold feet.

Now, four years later, at Nier's prompting, Ullrich began bearing his soul to another journalist who had made his name not collecting finish-line soundbites but reporting on elections and corporate fraud, Giuseppe Di Grazia of *Stern* magazine. Di Grazia travelled to Scherzingen and spent hours teasing out details that, Nier believed, would finally allow those who had condemned Ullrich to put his actions into their rightful context. They talked about Fuentes and doping, but also his childhood, his family, and his formative phases in Rostock, Hamburg and Berlin. 'I think there were a lot of details that would have made people really understand him,' says Nier.

The process ended up taking months. Meanwhile, the CAS verdict finally arrived in February 2012: the UCI's appeal was upheld . . . partly. Ullrich would be banned for two years, not life, and he would keep all results up to May 2005, the date from which there was clear evidence of his 'intensive' involvement with Eufemiano Fuentes. Ullrich also now admitted that relationship for the first time via a statement on his website. More important, he said, was that the ordeal was now over and he could 'look forward' to the rest of his life.

If only it were so simple. On 24 August 2012, the eve of that year's Ötztaler marathon, in which Ullrich was again due to take part, an old ghost returned to haunt him – Lance Armstrong. The USADA had concluded their investigation into Armstrong's alleged doping with the recommendation of a lifetime ban and the loss of all of his seven Tour de France titles. As the runner-up in three of those

Tours, Ullrich could now theoretically be considered a four-time champion, at least insofar as his results up to May 2005 remained officially if not morally intact.

Within hours, the German media had converged on Sölden. 'We arranged a little press conference, thinking there would be ten or fifteen Austrian crews, but every German channel turned up,' Nier remembers. They asked many questions but essentially got just one answer from a clearly uncomfortable Ullrich: in his eyes, Armstrong was still the winner because 'the race that mattered was the one that happened at the time'.

In fact, every one of the Tour's original podium finishers between 1999 and 2005 had now been found guilty of doping either during or after their careers, with the exceptions of Andreas Klöden, Fernando Escartín and Joseba Beloki. But a whole era had been desecrated. Hence, no one was surprised – and none of the aforementioned riders complained – when the Tour director Christian Prudhomme announced the 'Armstrong Tours' would remain winnerless.

When, in their Reasoned Decision a few months later, USADA called US Postal's 'the most sophisticated, professionalized doping programme ever', that definition not only seemed to overlook two decades of systematic, state-sponsored doping in the DDR, but also to gloss over what the overlords of cycling's biggest race had grudgingly acknowledged – next to none of its recent history was worth saving, including Ullrich's legacy. The fact that he had retained his place in the Tour's roll of honour owed not to a firm belief that his 1997 victory may have been clean; the Tour had simply taken the path of least embarrassment, as when they notionally stripped Bjarne Riis of his 1996 title following a belated confession . . . only to reinstate him a year later.

The story Ullrich had been telling Giuseppe Di Grazia could at least now complete its narrative arc. They met and talked for a final time in December 2012, *Stern* having slated the interview for publication in the New Year. As the date approached, though, Ullrich once again became anxious. Any notion that his sins were all forgotten received an ice-cold reality check from Armstrong – like so many of Ullrich's fantasies over the years. The American had lost almost his entire suite of personal sponsors on what he later called a 'brutal 75 million-dollar day'. Armstrong's cancer foundation ditched him shortly thereafter. All hope of a 'sweetheart deal' with USADA – a light penalty in return for useful evidence – had also been dashed in a fractious meeting in Colorado. One day in November, on his social media feeds, Armstrong had posted a photo of himself reclining in his Texan mansion, admiring the seven yellow jerseys framed on his wall. The message was one of defiance. The response was one of outrage.

Next, Armstrong retreated to Hawaii and weighed up his next move. He ordered an old friend to bag up all of his Nike sportswear, railed against USADA in private meals with friends – but also took tentative steps towards a previously unthinkable surrender. A conversation with an old friend, Oprah Winfrey, peeled back Armstrong's last reservations – and it was Oprah who would get the scoop. They sat face to face and the cameras rolled in Austin in the first week in January.

In Scherzingen, Ullrich's stress levels were spiking along with his alcohol consumption. Nier could sense his anxiety. And that he wasn't ready. Not to reveal his truth, nor for the consequences. Sure enough, Ullrich finally called Nier to request that *Stern* pull their article a few days before the publication date. At the time, he knew nothing of Armstrong's interview with Oprah.

Thus *Stern* went on sale, with no Jan Ullrich exclusive, on 12 January. And the next evening around 15 million people watched Oprah Winfrey asking Armstrong whether it was all true – the drugs, the lies, the bullying – and Armstrong tell her it was.

It now fell to Falk Nier to inform journalists that Ullrich hadn't even watched the Oprah interview and didn't want to comment beyond what he had told the news magazine *Focus*: 'I am certainly not going to go the same way as Armstrong and speak in front of an audience of millions of people.' He added that, as far as he was concerned, his and Armstrong's era belonged to ancient history and 'no longer has any influence on my life'.

So it was that a week supposed to finally begin the public rehabilitation of Jan Ullrich arguably delayed and jeopardized that process further. A long editorial in the *Frankfurter Allgemeine Zeitung* argued that even now, at his lowest ebb, Armstrong had left Ullrich trailing, for he at least had revealed a clear agenda, a path, a project. His 'I'm going to spend the rest of my life winning back people's trust' was, wrote Michael Eder, 'the sentimentally shaded printout of a clear calculation' – one that aimed to get him competing, earning and thriving once again. Meanwhile, Ullrich's paralysis prompted Eder to ask, and the rest of Germany with him, 'what does Jan Ullrich intend to do with the rest of his life?'

The same article made a further astute observation – that another area in which Ullrich had always lagged way behind Armstrong was in making enemies, and even that contributed to his current bind. The Armstrong investigation had relied heavily on the testimonies of individuals with axes to grind, whereas even in confessing their own cheating Ullrich's ex-comrades had taken great care to skirt around the issue of whether, how and when he had ever engaged in doping.

For a year there would be no prospect of that changing, or of anything else shaking him from his inertia until, in February of 2013, a French government commission gained access to the results of retroactive urine tests conducted on samples from the 1998 Tour de France for research purposes. A report was due to be published in July 2013. Meanwhile, the director of the Paris laboratory which had performed the 1998 re-tests told the commission that 'almost all' of the samples had tested positive for EPO.

Early in that summer of 2013, Falk Nier was getting married in Sardinia, with Ullrich among the guests. Nier took time out from rehearsing speeches and teasing flower arrangements to check in with his friend – or rather get something off his chest.

'Basically, there I told him that, with this Senate report coming, he didn't need a manager any more if he wasn't going to confess,' Nier remembers. 'I told him there was nothing for me to do any more. He could do a few things in Mallorca, some training camps with weekend riders or whatever, but there was nowhere to really go with any of it if he wasn't going to tell the truth. Our business relationship pretty much ended there.'

The Nier–Charly Steeb double act, which was itself about to fracture over an unrelated dispute, did take care of one last thing for Ullrich. The 2013 Tour de France would be the race's one hundredth edition and, to mark the anniversary, multiple major TV networks, magazines and newspapers had requested – and were granted – an interview with Germany's only winner. The news magazine *Focus* was the first to finally open the vault, Ullrich telling them that by doping he had simply been trying and, as it turned out, failing to

level the playing field, for it was now clear that Armstrong had bene-
fitted not only from the most high-tech drugs but also high-level
complicity on the part of the authorities.

Once more, there was no chorus of sympathy. On the contrary.
Ullrich's longest-standing critic, the microbiologist, Werner Franke,
now proclaimed him the 'world record holder of lying'.

In the contemporary peloton, too, there were groans. The best
German riders of the post-Ullrich generation were sick of a rider they
had once idolized but long since ceased to name among their heroes.
Now they faced a Tour de France in which, as the sprinter Marcel
Kittel said, 'all anyone will talk about is doping and not what we
achieve on the bike.' One German rider bedaubed as the national
saviour way back when he wore the yellow jersey for a day in 2007,
Linus Gerdemann, had temporarily quit the sport, partly in frustration at what he had described to me that spring. 'It felt like I'd been
sitting on a barstool talking to a German journalist about doping
every night for four years, but the conversation wasn't moving forward. The questions were still all the same.'

The new, would-be prophet Kittel took the first yellow jersey and
went on to win four stages. Tony Martin and André Greipel also
notched one each, making it Germany's most successful Tour since
the Ullrich era but far from its most watched, the state broadcasters,
ARD and ZDF, having binned their live coverage in 2012. The race's
sinking credibility in Germany was reflected in audiences that had
dropped from their 3.1 million average for live broadcasts in 2003
to 1.26 million in 2011. The ARD and ZDF bosses now also said it
was unlikely that live transmissions would resume any time in the
next few years.

The release of the French Senate report was finally delayed by a
few days, until the week after the Tour. But the bad news, yet more
of it, duly arrived: Ullrich's urine samples from the 1998 Tour were
'positive' for EPO, just like those of the race winner, Marco Pantani –
and those of Erik Zabel. After a first, untruthful confession in 2007,
Zabel had known what was coming – and dallied over a fuller admission for several days before finally summoning Andreas Burkert of
the *Süddeutsche Zeitung*. 'I'm the arsehole now,' he told Burkert. As
well as a mea culpa, though, Zabel's was a mournful ode to a period
and above all to a generation whom he had once envisioned growing
old like his eighty-year-old dad and his buddies, meeting up twice a

week and going on coffee rides. Instead, Zabel now glumly evoked a 'so-called generation of sinners' who, on the rare occasions when they had got together, showed each other their mobile phone displays before they said a word, to prove they weren't recording.

Some time, in fact years later, Zabel's reply to my interview request for this book suggested some wounds had healed while others never will. 'I went back over it all in 2013 to try to find closure. It was a good time overall but unfortunately, in retrospect, it was defined by the failings of my generation. That's the price we're paying. But it makes no sense to live in the past.'

In all, Falk Nier and Charly Steeb had spent two years trying and failing to catalyse the redemption of Jan Ullrich. In the end they stepped away with no hard feelings, but some frustrations and concerns.

'The lack of self-leadership was an issue, one hundred percent,' says Nier today. 'In a way it made it quite nice to work with him because we'd go to him with proposals and he's just say, "Ach, you know what's best for me, you decide." OK, Sara did a lot, but maybe she also did too much. She can't take on every role; she can't be wife, mother, secretary, manager – this never works. In the first few years after his career Sara did everything. Everything. When we started working together, it was hard for Jan to write emails. I remember once we had a long flight to Miami, and I used it to try to teach him a few basic things like how to respond to a letter. I think the first emails Jan ever wrote were when he started to work with us. Telekom also did absolutely everything for the riders. I remember checking into the hotel on that Miami trip and Jan asking me what he should wear the next day. It was a bit of a shock for someone like me who's used to tennis, where everyone organizes everything themselves. He wasn't very independent . . . He's a really nice, nice guy, with his heart in the right place, but you always needed to protect him.'

Nier's replacement was a goatee-bearded, slick-haired marketing agency director from Gütersloh, Ole Ternes. Just a few months older than Ullrich, Ternes partnered his client on bike rides and went with him on ski trips. He was fluent in marketing jargon, and could talk enthusiastically about 'repositioning the Jan Ullrich brand' and future book deals or even a biopic. Ternes was making some headway, notably signing Ullrich up to an endorsement deal with the upmarket apparel brand Rapha, when the next setback arrived in May 2014: a car crash a few kilometres from Scherzingen, caused by Ullrich's Audi smashing into the back of another vehicle stopped at a junction and spinning into another. Ullrich was relatively unhurt, but two of the passengers in the other vehicles needed hospital treatment. When word reached reporters from the Swiss tabloid *Blick* and they called to get Ullrich's version, he swore he had not been drinking and was travelling at 20 kph over the speed limit. 'These things can happen,' Ullrich said. In reality, Ullrich had been drinking with friends for much of the afternoon, was more than three times over the alcohol limit and somewhere between 52 kph and 63 kph over the 80 kph speed limit. The 'somewhere between' was significant, for anything over 60 kph would automatically mean jail time under Swiss law.

It would be more than three years, between assorted delays and disputes, before justice could be served. Finally, Ullrich was given a twenty-one-month sentence suspended for four years and a fine of 10,000 Swiss francs. Among the extenuating circumstances put forward by Ullrich's legal team was that, 'Mr Ullrich is an elite athlete. His body reacts differently to alcohol from other people's.'

While Ullrich was naturally relieved, others thought he had been lucky. Here was yet another stain on his image, a further reason for critics to either condemn or pity rather than forgive him. In 2014 he had also ridden tandem events with Matthias Kessler, the former T-Mobile teammate partially paralysed in a training crash four years earlier. But acts of philanthropy received minimal coverage compared to any news item re-emphasizing the established narrative. One journalist, Michael Ostermann, detected symptoms of what, in his view, is perhaps not just a German word but a national malaise, at least in the media: *Schadenfreude*. 'The public actually love Jan and show him that when he gets out there among them, but the lines of communication were broken because Jan stopped talking to the press and so did his friends and management, to protect him mainly. And the German media does tend to let people fall. Boris Becker also did some stupid things and you in Britain still love him, whereas in Germany he's just a joke. We don't see mistakes as charming; we love to take people down.'

This portrayal of Ullrich as a victim of an unforgiving,

bloodthirsty media has supporters, including Ullrich, who said to a sympathetic, nodding Becker in their made-for-TV bro-down in 2008, 'I still can't understand how they tear good people apart.' But in 2014 there were also those, like former teammate Rolf Aldag, who were struck less by the sadistic delight of reporters than Ullrich's umpteenth act of self-sabotage, at a time when judgements about his past may have been softening.

'You take the tabloid press, *Bild Zeitung*. They would love to have him back, celebrate him again, because for years the national treasures were Boris Becker, Michael Schumacher and Jan,' Aldag says. 'But then he does something like the car crash and they say it's clearly not the moment. I mean, just the way he dealt with that, and his PR people. "It shouldn't happen to a family man like me." It shouldn't happen to the binman! Drinking and driving is a pretty active thing. It's not like you're being hit by a thunderstorm.'

Infuriating, indefensible, seemingly incorrigible – and yet impossible to completely disown, for the part of the German psyche that identified a kindred spirit in the body of a physiological *Übermensch*. This paradox had perhaps been central to Ullrich's appeal from the start, as Aldag suggests. 'Zabel probably analysed it really well in 2004 or 2005. He said, "You know what, if I want to be a star like Jan, I should get divorced twice and go crazy . . ." Because that made Jan so popular in Germany.

'Erik was always perfection, and people don't love that, while every January, there's a photo of big fat Jan and a headline, "Dicker Jan", but what it really does is that common people read it and say, "See! He's having the same problems as me! Christmas was fucking shit, I had dinner with the family twice – that was three more kilos . . ." Then this fat guy goes and nearly wins the Tour de France. You know, you're the best bike rider in the world, and you run over twenty bikes with your 200,000 deutsche mark Porsche, that's kind of funny. People read it and think, you idiot, but, *ja*, that's Jan. And that really made him normal. Whereas Lance was totally different, totally impossible for most people to connect with. His girlfriend was from Hollywood, he's hanging out with Bono in his private planes . . . no one can connect with that as a fan. While Jan is one of 80 million Germans who are suffering here and there, having their good and bad times.'

*

On the twentieth anniversary of Jan Ullrich's Tour de France victory, the race returns to Germany for the first time since a 35-kilometre cameo in 2006. The 2017 edition of the race is to celebrate its Grand Départ in Düsseldorf – though the occasion is no homage to Ullrich, and indeed looks more like a version of the cult tragicomic film *Goodbye, Lenin!*, in which a woman in a coma in 1989 East Berlin regains consciousness after the Wall has fallen, and must be protected from finding out at all costs. Christiane Kerner's family ends up sealing her inside a private time capsule, in a parallel universe where capitalism (still) doesn't reign. Similarly, over a weekend in Düsseldorf, it is as though the Tour de France must be shielded and blinkered, lest it learn or be reminded of Jan Ullrich's existence.

Thomas Geisel, the mayor, has lured the Grande Boucle to the northern Rhine at a cost of nearly six million euros to the city and the same again to private sponsors. Geisel and the Tour organizers say they'll supercharge tourism and bike use while celebrating Germany's reconciliation with professional cycling after a decade in which the scene here – from teams to races to public interest and confidence – had dissolved to almost nothing.

On a weekend four months before the big day, Geisel reaffirms his pledge when we speak at a Saturday-morning event to drum up interest in the Tour among local schoolkids. To a question about Ullrich and whether he'll be welcome, Geisel responds, 'Everybody is welcome. Jan Ullrich is also welcome. As a Christian, I think that every rueful sinner has a second chance.'

There is a difference, though, between being 'welcome' and being honoured. Or even invited in any official capacity. The same weekend, over a coffee in the market square from which his race will roll out in July, the Tour chief Christian Prudhomme also seems, if not embarrassed when I broach the same subject, then at least reluctant to dwell. 'We're not particularly going to invite Jan Ullrich,' he says. 'We don't want to look back. But there's no acrimony. In Germany, even if roots are important, we mustn't forget what happened. We need to look forward. Regarding Ullrich specifically, I think he got caught in a spiral but had real, real qualities to be a champion.'

The politicking comes as no surprise, but something I hear on the same weekend stops me dead. A cluster of promotional stands on an esplanade overlooking the Rhine are publicizing the Tour's imminent arrival. I happen to be walking by when, at one of them, a gentleman armed with a megaphone is trying to whip up excitement among a small group of inquisitive locals.

'Who here knows the name of some German riders who'll be in the Tour de France?' he squawks.

Several seconds go by and no one as much as twitches. Laughing nervously, the MC decides to offer some assistance.

'OK, so what about Marcel Kittel, Tony Martin or John Degenkolb? And what about famous former German riders from the past? Who remembers the famous Telekom team? Names like Rolf Aldag, Jens Heppner . . .'

A former national hero is being extinguished, obliterated, cancelled before my eyes and ears. I am watching a real-life enactment of *Goodbye Ullrich!*

Even to German colleagues who saw a form of collective post-traumatic stress disorder take hold after 2006, the idea that Ullrich will be invisible come July seems realistic yet unfathomable. I find myself standing alongside Chris Hauke, the editor of *Procycling* magazine's German edition, while Geisel delivers another speech about the 'unique opportunity for Düsseldorf' in a packed town square. Hauke smiles meekly; he is also excited the city of his birth will welcome the sporting event that stole his heart, but, equally, taboos never sit easily, especially not with Germans.

'All of the new generation – the Kittels, Degenkolbs, the Martins – they all grew up watching and getting inspired by Ullrich and Zabel, so it's just weird Jan won't be there,' Hauke murmurs above the din. 'If the people here invite him to the Tour, they know that will just drag the conversation back to doping, and they would prefer just a bit of awkwardness, rather than that overshadowing the whole thing.'

Whether the same rationale would prevail elsewhere is a moot point. In traditional cycling powerhouses like Spain, Italy and Belgium, drug cheats are invariably condemned but almost never ostracized. Usually they return to competition or jobs in the media and their former place in fans' affections once their punishment is served. There is a tendency to attribute such willingness to cultural and religious stereotypes – Catholic precepts about sin and atonement – but a moral divide also exists between cycling's Old World and the sport's newer frontiers that owes partly to something else: the fact that, from the inception of drug testing in the 1960s to almost the end of the twentieth century, when the sport existed almost solely within the confines of Western Europe, doping was treated and sanctioned as a minor peccadillo, often with a suspension of no more than a few weeks or, at most, months.

Ben Johnson's positive test at the 1988 Olympics in Seoul (and some accompanying, implicitly racist coverage) was one event that contributed to heightening and changing sensibilities about illegal performance enhancement, as were revelations about state-sponsored doping behind the Iron Curtain. But it was cycling's Festina scandal in 1998 that caused a true paradigm shift, with its police raids, dripping syringes and the shocking realization that, in EPO, cycling had become hooked on a substance with the potential to upend whatever natural order was thought to exist. The World Anti-Doping Agency was created soon afterwards in acknowledgement that the game, or games, had changed – that sport had to get tougher on what were now no longer isolated acts of mischief but Frankenstein-ish, lucrative and sophisticated forms of treachery. Attitudes were remodelled accordingly, except in places with an entrenched professional cycling tradition and the less proud habit of overlooking, forgiving and minimizing doping. Germany had no such heritage, none of the same attachment to the sport's pockmarked history. As Zabel had already suggested in 1997, it had been a Jan Ullrich boom, not a cycling boom. And so it was now a Jan Ullrich bust.

But there was also something perhaps distinctly German in the way Ullrich had been not just cast aside but seemingly erased. As though his sins were in fact a mark of a nation's shame, an evil that had to be purged, scoured like an ulcer from Germany's own flesh. Germans, of course, have a word for this process of, if not self-excoriation, then at the least the rigorous exercise of reflection, recognition and atonement for the atrocities committed during the Second World War and the abuses of the SED dictatorship in the East. The endowments of this *Vergangenheitsbewältigung* are everywhere in modern-day Germany: in government texts, the monuments of every town, the almost daily headlines about the unmasking of some SS guard or Stasi informant, a whole sub-genre of literature and visual arts and, for inhabitants of Berlin or other major cities, literally on the pavements where we tread in the form of *Stolpersteine* – the little brass plates outside the former homes of SS victims, engraved with their names and how and when they met their death.

As the only journalist working for a major TV network anywhere in the world employed solely to report on doping, one could argue that Hajo Seppelt is himself a product of *Vergangenheitsbewältigung*, albeit one of its subtler offshoots. Seppelt agrees: when we meet in London in 2015, he says that ARD's decision to give him this unique mandate is in itself revealing. He believes that an inbuilt sense of national guilt after the Second World War in particular has, besides certain negative consequences, instilled in modern Germany a thirst for moral self-inquiry that may be unique in the world.

'Germans are very good at punishing themselves. In fact, we are world champions in that,' Seppelt explains. 'For example, the way we dealt with the whole issue of the Stasi files, the commitment to transparency, was an example for the rest of the world. I'm not a patriot, absolutely not, but this was very good, because you can only create something for the future if you learn from the past. I think the very, very bad experience we had with the Second World War created this sense that we had to be more conscious, more sensitive than other nations. You see it with the way we deal with so many things, from nuclear energy, to Israel, to other conflicts in the world. And you also see it with the way we reacted to Ullrich and the Telekom scandal.'

A simple sense of conscience and responsibility or a crippling moral prudishness bordering on sanctimony? Whatever it was, come July 2017, the reflex contributed to keeping Ullrich well away from VIP enclosures, celebration dinners and indeed all official ceremonies and events. In May, his surprise appointment as the race director of the Rund um Köln – followed four days later by his withdrawal – had served as a portent; the main broadcast rights holder for that race, WDR, had reacted so unfavourably to Ullrich's involvement that it became an impossibility.

Wounded by that experience, Ullrich decided to keep himself well away from Düsseldorf, although he could be found, and was by several journalists, at the side of the road in the little town of Korschenbroich, 75 kilometres down the route of stage two. Korschenbroich's mayor, Marc Venter, had reached out because no one more than Ullrich 'embodied the highs and lows of professional cycling in the last twenty years,' he said. Ullrich also proved to be a good and jovial guest, smiling and clapping as the peloton swished by. Later,

Venter called him onto a stage and a chorus of 'Ulle, Ulle!' echoed through the old town. When he was signing autographs, one elderly lady insisted on giving him a hug. Upon hearing about the Tour organizers snubbing his old rival, Lance Armstrong had pointed out that other convicted dope cheats worked on the race every year in prominent roles. 'Fuck ASO,' Armstrong hissed on social media. Meanwhile, Ullrich said it was 'all less dramatic than everyone had made out'. He could have gone to Düsseldorf, he insisted, but he wanted to be with his daughter, Sarah Maria, who was celebrating her fourteenth birthday.

He left Korschenbroich feeling heartened, accepted, even loved – just not by the kingmakers that Armstrong had also decried. Having publicly maligned the legacy of Ullrich and his generation for many years, now even the new crop of German riders, led by Kittel, said they disliked the way he was being treated. Times were a-changing, clearly. One day in the autumn of 2015, Sara and Jan had also taken the sudden decision to relocate from Switzerland to Mallorca; they were on one of their frequent walks on the Bodensee shore, huddled in their jackets, the hills around them submerged in fog, when they had begun asking themselves what was actually keeping them in Switzerland. They had many friends in Mallorca, as most wealthy Germans do, and the island was brimming with exactly the kind of cyclotourists who would pay handsomely to train or spend time with Jan. They also both liked the idea of immersing their three children in a new language and culture. Nine months later the family moved into their new home – a seven-bedroom, 500-square-metre villa with a swimming pool and an elaborate, landscaped garden dotted with sculptures, between Establiments and Esporles, fifteen minutes north-west of Palma.

They planned to suck it and see for one year, but by the summer of 2017 they were no longer sure if they would ever leave. The kids were settling in at school and becoming fluent in Spanish and English. Sara was also back in the classroom, studying holistic health and nutrition. Soon she would be raving to friends about a business idea that would surely keep both her and Jan busy – a health food and bike cafe where Jan could be a kind of maharishi in residence, riding with customers in the morning and spending afternoons dispensing tips and stories from the good old days over lattes and green juices. Jan's friend, Guido Eickelbeck, another former German pro, thought the cafe could be a goldmine. Meanwhile, Casa Ullrich was already spilling over with friends, children, toys and pets – 'like a scene from *Pippi Longstocking'* as one journalist who visited Ullrich, Johannes Krayer, wrote in the *Mallorca Zeitung*. Another reporter and long-time confidant, Philippe Le Gars of *L'Équipe*, flew in to interview Ullrich in June 2017 and came agonizingly close to cracking him open; the conversation meandered from the safe harbour of small talk to the brink of a soul-bearing confession, with Ullrich volunteering his memories of Fuentes and how he had trusted the doctor. Then Sara appeared on the terrace and reminded her husband of what they had agreed – that this topic was and would remain off-limits. It was time to face forwards, not back.

Throughout the summer, either side of the Tour, Ullrich reconnected with old teammates and other cycling buddies at charity events, conferences and training camps in Switzerland, Germany and back in Mallorca. Cycling was balsam for the spirit but, in Ullrich's case, not for a creaking, overstretched body: a cyst on his left knee, his 'good' one for most of his career, had flared up on rides over the summer and eventually stopped him riding altogether.

He would need an operation in mid-September and chose Erich Rembeck, a Munich-based specialist and Boris Becker's long-time doctor, to do it. The surgery was a success in that Rembeck did the necessary repair; it was disastrous in the sense that, according to a story later published by *Die Welt*, soon after the operation Ullrich lay surrounded by empty whisky and wine bottles and ashtrays brimming over with cigarette butts.

Not long later Sara was deciding that she and the children would move back to Germany. One of Ullrich's friends in Mallorca tells me this created two unbridgeable voids in his life. 'He says that he has attention deficit hyperactivity disorder [ADHD] and, if he can't work out, he has to move on to other stuff. The combination of the two things was disastrous.'

Others and Ullrich himself would argue that losing both his wife and his children is enough to send any man over the edge. To a devoted father like Ullrich, it was a doomsday far worse than Strasbourg in 2006.

'No one has a more badly scarred heart than me,' he would say one day that summer.

*

Reports of how Jan Ullrich had spent the evening of 3 August 2018 shocked and bewildered everyone except the few dozen friends with whom he had been in regular contact throughout the summer. For several weeks, he had been bombarding them with videos on Whats-App, sometimes at a rate of over a hundred a day, beckoning them through the keyhole of his new-found bachelordom on the island paradise known to Germans simply as 'Malle'. He sent so many of the clips that most of the recipients had stopped opening them, because they were horrified, not bored. The incessant notifications on his old mate Matthias Kessler's phone were keeping him up at night.

In one home video that later leaked to the German media, Ullrich filmed himself staggering around his empty villa, visibly drunk or high, alternating deranged boasts with dark laments about his dire predicament. He claimed to have set a new world record by smoking 999 cigarettes in nine hours. It was no doubt an exaggeration, although the rasp in his voice did make one wonder.

His ravings about old friends who could now 'lick his arse' fore-shadowed a text message that many of them had received on that same, eventful 3 August. The missive invited them to be grateful he hadn't 'gone the way of Cat Stevens and decided to call myself Ysufu'. He signed off on a tender, but emphatic note – he 'loved them all' despite their 'pessimistic predictions' about his future. For years he had lived an 'ascetic existence'. Now he wished they would 'leave him alone to enjoy his life'.

One member of his old support network in Mallorca says that one thing was abundantly clear: 'There was absolutely no way Jan wrote that.'

The inference – that he would now wilfully vanish from their lives – also turned out not to be true. For, within twenty-four hours, upon turning on their TVs and phones, they discovered that Ullrich had been arrested for breaking into the back garden of Til Schweiger, the much-loved yet also much-derided star of films like *Inglourious Basterds*, and Germany's most successful export to Hollywood. Schwei-ger was having a party to celebrate the end of filming on his latest project, *Honey in the End*, but Ullrich wasn't invited. In fact, it wasn't the first time that Ullrich had showed up unannounced at Schwei-ger's island hacienda that week, the actor told *Bild*. Or even the second. One day he had appeared suddenly in Schweiger's hallway and berated his neighbour for not telling him that he was home. A few hours later Ullrich was back, this time grabbing a fistful of Schweiger's hair and imploring the film star to 'Hit me! Hit me!' The next day, it was Schweiger visiting Ullrich. 'Get help,' Schweiger told him. Also: 'I don't want to see you on my property again.'

But within hours, Ullrich was trying to break in once more, finally leaving in tears after half an hour of negotiation with Schweiger through a locked door.

Then came Friday, the day of Schweiger's party. The gathering had decanted into the pool house, where, in happier times, Schweiger and Ullrich would kick back and watch Bundesliga games. Now Schweiger was showing his guests a music video when suddenly Ullrich's teetering, disorientated silhouette loomed behind them. According to Schweiger's account, Ullrich immediately lunged at one of Schweiger's friends with a broomstick, prompting Schweiger to call the police. Within minutes, a team of Policía Nacional officers was pouring onto the property. They would be there interviewing witnesses for several hours.

Ullrich was handcuffed and taken to a cell in Palma, where he would spend the night and most of the next day. Late the following afternoon, he stepped out of a police van and through the doors of one of Palma's main courthouses with four other detainees. By now, paparazzi and other emissaries of the German media's formidable Mallorcan colony had descended, prompting Ullrich to cover his face with a makeshift white shroud. He emerged later having been given a restraining order stipulating that he was no longer allowed within fifty metres of Schweiger, or to contact him electronically. 'I just want to go home now and to be left in peace,' he told the waiting reporters. Alas, within hours of him returning to his villa, the *Diario de Mallorca* would be publishing photos of him staggering across its tiled-roof.

Some months later, a few blocks from where Ullrich spent his night in police custody in Palma, I meet one of the adopted locals who knew and had become close to him and his family long before his 2018 summer breakdown. The friend prefers not to be named. They say they do not want to overplay their role trying to pull Ullrich out of the mire. Moreover, several months on, Ullrich's equilibrium remains delicate.

What the friend will tell me on a sunny December morning is that the events of early August were a surprise only insomuch as they and other friends of Ullrich had feared much worse for some time. A second knee operation in six months in February had been supposed to put Ullrich back on his bike – one of the only places he could free his mind. Instead, those who visited him after the surgery in Munich found him in a sorry state. A fond Easter tradition existed among the Ullrichs' Mallorca set – a brunch or lunch where families got together, the kids could play and the adults could guiltlessly embody a non-dom, island-life cliché, with its linen shirts, Breitling watches and endless conversations about housekeepers and international schools. Although everyone in the group knew about the Ullrichs' recent issues, they were pleased to discover that Sara and the kids would be joining them as usual and that Jan would also be there.

But Ullrich didn't show up to the Easter brunch. When, over the subsequent weeks, mutual friends told Sara how they would try to help her husband, she sounded grateful but demoralized. April was bad, May worse. Not that Ullrich necessarily agreed. One night he was eating in a restaurant in Palma when he spotted a pretty brunette at another table and sent over some flowers. A month later, the girl had moved into his villa in Establiments. She was thirty-four, Cuban, a former waitress. Her name was Elizabeth Napoles Prado.

The friend of Ullrich's that I meet in Palma says that Napoles seemed like a good influence – 'the only person in the house not doing drugs and drinking'. Ullrich showered her with gifts, but her affection seemed genuine, her intentions pure. Other acquaintances are less complimentary about the collection of rum characters who were increasingly casting a spell over Ullrich as spring turned to summer. A former pro rider named Jan Bratkowski arrived in mid-June and immediately assigned himself the role of Ullrich's personal trainer – as numerous videos later uploaded to Bratkowski's Facebook page demonstrate. In one we see a skeletal Ullrich in denim shorts and a trucker's cap woozily doing sit-ups on his pool terrace while the bald, muscular Bratkowski paces back and forth cajoling him. In another, Bratkowski plunges terrifyingly down a flight of outdoor steps on a mountain bike. Ullrich at one point tried to copy him and reportedly injured himself in the process.

Like Ullrich, Bratkowski had been hailed as a German cycling prodigy in the early 1990s, but became a journeyman misfit, more notorious than he was famous or successful. John Wordin, the manager of the US-based Mercury Mannheim team who signed Brat-kowski in 2000, will not forget him. Wordin's buyer's remorse kicked in roughly when Bratkowski was interrupting a group ride at the team's Los Angeles training camp to park his bike outside the front gates of Tommy Lee and Pamela Anderson's Mulholland Drive man-sion and beg her to come out. Or when, says Wordin, he rode solo, in full team kit, into the Chatsworth neighbourhood – otherwise known as the world capital of the porn industry – and demanded an audition at an adult film studio.

A row with a hotel receptionist about the 'quality' of the in-room entertainment at one race later in the season, whether real or apoc-ryphal, inspired Bratkowski's teammate Floyd Landis to pen a haiku: 'I don't pay for this. The titties are much too small. And the dicks are shit.'

John Wordin says that Bratkowski's Mercury career ended a few weeks later, when Wordin 'literally kicked him out of the car at a train station somewhere' midway through the Tour of Switzerland due to anomalies in his blood-test results that were highly indicative of doping. 'We knew what his natural values were,' Wordin says, 'so I told him his ass was fired and I never wanted to see him again.'

Bratkowski would race for a few more years before reinventing himself – as a kite-surfing instructor, then a sportswear impresario selling T-shirts and caps adorned with slogans like 'No Doping – No Fun – No Coca – No Party – No Porn'. Somehow, he had now also become one of Jan Ullrich's new gurus. This despite Bratkowski's own reckoning with the law in August 2018 – the announcement of his eighteen-month suspended prison sentence for fourteen counts of fraud arising from his latest gig, selling bikes and fitness equipment in Treuchtlingen in northern Bavaria.

The former ice hockey player Stefan Blöcher was another main-stay of Mallorca's German jet set and part of the old support network who despaired of Ullrich's 'new life'. Blöcher told *Die Welt* Ullrich would reach for an air rifle whenever, in the grip of his assorted paranoias, he thought he was being observed or in some way scru-tinized by a face that flashed onto his TV screen. He would then pepper the screen with pellets, destroying 'two or three TVs a week'.

One person could in fact 'spy' on Ullrich. *Stern* magazine reported that Sara had access to the villa's CCTV footage via an app on her phone. Whether she wanted to observe her old family home degenerate into the hellhole visitors later described – part frat house, part halfway house – was another question. Old friends couldn't fathom exactly who some of the now seemingly semi-permanent lodgers were or how Ullrich had become entangled with them. There was Bratkowski, but also one of his friends, a heavily tattooed, Ferrari-driving habitué of strip and boxing clubs from Schweinfurt in Bavaria, who in 2014 had been convicted of violent crimes. A passion for 'adult entertainment' appeared to be one common denominator between this pair and Richard Steiner. Born in Yugoslavia, Steiner had joined the French Foreign Legion as a young man and served time in a Brazilian jail, where, aptly, he claimed to have been enlightened by reading *Crime and Punishment* by Dostoevsky. More recently, Steiner had become well-known in Austria for two things: a bestselling memoir about his journey, as he put it, from 'red-light king to Buddhism', and a 2013 criminal trial in which he stood accused of exercising a 'reign of terror' over Vienna's bars, brothels and nightclub scene. The manhunt leading to Steiner's arrest had been the most expensive police operation in Austria's history, though resulted in only a modest conviction: a three-year, non-custodial sentence for tax evasion.

That was October 2013. Four-and-a-half years later, Steiner was enlisted by Guido Eickelbeck to transform Jan Ullrich in the same way that Steiner had supposedly transformed himself. A tattoo on Steiner's shoulder – 'Omertà' – augured poorly. Nonetheless, Steiner attempted a strong-arm 'detox'. But not even he could do much beyond keeping Ullrich alive.

There were indeed those among Ullrich's true friends who, far from lamenting the public nature of the Til Schweiger incident, considered it a blessing. Guido Eickelbeck, Charly Steeb and even Schweiger himself had come to believe that only force or law enforcement could help Ullrich. On the one occasion when Steeb and Eickelbeck succeeded in bringing him to a rehab clinic in Palma, he stayed around five minutes, the time it took for receptionists to produce an admission form. His mother flew in from Rostock and was rebuffed in much the same way, Ullrich 'kicking her out after two days', as one witness put it. Steeb and Eickelbeck feared that Ullrich quite simply wouldn't make it through the summer.

*

A month after Jan Ullrich's impromptu, forced entry to the Schweiger compound, I am standing outside the front gate of his villa in Establiments, on the spot where, a few days after the incident, a wild-eyed, bare-chested Ullrich angrily faced down a camera crew reporting on the latest stage of his meltdown.

Today, the property seems deserted behind its high walls. The label on the letterbox says 'Fam U', but reads like a forlorn rebuttal of what I know to be true – that the domestic idyll once created here has now been shattered.

Any doubt about that was erased by Ullrich's *hebdomas horribilis* – the infernal week that began in Schweiger's back garden and would end for Ullrich in the direst circumstances in Frankfurt. He had travelled to Germany on a private jet arranged for him by another of his dubious acquaintances, a gentleman referred to in the German press, for legal reasons, only as Gerd K. This individual, believed to be in his early fifties, had befriended Ullrich a few months earlier and was now giving him financial advice. Specifically, Ullrich's friends say that Gerd K persuaded him to shell out 18,000 euros on a 'nano wave' machine designed to diagnose and treat health problems that were either undetectable or untreatable by conventional means. Ullrich swore by it, just as he believed Gerd K's claim that Ullrich could double or triple his money if he sold the old family pile in Scherzingen and reinvested in cryptocurrency. Now, in mid-August, Ullrich had reportedly signed over complete control of his finances to the mystery friend.

Gerd K claimed to have Ullrich's best interests at heart; from Frankfurt they headed straight to a rehab clinic, where Ullrich would finally be able to reset. In Palma, he had alarmed airport staff with his bizarre behaviour – compulsively jumping on the spot while smoking three or more cigarettes at once. Now he was to spend his final hours of 'freedom', the twilight of his 'old' life, in Frankfurt's Villa Kennedy Hotel – and it was from there that he would leave the following morning, bound not (yet) for the Betty Ford Clinic in Bad Brückenau but, as it transpired, another police station. This time Ullrich had been accused not of trespassing but something much, much worse: in the early hours, some time after being ordered from the Kennedy's 'JFK' bar, Ullrich had allegedly physically attacked a woman whom every paper and news bulletin was referring to as a prostitute. Ullrich had been under the influence of drugs and alcohol, hence could not immediately be interviewed by police.

The alleged victim was able to give her full account to the police – and a few days later to the television network RTL. She identified herself as 'Brandi' and was thirty-one years old. Ullrich or his minders had hired her via the Diamond Escort website. Her eyes hidden behind dark glasses, her facial features pixelated and her voice electronically altered, she described being led to Ullrich's suite by one of his friends or associates and realizing after a first glance around the room that the party had long since started. Things progressed relatively normally for an hour or more until she took a moment to telephone and wake her young son. When the call ended, it was evident that Brandi was dealing with a different Jan Ullrich. She claimed Ullrich became violent and told her never to utter the word 'son' again. She was finally able to wrestle away and alert a member of the hotel staff, who promptly called the police.

From the police station, an ambulance took Ullrich to the Hohe Mark psychiatric clinic for a compulsory examination. Then, reluctantly, a few hours later he was driven to the Betty Ford addiction centre in Bad Brückenau that had been his original, intended destination. When they heard that Ullrich had been released from police custody, some of his friends in Mallorca were aghast. 'We all said, OK, great, now he's in custody and therefore he's safe,' says one of them, 'but they let him out of there when it was obvious the guy was out of his mind.'

Ullrich's complicated relationship with alcohol had been an open secret for years. What few outside his inner circle knew was that he had also become reliant on an amphetamine derivative which a doctor had prescribed years earlier for Ullrich's hyperactivity. Recently he had been taking as many as fifteen pills a day, Elizabeth told *Stern* – and by his own admission supplementing that with cocaine. His choice, he had told friends – 'My life is rock 'n' roll. Ozzy Osbourne, David Bowie, Iggy Pop . . . and Jan.' He didn't mention, but they had all witnessed, the less romantic side effects – the headsplitting insomnia and violent mood swings.

In the scramble to apportion blame, tender pity or just to understand, one of the more provocative contributions came from someone who did not know Ullrich personally but felt as though she had heard a version of his story many times before. Like Ullrich, Ines

Geipel was born in the DDR, selected for a KJS sports school at four-teen and went on to make sporting history as a quarter of a world record-breaking 4 x 100-metre DDR team in 1984. Where Geipel and Ullrich differed was in the way they looked back on their respective careers, Geipel having disowned hers on the basis that her achievements were chemically enhanced beyond reasonable com-parison. She had also embraced a new life as an acclaimed author and, for five years, the chairwoman of the Doping Opfer Hilfe – the organization set up to support and compensate victims of doping in the former DDR, whose offices I visited in late 2015.

Now, Geipel was struck by something about 'Generation Jan Ull-rich' that the author Mark Scheppert had also profiled – children of the DDR who had been teenagers when the Wall came down. They were well represented in some jarring, cautionary tales in recent German history: Robert Enke, the football goalkeeper who commit-ted suicide in 2009; Lutz Bachmann, another footballer and later the founder of the populist, far-right Pegida movement; other notorious figures of a similar political orientation to Bachmann. They were also numerous among the sick and crestfallen individuals that Geipel had been meeting for years at the DOH. 'They sat there and talked about what you'd call disorientation and being uprooted,' she wrote in the *Frankfurter Allgemeine Zeitung*. 'They know a lot about radical self-deception, lacking identity, emptiness, scars and erosion. All a kind of oblivion in which boundaries can melt away.'

Geipel didn't know – and it has never been firmly established* – whether Ullrich was, like her, a victim of State Planning Theme 14.25, an unwitting consumer of Oral Turinabol. But, while the DOH had for years been collecting evidence about the long-term neurological side effects of stimulants and steroids, she had also observed a form of existential rewiring that occurred irrespective of the athlete's

---

* On the record, Ullrich has always maintained that he received no more than flavoured sugar-cubes in the guise of performance-enhancement at Dynamo Berlin. Acquaintances have stated that, privately, he has shared quite different memories with them, but these claims seem speculative. Evidence for the systematic doping of teenaged endurance cyclists in the DDR has thus far been scarce, despite occasional, anonymous first-hand accounts like the one reported by Dr Achim Schmidt in the 2007 book *Doping Im Radsport* edited by Ralf Meutgens. The former track cyclist Uwe Trömer has also spoken at length about the dire consequences he suffered when he was unwittingly doped by a DDR doctor in 1983. Trömer has campaigned for and received financial compensation thanks to the Doping Opfer Hilfe.

particular poison. Again, it was to do with blurred lines – the creation of an inner mythology whereby a developing, perhaps already fractured sense of self became untethered from the developing body and medal-laden simulacrum. Eventually, when the spotlight went out, the parts somehow had to be rejoined – and for many this was too much to bear. Often it turned into a battle, said Geipel, 'between the original and the denial of the original'.

With one winner and, maybe in Ullrich's case in the summer of 2018, one clear loser.

Towards the end of Jan Ullrich's first week at the Betty Ford Clinic in Bad Brückenau, I receive a message in the middle of the night from Lance Armstrong. He assumes I'm following 'the Jan Ullrich situation'. Evidently, Armstrong has been aware since the early summer that Ullrich is spiralling, based mainly on messages from Ullrich himself. Now, Armstrong wants to help and, he tells me, has just landed in Germany. He hopes I keep that to myself for the moment. Nonetheless, in a few hours, on his social media feeds, he'll be posting the first picture of Ullrich in rehab, smiling and flanked by . . . Armstrong and Frank Wörndl.

Later, Armstrong will admit to being shocked by what he found. 'It was like his body had been taken over by an alien.'

Soon, there are other visitors to Bad Brückenau. A crew from RTL, whose peek behind the scenes of Ullrich's rehab is also far from reassuring. They film him manically doing press-ups, pull-ups and hitting a punchbag, then answering questions about his problems, the incident in Frankfurt and his future. He tells them it's wrong to call him a drug addict – that he has too much energy and amphetamines simply help to bring him down, like 'sleeping pills' for 'normal people'. In Frankfurt he 'didn't hurt anyone'. That his accuser was a prostitute shouldn't be a compounding charge or indeed anyone else's business, he said. His wife had left him and broken his heart. Plus, his new girlfriend, Elizabeth, had no objections. 'I need sex,' he said.

Hearing this, his friends back in Mallorca were understandably concerned. They believed the Betty Ford Clinic afforded too many freedoms – for instance to escape to the next-door Dorint Hotel, with all of its temptations, and to receive visitors who were less concerned with Ullrich's recovery than Armstrong and Wörndl.

The Betty Ford programme was also short. By the first week of September Ullrich was back in Mallorca with Elizabeth and Jan Bratkowski. He had plans to fly to Cuba with Elizabeth to meet her family, then travel to the United States to begin another stint in rehab. Meanwhile, he continued drinking and was again accused of lashing out at a photographer who approached him on a night out with Elizabeth. Adding to his sense of being followed, hounded, hunted was the fact that his villa had been broken into three times while he was undergoing treatment in Bad Brückenau.

Armstrong had wanted Ullrich to go next to a detox facility in Colorado, near Armstrong's Aspen home, but, finally, midway through October, Ullrich put his fate in the hands of another individual referred to in the German press only by his initials – who also forcefully requested not to be named in this book. The man was once a cyclist himself, but had since plotted a mazy, enigmatic career path on the fringes of the showbusiness world, often posing in photographs taken in exotic locations beside sports stars and world leaders. Now he was accompanying Ullrich from Germany to Miami – though not before Ullrich had allegedly attacked a waiter in Hamburg airport as he prepared to board his flight. The waiter had reported the alleged assault to police, who announced that they had started an investigation. Another friend of Ullrich's who had been with him at the time of the incident said that he had simply tried to give the waiter an exuberant hug.

On the flight itself, via London Heathrow, Ullrich had taken selfies with the crew and been recognized by fellow passengers. 'Stay strong! You can do it!' one American gentleman told him, clasping his hand around Ullrich's as they boarded. Ullrich smiled and nodded without making eye contact.

A few hours later he was checking into one of the most exclusive hotels in Miami, the Philippe Starck-designed Delano, ready for the start of his therapy the following day.

Jan Ullrich would not be pictured in public again for three more years.

Epilogue

The journey from Freiburg's main train station to Merdingen can be easily split into three parts, each of them no more than five kilometres or a few minutes by car: the first, a Queen's Gambit through the chessboard of the city's outer fringes, between glistening office blocks a few hundred metres in distance but centuries in architectural style from the half-timbered splendour of the Altstadt; the second, flat and straight westward, skirting the vast wooded expanse of the Freiburger Rieselfeld; and the third and last stretch, beginning in pretty little Opfingen, into a dreamy mini-verse of gently rolling hills dotted with vines and farmhouses bedecked with geraniums, and foregrounded by the larger outlines of the Black Forest's mountains.

Finally, a church spire appears, the whole village unfurls in the valley floor and the road dips to meet it. Jan Ullrich's first address in Merdingen was a little further down the same main street, just beyond the town hall, in a large gabled house belonging to Gaby Weis's parents. He later had a new property built a few blocks away before moving to Switzerland in late 2002. And now, two decades on, for reasons that even many who know him can't quite explain, Ullrich has returned to this oasis where he spent his most fruitful professional years.

The exact timing and motivation of Ullrich's return here sometime late in 2018 may be shrouded in mystery but Merdingen's appeal is there for all to see. The climate is the best in Germany and, sure enough, when I visit in the first week of March 2022, thatched roofs covered with solar panels sparkle like the edges of dazzling gemstones. 'Sleepy' seems an apt description – yet Merdingen has enough of a pulse not to feel isolated, dead or forgotten: three or four hairdressers; one cafe, a restaurant and a bakery; a large Rewe supermarket on the road that points towards the French border ten kilometres away; a variety of cars and houses that suggests the population nowadays is more white collar than brown overalls, despite the village's ancient winemaking tradition; swarms of children of all ages that disgorge from school buses halfway through the afternoon. A place, in short, where one could comfortably hide, recharge, reset without cutting the cord – either to the life already lived or the one that lies ahead.

One thing that has remained a constant in Merdingen over several decades is the Gasthof Keller. Its owner, Erich Keller, is himself a kind of institution. He orchestrated Ullrich fever in the 1990s, creating the first fan club and organizing the annual coach trips to the Alps, Pyrenees and Champs-Élysées. Now in his early seventies, he looks back on those years through misty eyes, telling me bluntly, 'They were the best times of my life.'

Certainly here, in March 2022, it must all seem terribly distant. Today at lunchtime the 'Jan Ullrich Platz' that doubles as a car park is deserted and the Gasthof's rooms are all empty. Soon, groups will start to arrive – cycling clubs and junior teams drawn by the weather, the climbs and the pristine tarmac that once lured Jan Ullrich. But Erich doesn't know how many more summers it'll all last. Three years ago, he lost his beloved wife to a heart attack. Nowadays, tourists also want different things. English, for example, which Erich doesn't speak. In fact, a friend who has interviewed Keller in recent weeks 'warns' that I may also find his Badisch dialect a struggle to understand. When I relay this, Erich cackles. He assures me he'll try to speak 'proper German'.

He says that Merdingen itself has also changed over the years. Once, to find a neighbour at any hour between dawn and dusk, the best place to look would be out in the vineyards. 'Hardworking folk . . . politically normal folk,' Erich says. He used to know everyone, or least it felt that way. 'But more and more are moving in,' he says, noting that the population now exceeds two thousand and would be much bigger if all of the planning applications were granted. He can understand them; Erich also says he never wants to leave. Even in March he can be skiing on the Feldberg in half an hour or on the Ballon d'Alsace in the French Vosges in forty minutes. And the cycling is paradise. Which is why, he reminds me, Ullrich came in the first place.

If there is an image, a memory that returns most vividly to his mind's eye, it is of those early summer days when Ullrich's focus would laser in on the Tour, and Erich would help to get him ready. Peter Becker's arrival would usually signify that the operation was about to enter its commando phase. Sometimes, Becker would hold court with journalists in the Gasthof's dining room – and Erich says with a chuckle that you could hear everything Becker said from the car park. At other times it was just Jan and Erich out in the hills, Jan aboard his Pinarello, Erich pacing him on a moped. Mornings in the mountains, then afternoons speeding down the Rhine from Breisach towards Basel, 'because there's not a single town and two junctions in sixty kilometres'. On that stretch, Ullrich would take a hand off his bars and signal to Erich to go faster, faster, until they hit 80 kph. 'You get to that speed and you're no longer talking about a human being; it's a machine,' Keller purrs.

Yes, those days may be long gone, but still Erich was delighted when, one day three years ago, he discovered that Jan was back and living in the village. In the two decades since he'd left he'd still been a regular visitor, mainly to see his daughter, Sarah Maria. Keller had also dropped in on Ullrich at his new 'home' in Switzerland. But as everyone dealt in their own way with the events of 2006 and their aftermath, so some relationships that had been knitted around Ullrich and his success survived while others frayed or broke. At times, like when a decision was made – Erich doesn't remember precisely when or by whom – to take down the 'Welcome to Merdingen: home of Jan Ullrich' sign greeting road users arriving from Freiburg, he thought that maybe some people in Merdingen had lost their minds, or at least that they were overreacting. But then he could also see how personally they took the affront, how deeply they felt let down. Some of the most disappointed were members of the fan club.

Now he doesn't see Ullrich every day or even every week in the village, but he seems to think his old friend is in good hands, and certainly in the right place to find himself again. Once Ullrich had Wolfgang Strohband, who sadly died in October 2021, to act as a filter, a buffer, a protector. That role has been taken by one of Ullrich's first friends in Merdingen, a jovial, now forty-something ex-German motorcycle-racing champion named Mike Baldinger. Erich has known Baldinger for longer than he can remember. A few months ago Keller also met another of the pillars in the life Ullrich is rebuilding – his girlfriend Elizabeth, who eventually moved with him from Mallorca. Other locals who have met her are impressed that she is learning German. 'A Cuban,' Erich says thoughtfully. He thinks she seems perfectly nice.

In the past three years a lot else has certainly happened, both within Ullrich's world and its wider orbit. Early in 2020, while almost total silence reigned about Ullrich's location and health beyond that he was 'in the Black Forest and doing better', Rudy Pevenage published his own autobiography and revealed further lurid details about the Ullrich years – despite telling me in 2015 that he would never commit his memories to print. Pevenage invited old pals to a launch evening near his home – and Eufemiano Fuentes sent a typically chortling, roguish video message to congratulate his old chum 'Rudicio'. The clip was projected on a screen and provoked gasps and laughter in the audience. Ullrich also sent a message, though Pevenage later admitted that Ullrich wasn't exactly thrilled with the book's revelations. Johan Bruyneel, too, was unimpressed with what he saw as Pevenage's belated stab at self-justification. In a follow-up interview with the Belgian daily *Het Laatste Nieuws*, Pevenage claimed that T-Mobile were mere 'amateurs' in all matters doping compared to Armstrong and US Postal. He said that US Postal and the UCI conspired together to protect Armstrong, the sport's golden goose, and that T-Mobile had 'no other choice' but to cheat. Bruyneel's caustic retort on social media – 'Rudy, it's all Lance's and my fault! WE made you do it . . . ' – was widely echoed.

Pevenage's case wasn't helped when Fuentes appeared on camera again a few months later, this time on the Spanish interview series *Lo de Évole*. That cameo was also vintage Fuentes, artfully sprinkled with winks, boasts and scurrilous half-admissions about his work with footballers and tennis players. Also typical of Fuentes is that, within hours of the broadcast, Real Madrid were threatening to sue him.

The more things change, the more they stay the same – as much as perspectives on the calcified prehistory of lives already lived can shift and acquire texture. People themselves can also evolve. Another production, Marina Zenovich's four-hour documentary for ESPN, *LANCE*, aired in the spring of 2020. It showed an Armstrong four years on from our game of golf early in 2015, four years more healed, four years more reconciled to the past, anchored in the present, arrowed towards his future. Which is not to say necessarily four years more redeemed or widely forgiven. 'I needed a nuclear melt-down and I got it,' he reflected at one point in the film. Perhaps most curious was how he was still taking the chance to take part in a process, even just in the conversation, unlike Ullrich. A few months later another feature-length documentary hit the screens, this time in Germany from the broadcaster NDR, its title *Deutschland: (K)ein Sommermärchen*, or *Germany: (No) Summer Fairy Tale*, its focus not a rehabilitation but a moment frozen in time: Ullrich's Tour win in '97. The talking heads included a few of the former teammates, gurus and critics interviewed for this book. 'I don't know how much anyone is still interested in hearing a Jan Ullrich confession,' was the journalist Andreas Burkert's closing thought – and indeed the whole film and its wistful indulgences seemed to sag with a distant, mostly unspoken but palpable regret. Images of Ullrich riding onto the Champs-Élysées were soundtracked by The National's 'Fake Empire', a song about denying uncomfortable realities. In his seminal book *The Body Keeps the Score*, the psychiatrist Bessel van der Kolk describes how individuals who are traumatized 'continue to organize their life as if the trauma were still going on – unchanged and immutable – as every new encounter or event is contaminated by the past.' Not long ago this diagnosis applied to the German public and its cycling scene vis-à-vis Ullrich. Nowadays it seemed to apply more to Jan Ullrich vis-à-vis them.

Former teammates Rolf Aldag and Udo Bölts both featured in the film and as always could draw on whatever words they needed to contextualize personal narratives. But, as mere domestiques, they also had a lot less to lose by owning and now retelling their truths. I wonder whether Ullrich doesn't feel about his career the way the author Maxim Leo feels about his youth in the DDR, as already discussed in Chapter 3. Just as East Germans don't get to wax romantic about the mundane pleasures of ordinary childhoods, lest they be accused of *Ostalgie*, so Ullrich may never summon the energy or language to persuade his countrymen that it wasn't all bad. To turn Leo's example into metaphor, that it didn't always rain in cycling in the 1990s. That drugs didn't make the emotions any less real. That talent existed. That his lungs still burned, his legs stung. That, in spite of all those days when he was being criticized or didn't want to train, it still felt like the time of his life and of theirs.

Ullrich couldn't bring himself to be interviewed for this book, either. That is one of the reasons why I have travelled to Merdingen in the first week of March 2022 – the idea that, if I can't have his voice, I can at least briefly frame myself in the context that he currently calls home. Parallel to this impulse is something that may also have been in the back of the NDR documentary-makers' minds in 2020: a desire to unspool the tape, rewind this story back to the mid-1990s and its happy beginning while we wait, lust, pray for a sunnier postscript. The delusion that by leaning in, embodying the original story, we might cajole Ullrich to break his paralysis, somehow thaw his trauma response.

It would be a stretch to say that the same unconscious desire was what made Jan Ullrich return here in 2018. One of his oldest friends, Mike Baldinger,* certainly wasn't aware of any such grand design. He mainly observed Ullrich's 2018 demolition derby from afar – that is, from here in Merdingen, just a phone call away but out of the front line – until his phone rang at around five in the evening one Sunday in October 2018, after Ullrich's detox in Miami. Baldinger stood surrounded by bricks and sacks of cement on a building site for the family's construction company. He didn't recognize the Spanish number but knew the voice at the other end. 'I'm in Basel. I'm in a bit of a desperate situation. Can you come and get me?'

An hour or two later Ullrich was climbing into Baldinger's car with only 'two suitcases, a pair of sunglasses and a phone with no credit on it'. Baldinger instinctively set off towards Merdingen and only later asked Ullrich where he wanted to go. Ullrich replied that he had no idea. 'So I just took him to my house. He ended up living with us for three weeks.'

Mike's twin brother Frank had an apartment that could provide a longer-term solution, and soon, without having planned or even really thought about it, Ullrich was back living in Merdingen nearly two decades after he'd left. 'He'd just come in here every day and smoke out of the window while I was working in the office next door,' Baldinger remembers as we sit in a meeting room of the family construction firm. At this point there wasn't so much a plan as hurdles to overcome, the damage of the previous months to repair. He had no driver's licence. An investigation into a serious alleged crime

---

* Mike and Dirk Baldinger, the former Polti rider who introduced Ullrich to Gaby Weis in 2004, have long been near neighbours but are only distant cousins.

hanging over him. Blocked credit cards. Debts. Shady individuals from the summer of mayhem still calling. A wife who wanted a divorce. Finally they retained a lawyer in Berlin, who helped to bring the case in Frankfurt to a speedy conclusion, with a sympathetic punishment: a 7,200-euro fine to go with what Ullrich paid the accuser privately in damages. Contact with his younger kids was restored. He was also now living around the corner from his eldest, Sarah Maria. Elizabeth had stuck around. He became less angry. His hands stopped shaking. He even stopped asking Baldinger to go to the supermarket to load up on cigarettes. As Baldinger says, 'We could see that he was getting better and better, more confident. Slowly coming back to earth.'

But it was not, couldn't possibly be, an overnight rebirth. Old traits hadn't been erased. 'If you put pressure on him, nothing works any more,' Baldinger observes. He provides the example of his attempts to get Ullrich back on his bike early in January 2019, when every prompting from Baldinger would bring a new excuse. 'First he couldn't do it because he had back pain, so we went to the doctor. Then it was his ears. We got that looked at . . . Then his knee. Eventually, I said to him, "Look, for every ailment you say you've got, I'll take you to another doctor or a physiotherapist until it's sorted. I won't leave you alone. Now I'm getting my dad's e-bike out of the garage and you're coming with me."' One ride through Ullrich's old, beloved vine-cloaked hills led to another, and it wasn't long before the motor in Mike's pedal axle was spluttering to keep up. 'The speeds he can go at, after just a little bit of training . . . It's brutal.' It was all the more shocking for Baldinger having seen the state to which Ullrich had reduced himself a few months earlier. 'Neither of us probably would have survived what he took and what he did to his body that summer in Spain . . .' Mike says solemnly.

Ullrich's organs had made a fast recovery. Even in 2018 a brain scan had reassured him that his excesses had caused no lasting damage. 'When there's nothing there in the first place, it can't get broken,' he joked at the time. But, in truth, his neural circuitry had always been a complex, tangled and sometimes contradictory web. There are still ticks that those who have known him for years can't understand. Like how, says Mike, he can go incommunicado, off the grid for days, apparently desperate to be left alone, yet still think it necessary or advisable to spontaneously call *Bild Zeitung* and impart some piece of personal news or insight. Or how he has no radar for parasites or bad influences. His issues with loneliness. Why he doesn't grasp that what he has survived says so much about his potential. And why he sometimes talks about his 'demons' and almost sounds as though he is romanticizing forces that have caused him immeasurable harm.

In Baldinger's frequent sighs, there is more affection than anger, more optimism than fatalism. Nonetheless, he says that his friend has to play his part, that there are certain provisos to his support.

'I've told him, if we offer you our help and you trample all over it, then we're going to remove that help. I'm going to try to keep you on the straight and narrow just as long as you show that you want it, as long as you prove that you want to make something of your life. Recently I read an article or interview with Robbie Williams, and he was talking about being hooked on espresso and Red Bull and various other things. The click came for him when his wife or partner basically said that if he didn't get therapy, she was leaving. She didn't expect him to be able to go cold turkey but he had to show willing. That's what I've told Jan. We'll always be there for him but he has to give something back.'

The latest reminder that it may be a long process came just a few weeks before Mike and I meet in Merdingen. Initial reports spoke of a relapse triggered by a brief split from Elizabeth. Ullrich denied them to *Bild*: drugs and alcohol weren't involved, he said, and he'd simply been unlucky to be struck by deep-vein thrombosis on a flight home from Cuba. What Ullrich did confirm was that he had somehow ended up in a hospital room in Cancún, Mexico, with Armstrong at his side. Only weeks earlier the old rivals had been enjoying a poignant reunion on a bike-touring trip in Mallorca that is one of Armstrong's many recent ventures. They had posted pictures from their rides and even recorded a podcast. On it, Ullrich admitted that he had 'nearly gone the way of Marco Pantani' in 2018, while Armstrong wanted their listeners to realize that Ullrich's was 'one of the biggest comebacks in the world'. Everyone on the trip was indeed thrilled to see Jan looking so happy and healthy. Even if, to one or two, things looked almost to be going too well, given what had come before.

The Cuba and Cancún scare brought a reality check. A warning. Another reset. 'There he sort of used up a credit,' Mike says, shaking his head. 'You're someone who needs the fire brigade, yet you're going about with a petrol can in your hand . . . He has to learn that's not always going to end well, that people will turn away.' More pep talks and home truths have been sent Ullrich's way since. New therapists enlisted. A support network that includes Armstrong, Johan Bruyneel and Andreas Schmid, one of the doctors behind the Freiburg-Telekom doping conspiracy, reinforced. Mike knows there'll be sneers. But for now the priority is Ullrich's health, not his image.

Anyway, Baldinger would defy anyone to tell him that Armstrong hasn't been a true friend over the last four years. He says that within hours of him calling, Armstrong was with Ullrich in Cancún. He's also willing to entertain the idea that sprinkled in with the generosity there could be pinches of guilt. 'I think there could be some of that, or at least a sense of responsibility. That's just the feeling I get. I think Lance knows that Jan was more talented . . .'

Nowadays, in their post-career lives, Baldinger agrees, the comparison is even more withering than when they were riders. Armstrong has 'an elephant's skin – you could shoot him with a bazooka and not knock him over'. Whereas, personality-wise, Baldinger says his friend more closely resembles another rider: 'Jan . . . vulnerable, can be thin-skinned, has addictive tendencies. More like Pantani . . .'

Pantani also became imprisoned in silence when accusatory fingers pointed in his direction in the late 1990s. The 'challenges' that Baldinger and I have discussed so far seem to exist in isolation from the vortex into which Ullrich disappeared in 2006. But as the conversation turns to the future, so we inevitably begin talking about conscience and the part that has also played. In short, Baldinger agrees that Ullrich's inability to open up, to recognize that shame cannot survive the light, has at least compounded his turmoil over the last few years. Part of the paralysis initially came from his fear of implicating or hurting others, to which was added a long-standing phobia of explaining himself though the media. Plus, of course, the knowledge that, as Mike says, 'Jan didn't invent doping.' But whatever the reasons, injustices and excuses, Baldinger is adamant that Ullrich *needs* to discharge his burden. And says that he will finally do so: a deal has been signed with a major film production company, and a multi-part series in which Ullrich reveals his whole truth will hopefully land on a major streaming service in the next few months.

'For three or four months he didn't want to [make the film], said that it would only cause more problems, then finally it became clear to him that maybe the solution to the problems he has is explaining how things were . . .'

Baldinger hopes the documentary will spell out and demystify several things. That a DDR sports system in which pre-pubescent teens learned to hang their whole identity on sporting success was not only dehumanizing but dangerous. That no product of that education, faced with the 'dope or be doomed' catch-22, could be expected to take the path of most resistance. That Telekom had their share of the glory but not of the ignominy. That now Ullrich wants one thing: 'a normal life'. That, as Mike says, 'he's basically a lovely, lovely guy . . . and if he finds his way again, he'll have come through an unbelievably hard time. I guess that's what I'd like people to see. That cycling was a gift and a curse for him. He wouldn't have earned those millions without it, but he's had to endure a lot of pain because of it.'

Right now Baldinger says that he's mainly concerned with 'preparing Jan for the summer'. Meaning that, with the twenty-fifth anniversary of Ullrich's Tour win on the horizon, requests will flood in, strobe lights will shine. Indeed, they are already flickering in early March. A handful of reporters have turned up unannounced on Baldinger's doorstep over the last few weeks; his mobile phone is under assault. His role as Ullrich's guardian angel but also de facto spokesperson is further complicated by another paradox – that Ullrich wants to be left alone, but also recognized, re-integrated into the cycling firmament. Just last autumn, Jan got Mike to text a major figure at the Tour de France organizers ASO to request an invitation to the 2022 route presentation. Nothing came back – not even a message to explain why it was, well, awkward. But Ullrich went to Paris anyway; via Instagram, he had asked the reigning champion Tadej Pogačar to meet for a coffee. And Pogačar obliged.

It's a similar story when Baldinger looks to the long term – at how they might solve the question posed by a German newspaper in 2013: what does Jan Ullrich intend to do with the rest of his life? In the summer of 2021, Mike, his namesake Dirk Baldinger and Ullrich unveiled at least part of a plan: a proposal to open a museum-cum-bike-cafe on land just a few paces from where we're sitting in the Baldingers' unit on the western edge of Merdingen. But faced with the mayor's decidedly lukewarm reception, the Baldingers are now in discussions with other locations in the area. 'The mayor was basically questioning whether there was any touristic value to it, saying stuff about Jan's doping and whether it sent the right message to kids . . . I think about the life that Jan's had, with all the highs and lows, which we also want to show. I think he's earned it, and there's so much interest – from collectors who would give us memorabilia to exhibit, to people who would want to visit. He's had a hell of a story. There are world-famous footballers whose lives and experiences are nothing in comparison.'

While Baldinger and I have been speaking, the sun has dipped below the Kaiserstuhl and adjacent smaller hills, bathing the village in an icy, lilac twilight that floods in through the window. Soon it'll be time for me to leave for a first assignment of the 2022 cycling season at Paris–Nice – and to get there, coincidentally, I'll be making the same journey that Jan Ullrich was due to complete in July 2006, from Strasbourg to Paris.

As Mike and I prepare to exchange farewells, he apologizes again that Jan couldn't be here to tell me the story of the last three years in his own words. Over the past month, he explains, he has tried to surround Ullrich with peace and serenity in the hope that will be reflected in his friend's mental and emotional bearing. 'It's all been calm and under control over the last couple of weeks,' he notes. Two or three times during our conversation, he has traced the wildly undulating trajectory of the last few years on the tabletop with his index finger. 'These extreme highs and lows. This "all or nothing" credo that he's also turned into a kind of motto. It has to stop . . .'

Before I head back to Freiburg to catch my train, he says there's one last thing that he nearly forgot: he wants a picture of me, and him, to 'send to Lance'.

Three days later, Mike sends a similar photo to my phone. In it, he wears the same fulsome smile, only now it is not me who stands to his left but, holding a thumb up to the camera, Jan Ullrich. A T-shirt hangs loosely from Ullrich's shoulders, the whites of his eyes sparkle and his grin is broad. He looks significantly younger than his forty-eight years.

It is a picture, if not of happiness, then at least one of hope.

Acknowledgements

The process of researching and writing this book began an almost unfathomably long time ago – seven years of transition, abject loss of confidence, an equal amount of bloody-mindedness and also great patience on the part of those who continued to believe it was a worthwhile odyssey. But the real seed was planted even further back, on an afternoon in Tuscany in July 1997, when my dear, cycling-agnostic father and I sat in our holiday accommodation and watched Jan Ullrich provide the image immortalized on the cover of this book by winning in Andorra. Indeed, if this journey took me all across the world, using all of the skills demanded by such a daunting challenge, it is entirely thanks to the opportunities afforded to me by my parents, out of which a passion and stuttering career eventually grew. To them, I will never be able to fully express my gratitude.

Similarly, the continued support and love of my other immediate family, particularly in these difficult last two years, cannot be quantified or repaid in words. Nonetheless, to Maria, Rob, The Sheriff and Verón, I will say it again here: thank you.

Word by word, day by day, Katie Green constantly encouraged and consoled and witnessed what it eventually took to see the project through. Without her it may still have happened – she knows my stubbornness – but her love and forbearance have filled life away from the laptop with hope, silver linings, laughter and joy. Sweetheart, you have amazed me.

In Berlin, over several years, Kati Bohnet also saw doubts, total dejection, confusion and tears but remained the stoic, compassionate domestique and directrice extra-sportive that I needed, exactly when she was needed, for this book and beyond. *Für alles, Kati, meinen allerherzlichsten Dank.*

Dozens of friends and colleagues contributed in vital ways, with practical help, advice or inspiration. I would particularly like to thank Felix Mattis, Michael Ostermann and Fran Reyes for their assistance with some of my early interviews for the book. Rob Hatch, as well as being a supremely gifted commentator and much better friend than I deserved, also provided key input back when I was still trying to turn my Spitaliano into Spanish. Many others read passages, passed on contact details or cuttings, or obliged with other favours: Ali Izhar Ahmed, Federico Meda, Brian Nygaard, Jeremy Whittle, Simone Benevelli, Jan Pieter de Vlieger, Leon de Kort, Herbie Sykes, Julien Pinot, Ken Sommer, Andreas Schulz, Claire Bricogne, Herbie Sykes, Kenny Pryde, Mark Cavendish, Guy Vermeiren, Ciro Scognamiglio, Saehra Kübel-Heising, Gregor Brown, Luca Gialanella, Daniel Brickwedde, Ole Zeisler, Pete Nattrass, Peter Cossins, Morton Okbo, Lionel Birnie, Andy Hood, Whit Yost, Scott Leaky, Stephen Farrand, Sam Dansie, Hugo Coorevits and the staff at the Biblioteca Pública Municipal de Sóller.

The subjects discussed here were so sensitive – and the person at the centre of narrative so assailed yet also beloved – that it was often difficult to persuade interviewees to go on the record. Nonetheless, next to the many who declined for understandable reasons, the following recognized the value of putting their stories into words, in some cases over several hours or days: Andreas Burkert, Ángel Casero, Bjarne Riis, Bob Stapleton, Brian Holm, Chris Hauke, Christian Prudhomme, Christian Vande Velde, Christophe Bassons, Daniele Nardello, Dario Pieri, David Millar, Erich Keller, Falk Nier, Fausto Pinarello, Félix García Casas, Filippo Simeoni, Frankie Andreu, Giovanni Lombardi, Giuseppe Guerini, Greg LeMond, Hagen Boßdorf, Hajo Seppelt, Hartmut Scherzer, Jacques Hanegraaf, Jan Schaffrath, Jens Heppner, Jeroen Swart, Johan Bruyneel, John Sessa, John Wordin, Jörg Jaksche, Jürgen Kindervater, Jürgen Werner, Katrin Kanitz, Lance Armstrong, Letizia Paoli, Linus Gerdemann, Luigi Cecchini, Lutz Lehmann, Marcel Wüst, Mario Kummer, Mark Scheppert, Michael Ostermann, Michael Rasmussen, Mike Baldinger, Patrice Clerc, Peter Becker, Peter Sager, Rafa Honigstein, Raphael Schweda, Rolf Aldag, Ron Sommer, Rudy Pevenage, Sandro Donati, Sylvia Schenk, Thomas Dekker, Tyler Hamilton, Udo Sprenger, Walter Godefroot, Werner Franke, Wolfgang Strohband.

I must also thank Jan Ullrich, who, although preferring not to speak in an interview with me himself, gave his blessing for several important figures to add their perspectives.

Additionally, I would like to acknowledge the inhuman patience and faith of my first editor at Pan Macmillan, Robin Harvie, who has been succeeded by a similarly staunch ally in Matthew Cole. Also at Pan Macmillan, Samantha Fletcher and Lyndon Branfield were unfailingly helpful in the dying metres of this epic stage-race(!), as was copy-editor Fraser Crichton.

Nearly last on this roll-call but always the first to reassure – or, when absolutely strictly necessary, commiserate over a delicious meal or bottle of Gigondas – is my long-suffering agent David Luxton. Joking and negronis aside, David and his colleague Rebecca Winfield empathized with, defended and indulged me throughout, in a way that was deeply touching and hugely appreciated.

Whatever joy or relief accompanied the final days of this project was sadly curtailed by the sudden passing in March 2022 of my friend and colleague, Richard Moore. At one of my lower ebbs, Richard kindly read half-baked chapters and tried desperately to breathe conviction into what was by then an empty vessel. I wish I'd asked for more help, because he was always there if I did – as generous as he was talented, selfless and magnanimous even when he didn't fully understand why I seemed to make such an elaborate, multi-course, taster menu meal of things. Most of all, Rich, I was looking forward to seeing you happy that I got there in the end, like the true mate you had always been.

Notes

1. Preface, p. 6: Speech at Frankfurt University, 5 February 1964.

2. Chapter 2, p. 17: Jan Ullrich, *Ganz oder Gar Nicht* (Econ, 2004).

3. Chapter 2, p. 28: ibid., p. 51.

4. Chapter 2, p. 31: Mike Dennis and Jonathan Grix, *Sport Under Communism: Behind the East German 'Miracle'* (Palgrave Macmillan, 2012), p. 191.

5. Chapter 3, p. 37: Benjamin Lowe, David B. Kanin and Andrew Strenk (eds.), *Sport and International Relations* (Stipes, 1978), pp. 348–9.

6. Chapter 3, p. 47: Ullrich, *Ganz oder Gar Nicht*.

7. Chapter 6, p. 77: Bjarne Riis, *Riis: Stages of Light and Dark* (Vision Sports, 2012).

8. Chapter 6, p. 77: Ferrari had by this time already been barred from any involvement in cycling events and from treating or consulting with any Italian Cycling Federation (FCI) licensee, per a ruling by the FCI on 13 February 2002. The FCI disciplinary committee had deemed Ferrari to have violated the UCI's anti-doping regulations on the basis of evidence gathered in a then ongoing investigation which would initially see Ferrari sentenced, in October 2004, to one year in prison (suspended), a fine of 900 euros and the suspension of his medical licence for eleven months and twenty-one days. Just under two years later, the judgement was overturned because the statute of limitations had expired on the charge of 'sporting fraud' (which, Ferrari's lawyer had argued in the initial trial, had been designed to combat corruption through gambling and not doping), while a second conviction for 'pharmacist misconduct' collapsed because

Ferrari had prescribed potentially harmful substances only sporadically and to a small number of individuals.

9. Chapter 7, p. 101: *Frankfurter Allgemeine Zeitung*, 20 September 1997.

10. Chapter 7, p. 102: *Der Spiegel*, 12 June 1999.

11. Chapter 8, p. 113: Udo Bölts, *Quäl dich, du Sau!* (Covadonga, 2006).

12. Chapter 10, p. 130: Lance Armstrong, *It's Not About the Bike: My Journey Back to Life* (Penguin, 2000).

13. Chapter 11, p. 141: Ullrich, *Ganz oder Gar Nicht*.

14. Chapter 12, p. 158: Lance Armstrong, *Every Second Counts* (Yellow Jersey, 2004).

15. Chapter 12, p. 159: Hamilton recounted these events both in his 2013 book *The Secret Race* and in a sworn affidavit to the United States Anti-Doping Agency. USADA concluded that 'Hamilton's detailed account of Lance Armstrong's doping is truthful, accurate and well corroborated'.

16. Chapter 12, p. 159: Johan Bruyneel, *We Might As Well Win* (Mainstream Publishing, 2011).

17. Chapter 12, p. 160: Donati's speculation about when Conconi first used EPO is partly based on evidence seized from the University of Ferrara in 1998, including details of Conconi's research projects funded with Italian Olympic Commission (CONI) grants. One study in particular, from 1987, focusing on the effect of acute and chronic variations in haematocrit on aerobic capacities, caught the attention of judge Pierguido Soprani but was deemed a 'clue' rather than proof that Conconi had started to administer EPO around this time. The first synthetic EPO to be approved for use in Europe was Eprex, in 1988.

18. Chapter 12, p. 160: Conconi was named president of the UCI's medical commission on 27 August 1993 (Alessandro Donati, *Lo sport del doping. Chi lo subisce, chi lo combatte* [Edizioni Gruppo Abele, 2013]). Two days earlier, the professor had given a now infamous speech at an anti-doping conference in Lillehammer in

Norway, announcing that he had begun a trial to test the effects of EPO on twenty-three amateur athletes. Years later, the prosecution in Conconi's trial for sporting fraud successfully argued that these amateurs were in fact world-class professional cyclists, although the doping charges against the professor were finally dismissed due to the statute of limitations having expired. Sandro Donati's book also details Professor Conconi's efforts to prove the efficacy of EPO with experiments . . . on himself. Between 30 July and 21 September 1991, according to Conconi's own notes recovered years later in police raids at the University of Ferrara in Italy, Conconi took just under fifteen minutes off his timed ascents of the Stelvio Pass, improving from one hour 21.01 minutes to one hour 5.29 minutes, thanks to what Donati describes as a 'horrifying' course of EPO treatment in the intervening period.

The International Olympic Committee funded Conconi's efforts to develop an EPO test method to the tune of $160,000. (*L'unità*, 1 December 1996, p. 11). Between 1979 and 1996, Conconi had received much bigger sums for other research projects and commissions from the Italian Olympic Commission (CONI). At a conference in Geneva in December 1994, speaking in his role as the president of the UCI's medical commission and with several leading riders in the audience, Conconi claimed the EPO detection method that he was helping to develop for the IOC was 'just a few months from being ready', in line with what he had already told Alexandre de Merode, the chairman of the International Olympic Committee's medical commission. Alas, in 1996, he was informing de Merode that, despite 'progress', his quest to find a valid EPO detection method was still 'a long way from its conclusion'. Later the same year, he wrote to de Merode that a successful outcome to his study would be 'a nice Christmas present for everybody' (Donati). De Merode responded by announcing to journalists on 16 December 1996 that the IOC would unveil its new EPO test 'the following week'. In fact, it would be four more years before a valid test, unrelated to the method proposed by Conconi, was rolled out in international sporting competitions.

19. Chapter 13, p. 177: Tyler Hamilton and Daniel Coyle, *The Secret Race* (Corgi, 2013).

20. Chapter 13, p. 181: Ullrich, *Ganz oder Gar Nicht*.

21. Chapter 14, p. 202: ibid.

22. Chapter 14, p. 211: ibid.

23. Chapter 15, p. 228: In November 2003 the Court of Ferrara acquitted Conconi of the charge of sporting fraud due to the statute of limitations having run out in August 1995, and a 'lack of evidence' for specific instances of doping thereafter. Conconi greeted the verdict by reaffirming that he had 'nothing to do with doping' and that to state otherwise would be akin to 'comparing a Goya nude to a pornographic photo'. Writing in the Italian newspaper *Corriere della Sera*, Giuseppe Toti called the verdict 'shameful'. Later, in June 2004, the anti-doping commission of the Italian Olympic Committee also dismissed their parallel case against Conconi for the same reasons. Nonetheless, as judge Giovanni Verdi wrote in his summing up, the picture that emerged from the case, and in particular evidence for Conconi's EPO doping, was 'demoralizing', shining a light as it did on 'doctors who show no scruples in studying the effects of doping substances on athletes, going to great lengths to do so, and also using public money obtained from CONI research grants and agreements with other federations and teams'.

24. Chapter 18, p. 273: Kelme became a title sponsor of the team previously known as Transmallorca-Flavia-Gios in 1980, and would remain its headline backer until the end of 2004. In the intervening period, team members would fail anti-doping tests leading to sanctions on seventeen occasions. When he took the stand in the Operación Puerto trial in 2013, Jesús Manzano claimed that he had only encountered one rider at Kelme who didn't dope, the Spanish journeyman Juan Miguel Cuenca. Kelme's long-time team manager, Vicente Belda, rubbished this accusation, declaring in court that Kelme were a 'clean' team. He also cast doubt on Manzano's credibility, explaining that he had renewed the rider's contract in 2002 only on

compassionate grounds after the death of Manzano's father. Belda suggested that Manzano's claims about Kelme were motivated by revenge, given that he was sent home from the 2003 Vuelta having been caught in flagrante with a woman who wasn't his girlfriend in the team hotel – and never raced for the team again.

25. Chapter 18, p. 276: C. G. Jung, *Aufsätze zur Zeitgeschichte* (Rascher, 1946), pp. 73–117.

26. Chapter 20, p. 303: Saiz was acquitted of crimes against public health when Operación Puerto went to trial in 2013. Saiz had testified that, although he had employed Fuentes in his teams in the 1990s, he had 'never been present when a cyclist was consulting Fuentes', 'didn't know what the team doctors were doing for 280 days a year', and had 'never given [my] riders banned medicines or blood transfusions'. He claimed that the meeting in the Hotel Pio XII which had led to his and Fuentes's arrests had to been set up to discuss the possibility of helping the doctor's daughter to obtain a job at ONCE, a Spanish charity for the blind and Saiz's former team sponsor, after her treatment for cancer.

27. Chapter 21, p. 317: Nearly seven years after Eufemiano Fuentes's arrest, Operación Puerto finally came to trial in April 2013. Fuentes and four other individuals were accused of crimes against public health – Manolo Saiz; Fuentes's sister and fellow former Kelme doctor Yolanda; and the former Kelme directeur sportif and team manager respectively, Ignacio Labarta and Vicente Belda. Finally, only Fuentes and Labarta were found guilty, the former receiving a one-year suspended prison sentence and the latter a four-month term. Judge Julia Patricia Santamaria said that Fuentes's blood transfusions represented 'a significant risk to the health' of his patients. Both Fuentes and Labarta appealed – and three years later both men were cleared on the basis that blood transfusions could not be considered 'medicines' and therefore fell outside of the realm of the alleged crimes. In 2019, the World Anti-Doping Agency (WADA) was finally able to perform DNA tests on hitherto unidentified blood bags seized from Fuentes's Madrid apartments but said that it would not disclose the results as their statute of limitations for disciplinary

action had expired. In January 2022, WADA did not respond to a query about whether athletes are formally banned from being coached or treated by Eufemiano Fuentes, given that he does not feature on WADA's Prohibited Association List, unlike Michele Ferrari and other doctors who have previously faced allegations of doping cyclists.

28. Chapter 21, p. 320: Christian Frommert, *Dann iss halt was!* (Mosaik, 2013).

29. Chapter 21, p. 329: *La Gazzetta dello Sport*, 8 May 2007.

30. Chapter 22, p. 349: DDR doping czar Manfred Höppner admitted in 1991 that most of the documents pertaining to East Germany's systematic doping programme, or 'State Planning Theme 14.25', were shredded or in some other way destroyed in the months that followed the fall of the Berlin Wall, as the regime's former chiefs scrambled to cover their tracks. Evidence from the late 1980s was particularly scarce and difficult to piece together. Höppner's own 'Stasi' files do indicate that blood transfusions were at least an area of interest for the East German sports leadership from August 1986, three months after the technique was banned by the IOC. EPO was first approved for the treatment of anaemia in Europe two years later, shortly before the Peaceful Revolution, and there is little evidence to suggest that it became East German athletes' blood-boosting method of choice. Nonetheless, citing newly examined files from the DDR Health Ministry, *Der Spiegel* reported in 2013 that West German EPO manufacturer Boehringer Mannheim had performed clinical EPO trials on thirty prematurely born babies in Berlin's Charité hospital. The magazine presented evidence that Boehringer was one of several West German pharmaceutical companies that, between them, paid modest sums to recruit around 50,000 East German volunteers for experimental treatments in the late 1980s. Participants in several of the trials are believed to have died.

31. Chapter 22, p. 359: Godefroot sued D'Hont for alleging in his book that Godefroot had organized and financed Telekom's

doping programme. The presiding judge ruled in March 2010 that there was insufficient evidence to support the claim, although Godefroot was aware of doping in the team. D'Hont was ordered to pay 7,500 euros in damages.

Selected Bibliography

BOOKS

Albergotti, Reed and O'Connell, Vanessa, *Wheelman: Lance Armstrong, the Tour de France, and the Greatest Sports Conspiracy Ever* (Avery, 2014)

Armstrong, Lance, *Every Second Counts* (Yellow Jersey, 2004)

Ballester, Pierre and Walsh, David, *L.A. Confidentiel: Les secrets de Lance Armstrong* (La Martinière, 2004)

Bassons, Christophe, *Positif* (Stock, 2000)

Becker, Peter, *Der Trainer – Ein Leben für den Radsport* (Scheunen, 2004)

Berendonk, Brigitte, *Doping Dokumente* (Springer, 1991)

Blume, Klaus, *Des Radsports letzter Kaiser?* (Covadonga, 2011)

Bölts, Udo, *Quäl dich, du Sau!* (Covadonga, 2006)

Braun, Stuart, *City of Exiles: Berlin from the Outside In* (Noctua Press, 2015)

Bruyneel, Johan, *We Might As Well Win* (Mainstream Publishing, 2011)

Burkert, Andreas, *Jan Ullrich: Wieder im Rennen* (Goldmann Wilhelm, 2004)

Cleiß, Peter, *Der Fall Jan Ullrich . . . unser Fall?* (Books on Demand, 2007)

Coyle, Daniel, *Lance Armstrong's War* (HarperCollins, 2005)

D'Hont, Jef, *Memoires van een Wielerverzorger* (Pelckmans, 2011)

Dennis, Mike and Grix, Jonathan, *Sport Under Communism: Behind the East German 'Miracle'* (Palgrave Macmillan, 2012)

Di Luca, Danilo, *Bestie Da Vittoria* (Piemme, 2017)

Donati, Alessandro, *Lo sport del doping: Chi lo subisce, chi lo combatte* (Edizioni Gruppo Abele, 2013)

Frommert, Christian, *'Dann iss halt was!': Meine Magersucht – wie ich gekämpft habe – wie ich überlebe* (Mosaik, 2013)

Funder, Anna, *Stasiland: Stories from Behind the Berlin Wall* (Granta Books, 2021)

Hamilton, Tyler and Coyle, Daniel, *The Secret Race: Inside The Hidden World of the Tour de France* (Corgi, 2013)

Haney, Hank, *The Big Miss: My Years Coaching Tiger Woods* (Crown Archetype, 2013)

Honigstein, Raphael, *Das Reboot: How German Football Reinvented Itself and Conquered The World* (Vintage, 2016)

Leo, Maxim (trans. Shaun Whiteside), *Red Love: The Story of an East German Family* (Pushkin Press, 2014)

Lowe, Benjamin, Kanin, David B. and Strenk, Andrew, (eds.) *Sport and International Relations* (Stipes, 1978)

Macur, Juliet, *Cycle of Lies: The Fall of Lance Armstrong* (HarperCollins, 2014)

Meutgens, Ralf, *Doping Im Radsport* (Delius Klasing Verlag, 2007)

Moore, Richard, *Étape: The Untold Stories of the Tour de France's Defining Stages* (HarperSport, 2014)

Ohler, Norman, *Der totale Rausch: Drogen im Dritten Reich* (Kiepenheuer and Witsch, 2017)

Riis, Bjarne, *Riis: Stages of Light and Dark* (Vision Sports, 2012)

Scheppert, Mark, *Der Mauergewinner oder ein Wessi des Ostens* (Books on Demand, 2009)

Schneider, Peter, *Berlin Now: The City After the Wall* (Farrar, Straus and Giroux, 2014)

Spitzer, Giselher, *Doping in der DDR: Ein historischer Überblick zu einer konspirativen Praxis* (Sportverlag Strauß, 2018)

Ullrich, Jan, *Große Schleife die Zweite* (Sportverlag, 1997)

Ullrich, Jan, *Ganz oder Gar Nicht: Meine Geschichte* (Econ, 2004)

Ungerleider, Steven, *Faust's Gold: Inside the East German Doping Machine* (CreateSpace, 2013)

Van Ierland, John, *Der Rudy: Biografie van Rudy Pevenage* (Uitgeverij, 2020)

Walsh, David, *Seven Deadly Sins: My Pursuit of Lance Armstrong* (Simon & Schuster, 2013)

Whittle, Jeremy, *Bad Blood: The Secret Life of the Tour de France* (Yellow Jersey, 2009)

FILMS

B Movie: Lust and Sound in West Berlin, directed by Jörg Hoppe, Klaus Maeck and Heiko Lange (DEF Media, 2015)

Betrifft: Doping und die Freiburger Sportmedizin, written by Patrick Hünerfeld (SWR, 2008)

Deutschland: (K)ein Sommermärchen – Die Tour de France '97, directed by Ole Zeisler and Ben Wozny (NDR, 2020)

Die Goldmacher, Sport in der DDR, directed by Albert Knechtel (Provobis, ZDF and MDR, 2008)

Höllentour, directed by Pepe Danquart (Quinte Film, Multimedia Film, Dschoint Ventschr Filmproduktion AG, 2004)

Jan Ullrich: Ein Champion auf der Siegerstraße, directed by Bernard George (La Sept ARTE and PdJ Production, 1997)

Jan Ullrich: Het wonderkind wacht, directed by Guillaume Graux, written by Dirk Van Nijverseel and Jan Antonissen (Belga Sport, 2010)

Jan Ullrich: Zwischen Licht und Schatten, directed by Bernard Debord (2004)

Wissenschaft auf schmalen Reifen Team Telekom 1997 (Süddeutscher Rundfunk/Studio Mannheim, 1997)

KEY REPORTS

'Abschlussbericht der Expertenkommission zur Aufklärung von Dopingvorwürfen gegenüber Ärzten der Abteilung Sportmedizin des Universitätsklinikums Freiburg' (Freiburg expert commission, 2009)

'Analyse der Live-Kommentierung der Tour de France 2000, Ein Vergleich der Sender ARD, ZDF und Eurosport' (Heike Vanselow, 2001)

'Doping beim Team Telekom/T-Mobile: Wissenschaftliches Gutachten zu systematischen Manipulationen im Profiradsport mit Unterstützung Freiburger Sportmediziner' (Andreas Singler with Lisa Heiner, 2016)

'Armin Klümper und das bundesdeutsche Dopingproblem – Wissenschaftliches Gutachten im Auftrag der Albert-Ludwigs-Universität Freiburg' (Andreas Singler with Lisa Heiner, 2017)

Cycling Independent Reform Commission Report to the President of the Union Cycliste Internationale (UCI, 2015)

'Evaluierungskommission Freiburger Sportmedizin: Joseph Keul: Wissenschaftskultur, Doping und Forschung zur pharmakologischen Leistungssteigerung' (Andreas Singler and Gerhard Treutlein, with Lisa Heitner, 2015)

'Rapport fait au nom de la commission d'enquête sur l'efficacité de la lutte contre le dopage' (French Senate, 2013)

Report on Proceedings Under The World Anti-Doping Case and the USADA Protocol, USADA v. Lance Armstrong, Reasoned Decision of the United States Anti-Doping Agency on Disqualification and Ineligibility (USADA, 2012)

Picture Credits

FIRST SECTION

Page 1: Both photos courtesy of the author.

Page 2: Peter Sager (*top*); Graham Watson (*bottom*).

Page 3: Graham Watson (*top*); courtesy of the author (*bottom*).

Page 4: Courtesy of the author (*top*); IMAGO/Heuberger (*bottom*).

Page 5: Both by Graham Watson.

Page 6: Ruediger Fessel/Bongarts/Getty Images (*top*); Mike Powell/ Allsport via Getty Images (*bottom*).

Page 7: Both by Graham Watson.

Page 8: Bongarts/Getty Images (*top*); Ruediger Fessel/Bongarts/ Getty Images (*middle*); Graham Watson (*bottom*).

SECOND SECTION

Page 1: Pascal Pavani/AFP via Getty Images (*top*); Graham Watson (*bottom*).

Page 2: All by Graham Watson.

Page 3: STF/AFP via Getty Images (*top*); Andreas Rentz/Bongarts/ Getty Images (*middle*); courtesy of the author (*bottom*).

Page 4: Courtesy of the author (*top*); IMAGO/Ulmer (*middle*); Alexander Hassenstein/Bongarts/Getty Images (*bottom*).

Page 5: Graham Watson (*top*); Michael Latz/DDP/AFP via Getty Images (*middle*); Tim De Waele/Getty Images (*bottom*).

Page 6: Friedemann Vogel/Bongarts/Getty Images (*top*); Franck Fife/AFP via Getty Images (*bottom*).

Index